The Centrality of Slavery

EARLY AMERICAN STUDIES

Series editors: Kathleen M. Brown, Roquinaldo Ferreira,
Emma Hart, and Daniel K. Richter

Exploring neglected aspects of our colonial, revolutionary, and early national history
and culture, Early American Studies reinterprets familiar themes and events
in fresh ways. Interdisciplinary in character, and with a special emphasis on
the period from about 1600 to 1850, the series is published in partnership
with the McNeil Center for Early American Studies.

A complete list of books in the series is available from the publisher.

The Centrality of Slavery

Empire and Enslavement in
Colonial Illinois and Missouri

John Craig Hammond

PENN

UNIVERSITY OF PENNSYLVANIA PRESS

PHILADELPHIA

Published by
University of Pennsylvania Press
Philadelphia, Pennsylvania 19104-4112 USA
www.pennpress.org

EU Authorized Representative:
Easy Access System Europe - Mustamäe tee 50,
10621 Tallinn, Estonia, gpsr.requests@easproject.com.

Printed in the United States of America on acid-free paper
10 9 8 7 6 5 4 3 2 1

A Cataloging-in-Publication record is
available from the Library of Congress

Hardcover ISBN 978-1-5128-2842-9
eBook ISBN 978-1-5128-2843-6

For Hallie, Hannah, and Addie, always

*And for Pep Hammond: father, grandfather,
union steamfitter, 1941–2024*

CONTENTS

Sovereignty, Slavery, and Empire in the Mississippi Valley

This book focuses on a small place in Middle America: the Middle Mississippi Valley, a riverine region surrounding the confluences of the Mississippi River with the Illinois, Missouri, Kaskaskia, and Ohio Rivers.[1] This small area played a vital role in the larger history of empire, enslavement, and emancipation in North America in the eighteenth and early nineteenth centuries, culminating in the Missouri Crisis, an extended conflict over the future of empire and enslavement on the North American continent. Before then, between 1720 and 1820, European colonizers, dynamic Indigenous polities, competing empires, and enslaved people created different systems of slavery under diverging imperial sovereignties and regimes. From 1820 through 1860, the Middle Mississippi Valley became a contested borderland, between Indigenous people and U.S. conquerors and colonizers, between Illinois and Missouri, and between the advocates of free-soil imperialism who came to dominate the Upper Mississippi Valley and the Great Lakes, and the advocates of an aggressively expansive empire for slavery who came to dominate the Lower Mississippi Valley. Empire and enslavement created the Middle Mississippi Valley, shaped its subsequent history, and then influenced the larger imperial trajectories of the United States and the North American continent.[2]

Like any geographical area, the Middle Mississippi Valley became a region due to the way that peoples and polities interacted with one another and defined it.[3] The mobility and reach of the rivers converging in the Middle Mississippi Valley amplified the importance of the region to the peoples, polities, and empires who inhabited a vast swath of the North American continent. Going northward, the Mississippi and Illinois Rivers provided access to the eastern and western Great Lakes, and from there to important colonial entrepôts at Detroit and Montreal. The Ohio River connected the region to Pittsburgh and onward to cities on the Atlantic coast, such as Philadelphia and Baltimore. The Missouri River follows a more or less east-west line from St. Louis to Kansas City; from there, the Kansas River continues westward while the Missouri turns to the northwest, with both rivers providing access deep into the Great Plains. Running southward, the Mississippi River provides a direct outlet to the region's most important entrepôt, New Orleans. In all directions, fields, forests, prairies, and woods promised economic abundance for the staples of the colonial North American economy, whether furs and skins, commercial agriculture and stores such as lead, or cash crops, including tobacco and hemp. The Middle Mississippi Valley sat at the center of the peoples, polities, and empires who vied for sovereignty and supremacy between the Appalachians and the Rocky Mountains, the Great Lakes and the Gulf of Mexico. It sat astride the crossroads of imperial North America. The practices of empire and enslavement forged and fought over there exerted an outsized influence on the imperial history of slavery in North America and the United States.

How did Illinois and Missouri, intimately connected and joined by the Mississippi River from the 1720s through the 1760s, become distinct places between the 1760s and the 1810s? How did the practices of enslavement and empire lead to such radically different outcomes when these territories sought statehood in 1818 and 1819? Why did a Missouri Crisis erupt in 1819, but a potential Illinois Crisis was averted in 1818? Histories of enslavement and empire in the Middle Mississippi Valley before 1820 have typically been written from two historiographical perspectives: the politics of enslavement and emancipation in the early U.S. republic, and the new history of slavery and capitalism.[4] In the historiography of slavery and politics in the early American republic, the Missouri Crisis has rightfully come to occupy a central place. Some historians have used the Missouri Crisis as the conclusion to an early epoch of the politics of slavery that began with the American Revolution and closed with the Missouri Compromise.[5] Others have found in the Missouri Crisis the genesis of a new form of national political parties committed to protecting slavery.[6] Others still have used the Crisis as an inflection point to examine why southern whites adopted a proslavery ideology, or why white northerners engaged with or retreated from antislavery politics.[7] A two-volume edited collection, marking the bicentennial of the Missouri Crisis, analyzes the politics of enslavement and emancipation in the early American republic from all of these perspectives while developing several new ones.[8]

Yet almost all of these works situate the stories of empire and enslavement in the Middle Mississippi Valley in the context of United States history and the politics of emancipation and enslavement in the early U.S. republic. Likewise, major works focusing on slavery in the trans-Appalachian and trans-Mississippi West through the Missouri Crisis have focused almost exclusively on white people from the United States arguing about Missouri and Illinois slavery in the abstract, or extending their conflicts between emancipation and enslavement from the East to the West.[9] Taken collectively, these works separate and exceptionalize the histories of Missouri and Illinois while overlooking the long, interconnected histories of enslavement and empire in the Middle Mississippi Valley that predated U.S. dominion. What's missing are analyses of habitants, free and enslaved Indigenous people, francophone Africans, and Spanish imperial officials creating, transforming, transferring, challenging, and dismantling systems of slavery in colonial Illinois *and* Missouri. These same people challenged borders, ignored borders, or made borders meaningful, depending on circumstances and their particular interests.

The new history of slavery and capitalism should provide some redress to this oversight. These works rightfully insist on understanding both the conquest and dispossession of Indigenous peoples, as well as the creation of an enslaving regime across the southern interior and in the Lower Mississippi Valley, as imperial projects that amounted to something much more than mere "expansion." These authors have been invaluable both for elucidating the processes by which white people from the United States created volatile enslaving regimes and for examining the never-ending challenges, crises, and disruptions that threatened to collapse these regimes.[10] Despite sweeping titles and subtitles, though, these works are really regional histories of slavery in the interior South and the Lower Mississippi Valley, coupled to histories of Anglo-American finance and capitalism. As a result, these otherwise excellent monographs overlook the processes by which settler-colonizers and imperial powers created and transformed slavery in the Middle Mississippi Valley, and how the Middle Mississippi Valley fed and sustained plantation revolutions in the Lower Mississippi Valley. This omission is striking, given that the slave societies of the Middle Mississippi Valley and the southern interior both grew out of the Atlantic plantation complex's "second slavery," a period between the 1770s and the 1810s that resulted in the great growth and expansion of slavery from its eighteenth-century core in places such as Saint-Domingue, Jamaica, and the coastal colonies of British North America to once-peripheral places such as Cuba, Louisiana, the southern interior, and the Ohio and Missouri Valleys, including Illinois and Missouri.[11] Enslavers and empires in the Middle Mississippi Valley tied their fortunes to enslavers and empires in the Lower Mississippi Valley; indeed, enslavement and empire in the Middle Mississippi Valley provisioned the growth of empire and enslavement in the Lower Mississippi Valley. The histories of empire and enslavement in those regions remained distinct, but they were always connected and depended on each other, whether in the 1720s or the 1820s.

Recently, historian Walter Johnson has situated Missouri in "the history of 'racial capitalism': the intertwined history of white supremacist ideology and the practices of empire, extraction, and exploitation." Johnson identifies St. Louis as "the crucible of American history": the "morning star of U.S. imperialism" from whence sprung "the juncture of empire and anti-Blackness." Johnson's claims ring true enough, and he provides an excellent guide to understanding "the practices of empire, extraction, and exploitation" in the Middle Mississippi and Missouri Valleys in the nineteenth and twentieth centuries. Yet Johnson's argument proceeds *from* the Louisiana Purchase and the Lewis and Clark expedition of 1803.[12] As a result, Johnson's racial capitalism in Middle America becomes myopic, removed from the long, contested histories of empire and enslavement that stretched back to the early eighteenth century. The racist, imperial dreams of white Americans appear *ex nihilo* in post–Louisiana Purchase and then post-statehood Missouri. In the process, the long eighteenth-century history of empire and enslavement—including the enslavement of Indigenous peoples—is subsumed into the nineteenth- and twentieth-century history of U.S. capitalism, slavery, and white supremacy.[13]

In doing so, Johnson and other new historians of slavery and capitalism deemphasize the enslavement of Indigenous peoples under successive French and Spanish regimes, while implicitly following the Tannenbaum thesis and scholarship, which held that Franco-Hispanic slavery in the Americas was somehow less predatory, less racially rigid, and less violent than the forms of Anglo-American enslavement spawned by nineteenth-century capitalism. By omission, these works imply that the Franco-Spanish empires and habitant enslavers in the Middle Mississippi Valley were somehow indolent and not capitalistic; that the forms of enslavement and racial subjugation that they inflicted were less rapacious; and that their commerce was less extractive and exploitative because its genesis laid outside of the new forms of capitalism arising out of the U.S. plantation South.[14] As with so much of the new history of slavery and capitalism, in Johnson's Mississippi Valley, enslavement, empire, and dispossession arrive only with the Louisiana Purchase of 1803, followed by the fuller extension of the U.S. empire for slavery after 1815. Under the terms of the new history of slavery and capitalism, until 1803 peaceful Indigenous people and indolent habitants engaged in a noncapitalistic form of the fur trade under the auspices of more humane systems of racial differentiation and bondage.[15] Under the new history of slavery and capitalism, the systems of empire and enslavement created by the United States in the Middle Mississippi Valley were not only *ex nihilo*; they were also *sui generis*, categorically distinct from the systems of empire and enslavement that preceded U.S. claims of sovereignty and dominion.

Taken collectively, the new history of capitalism and slavery and the robust literature on the politics of enslavement and emancipation in the new American nation approach the history of enslavement and empire in the Middle Mississippi Valley from the perspective of United States history, assuming that the United States, as an imperial power, stood singularly committed to the concomitant expansion of empire and enslavement. These works typically begin with the Northwest Ordinance of 1787 in the case of Illinois, or with the Louisiana Purchase of 1803 in the case of Missouri—if they write on enslavement in either of those places at all.[16] In doing so, these works subsume colonial, imperial, and Indigenous history into U.S. history, overlooking the eighteenth-century histories of empire, enslavement, and Indigenous history that shaped the nineteenth-century practices of U.S. empire and enslavement. The broader history of North America is reduced to proto-U.S. history. Yet habitants and French and Spanish imperial officials in the Middle Mississippi Valley were as committed to using imperial state power to create, maintain, and expand systems of slavery as any U.S. colonizer or imperial official. They were equally committed to forms of capitalism that relied heavily on enslaved labor and to social and political systems that elevated men of property and capital. The colonial legacies of enslavement and empire ran deep in the Middle Mississippi Valley in the eighteenth century. The history of enslavement and empire in Missouri begins with Auguste Chouteau and François Vallé in the 1760s and with middling enslavers of Indigenous people in Illinois in the 1730s more than with William Clark in the 1810s.

The new history of slavery and capitalism also overstates shared white commitment to slavery's expansion after 1780 while understating the significance of the Northwest Ordinance. Historian Edward Baptist thus claims that, by the early 1790s, "support for slavery's expansion had already become one of the best ways to unite southern and northern politicians."[17] Such interpretations conceive of the United States as an empire simultaneously monolithic, unitary in its determination to spread slavery across the North American continent, and hegemonic in its ability to do so. They also posit a vast consensus among white people from the United States, incorrectly asserting that northern whites, as much as their southern counterparts, made slavery's expansion and the privileging of enslavers coeval with U.S. empire. White northerners from Maine to Missouri shared a more or less consistent set of anti-Black beliefs and practices, to be sure. Their white supremacist consensus, however, did not preclude the formation of meaningful forms of antislavery imperialism or antislavery politics.[18] Almost universally, northern whites desired a semicontinental, imperial union, free of slavery, Black people, and Indigenous peoples.[19]

As a union and as an empire, the United States was hardly monolithic, unitary, or hegemonic; it was simply too big, too diverse, and too overextended to be so. From its creation in the 1770s, the United States operated as a composite rather than as a unitary empire, especially with regards to slavery.[20] That composite empire always contained diverse and clashing interests over slavery, both at the seat of imperial power and in the places it sought to claim, conquer, and control. In many ways, the men who fought hardest to construct a union and empire in the United States in the 1780s did so to mediate sectional and regional conflicts, many of which had their origins in the relative importance of slavery between sections, and expectations for conquest and incorporation of the trans-Appalachian West by those sections.[21] In creating a historiographically homogeneous U.S. empire, the new history of capitalism and slavery conflates northern and southern white conceptions and practices of empire.

At the same time, the new history of slavery and capitalism understates the similarities and continuities that the U.S. empire shared with its enslaving imperial rivals and predecessors on the North American continent. In homogenizing and exceptionalizing early U.S. empire, these works minimize both how the Northwest Ordinance created a significant historical change in the trajectory of colonial and imperial North American history, and how the United States built on its imperial predecessors in the Middle Mississippi Valley. A divided, fractious union with continental aspirations, the United States acquired and built on previous imperial regimes in the Middle Mississippi Valley far more than it projected its own ideological proclivities onto the region. The United States accelerated processes of enslavement, Indigenous evisceration, and emancipation long underway, far more than it imposed a new ideological vision on the Middle Mississippi Valley.

Until the late 1700s, imperial North American history had been charac-terized by the mutual creation of sovereign imperial spaces and systems of enslavement. Empires expanded through enslavers, and enslavers relied on imperial state power to establish systems of slavery. In short, until the 1780s, wherever European imperial powers established sovereignty, they created new systems of enslavement and bondage while expanding and modifying old ones. Imperial European states saw enslavers as important tools of empire building across the North American continent. At the same time, enslavers sought imperial state institutions and infrastructures to empower themselves against the people they enslaved. State formation in European colonies fol-lowed from the interests and imperatives of colonizing elites; those local elites were almost always enslavers, or they scrambled to become so soon after arrival. In the long history of imperial North America from the 1660s through the 1860s, European sovereignty and racialized systems of enslave-ment almost always advanced together. Even when European imperial pow-ers sought to limit the scope, practices, and extent of enslavement, local elites and potentates evaded those regulations with near impunity.[22]

Imperial state collaboration with enslavers was the norm in the imperial history of the Americas from the mid-1600s well into the nineteenth century. And that's why the Northwest Ordinance of 1787 mattered, both historio-graphically and historically. The Northwest Ordinance of 1787 significantly changed the course of imperial U.S. and North American history in the *longue durée.* The Article VI ban on slavery, along with the differing impe-rial and colonial histories of Britain's North American colonies, encouraged at least some white colonizers and invaders to imagine a competing set of imperial visions that treated enslavers as detriments to and drags on empire, rather than as assets. Since the 1980s, historians either have minimized the significance of Article VI of the Northwest Ordinance of 1787 or have consid-ered its importance in moral terms, rather than analyzing its historical impli-cations.[23] Baptist, for one, claims that passage of the Northwest Ordinance "was no great moral or political feat."[24] Other historians either seek to con-demn the U.S. government for failing to live up to the promise of Article VI, or they seek to explain away the persistence of slavery by identifying heroic individuals who saved Illinois from slavery. By analyzing Illinois slavery as a moral failing (or, as in other historiographical iterations, its defeat as a moral triumph), historians leave themselves unable to explain not only the pro-foundly different tracks of empire and enslavement in Illinois and Missouri, but also the growing differences between ostensibly free and slave states after

1820, especially with regards to conquest, expansion, and empire, and the causes of disunion and civil war in the 1860s.[25]

The historiographical challenge here is not to condemn, excuse, or celebrate; rather, it is to explain the persistence of multiple things at once: the slow erosion of chattel slavery in Illinois and the persistence of various forms of unfree labor in a region where it was presumably banned; Congress's refusal to rescind or modify Article VI along with its concomitant refusal to enforce its plain terms and meaning; and the rapid growth of slavery in Missouri and its stagnation in Illinois. Why does Walter Johnson locate the broken heart of America in St. Louis rather than in Chicago or Peoria, Kaskaskia, or Cahokia? The trajectories of empire and enslavement developed differently in Illinois and Missouri—it remains important to explain how and why that happened and to understand why those differences mattered. Implementation of the Northwest Ordinance of 1787 in Illinois might have been "no great moral or political feat," but it was politically and geopolitically significant in the broader imperial history of North America through 1860. Northern imperialists' refusal to rescind it from 1788 through 1818, and then their attempt to force a version of Article VI on Missouri through the Tallmadge Amendment in 1819, made it historically and historiographically significant, too.

While the main thrust of the historiography on enslavement and empire in the Mississippi Valley proceeds from the assumption that the United States fastened slavery and empire there, an entirely different body of literature that has developed over the past two decades seeks to understand the peoples and polities of the Middle Mississippi Valley in the eighteenth and early nineteenth centuries on their own terms. In 2006, Kathleen DuVal and Stephen Aron published two important works that focused on interactions among Indigenous peoples, European colonizers, and imperial powers in the broader Mississippi Valley.[26] Since then, additional monographs have examined how Native Americans, European interlopers, and competing European and Indigenous empires created frameworks for cooperation, competition, cohabitation, and conflict in the Middle Mississippi Valley and its major tributaries, including the lower Missouri, Ozark, and Ohio River Valleys, and the Great Lakes, in the eighteenth and early nineteenth centuries. As these works demonstrate, Indigenous and European inhabitants of the Middle Mississippi Valley formed extended kinship networks that embedded themselves in and across polities and empires. As these works also demonstrate, Indigenous power outpaced European empires and local colonizer polities far into the eighteenth century. Only in the late eighteenth and early nineteenth centuries did European empires erode Indigenous power to the point that European empires and colonizers could insist on inhabiting the Middle Mississippi Valley on their own terms.[27]

These works, which collectively form something like a "midcontinent borderland" interpretation of North American history between 1720 and 1820, remain invaluable for understanding the intertwined histories of Indigenous peoples and European colonizers in the interior of the North American continent.[28] This broader interpretation also correctly emphasizes the significance of Native Americans and francophonic colonizers in the imperial and Indigenous histories of the Middle Mississippi Valley into the early 1800s. Unfortunately, these works tend to minimize the significance of slavery and the intertwined facets of empire and enslavement that joined together diverse peoples—Indigenous, African, and European—in the Middle Mississippi Valley. Like the new history of slavery and capitalism, these works push off the significance of chattel slavery in the region until the Louisiana Purchase. Midcontinent borderland works also tend to overlook the broader significance of Indigenous enslavement to European colonizers and empire, even as they recognize the significance of Native enslavement to Indigenous polities.

The Centrality of Slavery builds on this new body of scholarship to understand better the processes by which the changing peoples and polities of the Middle Mississippi Valley constructed and contested systems of race and slavery under shifting imperial sovereignties. The creation and maintenance of racialized enslavement in the Middle Mississippi Valley was part of several imperial projects. Systems of slavery were made possible only by the mobilization of imperial state power, in local polities, to enslave people of African and Native American descent.[29] Enslaved Africans and Native Americans repeatedly challenged their enslavement, created and exploited cracks in the weaknesses of local polities and imperial territorialities, and threatened to undermine the fragile systems of enslavement constructed under the auspices of imperial France, Spain, Britain, Virginia, and then the United States, from the 1720s through the 1810s. In turn, European-American colonizers and imperial officials used the accoutrements of state power, state-sanctioned violence, and the emoluments divvied out by imperial states to keep men and women enslaved. Historian Gregory Ablavsky has written that, in the trans-Appalachian West in the 1790s, "the federal government was less an institution than a resource, a font of law and money."[30] More broadly, in the Middle Mississippi Valley, the resources and ideological sanction granted by imperial states were sources of power. Enslaver-colonizers sought out that power;

enslaved people tried to escape it or to use it for their own ends. Imperial sovereignty became real when enslavers used imperial state power to create and maintain systems of slavery in their local communities.

European-American colonizers inextricably linked imperial sovereignty to slavery and local self-government; they also proved bourgeois to the last, whether as habitants in Illinois in the 1720s or American enslavers in Missouri in the 1810s. Empire and enslavement became the means by which bourgeois colonizers satisfied their ambitions and realized their pretensions in the Middle Mississippi Valley. In turn, the creation, maintenance, and growth of slavery served as an important tool of empire building in the Middle Mississippi Valley, just as it did elsewhere in colonial North America. French, Spanish, British, Virginian, and U.S. imperial agents turned French-speaking habitants and Americans into loyal subjects or citizens by using imperial state power to assist them in continuing to enslave Africans and Native Americans while acquiring more slaves. No imperial state in the Middle Mississippi Valley evinced much ability to exert coercive authority over the free subjects they ostensibly governed, and most lacked the kinds of strong coercive institutions necessary to govern free subjects in either case. Even when they wanted to, imperial states found it difficult to govern far-off colonies and territories in the interior of the North American continent. Imperial states instead worked to empower local potentates and free subjects. These groups then governed their supposed subordinates according to race, rank, and gender. State formation, along with the laws, policies, and customs that governed everyday life, proceeded from the ideological and material interests of local potentates and property-owning subjects. Their interests centered primarily on land, relations with Indigenous peoples, and enslavement of racialized peoples. At the most local level, empire and colonialism for middling and grand subjects centered on enslavement and on keeping enslaved people in slavery while acquiring more. Colonizers and imperial officials wanted the same things.

For European-American settler-colonizers, access to imperial state power served as a necessary precondition for creating and maintaining systems of slavery. White settler-colonialists in the Middle Mississippi Valley evinced no strong preference for living under any particular imperial power; they only insisted that whichever empire claimed sovereignty use state resources to keep enslaved people in slavery. Imperial officials and agents responded to these imperatives by enhancing imperial state power to attract enslavers and then placing the coercive powers of the imperial state at their disposal. Enslavers followed imperial state power, laid claim to it, and then used it on the people whom they enslaved. More than simply taking over coercive institutions, enslavers built them with imperial officials on the ground. Thus, when British imperial power faltered in Illinois in the 1760s and 1770s, habitant enslavers crossed to Spanish Upper Louisiana, where they built a robust enslaving regime with local officials. Likewise, when U.S. imperial state power failed to sanction slavery in Illinois or to prop up the enslavers who remained there, American enslavers left Illinois or bypassed it for Missouri. Enslavers thrived in Missouri from the 1750s through the 1810s—systems of slavery grew and stabilized there—because the French, Spanish, and then U.S. imperial states devoted resources to propping up enslavers. Empire and enslavement advanced together. Enslavers languished in Illinois when successive British, Virginian, and then U.S. regimes proved unable or unwilling to use imperial state power and sanction to sustain systems of slavery.

Through the 1780s, North American imperial regimes readily obliged free subjects who sought to enslave others in order to strengthen their own claims of sovereignty and to expand the territory they could effectively claim and exploit. Empires expanded through enslavers, and enslavers relied on imperial state power. Even when the ability of imperial states to exercise power proved limited, the projection of small amounts of state power could have outsized effects due to the strategic geopolitical location of the Middle Mississippi Valley and the presence of competing empires, polities, and peoples. The presence of a functioning judicial system, coercive institutions, and state-sanctioned violence in Upper Louisiana, and their absence in Illinois, for example, was enough to entice Illinois enslavers to Upper Louisiana. The power of enslavers—and the corresponding autonomy of enslaved individuals—rose and fell according to the amount of ideological sanction and material support that imperial states provided to enslavers. European-American colonizers exploited imperial aspirations in the interior of the North American continent to channel the limited powers of imperial states to create systems of slavery, to continue to enslave Africans and Native Americans, and to acquire more. Where this happened—first in Illinois from the 1720s through the 1750s, and then in Missouri, from the 1760s through the 1810s—slavery grew and expanded. When imperial states proved unable or unwilling to extend imperial state power and sanction to enslavers, as happened in Illinois beginning in the 1760s, enslavers and enslaved people halted slavery's growth and hastened its decline. Article VI served not as an active tool of emancipation but as the means by which a group of antislavery imperialists passively denied imperial state sanction to local enslavers. Slavery

Middle North America, 1760s

CANADA

Montreal

Meskwaki

Michilimackinac

Green Bay

Sauk

Detroit

Haudenosaunee

Prairie
du Chien

Potawatomi

Delaware

Fort Duquesne
(Pitt)

Little Osage

Ft. St. Louis
(Peoria)

Shawnee

Cahokia

Vincennes

St. Louis

Ft. de Chartres

Ste. Genevieve

Kaskaskia

Great Osage

Chickasaw

Appalachian Mountains

BRITISH COLONIES

Arkansas Post

Natchez

LOWER
LOUISIANA

Mobile

New Orleans

0   90   180
Miles

Map 1. Middle Mississippi Valley, 1760.

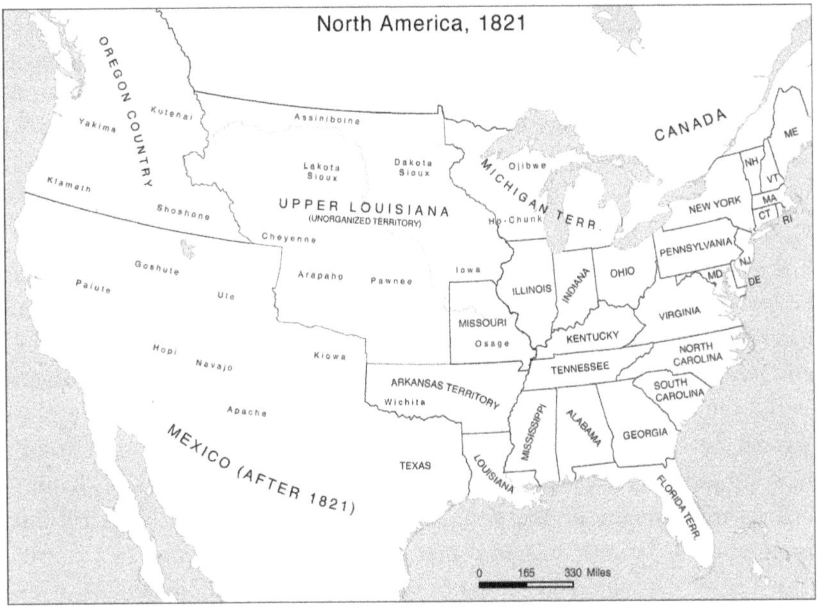

Map 2. Middle Mississippi Valley, 1821.

developed differently in Illinois and Missouri from the 1760s through the 1780s because imperial states deployed state power on behalf of enslavers differently in those places. Article VI reinforced and accelerated those dynamics after 1787, as the United States merely tolerated the continuation of slavery in Illinois, while Spain and the United States actively supported enslavers in Missouri. Imperial support or indifference for enslavers affected the trajectories of empire and enslavement. Article VI proved effective, even if not in the ways that U.S. policy-makers or later historians expected it to be.

Nonetheless, the effects of imperial policies were slow to be felt. Imperial regimes could issue decrees, but they rarely determined local practices of enslavement and emancipation. In 1769, Spanish officials issued a proclamation banning the enslavement of Native Americans in Spanish Upper Louisiana. Habitants objected, and Spanish officials on the ground in Upper Louisiana spent the next three decades working with habitants to shape and evade Spanish imperial regulations regarding enslaving Indigenous people. By the late 1790s, Spanish officials and habitants had, on paper, transformed enslaved Native Americans into enslaved African Americans. With that, Spanish officials and habitant enslavers both obeyed and complied with

imperial regulations while also placing the local powers of the Spanish imperial state at the service of enslavers. U.S. imperial agents in Illinois did much
the same thing. The United States prospectively banned slavery in Illinois in
1787. Local enslavers and U.S. imperial officials worked to overturn Article VI
and to dictate the terms of enslavement. They protected the forms of slavery
that preceded U.S. sovereignty; they created new systems of indentured servitude; they skirted and evaded the clear meaning and intent of Article VI.
They could do so because, in the Middle Mississippi Valley, local officials
enforced imperial decrees in manners that best addressed the interests of
local potentates and middling property owners, most of whom were enslavers. Local imperial officials were themselves local potentates and enslavers,
or they quickly became so. As a result, the effects of imperial decrees against
slavery that directly affected the material and ideological interests of prominent subjects were realized only in the long term. Spanish officials banned
Native American enslavement in 1769; it remained legal through thirty-four
more years of Spanish rule and then another thirty-four years of U.S. rule.
The United States banned slavery in the Northwest Territory in 1787; nonetheless, various forms of bondage continued in Illinois until the late 1840s.

The relationship between empire, enslavement, and emancipation in the
Middle Mississippi Valley would not be solely determined in the halls of
Congress, any more than it was created in palaces in Madrid or Paris. Impe-
rial state power and decrees shaped local practices of slavery, to be sure.
However, from the 1720s through the 1810s, imperial policy-makers, imperial officials, local enslavers, and enslaved people all fought to determine the
local meanings and practices of slavery and emancipation. They contested
imperial decrees. They wielded imperial decrees to safeguard their interests.
They battled with each other in larger imperial structures and local polities.
The relative power of enslavers and enslaved people shifted. The viability of
systems of slavery proved dynamic. The story of empire, enslavement, and
emancipation in the Middle Mississippi Valley remained contingent from
1720 through 1820. Then, the Missouri Crisis inextricably yoked the region
to new, larger conflicts over empire, enslavement, emancipation, and exile
on the North American continent, ultimately leading to the U.S. Civil War.
Understanding empire and enslavement in the Middle Mississippi Valley,
along with the origins and significance of the Northwest Ordinance and the
Missouri Crisis, requires going back a century to five modest French villages
in *le pays des Illinois*, "the country of the Illinois."

CHAPTER 1

Making and Re-Making Slavery and Empire
in the Middle Mississippi Valley, 1720–1790

Various forms of Native American slavery, captivity, and bondage existed in the Middle Mississippi Valley long before the arrival of European interlopers. But when French colonizers and imperial officials began establishing permanent settlements on the east bank of the Mississippi River in the early 1700s, they drew on the kinds of racialized chattel slavery that they and other European colonizers had created in the broader Americas. They also brought with them the forms of Native American enslavement that were familiar to them in French Canada, while adapting to and then transforming the kinds of Native American captivity and bondage already prominent in the Great Lakes and the Mississippi and Missouri Valleys. Using the resources of the French imperial state, by the 1730s, habitants, *voyageurs*, and *coureurs* had created distinct forms of triracialized enslavement that they embedded in larger imperial structures. By 1750, habitants and French imperial officials overseeing the five French villages in Illinois racially categorized approximately 40 percent of the 1,300 residents as *sauvage* or *negroe* and held them in various states of enslavement.[1]

By midcentury, habitants had also oriented economic, political, and diplomatic life in the Illinois Country in two directions. One axis directed patterns of exchange, interaction, and diplomacy from French Canada, through the Great Lakes, down to the French villages, and then up the Missouri River toward present-day Kansas. Another axis stretched from the French villages down the Mississippi River to Lower Louisiana, where enslaved Africans and Native Americans had thwarted earlier French plans to establish a robust slave regime centered on New Orleans and Natchez. Mirroring these orientations, Illinois habitants created systems of slavery that comingled Native

American enslavement and the fur trade with African American enslavement and the production of foodstuffs and stores for New Orleans.

Slavery's establishment and growth in present-day Missouri occurred in
the twenty-five years following the 1763 division of the Middle Mississippi
Valley. Spain claimed the west bank, which remained part of Spanish Upper
Louisiana until 1803. On the east bank, Britain initially claimed dominion
in 1763, but Virginia and then the United States staked claims to the region
in the 1770s and the 1780s. The new imperial borders had little immediate
effect on the day-to-day lives of habitants and enslaved Native and African
Americans. Habitants and enslaved men and women moved across the river
and the border it created with little regard to imperial dominions and claims
of sovereignty. Though technically banned in Upper Louisiana and of murky
legality in Illinois after 1763, the enslavement of Indigenous people continued apace. But if empires made slavery, they also remade it. In the late 1780s,
the enslavement of Native Americans in Upper Louisiana ended—on paper
at least—as habitants transformed enslaved Native Americans into African
American slaves, matching their local practices with imperial decrees. It
would not be the last time that particular forms of slavery persisted long after
imperial decrees banned them.

Between the 1760s and 1780s, habitants and Anglo-American colonizers sought to work with imperial agents from Britain, Spain, and Virginia to
make African American slavery a central feature of European imperialism in
the Greater Mississippi Valley. By 1790, rival imperial powers had created a
distinct Mississippi Valley plantation complex centered in New Orleans but
part of a broader Atlantic and North American world of competing empires.
Whether in the employ of Spain, Britain, Virginia, or the United States, imperial agents all deemed the enslavement of African-descended peoples for the
production of staples, stores, and foodstuffs for the Lower Mississippi Valley
as central to the furtherance of their imperial projects in the Middle Mississippi Valley. Whether in Ste. Geneviève or St. Louis, Cahokia or Kaskaskia,
elites and middling families made claims on imperial states as they sought
to mobilize imperial power locally. Once empowered locally, they used their
power to enslave African and Native Americans and then keep them in slavery. Imperial agents and officials, eager to best their rivals and solidify claims
of sovereignty, readily indulged enslavers and would-be enslavers. Imperial
agents realized their claims of imperial sovereignty by using state power to
assist local colonizers in creating and maintaining systems of slavery. In the
Middle Mississippi Valley, enslavement, imperial state power, and sovereignty

reinforced each other. Imperial agents and colonizers made slavery the main business of empire.

Until the 1750s, the immediate west bank of the Mississippi River in present-day Missouri constituted something of a barely inhabited, neutral ground between competing Native American nations. In the Lower Missouri Valley, the Osage, as intermediaries, governed interactions between European merchants and the numerous Native American nations farther up the Missouri and Kansas Valleys. On the east bank of the Mississippi River lived a diverse group of Native Americans that included Cahokias, Kaskaskias, Peorias, and other Illiniwek. Joining them in their Mississippi Valley homeland since the late 1600s were refugees who had fled Haudenosaunee (Iroquois) attacks in the Great Lakes region and the Upper Ohio Valley. Collectively, these Native American nations formed the Illinois, a loose confederacy with no central or formal political structure.

By the 1730s, French Canadians had established a series of five villages on the east bank of the Mississippi River. Cahokia, located adjacent to an important Native American settlement, sat farthest north, across the river from present-day St. Louis. Kaskaskia lay fifty miles to the south, across the river from present-day Ste. Geneviève. Like Cahokia, it too sat adjacent to an important Native American settlement. The more minor villages of St. Phillipe, Prairie du Rocher, and Fort de Chartres lay in between. These French villages existed at the sufferance of the Illinois, the Osage, and other nations to the north. Rather than being part of a larger French empire in North America, the five habitant villages operated as imperial exclaves that existed only as long as they served the interests of the Illinois and other Indigenous peoples and polities in the region, along with the larger French empire in North America. The villages served the interests of both by operating as the nexus of the fur trade, which connected Native Americans with French merchants in Canada and New Orleans, and by serving as an important source of grain for France's fledgling plantation regime in the Lower Mississippi Valley.[2]

Habitants—entirely unable to impose their ways on Native Americans—incorporated themselves into already-existing Native worlds that were undergoing deep changes. Through the 1700s, Native Americans in the Mississippi Valley proved as powerful and as essential as any other imperial power in keeping captive African Americans and Native Americans enslaved. Native American power, whether from the Illinois or from nations up the Missouri River, remained essential in creating Native American enslavement and maintaining both Native and African American enslavement from the 1720s through the 1780s. Indeed, until the 1780s, the history of the Middle Mississippi Valley was not so much a story about European colonization as much as it was a story about European interlopers establishing outposts among and between competing Native American groups and polities.[3]

During the entirety of the eighteenth century, European colonial exclaves—and their institutions and practices, such as the enslavement of Native Americans and African Americans—existed at the sufferance of the numerous and still-powerful Native American nations and confederacies that surrounded them. In 1739, Chickasaws forced an habitant enslaver to return an enslaved woman who had been sold to him by the French West Indies Company.[4] In 1765, French officials ordered an enslaved Mesquakie woman named Marie to be "declared free" and returned to her family. French officials did so at the demand of "the great chief of the Fox Nation" and explicitly cited French officials' determination to avoid war with the Mesquakie and their allies.[5] Five years later, Chickasaws abducted three enslaved men working the lead pits outside of Ste. Geneviève. Habitant enslavers hired two couriers to facilitate the return of their valuable property. The couriers in turn demanded funds to hire "three Ark[ansa]s" and "an interpreter" to assist them in their negotiations with the Chickasaw.[6] Native Americans could free or seize enslaved Native Americans and African Americans at will. Likewise, they would return those they had seized only on their own terms. Through the 1770s, Indigenous power far exceeded European power in the Middle Mississippi Valley. Habitants could establish small but thriving slave societies in Illinois only with the consent and cooperation of the numerous and powerful Native American nations and confederacies that could annihilate the French settlements or free all those held in slavery. They did not, however, because, like the French, the Illinois and other Native Americans in the region possessed a long history of enslaving others, and they benefited from the presence of French colonizers who enslaved Africans and Native Americans that both groups deemed outsiders.

Habitants drew on Native American and European imperial practices to make slavery a central part of their primary economic activities, political interactions, and social hierarchies. Bondage, captivity, and various kinds of unfreedom were more or less ubiquitous among the diverse peoples and polities of the Middle Mississippi Valley and colonial North America in the eighteenth century. The enslavement of people of African and Native American descent formed a core part of the habitants' economy. Likewise, the trade in captive Native Americans from the Great Plains and the Upper Mississippi Valley formed an important point of cultural, political, and economic relations between habitants and the Osage, Missouria, and Illinois. Finally, ownership of enslaved African and Indigenous bodies enhanced the social and political prestige of habitants and the Native Americans whom they most frequently interacted with. By 1750, the French villages counted nearly 1,400 residents; habitants held approximately 40 percent of the population in slavery.[7]

Of the approximately five hundred enslaved African Americans in the French villages in the 1750s, most were second- and third-generation creoles whose ancestors had been forced upriver from New Orleans in the 1720s and the 1730s. In the 1720s, France initiated designs on building a full-fledged plantation regime in the Lower Mississippi Valley. The first article of the French Company of the Indies' prospective and ordinances for Louisiana and Illinois promised that "the Negroes" procured by the French imperial state "will be sold" to colonizers "at the price of six hundred livres each."[8] Between 1719 and 1731, the Company of the Indies oversaw the shipment of approximately six thousand African captives to Lower Louisiana.[9] In that brief, crucial period, French colonizers and the French imperial state established an incredibly persistent form of African American enslavement in the Lower and Middle Mississippi Valley. As French imperial officials formulated plans for a plantation regime in the Lower Mississippi Valley, Louisiana Governor Jean-Baptiste Le Moyne, Sieur de Bienville, noted that "the lands higher up appear to be more suitable for the other grains such as wheat, rye, barley and oats etc." Bienville expected those staples to "grow there more abundantly in proportion as the settlers there have more slaves to cultivate the land." In the early 1720s, Bienville counted "ninety negro workmen" held by the 195 registered habitants in Illinois.[10] From the beginning, the French imperial project in the Mississippi Valley tied a plantation regime in Louisiana to a provisioning colony in Illinois, with both dependent on enslaved labor.

In the 1720s, merchants and officials sent small groups of enslaved Africans upriver to the Illinois settlements, where they became instrumental in producing Illinois's main export, wheat for New Orleans.[11] In the 1720s, wheat produced by enslaved Africans in Illinois then became the main source of revenue for purchasing enslaved Africans in New Orleans. A 1732 census counted 275 enslaved Africans, and roughly half of the households in the Illinois Country claimed ownership of an enslaved person. At a more granular level, the 1732 census counted 102 enslaved Africans at Kaskaskia, with 37 enslaved Africans at the settlement around Fort de Chartres.[12] Enslaved

Africans were also forced to perform other basic duties in erecting French settlements. In 1725, Commandant Claude Charles du Tisné agreed that the Company of the Indies would provide the settlement's "master pit saw-yer" with an enslaved African to facilitate lumber production in Illinois. The enslaved African provided by the Company would supplement the two Africans whom the sawyer already enslaved. French colonizers constructed homes and boats with planks and beams cut by enslaved Africans.[13]

The fate of slavery in Illinois was inseparable from Lower Louisiana. French imperial designs in Lower Louisiana crashed due to Native Ameri-can and African American resistance, with ramifications for enslavement and empire upriver. In 1729, Natchez Indians launched a surprise attack against the fledgling French plantation settlement at Fort Rosalie (present-day Natchez), destroying the French outpost and killing or capturing its colonizers, enslaved Africans, and officials. The French imperial project in the Lower Mississippi Valley—already battered by the financial pressures of building a plantation regime from scratch in less than ten years—nearly collapsed. Native Amer-icans and enslaved Africans halted efforts to build a plantation regime. The trans-Atlantic and inter-Americas slave trade to the Mississippi Valley crashed as well, as New Orleans sat far outside the main routes of the trans-Atlantic slave trade, while New Orleans merchants lacked the capital, credit, and con-nections possessed by enslavers in places like Saint-Domingue.[14]

As shipments of newly enslaved Africans became scarce in New Orleans, the forced migration of enslaved Africans upriver declined dramatically in the 1730s and 1740s. Rather than large, forced migrations, enslaved Africans now came upriver singularly or in small groups, often the product of deals brokered between individuals in Illinois and New Orleans. In 1734, a French mason offered to rebuild a fort on the condition that he receive "in payment a negro" from New Orleans.[15] In 1747, French officials issued an ordinance "forbidding the transportation of negroes to the Illinois" altogether, ending officially what had largely ceased in practice fifteen years earlier.[16] Enslavers and officials in Lower Louisiana remained "very much interested in that pro-hibition on account of the scarcity of negroes occasioned by sending them off to the Illinois, especially since none had been brought" to New Orleans for such a long period of time.[17] Imperial policy created African enslavement in the Illinois Country in the 1720s; changes in imperial policy and fortunes markedly slowed its growth from the 1730s through the 1750s.

With enslavers downriver scrambling to hold on to every enslaved per-son they could find, merchants sold few enslaved Africans upriver, despite demands from habitants and officials in Illinois. Slavery in the Americas was an imperial creation. With imperial support, it grew; without imperial support, it stagnated. Imperial agents and habitants alike identified imperial state power with the ability to procure enslaved Africans. In the early 1750s, New France Governor Jacques-Pierre de Taffanel de la Jonquière complained to his superiors that "there was no other means to induce" habitants "to cultivate their lands" without enslaved Africans. According to the governor, habitants "left the land entirely to the labor of their negroes and remained in indolence from which nothing else could draw them." If French officials expected habitants to produce wheat for New Orleans or Fort Duquesne, they demanded that the French imperial state assist them in procuring enslaved Africans. "The good inhabitants of the Illinois could no longer enlarge their farms," he advised, because of their inability to procure more enslaved Africans. He then directed officials in New Orleans to send as many enslaved Africans as they could, as the habitants would "make use of all the advantages that these negroes can give them in the cultivation of their lands." The grain produced by enslaved Africans would then redouble in its benefits to the French empire, supplying forts up the Ohio River and residents downriver in New Orleans.[18] A year later, Barthélemy de Macarty Mactigue, the new commandant of the main fort in Illinois advised his superiors "that it is only those who own negroes who make good harvests."[19] Good harvests sustained French imperial settlements in North America; good harvests required enslaved people. Enslaved people were procured through empire.

Habitants and officials also made enslaved labor central to lead mining, and they conceived of enslaved Africans as seed capital for lead-mine operators. Lead proved difficult to extract and process because the main mine operator possessed "no negroes and white labor costing considerably here."[20] Two years later, an official attributed the paucity of output to "the shortage of his labor which consists I believe of one negro." To facilitate mining, the operator requested that officials "advance him some negroes for which he will soon pay, putting himself in a situation to buy others."[21] Lead became shot for rifles and proved a most valuable imperial commodity in the Middle Mississippi Valley, useful as a gift to Native Americans and for defending French holdings from European rivals. Habitants and French officials agreed that lead mining required enslaved labor. Habitants and officials demanded that the resources of the French imperial state be used to procure more captive Africans. European empires in North America ran on enslaved labor. As both imperial officials and European-American colonizers understood matters, a paramount purpose of imperial state power was to assist subjects and agents in acquiring enslaved people. Habitants constantly sought new sources of enslaved Africans, but French officials and merchants could not extend the trade routes that fed the enormous growth of African enslavement in the Caribbean and other parts of North America in the 1700s to New Orleans and the Mississippi Valley. As a result, very few enslaved Africans or creoles arrived in Illinois between the 1730s and the 1760s. Many habitants welcomed British and Spanish regimes in the 1760s, in no small part because they expected the new imperial regimes to help facilitate the forced migration of enslaved Africans to the Middle Mississippi Valley.

In the 1760s, British officials and merchants made concerted efforts to forcibly migrate hundreds of enslaved Africans from Jamaica and Philadelphia. Despite the might and extent of the British empire and merchants, only twice did British officials and merchants forcibly transport enslaved Africans to Illinois in the 1760s.[22] Illinois remained too far afield from the main currents of the trans-Atlantic slave trade for the French and British imperial states to supply the demands of habitant enslavers and would-be enslavers. The French imperial state had proved instrumental in establishing African American enslavement in Illinois in the 1720s. When the French imperial state faltered in the Mississippi Valley in the 1730s, and when the British imperial state also failed to extend state power and commerce to Illinois in the 1760s, the growth of African American enslavement stagnated.

French interlopers in the Illinois Country supplemented the enslavement of African Americans with enslaved Native Americans. As with enslaved Africans, enslaved Indigenous people appear in the earliest records of the five French villages; a 1723 estate inventory from Kaskaskia included an assessment on "Indian slaves," and enslaved Indigenous people appear frequently in property records and transactions.[23] The trade in enslaved Native Americans was Indigenous and ritualistic, but highly modified by contact with European interlopers and the destruction of Native American polities through war and disease. Native American nations had long traded captives—almost always women and children—as a means of creating, maintaining, and expanding their relations within and between families, villages, and nations.[24] The Illiniwek incorporated habitants into this long-standing system from the beginning of French settlement. For a brief period in the early 1700s in the southeast and southwest quarters of the North American continent, the Native American slave trade became regularized, systematic, and tied to imperial expansion among both Native American and European powers.[25]

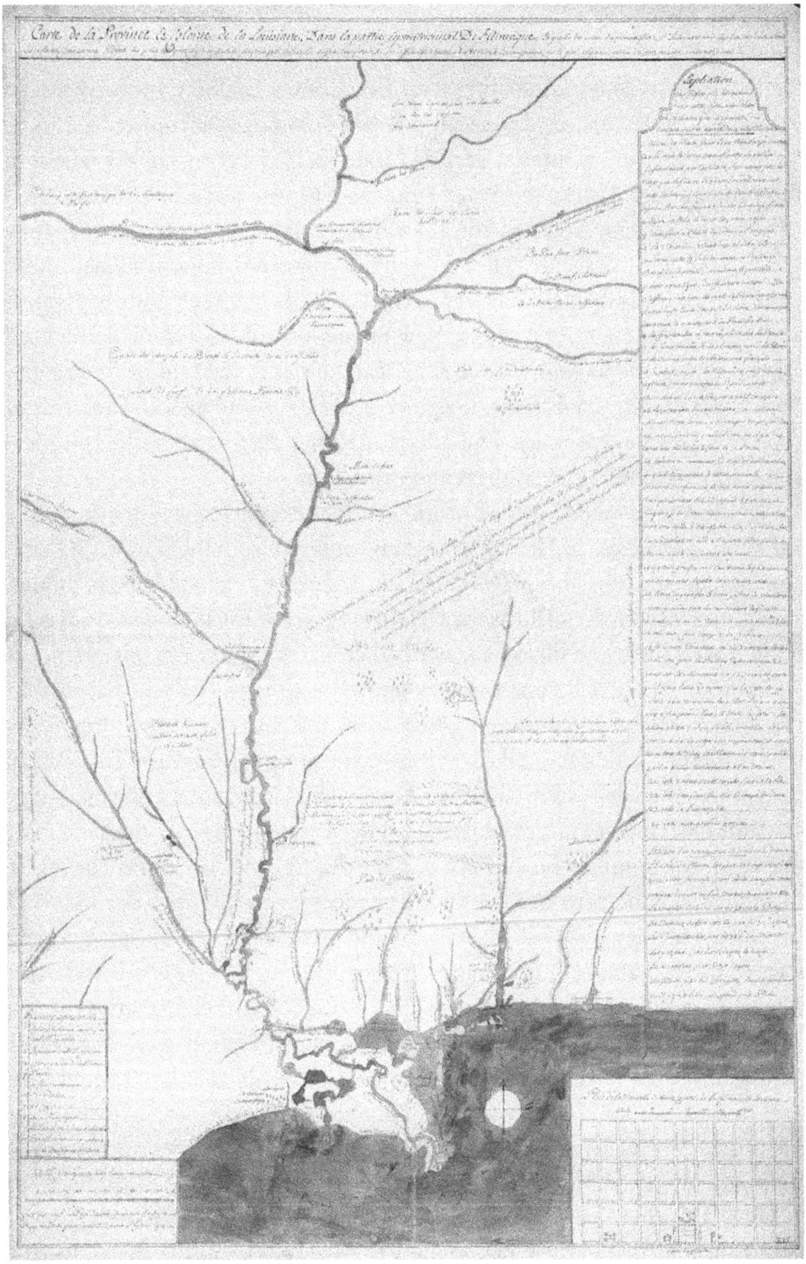

Figure 1. Map of the province and colony of Louisiana, in the northern part of America, 1735, G4042.M5 1735.L4, Geography and Map Division, Library of Congress.

Parts of this expansive and deliberate system of enslaving and exchanging Native Americans occasionally reached the Illinois Country. In the 1730s, an unnamed captive Native American woman, commonly acknowledged to be "a Natchez Indian," arrived at Fort de Chartres, likely as part of the fallout of the Natchez and Chickasaw Wars.[26] But, as with the trade in enslaved Africans to the Illinois Country, the French imperial state remained too weak in the Middle Mississippi Valley to facilitate a more regular, systematic, and commercial trade in enslaved Native Americans, as had been done by English and French traders from Canada, New England, and Charleston, South Carolina. In turn, the trade in Native American bodies in the Middle Mississippi Valley was mostly small-scale, irregular, and tied to Indigenous practices of captivity, kinship, exchange, and alliances rather than large-scale, commercial, and tied to imperial rivalries and expansion

To create and maintain good relations with the French, the Illinois supplied habitants with enslaved Native Americans captured from the Illinois's historic enemies, mostly the Chickasaws to the south and the Fox to the north, though sometimes from as far afield as the Haudenosaunee.[27] The Illinois also engaged in their own trade and diplomacy with other Native Americans, including the Potawatomi, and this became another source of enslaved Native Americans in the French villages. Potawatomi gifted or traded enslaved Native Americans to the Illinois, solidifying alliances and confirming friendships. The Illinois then gifted or traded enslaved Native Americans to habitant merchants, farmers, and officials. In 1752, as tensions between the Illinois and their enemies escalated, the commander of Fort de Chartres, Barthélemy Louis Daniel de Macarty Mactigue, provided the Illinois chief Patissien with "powder and ball." In return, Patissien "offered" Macarty "an Indian slave." Enslaved Native American women solidified political and diplomatic alliances between French and Illinois men.[28] In another instance, a French trader found refuge in an Illinois village after his boat overturned. A Native American family from a different nation, who had relatives held as prisoners by French officials, "offered" the French trader "a slave" in exchange for his assistance in ransoming their family members.[29] In other cases, Native Americans used enslaved people to ransom family members who had been captured by rival nations. Thus, in 1752, a Native American man, Pattissier, arrived in Kaskaskia with "an Indian slave" to "obtain" the "deliverance" of his family from Native Americans friendly with the French.[30]

A second vector of trade, captivity, and forced migration originated in the Missouri, Kansas, and Osage Valleys. The growing availability of French trade goods encouraged nations west of the Mississippi River, primarily the Osage and Missouria, to use enslaved Native Americans for trade and diplomacy with French hunters and traders. French traders who went up the Missouri, Kansas, and Osage Rivers acquired small numbers of captive Native Americans—typically women and children—through trade and diplomatic ceremonies, which were inseparable from each other. The transfer of captive Native American women to habitant hunters and traders then tied a particular habitant to a specific Native American village.[31] Sometimes, some Native American hunters and diplomats gifted captive Native Americans to Illinois villages or habitants. Sometimes, French traders acquired enslaved Native Americans in the Missouri Valley, primarily from the Osage, Kansa, and Missouria. Enslaved Native Americans who typically came from regions beyond present-day Kansas City were either captured by the Osage, Kansa, and Missouria or were acquired by them through trade and diplomacy. Generically referred to as Panis or Pawnee, these enslaved Native Americans typically came from Native American nations in the Great Plains or the Southwest. Osage, Kansa, and Missouria villagers then traded or gifted these enslaved Indigenous peoples to Illinois-based merchants. As late as 1779, French traders "entered into the river of the Kans . . . in order to hunt, and from there to buy slaves" from the Kansa.[32] The cumulative effects of these irregular and haphazard exchanges created a small but steady forced migration of enslaved Indigenous women and children into the French villages.

After enslaved Native Americans came into the possession of habitant traders, they were forcibly marched to the French villages. There, French officials duly recorded them as property through a "declaration" that turned captive Indigenous people into enslaved European chattel.[33] Habitants then purchased, sold, rented, leased, gifted, and willed enslaved Native Americans as personal property, protected by French imperial law and local regulations and customs. In the French villages, captives became commodities to be bought and sold. Habitants valued enslaved Native Americans both for their economic worth and for the social and political prestige they conferred on enslavers. Coerced Indigenous labor produced wheat, salt, and lead; prepared furs and skins; labored in households; were sexual slaves and forced mistresses; and enhanced the status humble farmers and traders, along with prominent merchants and officials.[34]

Whereas enslaved Native Americans became central to economic production for a brief period in Virginia and South Carolina in the late 1600s and the early 1700s, in the Middle Mississippi Valley the labor of enslaved Indigenous people was supplemental more than it was central to economic production. And while the forced migration of enslaved Indigenous women and children to the French villages remained steady from the 1720s through the 1750s, the relative number of enslaved Native Americans remained low. Habitant men frequently forced Native American women into concubinage. Sometimes these women became wives, and, if married in the Catholic Church, they became free. At other times, habitant men freed the children they had fathered with Native American women. Even though the cumulative number of enslaved Native Americans forced to the five villages probably equaled the number of enslaved Africans forced there, the population of enslaved Native Americans remained comparatively lower, as enslaved Indigenous women and children more frequently became free due to marriage, parentage, and other factors.[35] Whatever the case, by the 1750s, approximately 13 percent of the populations of the five French villages on the east bank consisted of enslaved Native Americans.[36]

Colonization on the west bank of the Mississippi River included enslavement from the start. In the 1720s, habitants and the people they enslaved began crossing the Mississippi River to mine lead, produce salt, and trade with the Osage and Missouria. By the 1750s, trading, mining, and salt camps began to take the form of more permanent agricultural, trading, and diplomatic settlements, giving rise to Ste. Geneviève in the early 1750s, St. Louis in the early 1760s, and a series of mining and salt hamlets along the region's smaller rivers.[37] Of the earliest colonizers on the west bank, Henry Marie Brackenridge wrote "slaves were regarded" by them as "the highest species" of "real property."[38] In 1766, habitant Jean Lagrange ran a salt-boiling operation at La Saline outside of Ste. Geneviève with "seventeen heads of negroes,"[39] including an enslaved man "named Mercure, his wife and three children."[40] Daniel Blouin's salt-boiling and lead operation included six enslaved Africans, "Cezar and Janeton his wife," along with Maturin, Batiste, Nagos, and Jasmin.[41] Joseph Dubond's salt and lead camps likewise expropriated the labor of seven adult African Americans: Mara, Polite, Michael, Pierre, Jean, Beaujemain, and Elizabit, along with her three children, Joseph, Jean Baptiste, and Alexandre. Dubond also claimed ownership over enslaved Native American man Jacob, though he had run away "two years" earlier.[42] François Vallé, the most prominent resident of Ste. Geneviève, claimed ownership of more than sixty enslaved Native and African Americans, most of whom worked his extensive agricultural operations. The 1766 Spanish census of Ste. Geneviève, and its satellite settlements La Saline and Mine LaMotte, counted 228 enslaved men and women, slightly over 40 percent of the 547 residents recorded.[43] Empire and enslavement defined the first colonial settlements in what would become Missouri.

While the economy of Ste. Geneviève revolved around lead mining, salt, and commercial agriculture, the economy of the newer settlement of St. Louis centered on trade with Native Americans in the Missouri Valley. Despite these differences, slavery remained vital to both. Trade with Indigenous peoples financed habitants' efforts to procure enslaved Africans in Lower Louisiana. In 1768, fur trader Alexander Langlais entered into an agreement with merchant Antoine Hubert. In exchange for "eight hundred livres in peltries," Langlais requested "a negro . . . on the arrival of the convoy from New Orleans."[44] The following year, when Pierre Laclède Liguest bought out his New Orleans partner, Gilbert Antoine de St. Maxent, the settlement included "12 slaves, as many big as little." Officials valued the enslaved adults and children at 14,000 livres, the firm's second largest asset after the 25,000 livres in furs they had acquired.[45] From the start, then, Laclède's St. Louis operations included twelve enslaved African Americans from New Orleans. In February 1772, brothers Louis and James Perrault settled debts related to their operations, which ran between New Orleans, St. Louis, and Quebec, by acquiring "six negroes, including a negress."[46] Overall, the 1766 census for St. Louis counted 75 enslaved people, accounting for approximately 23 percent of the 257 people recorded. Over the next half-century, the population of enslaved people in St. Louis and Ste. Geneviève would continuously hover around 20 percent.[47]

By the 1750s, habitants and French imperial power had managed to create a collection of seven villages in the Middle Mississippi Valley. In the 1760s, imperial conflicts led to the division of the French Illinois Country into British Illinois and Spanish Upper Louisiana, and then to the transfer of Illinois to Virginia and the United States. While those villages remained comparatively small in size, slavery remained central to their place and significance, both in the mid-eighteenth century and to the long-term development of slavery and empire in the Middle Mississippi Valley. The systems of slavery established by habitants and imperial officials beginning in the 1720s proved remarkably persistent over the next century, even as they shifted between one side of the river and the other.

Imperial officials in the Middle Mississippi Valley, whether French, Spanish, or British, all viewed enslaved people and enslavers as imperial assets, valuable in building and solidifying claims of sovereignty in the contested imperial regions of North America. Underscoring the importance of slavery to empire, formal and informal imperial agents frequently sought to count the number of inhabitants in any given settlement, and they always sought to identify the size of the enslaved population. Upon assuming command of Upper Louisiana in 1751, Commandant Macarty was ordered to perform "every year a general roll of the militia and a general census of all the French, men, women, down to infants at the breast, together with the number of red and black slaves in each settlement."[48] French priest Louis Meurin wrote to his superiors that "this country of the Illinois is nothing more than six villages of about fifty to eighty fires each not including the slaves whose number is sufficiently great." Across the river in St. Louis and Ste. Geneviève, he counted an equally large number of "inhabitants" along with "slaves red and black."[49] British imperial agents proved especially interested in counting the number of enslaved people in the French villages in the Illinois Country, and British policy favored keeping them on the British side of the river. A British census of 1767 recorded 303 enslaved persons out of a total population of 900 at Kaskaskia.[50] Philip Pittman, a British engineering officer stationed at Fort de Chartres, conducted an extensive inventory of the French villages on both banks. In Kaskaskia he took note of "Mons. Beauvais, the richest of the English subjects in this country," who "keeps eighty slaves; he furnished eighty-six thousand weight of flour to the king's magazine, which was only a part of the harvest he reaped in one year." In Saint Philippe "the captain of militia has about twenty slaves, a good stock of cattle, and a water-mill for corn and planks." In Ste. Geneviève, he took note of François Vallé, "the richest inhabitant of the country of the Illinois. . . . [H]e has one hundred negroes, besides hired white people, constantly employed."[51] Cartographer Thomas Hutchins was especially keen to count the number of enslaved African Americans in the Illinois Country. Hutchins noted that Kaskaskia contained "between four and five hundred negroes"; Prairie du Rocher, "80 negroes"; and St. Louis, "about 150 negroes."[52] In the Middle Mississippi Valley, censuses served as instruments of empire, and imperial officials categorized enslaved African and Native Americans among a regime's most valuable resources.

Imperial rivalries in the Mississippi Valley in the 1760s added to the urgency of connecting empire to enslavement. In the 1760s, British imperial designs for the Mississippi Valley, from Fort Pitt to the Illinois Country to Natchez and West Florida, centered on building fortified trading posts to entice enslavers to British dominions. According to one British official, settlements with trading posts were necessary to retain and attract "the most opulent French Inhabitants with their Slaves" to settle in British Illinois and Natchez in the aftermath of the Seven Years' War.[53] As British and Spanish officials understood, habitants wanted to purchase enslaved people. Habitants seemed eager to work with any imperial power who could supply them with enslaved bodies. With British subjects cut off from the markets at New Orleans, Illinois habitants crossed the Mississippi River to become Spanish subjects. British officials in Illinois expressed alarm that "many Frenchmen" in Illinois were "preparing to depart for New Orleans on no other acc't than to purchase slaves,"[54] slaves that proved difficult to purchase through imperial British channels. Illinois habitants who purchased enslaved people in New Orleans became subject to a host of British fines and punishments, including possible seizure of the people they enslaved. Rather than dealing with the British imperial-administrative state that impeded their access to enslaved bodies, they simply relocated to Spanish Upper Louisiana.

Imperial officials offered incentives and support for merchants who could acquire and sell enslaved Africans in the Middle Mississippi Valley. To counteract the stream of habitants fleeing British Illinois for Spanish Upper Louisiana, British officials assisted the Philadelphia merchant firm of Baynton, Wharton, and Morgan in forcing two large groups of enslaved African Americans to the Illinois Country. While one group was forced to march to Kaskaskia from Philadelphia, the other group came from Jamaica via New Orleans.[55] Baynton, Wharton, and Morgan laid out at least 1,853 pounds' worth of food, clothing, and other supplies to transport the enslaved group from Philadelphia to Fort Pitt to Kaskaskia.[56] In Kaskaskia, the firm sold each enslaved man for 2,000 to 2,250 livres; each woman for 1,800 to 2,000 livres; and each child for 1,400 to 1,600 livres, more than double the typical cost of purchasing enslaved humans in the Middle Mississippi Valley in the 1760s.[57] Illinois habitants initially balked at Morgan's high prices but eventually bought him out. Testifying to the great demand for enslaved bodies, one habitant purchased "4 Men & 2 Girls" with pork, flour, promissory notes, and "a Gold Watch" valued at 425 livres.[58] The following summer, the firm purchased "a Negro Wench named Fanny" at Fort Pitt to add to the four batteau of goods they sent from Fort Pitt. Fanny would work her way down the Ohio and up the Mississippi and then be sold in Illinois.[59]

British officials also believed that effective imperial administration required that they assist enslavers in capturing any enslaved men and women who fled. Shortly after taking control of the Illinois settlements, a group of British officials went to extraordinary lengths to recover three enslaved men who had escaped from Kaskaskia. "A Negro named Bill, a Mulatto called Sam, and a Panis by the name of Antoine" fled British Kaskaskia and allegedly made their way to Chickasaw Territory. Agents of the British imperial state across North America contributed to the capture of these enslaved men. The British "intendant of the Chickasaw tribe," licensed traders, an army officer in New York, and an imperial agent in Pensacola spent over a year arranging for the Chickasaw to return the three enslaved men. British authorities sought to establish their worthiness as sovereigns over habitants by extending the tentacles of British state power from New York, to Kaskaskia, to Pensacola, to Chickasaw Territory, all in pursuit of three enslaved men.[60] British imperial officials and habitant enslavers instinctively drew connections between imperial state power, sovereignty, and slavery. British sovereignty in Illinois was as good as the British imperial state's ability to procure enslaved people and keep them enslaved.

Spanish officials agreed with their British counterparts on the close connections between gaining the loyalties of subject-colonizers, establishing effective imperial sovereignty, and increasing imperial state support for slavery. Upon first arriving in Upper Louisiana in 1769, Lieutenant Governor Pedro Piernas enthused that Ste. Geneviève counted among its inhabitants "some who are wealthy enough to cultivate their lands, and raise cattle, hogs, and horses, and have a considerable number of slaves." Piernas appreciated the agricultural potential of St. Louis but lamented that "there are not so many slaves" in St. Louis, "as it is the last settlement that has been formed, they have not yet acquired the means to have slaves."[61] Nearly a decade later, the population of enslaved African Americans in St. Louis remained low compared to surrounding settlements, prompting Spanish officials to remark on "the weakness of the population" and to issue pleas for imperial assistance in obtaining enslaved Africans via Havana and New Orleans.[62] Another Spanish official, Bernardo Gálvez, brooded over "the weakness of the population" in St. Louis and its surrounding villages due to the insufficient number of enslaved people. Without slaves, the habitant settlements were "weak," a hindrance to empire rather than an asset. To rectify the situation, he counseled his superiors to appeal to "the compassion of the King" to "provide them with negro slaves on credit, for whom they may pay with the crops."[63] Imperial officials mobilized imperial state resources in favor of enslavers, bolstering efforts to establish a base of commercial agriculture in support of the plantation regime downriver.

St. Louis enslavers' preference for the fur trade over commercial agriculture rankled Governors Bernardo Gálvez and Fernando de Leyba. Leyba viewed the strength of empire as lying in cash-crop production, commercial agriculture, and African enslavement. The region around St. Louis contained "many square leagues of beautiful meadows" suitable "for all kinds of crops" that could supply growing plantation operations downriver. Yet "there is always a scarcity of food at this place." Without sufficient slave labor to exploit, "the people are interested in" trading with Native Americans "and not in farming because the latter gives them little or no gain, while the former supports them and even makes them rich." As Leyba understood matters, habitants would engage in commercial agriculture only if it was profitable, but profitable commercial agriculture could only be realized with more enslaved labor. To encourage the expansion of commercial agriculture in Upper Louisiana, leading habitants again requested that officials in New Orleans and Havana "advance Negroes" on credit from the empire. The cost of enslaved Africans would then be repaid with taxes and profits on increased agricultural output.[64] Leyba's superior, Gálvez, authorized him to "advise the said settlers that I have proposed to the King that he furnish them with negroes in order to develop more quickly the crops."[65] The request made its way to Madrid. Top-level officials, "having informed the king of all this," received royal sanction to "take the best and most opportune measures for sending negroes."[66] That same year, as Spain undertook the Bourbon Reforms, Council of the Indies member José de Gálvez informed Upper Louisiana Lieutenant Governor Francisco Cruzat that "His Majesty has decided to make provision for supplying them with the negroes, in such manner as may be practicable."[67] For two years, Spanish officials in St. Louis, New Orleans, and Havana worked together to "make easier for them the method by which they might acquire some negro slaves."[68]

Like early European colonizers everywhere in the Americas, habitants insisted that active and abiding state support for slavery was a precondition for establishing permanent settlements that would be integrated into the larger political economies of the Mississippi Valley, imperial and Indigenous North America, and the Atlantic world. In the 1770s, Spanish and British officials, whether in Kaskaskia, New York, St. Louis, New Orleans, Havana, or Madrid, faced difficulties in incorporating habitants into the sprawling Spanish and British empires. In response, officials became sympathetic to demands made by colonizers in places like St. Louis and Kaskaskia. Habitants, sensing an opportunity to use the resources of the Spanish and British states to acquire enslaved Africans far away from the main routes of the trans-Atlantic slave trade, pressed imperial officials to provide active support for a slave trade that carried enslaved Africans from the Caribbean, to New

Orleans, to St. Louis, and from Philadelphia, to Pittsburgh, to Kaskaskia. In the Middle Mississippi Valley, as in much of eighteenth- and nineteenth-century North America, enslavement, imperial state power, and sovereignty operated together.

In 1769, Spanish officials in New Orleans issued a ban on Native American enslavement in Upper Louisiana. Habitants and imperial officials in Upper Louisiana responded by devising ways to conceal and prolong systems of Indigenous enslavement throughout the entirety of Spanish dominion in Upper Louisiana.[69] Habitants who crossed to the west bank of the river in the 1750s and 1760s made the enslavement and trade of Native Americans routine from the beginning of colonization. In 1768, St. Louis founder Pierre Laclède gifted "three negro slaves" and "two Indian slaves" to his common-law wife, Madame Marie Therese Bourgeois Chouteau, and her children.[70] Of the thirteen recorded transactions involving enslaved people recorded at Ste. Geneviève between 1767 and 1770, three involved enslaved Native Americans.[71] In the late 1760s, the Jautard family found themselves owing 17,553 livres to New Orleans merchant Pierre Poupet. The Jautards partially settled the debt with "two slaves, one of whom is a negro named Francois, and the other a Panis Indian name Pierrot."[72] Enslaved Native Americans also served as collateral on loans. In 1769, Ste. Geneviève merchant Francis Duchouquet lent 472 livres to St. Louis trader Joseph Pouillot. Pouillot secured the debt with "an Indian female slave named Angelique, aged about twenty years, pregnant and near her confinement."[73] Enslaved Native Americans served as a form of capital in Upper Louisiana in addition to serving as an important source of coerced labor and font of prestige. Neither habitants nor local imperial officials—many holdovers from the French regime—had any intention of doing away with it, regardless of imperial decrees.

Spain's 1769 ban on Native American enslavement threatened to disrupt the burgeoning systems of Native American enslavement in the nascent settlements on the west bank. Since the 1500s, Spanish officials had condemned outright chattel enslavement but condoned and supported various forms of captivity and bondage for Native Americans. By the mid-1700s, practices of Native American bondage and slavery in Spanish dominions had become a pragmatic matter, subject to local governors' relations with Native American nations and leading local families. While the outright enslavement of Native Americans had long been banned, local officials and colonizers had created innumerable means of binding and enslaving Native Americans across the

Spanish empire.[74] In 1769, newly appointed Louisiana Governor Alejandro O'Reilly met with representatives from numerous Native American nations with whom imperial France had maintained relations. Shortly after their meeting, O'Reilly issued a proclamation seemingly banning Native American enslavement in both Lower and Upper Louisiana. His proclamation warned that Spanish law "very expressly forbid any subject of any quality or condition whatsoever to make any Indian a slave or to possess any such, under any pretext whatever, even though there be an open war against that Indian's nation." O'Reilly's proclamation also warned habitants that "all subjects of His Majesty, and even all transients, are expressly forbidden to acquire, purchase, or take over any Indian slave, beginning from the day of publication of this order." The trade in Native American slaves was expressly forbidden. "The present owners" of enslaved Native Americans were henceforth "unable to part with those they now have in any matter whatsoever, except to give them back their liberty, until receipt of orders from His Majesty."[75]

At minimum, O'Reilly's decree and later instructions had the intent of stripping away enslaved Native Americans' status as chattel property, converting moveable, sellable, and inheritable property into a form of noninheritable servitude more in line with Spanish practices elsewhere. Imperial officials in Madrid never followed up with more precise instructions on O'Reilly's decree, leaving its implementation and enforcement in the hands of local Spanish officials. Local officials and enslavers immediately set about manipulating the proclamation's meaning and terms. Anticipating lax U.S. enforcement of Article VI of the Northwest Ordinance in Illinois, habitants and resident Spanish officials (many of whom were francophonic habitant enslavers themselves) spent the next two decades interpreting and applying the proclamation in ways that best suited their interests. While enslavers and imperial officials obeyed the proclamation, they rarely complied.[76] Spanish officials and habitant enslavers made the terms of Indian enslavement deliberately indeterminate. That indeterminacy allowed enslavers to perpetuate Indigenous enslavement in Upper Louisiana and Missouri until the 1830s.

Having already made Native American slavery central to life in St. Louis, white St. Louisans immediately defied the ban. Sometime in 1770 or 1771, "various inhabitants" of St. Louis "had engaged" with traders "to buy Indians and had even advanced money" for the purchase. "As a result they had acquired fourteen," who had already been sold. Faced with a hostile subject population, Spanish authorities feared challenging St. Louis enslavers. Thus, new Louisiana Governor Luis de Unzaga instructed his subordinates in

St. Louis that "the fourteen Indians bought by the inhabitants of Saint Louis, even after the publication of the ordinance, may be kept by their owners as slaves, but not sold pending the decision of his majesty." These instructions were followed by a warning to "all others in that jurisdiction, not to buy any Indians henceforth nor subject them to slavery."[77] Spanish imperial officials indulged white St. Louisans who purchased enslaved Native Americans, attributing their actions to ignorance of Spanish regulations. They had little choice. Spain's tenuous hold over habitants in Upper Louisiana left them in no position to challenge the actions of subjects in far-off St. Louis. Better to indulge habitants and make them part of the Spanish empire than to drive them into the arms of the British empire across the river.

Habitants and officials devised numerous means to circumvent the ban. The 1769 decree prohibiting Native American enslavement came with orders for a census. O'Reilly instructed enslavers of Native Americans "to make a declaration to the record office of the name and nation of the said Indians, and to set a value on them." To better enforce the ban, O'Reilly ordered all "post commandants to make an exact census of all the Indians who are in slavery in the entire area of their commands. This census shall contain the names of the said slaves, their age, their sex, and their descent, together with the names of their masters, and the price and valuation of the said slaves."[78] Upper Louisiana Lieutenant Governor Pedro Piernas accordingly ordered census takers to count the "*esvlavos Indiuos* that are found in your power" in the "*pueblos de San Luis y S'ta Geneveba.*"[79] Spanish officials—who would themselves soon enough enslave Native Americans—then appointed habitant enslavers to the very offices charged with executing the census.

The census is riddled with obvious errors, omissions, and evasions, suggesting that enslavers and officials deliberately undercounted and re-racialized enslaved Native Americans. In Ste. Geneviève, François Vallé headed up the census. Vallé had long been involved in the enslavement of Native Americans. In 1748, Vallé gifted to his goddaughter "a young Indian slave named Baptiste."[80] In the 1780s, Vallé orchestrated a scheme with Cruzat to re-racialize and then sell "various slaves" who were almost certainly of Native American descent. In St. Louis, Piernas undertook the census. Like Vallé, Piernas became deeply enmeshed in Native American enslavement. In the 1770s and 1780s, he actively assisted prominent enslavers such as the Chouteau family and Louis St. Ange in re-racializing the children of enslaved Native American women as negroes. It is easy to imagine prominent habitants working with Spanish officials to devise schemes to keep enslaved Native Americans in slavery. Enslaver Antoine Diel claimed ownership of Indigenous woman Rose and her six-year-old son. Officials recorded Rose as a "savage . . . of the Pawnee nation." However, they listed her son as a "male negro child, six years of age." With that, Diel re-racialized Rose's son from an enslaved "sauvage," who possessed a possibility of emancipation and whose status prevented his sale, into a "negroe," sellable chattel facing lifetime enslavement for himself and his heirs.[81] Census officials and habitants omitted other enslaved Native Americans from the census entirely. In 1769, St. Louis merchant Joseph Pouillot used enslaved Native American woman Angelique as bond for a 472-livre debt to Francis Duchouquet. However, Angelique, Pouillot, and Duchouquet do not appear in the St. Louis or Ste. Geneviève Indian slave censuses.[82] Likewise, in 1768, habitant enslaver Hunion Huberdeau sold a "savage woman" to Poitvin. Again, Huberdeau, Poitvin, and the enslaved Native American woman do not appear in the 1770 census, and it is likely that Poitvin simply reclassified the enslaved woman as African, as habitants continued to do for the next three decades.[83]

Habitants circumvented the ban for years after the census. The 1770 census recorded in the household of Antoine Aubuchon "one savage woman named Marianne" and her two children, "a boy named Baptiste, seven years old," and "Louis, four years old, both creoles baptized." In 1778, their enslaver, the widow Aubuchon, remarried, leading to an inventory of her estate. Marianne does not appear in the inventory, as she had fled to the woods in 1773 with Céladon, a hunter of mixed Native American and French descent. Marianne's sons, Jean-Baptiste and Louis, however, appear in the estate inventory as simply "slaves," and the family member overseeing settlement of the estate "declared to have sold" the enslaved siblings to other members of the family to settle the terms of the will and estate. The Aubuchon family treated Jean-Baptiste and Louis as chattel to be sold, transferred, and inherited, despite clear Spanish prohibitions.[84] With that, an imperial Spanish regulation was defied, enslaved Native Americans were transformed into enslaved African Americans, and enslavers perpetuated seemingly banned forms of slavery.

Other families continued to hold, trade, and transfer enslaved Native Americans. The 1778 estate inventory of merchant Charles Marois, who split time between St. Louis and Cahokia, included at least two enslaved "sauvages," Etienne and Alexis. Marois's executor sold Etienne to Joseph Tayon (sometimes Taillon) who, according to the 1770 census, already enslaved Native American woman Marie-Louise and her three children. In addition to thirteen enslaved African Americans, two enslaved persons in Marois's estate were not explicitly racialized in the estate inventory, suggesting that Marois and his executor had deliberately omitted their maternal Native American descent. And if the executor and heirs of Marois's estate followed precedent, they also transformed these enslaved Native Americans into enslaved African Americans.[85] Local officials charged with enforcing Spanish regulations simply changed *sauvage* and *rouge* to *negro*, or dropped racial modifiers altogether. In the process, the limited-term, nontransferable servitude decreed by Governor O'Reilly reverted to permanent, inheritable chattel enslavement in the hands of local officials. Local polities made and remade slavery within the boundaries of imperial dictates, often with the connivance if not direct assistance of imperial officials.

Unless directly prompted to do otherwise by their superiors, Spanish officials ignored the restrictions on Native American enslavement and permitted habitants to continue treating enslaved Native Americans as chattel. More than this, they actively assisted habitants in evading imperial regulations. Louis St. Ange, the longtime commander of French forces in Illinois, moved to St. Louis in 1765 after transferring Fort de Chartres in Illinois to British officers. Appointed commandant at St. Louis by Spanish officials, he served as something like an informal co-lieutenant governor and adviser for Spanish officials. He was also crucial in reforging old French and Indian alliances into Spanish-Indian alliances, and in maintaining the Missouri River trade. According to the 1770 census, St. Ange owned at least three adult enslaved Native Americans, François, Lizette, and Angelique, along with three enslaved children, Jean-Baptiste, Louis, and Ignace (Angelique's daughter Charlotte is not listed in the 1770 census). Over the next four years, Angelique gave birth to at least one son, Antoine. In 1774, as St. Ange lay dying, he reviewed his will with Piernas, the very official charged with conducting the 1770 census and with upholding Spanish regulations barring the enslavement, sale, and transfer of enslaved Native Americans. St. Ange's will included "three slaves": Angelique, "an Indian woman," and her children "Charlotte, aged about nine years, and Antoine, aged about 16 months." St. Ange willed to his niece the children Charlotte and Antoine as slaves "until they attained the age of 20 years," at which point "the said two children be free." As for the mother, Angelique, St. Ange willed her to his niece "as a slave for life." Here, two of the leading imperial officials in St. Louis divvied the enslaved bodies of Native Americans, concurrently pushing the permissible boundaries of enslavement and Spanish law, which required that Native Americans could only be held by their original owners or otherwise freed. In addition, by 1774, two enslaved adults and two enslaved children who appeared in the 1770 census are absent from St. Ange's 1774 will. Given St. Ange's treatment of Angelique and her children at his death, it seems likely that St. Ange sold or gifted François and Lizette, along with Jean-Baptiste, Louis, and Ignace, before his death in 1774.[86]

Piernas assisted other enslavers in re-racializing Native Americans. After compiling the first registry of enslaved Native Americans, Piernas issued an ordinance that held that "all those who would not conform to the ordinance of O'Reilly should forfeit their right to the slave Indian." Piernas's order satisfied the demands of his superiors in Havana and Madrid, but it also provided a convenient ruse for enslavers of Native Americans who had evaded the first census in 1770. In 1772 and 1773, Piernas ordered a new census of Ste. Geneviève and St. Louis. Rather than using the customary French racial designations of *mulatto* and *negro*, *sauvage* and *metis*, Piernas simply recorded the number of "slaves" in each village, hiding from imperial officials in Havana and Madrid the continuing enslavement of Native Americans in Upper Louisiana.[87] Piernas and enslavers of Native Americans then used censuses to record their ownership of enslaved persons of maternal Native American descent, but switched their maternal and paternal lineages. Thus, enslaver Joseph Tayon "reported Marie Louise and other Indian slaves" but claimed that they descended from a "mulattress of Nigro blood." Supporting enslaver Tayon's testimony, leading habitant Auguste Chouteau presented himself to Piernas "and said that he was the godfather of Marie Scipion and his wife the godmother, and that she was the daughter of a negress." Piernas "declared" Chouteau's testimony "sufficient." He then ordered that Tayon had acted "in pursuance of the Ordinance of O'Reilly of sundry Indians owned as slaves." Marie Louise Scypion and her daughters did not have to be "reported" on the registry of enslaved Native Americans because their mother had been re-racialized from *sauvage* to *negro*. More broadly, Spanish officials assisted prominent habitant enslavers in recording that enslaved Native Americans "had Indian Blood by father, not by mother," thereby reclassifying enslaved Native American women as "mulatresses" and ensuring that their children, too, would fit the legal categories for inheritable chattel enslavement.[88] Re-racialization of the people they enslaved came easily enough for prominent habitants and Spanish officials.

Nine years after publication of O'Reilly's ordinance, a dispute between traders indicated that the capture, purchase, and sale of Native Americans remained active in Upper Louisiana. A hunter illegally traded along the Kansas River with Native Americans outside his permitted trade area, and a lawsuit followed. In the suit, Louis Beaudoin casually testified that he "had entered into the river Kans in order to hunt, and from there to buy slaves," suggesting that the trade in captive Native Americans remained routine and de facto legal in the late 1770s. Beaudoin further insinuated that when his permit to trade was issued, officials knew he intended to acquire enslaved Native Americans. Recognizing that their unofficial imprimatur of the Indian slave trade now sat in official records that could go to New Orleans, Havana, and Madrid, the officials covered for their affirmation of the trade in enslaved Native Americans. The officials interrogated Beaudoin on why he was "going to do slave business, as he must not ignore that such business is prohibited and forbidden, the ordinances having been published before": so much special pleading from imperial officials covering their complicity in the trade in enslaved Native Americans. In the end, the trader admitted that he had "entered the river Kans" intending to "trade in slaves." However, the Kansa refused him passage upriver, which "forced him to trade his merchandise" intended for the slave trade with the Kansa. The Kansa provided him with skins and pelts rather than the enslaved Native Americans he had set out for, or at least that's what the official records stated. In either case, in issuing the judgment and sentence, Fernando de Leyba covered for official connivance in the Indian slave trade, reiterating that Spanish law "expressly forbids the trade of *rouge* slaves" as well as unlicensed trading with Native Americans. But in the end, Leyba punished the trader—not for engaging in the slave trade but for trading with Native American groups residing outside of his permitted territory.[89]

In the 1770s and 1780s, the status and racial classification of enslaved Native Americans on both sides of the river became dynamic, subject to the whims and power of enslavers and officials. Actions by local officials on both sides of the river continued to sanction the enslavement of Native Americans in other ways. In 1781, new lieutenant governor Francisco Cruzat issued a set of slave codes governing the actions of enslaved Native and African Americans. Testifying to official sanction for the continued enslavement of Native Americans, he directed his ordinances against "the savages, both free and slaves, and the negroes."[90] Virginia took control of Illinois from Great Britain in the late 1770s, and Native American slavery remained ubiquitous there. In 1779, officials in Illinois issued a decree concerning "red and black slaves," while George Rogers Clark, de facto governor of the Illinois settlements, issued a proclamation decrying the "too great liberty enjoyed by the red and black slaves."[91] Four years later in Kaskaskia, two habitants agreed to use "a *griffe* slave, named Louison," as collateral on a loan.[92] Habitants in Illinois continued to buy, sell, and transfer enslaved Native Americans well into the 1780s.[93]

Imperial officials and prominent habitants in Upper Louisiana concealed and perpetuated the enslavement of Indigenous people in myriad ways. More than any other official in Upper Louisiana, Francisco Cruzat understood the extent of Native American enslavement in Upper Louisiana. He was also best positioned to elude the prohibitions he was supposed to enforce. To do so, Cruzat and prominent habitant enslavers simply stopped referring to enslaved Native Americans as "Indians." In 1775, Cruzat purchased a seventeen-year-old enslaved woman whom he listed as a "*Negra*," an enslaved female of African descent. It seems likely that this unnamed, enslaved girl was María, a Métis woman who gave birth to two children fathered by Auguste Chouteau.[94] Cruzat simply labeled María "*Negra*" to evade the ban on purchasing enslaved Native Americans.[95] Cruzat conspired on other dubious deals with Ste. Geneviève's leading habitant family, the Vallés. In 1783, Cruzat purchased "various slaves" from them. The Ste. Geneviève archives record only a mysterious sale of "various slaves" by Pélagie Carpentier Vallé, the estranged wife of Charles Vallé. The Vallé clan likely drove Pélagie back to Canada after she sought a divorce from Charles, whom she charged with "drink, gambling, and concubinage, which are the three capital sins." She also alleged that Charles had absconded with three enslaved people whom Pélagie had brought into the marriage without her "knowledge."[96]

Around the same time that Pélagie Carpentier sought the judicial return of three enslaved people that her husband and his family had taken from their residence, the Vallé family engaged in a trade with Cruzat. "Various" enslaved people were sold in Pélagie's name to Cruzat, with no racial identifiers. Four years later, Cruzat prepared to leave Upper Louisiana for a new post in East Florida. Before departing, Cruzat and the Vallés consummated another sale of enslaved people, this time recorded as "an exchange of slaves" between "Don Fois Cruzat and Don Carlos Valle." Again, they recorded no racial identifiers in this "exchange," which likely involved transferring the enslaved people whom Cruzat had acquired in 1783 back to the Vallés before Cruzat's departure for New Orleans in 1787. Every enslaver who sold an enslaved person in the Ste. Geneviève records between 1777 and 1789 used a racial identifier, marking each sold person as "negro" or "mulatto." The only exceptions were the exchanges between the Vallé clan and Cruzat. Given these circumstances, it seems likely that the Vallé clan used the name of an exiled and estranged female in-law to sell enslaved Native Americans to the governor. Before departing for New Orleans, Cruzat in turn sold them back to the Vallé family. With the imprimatur of the departing governor, enslaved Native Americans claimed by the Vallés—*sauvage esclaves* and *esclauvages*—became "various slaves."[97] Aided and abetted by the chief imperial officer in Spanish Upper Louisiana, enslavers such as the Vallé family re-racialized enslaved Native Americans. By the late 1770s, registrations and sales of enslaved Native Americans largely disappear from official records in St. Louis and Ste. Geneviève. The keepers of those records: the Vallé and Chouteau families, enslavers of the largest number of Indigenous people in Ste. Geneviève and St. Louis, respectively. Habitant enslavers and officials like the Vallés and Chouteaus simply dropped the modifier *sauvage* from *esclavauge*. Enslaved Native Americans were now simply "slaves."[98]

Officials such as Cruzat and Chouteau found other ways to tighten their grasp on enslaved Native Americans, even as some found ways to escape their bondage. In St. Louis in 1785, a group of eight Native Americans and "several" African Americans fled their enslavement for several weeks. While pursuing the group, the slave patrol and Spanish soldiers accidentally killed an enslaved African American man, Baptiste. Baptiste's death prompted a lawsuit and an investigation when enslaver Marie Therese Bourgeois Chouteau sued to recover the value of Baptiste. The witnesses, scribes, and notaries, including several Spanish soldiers and officers, repeatedly used phrases such as "the runaway Indian slaves who had fled from the village some time ago," the "fugitive Indians," the "runaway Indians," and "the Indian slaves." Joseph Marie Papin, a well-educated, on-and-off Spanish official, was the only participant to avoid referring to the Native Americans as slaves, instead denoting them "eight free Indians, former slaves." The lawsuit also listed the names of the enslavers of the Native Americans who ran away in 1785; at least three of these enslavers do not appear in the 1770 census of enslaved Native Americans in St. Louis.[99]

The 1785 lawsuit over Baptiste drew in Louisiana Governor Esteban Miró, who had to approve the settlement for Baptiste. The settlement included dozens of pages of testimony concerning escaped Native American slaves. Having issued a "judgement" regarding "several fugitive Indians, who have been held as slaves despite the ordinances," Miró could no longer ignore habitants' and officials' flagrant disregard of O'Reilly's 1769 decree. He ordered Cruzat to reissue and repost the original ban on enslaving Native Americans. Following Miró's orders, Cruzat reissued the 1769 prohibition on Native American slavery, which held "that the wise and pious laws of his Majesty most strictly forbid any subject, of whatever rank or condition he may be, to make any Indian a slave, or to hold one as such, under any pretext whatsoever." The reissued decree also warned "that the present owners of the said savages, slaves, shall not be allowed to get rid of those whom they have, in any manner whatsoever, except it be by giving them their freedom."[100]

Miró's order could be easily disobeyed, even exploited, especially when enslavers were the ones charged with enforcing them. The escape of enslaved Native Americans and the subsequent lawsuit that made its way to New Orleans afforded Cruzat an opportunity to re-racialize enslaved Native Americans yet again. Shortly after details of the escape arrived in New Orleans, Spanish officials called for a new census of Upper Louisiana. In those censuses, Cruzat used the racial terms *negro* and *pardo* (meaning tan or brown) instead of the traditional categories of *sauvage*, *griffe*, *mulatto*, or *metis* to record enslaved persons of Native American ancestry. In doing so, Cruzat designated enslaved persons of Native American descent to be of African descent, defying imperial regulations and turning bonded people of questionable legal status into chattel slaves. Prominent enslavers such as the Chouteau clan directly benefited from Cruzat's mischief. In the 1787 census, the Chouteaus are listed as owners of thirteen enslaved *pardos*.[101] As of 1791, Native American enslavement no longer existed in Upper Louisiana, at least on paper. Cruzat, other officials, and habitant enslavers folded the mixed forms of Native American enslavement that had developed over the previous seventy years into African American slavery. All told, the 1787 and 1791 censuses of St. Louis and Ste. Geneviève listed approximately 7 percent of the population as *pardo esclavos* and approximately 23 percent of the population as *negro esclavos*. Overall, habitants held approximately 30 percent of the population of Spanish Upper Louisiana in some state of enslavement.[102] Under the auspices of the Spanish empire, habitants and officials had overseen a steady growth in the absolute number and relative percentage of enslaved people in Upper Louisiana.

Official emancipations of enslaved Native Americans remain sparse in the surviving records from St. Louis and Ste. Geneviève. The surviving Ste. Geneviève archives contain thirty-two records involving enslaved Native and African Americans between 1766 and 1780. Only one resulted in "emancipation," which was granted and recorded by Louis de Noyon to a "*savagesse* named Jeanette." That came with stipulations, and Jeanette's lifetime of slavery seems to have been converted into some kind of conditional-term slavery.[103] Most other enslaved Native Americans remained trapped in slavery. Twenty years after the initial ban on Native American slavery, the 1790 estate of the widow Bauvais listed among its assets "an Indian woman named 'Manon,' fourteen years old."[104] Habitants and Spanish officials created an extra-legal norm that the children and descendants of enslaved Native Americans would inherit their status, even though Spanish law suggested otherwise. Short of gaining freedom through concubinage or French paternity, the only chance for enslaved Native Americans to gain their freedom was to present their case in New Orleans during a short period in the early 1790s when a new group of Spanish officials seemed sympathetic to Indigenous claims to freedom.

The travails of an Indigenous family enslaved by Cruzat illustrate the machinations and limits of Indigenous enslavement, and how local officials used their personal power to maintain forms of slavery that directly contradicted imperial decrees. Around 1780, Auguste Chouteau fathered two children with a Métis woman, María Page, who was enslaved by Cruzat. Chouteau apparently wanted his children released from slavery, and he sought possession of them from Cruzat (and María). Cruzat forced Chouteau to purchase the rights to at least one of the enslaved Native American children, who was baptized as Auguste Cruzat. The second child, a daughter, was baptized "Victoire, daughter of Marie, *métisse* slave of Don Francisco Cruzat." After gaining possession of these children, Chouteau likely placed them with the families of children he or his brother had fathered among Osage members in the 1770s. French paternity could be one route to freedom.[105] Meanwhile, María remained enslaved in Upper Louisiana. When Cruzat was transferred to New Orleans in 1787, he forced María and her brother Pierre (sometimes Pedro) to join him. Cruzat's dominion over the lives and labors of enslaved Native Americans was personal, direct, and bound by place. Cruzat died in 1790, and his heirs sought to sell María and Pierre in New Orleans. María and Pierre instead fled, filed freedom suits, and won. Their brother Baptiste, enslaved in Ste. Geneviève, was sold in 1788 as a "mulatto," even though he, too, was of maternal Native American descent. When his enslaver used his labor on a trip to New Orleans, Baptiste fled, hid, and successfully sued for his freedom. María, Pierre, and Baptiste gained their freedom only after the death of Cruzat, when they were able to present their case before high-ranking imperial officials in New Orleans.[106]

At least one other enslaved Native American from Upper Louisiana successfully fought their way out of slavery after going to New Orleans. In 1790, the recently widowed Marie Rose Devaignay filed a suit against merchant Simon Hubardeau. Devaignay's deceased husband had hired out an unnamed, enslaved Indigenous man for a trip to New Orleans and back.

Once in New Orleans, the enslaved man fled from Hubardeau and obtained his freedom, prompting Madame Devaignay's lawsuit seeking compensation for loss of her property.[107] In 1806, an habitant testifying in a freedom suit claimed that in the early 1790s "Indian slaves were going to New Orleans for their freedom," but evidence of such freedom suits is scarce.[108] Whatever the case, Lower Louisiana enslavers, who were losing far more enslaved Indigenous people to freedom suits than Upper Louisiana enslavers, demanded a change in policy. By 1794, Governor Francisco Luis Héctor Carondelet effectively ended the viability of Indigenous freedom suits in both Louisianas.[109]

Imperial decrees might have been drawn up in the parlors of Madrid palaces and Havana fortresses, but local officials and persons of prominence ran the day-to-day operations of empire in places like Ste. Geneviève and St. Louis. In the Middle Mississippi Valley, as with imperial regimes elsewhere in North America, local imperial officials cultivated imperial sovereignty and authority by propping up a regime's most powerful local subjects, enslavers. Enslavers used instruments of empire such as censuses to reinforce their hold over the people they enslaved. Local potentates and imperial officials easily enough re-racialized enslaved people, aligning local practices with imperial dictates. In the process, habitants became loyal subjects of the Spanish empire; enslaved Indigenous people became *pardos* and chattel slaves. In the Middle Mississippi Valley, local officials and potentates implemented imperial edicts in ways that most favored themselves by building and mobilizing imperial state institutions and instruments in local polities. In the process, they made, remade, and perpetuated systems of slavery.

Empire and enslavement proved vital to the history of the Middle Mississippi Valley over the course of the eighteenth century. Various forms of bondage, captivity, and slavery were already widespread among Indigenous people in the Middle Mississippi Valley when French hunters and traders began passing through the region in the late 1600s. When French colonizers began establishing permanent outposts in the early 1700s, they brought with them new forms of slavery and unfree labor, mostly from Canada, but also from the Caribbean. In the late 1710s, French colonizers forced the first enslaved Africans into the region upriver from New Orleans. By the late 1750s, approximately 40 percent of the population of the French villages were enslaved. The French imperial state oversaw, coordinated, and financed the private and state-sponsored enterprises that drove French participation in the burgeoning trade in enslaved Africans that stretched from West Africa to the

Caribbean and New Orleans and then upriver to Illinois. In the 1760s, European imperial rivals divided the Middle Mississippi Valley between Spain and Britain. Both imperial powers tied sovereignty and empire to slavery. In the Middle Mississippi Valley, enslavement was central to empire and colonial settlement; systems of slavery were central to claims of imperial sovereignty. Empire and enslavement shaped the contours of daily life for the peoples of the Middle Mississippi Valley, along with the long-term sovereignties of competing imperial powers. But not all imperial powers in the Middle Mississippi Valley could devote equal resources to slavery. Empire and enslavement thrived when imperial states could extend the ligaments of imperial state power to enslavers; empire and enslavement faltered when imperial officials found themselves distracted, unable, or unwilling to prop up enslavers. The power of enslavers, the autonomy of enslaved people, and the vitality of slave societies in the Middle Mississippi Valley would begin to diverge in the 1760s.

CHAPTER 2

Challenging, Undermining, and Strengthening Slavery in the Middle Mississippi Valley, 1750–1790

Imperial state power kept Native Americans and African Americans in slavery through violence inflicted on enslaved bodies. Violence was endemic to the systems of slavery created by habitant enslavers and imperial officials. Violence made slaves. Violence kept enslaved people in slavery. Despite the centrality of state-sanctioned violence to enslavement, the conditions under which imperial regimes projected violence and terror onto enslaved men and women proved dynamic and variable, especially after the imperial division of the Middle Mississippi Valley beginning in the 1760s. When the power of imperial regimes in the Middle Mississippi Valley waned, enslaved men and women loosened the bonds of their enslavement, sometimes jettisoning them altogether. The environments in which habitant enslavers created their systems of slavery proved dynamic under the most advantageous circumstances; they became volatile when imperial regimes changed and imperial power withered. Under these circumstances, enslaved men and women either sought flight when opportunities presented themselves, or they sought to define the terms of their enslavement in ways that allowed them to exercise greater control over their personal and laboring lives.

Wherever colonizers established slavery, enslavers relied on the traditional accoutrements of imperial state power: access to trade, including the trade in enslaved peoples; institutions that stigmatized enslaved peoples and maintained hierarchies; titles and offices that elevated enslavers; regular soldiers to back up militias and the slave patrol; functioning courts; clearly defined legal impositions on enslaved peoples; and effective mechanisms for imposing violence and terror on enslaved people. In 1730, enslaver François Bastien tried to assault enslaved man Jean Baxe after Baxe refused his commands. Baxe fought off Bastien, leading imperial agents and officers to try Baxe for violating the code "against the negroes who would rebel against free whites." Officials spared Baxe from execution, likely because enslaved men were too hard to come by in Illinois. They instead ordered "a public punishment to make an example." Officials sentenced Baxe to make a public apology "on his knees"; to be "flogged on three separate days"; and that he "bow before" Bastien whenever he encountered him.[1] The violence delivered to enslaved bodies by French officials alone allowed enslavers like Bastien to keep men like Baxe in slavery. The centrality of state violence to slavery manifested itself again a little over a decade later, when French officials suspected that a group of Native Americans and African Americans had "made a pirogue" to "desert" their enslavement by fleeing somewhere in the Mississippi Valley. French authorities deemed "the crimes of" plotting "desertion and insubordination" deserving of severe physical punishment, sentencing all to "several blows of the whip."[2] Imperial state power, mobilized and manifested in local communities, made and perpetuated slavery. Colonizers in the Americas established lasting slave societies when the institutions and practices of imperial powers placed the resources of the imperial state at the disposal of local enslavers.

France did so successfully in the Illinois Country in the 1720s and the 1730s. When French imperial state power attenuated in the 1750s, the slave societies in Illinois stagnated. The 1763 division of the Illinois Country into Spanish Upper Louisiana and British Illinois tangled claims of sovereignty while the ligaments of imperial state power in Illinois faltered. The Illinois settlements sat far outside the regions in which Britain, Virginia, or the United States could deploy imperial state power. Faced with pressing colonial issues along the Atlantic seaboard and in Canada, and Native American opposition in the Ohio Valley and Great Lakes region, Britain had scant resources to spare on governing habitants in the Illinois Country. Virginia's conquest of British Illinois in 1778 brought new disruptions to the routines of state violence and terror that kept enslaved people in slavery. In the early 1780s, Virginian and U.S. authorities more or less abandoned Illinois. Britain, Virginia, and then the United States failed to extend basic imperial functions to Illinois from the 1760s through the 1780s. In turn, the power of enslavers declined in Illinois as enslaved men and women claimed control over their personal and laboring lives. Enslaved people who undermined slavery in Illinois from the 1760s through the 1780s made the Northwest Ordinance and its

Article VI prohibition of slavery possible by driving significant portions of Illinois's enslaving regime across the river to Spanish Upper Louisiana.

Enslavers in the Middle Mississippi Valley followed imperial state power. While the power of enslaving regimes in Illinois waned, Spanish officials in Upper Louisiana made concerted efforts to create an effective slaveholders' regime that girded the power of enslavers by threatening and exercising violence on the bodies of enslaved men and women. Spanish officials mobilized imperial power in their local communities and put it at the service of enslavers. Habitant enslavers in the Middle Mississippi Valley recognized that Spanish Upper Louisiana offered the kinds of state support for slavery that Britain, Virginia, and the United States could not provide from the 1760s through the 1780s. In response, habitant enslavers steadily fled Anglo-Illinois for Spanish Upper Louisiana, further diminishing the power of enslavers in Illinois while adding to the strength of the enslaving regime in Upper Louisiana. As enslaved men and women in the Middle Mississippi Valley discovered, different enslaving regimes exercised vastly differing degrees of mastery, sovereignty, and control over their lives. As the power of enslavers within imperial and local polities shifted, so did the ability of enslaved men and women to claim greater control over their laboring and personal lives.

In the early 1750s, an unnamed Native American woman and Lusignans, of mixed African and Indigenous descent, fled their enslavement. They did so by taking advantage of the weaknesses of French polities undergoing expansion, competition between French and English traders, the in-between spaces that separated French enclaves in the Middle Mississippi Valley, the presence of numerous and powerful Indigenous nations and bands, and the potential for finding kinship with nearby Native American groups. By the early 1750s, habitants from Kaskaskia established a permanent settlement across the river at Ste. Geneviève, along with semipermanent settlements at the salines that lay close by. French claims of sovereignty might have crossed the river, but imperial and local power did not always follow habitants and the people they enslaved. While working on the outskirts of Ste. Geneviève, Lusignans and other enslaved men and women held a party, where Lusignans "assaulted" a Native American woman "when he was drunk." The unnamed Native American woman defended herself by delivering "a blow with a tomahawk" to Lusignans. Local authorities promptly had Lusignans "put in prison." By his own words, he escaped confinement "to avenge himself" against the female Native American who had fended off his assault. Lusignans next joined up with "a

Chickasaw" woman who had also recently escaped enslavement. Lusignans and the Chickasaw woman then found their way to a band of Chickasaws who were raiding French and Illinois hunters and traders around Kaskaskia, Ste. Geneviève, and the salines. The Chickasaw raiding party offered kinship to Lusignans and the woman, both of whom joined the raids.[3]

Officials deemed Lusignans especially dangerous, as "he knows this neighborhood since he has hunted here since he was very young." Imperial officials' concerns proved correct. Lusignans, the woman, and the Chickasaw attacked a group of habitants out to hunt. The group decapitated and "disemboweled" Pagé, one of the French hunters. They also left on his body "a mark of two little bows and eight arrows, and a thong of English gartering dripped in blood." The hunting group included the son and nephew of Lusignans's enslaver; likely at Lusignans's direction, the group kidnapped both. Holding his enslaver's family hostage, Lusignans and the other Chickasaws remained in the area and sought food and other assistance from enslaved people, including four African Americans who had been sent into the woods "to gather pecans." While Lusignans and his party raided habitants and commiserated with enslaved African Americans, the commandant of the Illinois settlements expressed his desire "that Lusignans could be captured for he is very dangerous among our enemies." To track down a runaway man and woman who had joined up with a party of Chickasaw raiders, Commandant Barthélemy de Macarty Mactigue sent out sixty-three soldiers, militia, and French and Native American hunters to find the raiding party, all to no avail. The search party failed to find Lusignans and his band, but they did presumably force them away from the French settlements into Chickasaw territory. Lusignans disappears from the historical record at that point, as he likely found refuge and kinship with Chickasaws in what is now western Tennessee and northern Mississippi.[4] Vast contested and Indigenous spaces, enslaved people's geographical knowledge gained through their forced labor in a mixed-exchange economy, the impossibility of continuously monitoring enslaved people, and the possibility of kinship with Native peoples all permitted Lusignans and an unnamed Chickasaw woman to flee their enslavement.

In the early 1760s, enslaved Indigenous man Louis Mahas took advantage of the unique circumstances of the Middle Mississippi Valley in the midst of imperial transfers to free himself from slavery. Because Mahas was denied kinship with Indigenous nations, his experiences of freedom would differ considerably from that of Lusignans and the unnamed Chickasaw woman.[5] In the late 1750s, "Monsieur Darpentigny [De Repentigny], captain of the troupes of Canada," held Mahas as a slave in Illinois and Michigan. After France ceded its sovereignty in North America to Britain, De Repentigny sold Mahas "as a slave to an English merchant" in Illinois. Sensing an opportunity to dash for freedom, Mahas allegedly delivered a "blow" that "killed the said English merchant." Violence put Mahas into slavery. Mahas used violence to get himself out of slavery. The world that Mahas freed himself into included confused sovereignties between Britain, France, and Spain; fluid identities among and between Native Americans; and expansive stretches of territory that were either contested, uninhabited, or controlled by Native Americans. Mahas seized on these confused geographies and fluid identities and "fled into the nations of this continent." There, he found refuge if not permanent kinship with an unnamed Native American nation.[6]

For unknown reasons, the Indigenous people who provided refuge to Mahas later expelled him. After "being chased" away from Indigenous territory, Mahas made his way toward St. Louis. There, he survived as something of a renegade *coureur des bois*. "For 6 or 7 years" Mahas "lived, at intervals, in this village and in the woods." Unable to live as a free person under Spanish or British sovereignty, or to claim kinship with a Native American nation, Mahas wandered the woods, hunted, pillaged farmers, and engaged in clandestine trade. Mahas also met frequently with enslaved men and women when they took to the woods for nocturnal parties; they returned Mahas's favor by offering him shelter and supplies. Authorities pegged numerous "outrages" on Mahas, including "stealing, running off cattle, debauching slaves with liquor, and insulting habitants, even trying to shoot some one, committing all sorts of atrocities, threatening to take the scalps of French and Spanish." All of these actions made Mahas a wanted man by habitants and Spanish officials alike.[7]

Like other *esclaves* who fled their enslavement, Mahas lived in a netherworld between slavery and freedom, Native American and European sovereignty, all the while evading imperial and local mechanisms of enslavement and captivity. For Mahas, conflicts and competing sovereignties between imperial powers and Native American nations created opportunities for freedom. But, as Mahas discovered, Native American nations treated individuals like him opportunistically. Indigenous groups welcomed Mahas when it was advantageous for them; they expelled him when he became a liability, proved burdensome, or was simply unlikable. An inventory of Mahas's possessions testifies to his meager existence as a condemned fugitive and refugee unable to claim either kinship with any Native American nation or subjecthood under the English or Spanish regimes. Mahas possessed, in addition to his rifle, "about 10 jars" of "bear butter," "seven deer pelts, one bear pelt, not cured," along with sundry items, including "one straw bag of various knick-knacks of savages." Life was hard for fugitive Native Americans unable to find asylum in Native American villages. Lacking kinship with Indigenous people and subjecthood with European colonizers, Mahas wandered the woods or found refuge in his lonely cabin.[8]

A group of hunters captured Mahas in late 1778 when he attacked them in Illinois, which had recently been claimed by Virginia. Illinois had no real functioning government or court system in 1778. Furthermore, Mahas's most recent alleged crimes took place on the Spanish side of the river, even if he had apparently murdered his enslaver on the British side. Testifying to the confused sovereignties, territorialities, and slaveries that crossed rivers and imperial states, the hunters returned him to the west bank of the Mississippi, where they handed him over to Spanish officials in St. Louis. Though testimony against Mahas demonstrates that most habitants considered him to be a slave, the imperial edicts on Native American slavery in Upper Louisiana made it difficult for Spanish officials to treat Mahas as such. Thus, official records repeatedly refer to Mahas as a "savage, formerly slave, at present calling himself free." Spanish officials could not return Mahas to slavery legally, and, given his history, they likely would not want to do so in any case. Thus, Lieutenant Governor Fernando de Leyba sentenced Mahas to "be expulsed from this post permanently, and remitted to" New Orleans, where he would become the problem of the governor general. Upper Louisiana authorities sentenced Mahas to banishment on January 3, 1779. He would be jailed until the ice cleared the Mississippi River and water levels rose, allowing his forced passage to New Orleans. Yet the mechanisms of state and local power could only ensnare someone like Mahas for so long. Barely three weeks after being confined, Mahas "escaped through a fracture which" he "made in the wall" after using "a file" to remove "the irons that the said Mahas had on his feet."[9] At that point, he disappeared from the historical record. Perhaps he found refuge and kinship this time. Perhaps he also died alone in the woods or along a frozen creek or river. Flight and maroonage was difficult for enslaved men and women who pursued freedom without kinship or subjecthood.[10]

The disruptions in the routines of everyday life that accompanied the division of the Illinois Country into British Illinois and Spanish Upper Louisiana, the arrival of British colonizers, and the forced migration of enslaved African Americans created additional opportunities for flight. In 1770, "a Negro named Bill, a Mulatto called Sam, and a Panis by the name of Antoine" disappeared from British Illinois. The flight of these three enslaved men probably began when habitant Fagot La Garciniere determined to sell Sam in New Orleans. La Garciniere placed Sam in the custody of merchant Daniel Blouin, who was instructed to sell Sam. While in the custody of Blouin, Sam met with Antoine, a Native American man enslaved by Blouin. Together, they joined with the enslaved African American man Bill, who had arrived in Illinois with Anglo-American colonizers. British authorities and enslavers suspected they had been "enticed to run away by the Chickasaw Indians"—whether they did so with or without Chickasaw assistance remains unclear. In either case, imperial transfers, the weaknesses of state power in British Illinois, the arrival of newcomers, and the unsettling of the day-to-day routines of enslavement allowed Bill, Sam, and Antoine to successfully flee their enslavement.[11]

Three years later, similar circumstances allowed two enslaved Native American women to flee their captivity with the assistance of a Métis *coureur des bois*. On a Sunday evening in the early spring of 1773, the enslaved Native American woman Marianne, from Ste. Geneviève on the west bank, joined a motley collection of recently arrived Spanish soldiers, long-resident habitant and Métis merchants and hunters, and enslaved men and women. The group crossed the Mississippi River from Ste. Geneviève to Kaskaskia, where they partied at the home of an arriviste English couple. At the party, a Métis *coureur des bois* named Céledon met with Marianne and an unnamed Native American woman from Kaskaskia. Céledon expressed his desire to have a woman join him on his long excursions into the woods; the women shared their desire to flee their enslavement. A plan to flee was hatched.[12] The following Wednesday, the unnamed Native American woman from Kaskaskia "disguised" herself "as a man" and fled with Céledon, crossing from Kaskaskia to the Ste. Geneviève hinterlands. They had apparently planned to have the woman hide in the woods south of Ste. Geneviève. Céledon was then to ride to Ste. Geneviève, where he would assist Marianne and her sons in escaping. The plans went awry when an accidental gun discharge killed the unnamed Native American woman. The gunshot attracted the attention of authorities from Ste. Geneviève at about the same time that the "Lord Commandant of the Kaskasias on the English part" sent word that the unnamed Indigenous woman had fled from Kaskaskia. Céledon fled into the woods alone. Authorities suspected Marianne's involvement in the original escape. After interrogating her, they ordered that she be "held in chains" in a room with "wooden bars" on the window.[13]

A month later, Céledon arrived at Marianne's window, asking her to flee with him. Marianne implored her nine-year-old son, Baptiste, "to come with her." Baptiste declined, "saying that he didn't want to go without his little brother," six-year-old Louis. Marianne refused Baptiste's request because Louis "would hamper" their quick escape. Marianne thus left her sons but promised to return. Marianne was "going into her country," she told Baptiste, promising "that this winter she would come back to get him with some *sauvages*." With assistance from Céledon, Marianne "removed the chain from her feet" and fled. Authorities led by François Vallé "sent a detachment of ten militia in pursuit," but Marianne and Céledon managed to escape. Céledon and Marianne settled in the Black River Valley, far outside the reach of Spanish and habitant authorities, on the edge of Quapaw Territory in northern Arkansas. Marianne and Céledon never managed to liberate her sons, whom the Aubuchon family continued to hold as slaves through at least 1787.[14]

Marianne's netherworld between slavery and freedom proved especially cruel. A group of hunters from Ste. Geneviève happened upon Marianne and Céledon's camp in the woods the following fall. "As soon as she saw" the hunters, "she started to cry." The sight of *coureur des bois* from Ste. Geneviève provoked strong feelings of loss for her children. Marianne "asked them where her children were." She begged a second hunter "to entreat those responsible for her children to raise them in the fear of God." When a third hunter spoke with Marianne, "she told him that she didn't want to come back to the village" of Ste. Geneviève. Céledon wished "to pay Madame Aubuchon" for Marianne's freedom, but the circumstances of their escape and the death of the unnamed Native American woman meant that they could never return to Ste. Geneviève. Fear of capture meant that Marianne and Céledon could never even establish "a fixed camp" for themselves, so they were "always moving around" due to their "fear of being followed." To mask herself further, Marianne often "disguised" herself as a "man."[15]

Meaningful "freedom" for enslaved women like Marianne was hard to come by. Whatever kinship Marianne could claim with Indigenous people had apparently been stripped away by French enslavement, consigning her to roam the woods with Céledon. Freedom also meant flight far away from the ability of Spanish authorities to re-enslave her, along with the abandonment of her two sons. All three found themselves trapped in a special kind of captive hell created by enslavers across the North American continent for three centuries. Freedom from slavery in the Middle Mississippi Valley often meant self-imposed exile, compounding the difficult decision of enslaved men and women to flee, but also impelling many to remain in a state of slavery where they supported and received support from their friends, families, and loved ones. Kinship could be found within slavery for some; kinship outside of slavery proved elusive for Marianne and Mahas. Enslavers—and the imperial states that empowered them—created a series of impossible choices for the men and women whom they enslaved. The impossibility of those choices served as an invisible set of chains that trapped many. As Marianne's agony at the thought of her children demonstrates, enslavers and the empires that supported them possessed a vast arsenal of control that included but extended far beyond violence.

Lusignans and the unnamed Chickasaw woman, Louis Mahas, Marianne, Bill, Sam, and Antoine were outliers who escaped chattel bondage and remained free for extended periods of time. Other enslaved Native and African Americans could only find greater freedoms within their continued legal enslavement. Imperial transfers that began in the 1760s fragmented the interlocking matrices of imperial, local, and personal power that enslavers used to keep Native Americans and African Americans in slavery. Enslaved people in Illinois used these circumstances to claim and gain greater control over their own lives.

The enforcement of local regulations, including those used to govern slaves, dissipated quickly in Illinois when numerous French officials and leading Illinois habitants migrated to Spanish Upper Louisiana beginning in 1764. In Illinois, these French officials and leading habitants stood at the intersection of imperial power, local hierarchies, and the kinds of social prestige and political power that enslavers relied on to maintain bondage. Absent a powerful imperial presence, habitant enslavers fled to Spanish Upper Louisiana when their personal circumstances permitted it. Prominent habitants who fled to Spanish Upper Louisiana carried with them the local sources of power needed to regulate slavery, including the militia and slave patrols, courts that doled out punishment to enslaved people, and grandee enslavers who deployed their personal power on behalf of themselves and other enslavers. The embodiment of local and imperial infrastructures of enslavement crossed the river to Spanish Upper Louisiana, where imperial officials and local potentates reconstructed it. A growing number of enslavers followed.[16] When French officials and enslavers evacuated British Illinois for Spanish Upper Louisiana, they took with them the laws, regulations, mechanisms, practices, social powers, and customs that had been used to keep enslaved Native and African Americans in slavery over the previous half-century.

British officials, operating in a badly overextended empire amid multiple imperial crises, faced difficulties in stretching the sinews of imperial state power to Illinois. Consequently, British officials and imperial agents in Illinois exerted little power or influence over Native Americans, habitants, or enslaved people. As of 1765, the British presence in Illinois consisted of an undermanned garrison at Fort de Chartres. Parliament, distracted by other pressing matters, failed to create a civil government for Illinois or Canada, and day-to-day governance fell to a small contingent of harried military officers. When British merchants and habitants continued to use the Mississippi River and New Orleans for commerce, British officials lamely issued "a Placart forbidding the Inhabitants" from sending goods downriver.[17] Illinois habitants and British merchants ignored the placart with impunity. In doing so, however, they undermined the very authority they relied on to keep enslaved people in slavery.

More than any other factor, the comparative ability of rival imperial powers to build and sustain state power determined where enslavers would thrive and also where enslaved people could create new freedoms for themselves while undermining the power of slaveholder regimes. The weaknesses of the British imperial state in Illinois allowed enslaved men and women to break down the mechanisms that had kept them in slavery. Citing a "want of power," one British official expressed disgust at a spate of murders, including a "Frenchman" who "committed that horrid crime on a poor Negro." He "lamented that no steps can be taken to try matters of that kind in so distant a Country." The same circumstances that permitted an enslaver to murder an enslaved man free of consequences also weakened the state power that enslavers relied on. The officer more broadly feared that the lack of British state power "may be productive of the worst of Consequences," a degeneration into a Hobbesian society of all against all. Turning to the relationship between slavery and state power, he concluded that "some Laws, Regulations, or powers is become absolutely necessary, particularly with regards to the Slaves now become numerous, by their increase and late importations."[18] British officers recognized that imperial state power sustained slavery.

Parliament did not create a government for Illinois until 1773. Before then, British officials and agents, along with habitants, created their own ad hoc regime that was plagued by infighting, duplicity, and a constant rotation of British and habitant personnel. British officials and habitants understood the

necessity of creating a legal regime—and the disciplinary mechanisms it created—to maintain the systems of slavery that habitants had created and maintained over the previous three decades. In 1765, a British official in the Illinois
Country appointed an imperial agent "to decide all disputes that might arise
amongst the Inhabitants according to the Laws and Customs of the Country."
This new court quickly failed due to the exodus of habitant bureaucrats, bilingual notaries public, imperial agents, and local potentates to Spanish Upper
Louisiana. As a result, the remaining habitants' "knowledge of the law," whether
French, British, or local, "is not sufficient as it ought to be," complained British
officials in Illinois. British officials then deemed it "necessary that Judges be
sent [t]here to administer justice."[19] In 1768, British officials sent Lieutenant
Colonel John Wilkins to Kaskaskia to establish courts. Wilkins instead joined
with habitant Robinet to swindle Madame LaFlaim out of two enslaved people
while her husband was "trading with the Indians."[20] With Wilkins's credibility
undermined, habitants created their own quasi-legislative and judicial courts
in their own localities. Citing the "Great expence and inconvenience attending
the Inhabitants being obliged to go to Fort Chartiers," by 1770 habitants were
holding their own rogue court sessions in Kaskaskia. But with no real British presence in Kaskaskia, habitants and English interlopers could do little to
enforce the rulings and decrees issued by British officials or local courts.[21] The
erosion of imperial state power created cracks in the regime of enslavement
that had been nurtured by habitants and French officials. Enslaved men and
women sought to split these cracks wide open.

Shortly after the transfer of Illinois to Britain, an unnamed enslaved man
refused his enslavers' commands, insulted the mistress of the household, and
allegedly stirred up a slave rebellion. But British officials in Illinois, lacking
any British legal system due to delays in London, could not decide how to
punish the enslaved man and discourage further acts of defiance. Paul Derisseaux (or Des Ruisseaux) had emigrated to "Paincourt" (St. Louis) and then
"lately settled himself on this side" of the river in Illinois, likely to flee debts
he had accrued in Spanish Upper Louisiana.[22] Somewhere along the way, he
purchased an enslaved man. The enslaved man sensed that the breakdown of
the imperial state power that enslavers could call on shifted circumstances
in his favor. The enslaved man insulted and disobeyed Derisseaux, who was
"mighty quick and hasty" in punishing him. The enslaved man remained
defiant, and Derisseaux feared that he could no longer control him. When
the enslaved man began talking of rebellion with other enslaved people,
an exasperated Derisseaux turned him over to British officials. The leading

British official in Illinois, Colonel Thomas Reid, was perplexed about what to do with the enslaved man, as Britain had yet to issue a slave code for Illinois. Reid wanted to beat and punish the enslaved man publicly to demonstrate the power of the British imperial presence to enslaved men and women, but he had no authority to do so. Reid turned to the commanding British officer for North America, General Thomas Gage, stationed in New York. Gage had "no doubt" that the enslaved man refused and insulted his enslaver and plotted rebellion. Gage also agreed that the enslaved man "ought to have been punished by authority" in public, rather than simply by his enslaver in private. Gage, however, had little else to offer. Eventually, British officials returned the enslaved man to his enslaver.[23]

Gage and Reid understood that enslavers could use private power to maintain slavery for only so long. Systems of slavery could be maintained only when imperial state power propped up the private power of enslavers and publicly inflicted coercive violence on the bodies of enslaved men and women. More, Gage and Reid understood that habitant enslavers would continue to flee British Illinois until British authorities could constitute an effective enslaving regime. Yet, with British authority all but nonexistent, with the enslaver Derisseaux unable to control the enslaved man due to the weakness of British authority, the best Gage could do was to recommend that local officials "examine into the affair, and do justice in it."[24]

British officials' implementation of Gage's orders only undermined their authority further. Two British officers, allegedly acting on orders from the British governor, seized the enslaved man again after returning him to Derisseaux. The British officers held him for at least six months, making use of the enslaved man's labors for themselves. In effect, British officers stole the enslaved man from Derisseaux and then stole his labor. Derisseaux petitioned Kaskaskia's ad hoc court for a warrant asking the British officials to return the enslaved man and pay damages. The most that the ad hoc court could offer was a request that the officer "make known to them why and wherefore he did take the Negro." The court also threatened to open proceedings to reclaim the enslaved man, but they were powerless to actually seize him from the British officers.[25] Thus, even when British officials used state power to punish allegedly wayward enslaved men and women, they did so in a manner that alienated habitant enslavers while undermining their ability to control the people they enslaved. The power of individual enslavers over the men and women whom they enslaved withered under circumstances that pitted enslavers against imperial authorities and agents.

The weaknesses of new imperial states also created new opportunities for enslaved men and women to gain greater control over their personal and laboring lives, if not to flee outright. In 1767, Pennsylvania trader George Morgan provisioned the enslaved people he had forcibly migrated to Illinois by "purchasing from the French Negroes."[26] By 1767, enslaved men and women in Illinois had claimed enough control over their own laboring lives that they were able to sell the fruits of their labor to English merchants. A year later, enslaved man Jupiter engaged in enough independent economic activities that he was able to establish his own account with Morgan.[27] Under British rule, enslaved people increasingly worked for themselves. Other enslaved people fled. In addition to Bill, Sam, Antoine, and the Indian "woman disguised as a man" who fled Kaskaskia, scattered fragments of remaining documents give glimpses of "missing" enslaved men and women who had apparently fled their enslavement during the brief period of British rule.[28] The harried demands of habitants upon the arrival of Virginia interlopers underscored the extent to which enslaved men and women in Illinois used the breakdown of British imperial authority in Illinois to their own advantage.

In July 1778, Virginian George Rogers Clark marched a small contingent of Virginia troops to the Illinois Country on his way to capture the British outpost of Detroit.[29] Clark and his soldiers easily forced the surrender of the meager British forces stationed in the Illinois Country, and habitants initially welcomed the Virginians. Britain had done little to govern the Illinois Country, providing neither a clear set of laws, an adequate number of officials and soldiers to enforce them, or the promised commercial benefits of the British empire. Habitants hoped that a new regime might provide the stability and state power that had been badly attenuated under British rule.[30] Shortly after Clark assumed control of the Illinois settlements, habitants served him with a litany of complaints about seemingly endemic "disorders, abuses, and brigandage" committed by enslaved Native and African Americans over the previous decade.[31]

Enslaved Native and African Americans who had steadily less fear of punishment from an imperial state, from local polities, or from their individual enslavers increasingly lived their lives on their own terms. They defied their enslavers by keeping and selling the food they grew, the wood they chopped, and the goods that they produced and procured. They took to the woods—and increasingly within the villages—for drinking, singing, and gatherings. They claimed and asserted greater control over their daily lives. For enslavers and their imperial enablers, however, increased autonomy exercised by enslaved people spelled doom. Unless Virginia could project the kind of imperial state power that enslavers relied on, Clark and habitants feared "the total loss of this colony." As both Virginians and habitants understood, enslaving regimes survived only when imperial state power buttressed enslavers and hounded the enslaved. Clark quickly decreed an extensive set of regulations governing "*les Esclaves rouges et noirs*" (the slaves red and black). Clark and his associates had witnessed firsthand how the breakdown of imperial authority and war in Virginia led to slave flight and resistance in Virginia over the previous few years. They stood determined to avoid the same situation in Illinois.[32]

According to Clark and habitant enslavers, the weakness of imperial state power over the previous decade had allowed enslaved Native and African Americans to claim for themselves "great liberty" and to ignore "the different pieces of work in which their masters employ them." Clark's proclamation made clear that enslaved men and women performed more work for themselves and less work for their enslavers. They also traded with non-enslaver whites, who found themselves free from the dominion of prominent habitant enslavers and French officials who had fled to Upper Louisiana. By the 1770s, nominally enslaved Black people and non-enslaver white people had created an economy and social system no longer predicated on exalting enslavers with access to imperial power. The proclamation correspondingly "forbid all persons to buy from, or exchange with, the said red or black slaves any goods, commodities, pigs, wood, or other things whatsoever."[33] As Clark's proclamation indicated, enslaved people now raised pigs for themselves and sold them to others; they chopped wood for themselves and sold it to others; they acquired and traded various goods and commodities. Over the previous decade, enslaved people and non-enslaver whites had created their own economy within which enslaved people exercised a large degree of autonomy over their labor. Absent imperial authority and institutions, there was little enslavers could do to stop them.

Enslaved Native and African Americans also claimed greater control over their personal lives. In the absence of imperial authority and prominent habitants, enslaved men and women gathered more frequently for celebrations and get-togethers. Nocturnal soirees that once took place in the woods were increasingly taking place in the French villages, at homes and farms let out by non-enslaving whites. Nominally enslaved Black people and non-enslaving white people created for themselves a social world free from the self-interested demands of habitant enslavers and imperial officials. In turn,

Clark "forbid all persons to lend or rent gratuitously to any red or black slaves their house, buildings, and courts, after sunset or for the night, for the purpose of dancing, feasting, or holding nocturnal assemblies." Partygoers fueled their "nocturnal" gatherings with alcohol, and Clark "forbid and prohibit[ed] very expressly all persons of whatsoever quality they may be from selling to, causing to be given to, or trading with the red or black slaves any intoxication liquors under any pretext whatsoever and in any quantity, little or big." Clark and leading habitants also suspected enslaved men and women of financing their gatherings with nighttime "thefts and robberies." Clark correspondingly forbid "red and black slaves" from leaving the properties of their enslavers after the "*retraitte Battue*," the beating of the nighttime drum in the village.[34]

Clark intended to bring the full force of the Virginian imperial state to bear on enslaved people. Any enslaved man or woman who violated these prohibitions faced a punishment of "thirty-nine strokes of the whip," administered "in a public place." Clark "enjoined all captains" and "officers of the militia" to "enforce" the proclamation, and he ordered "all white men to arrest the red and black slaves" found outside their enslavers' properties after the beating of the *retraitte Battue*. Any "white men" who arrested offending slaves received a reward of "*qua* [sic] *paistres*" for each enslaved person apprehended.[35] Habitants and Virginia interlopers now had a legal code that empowered them to govern more closely the daily lives of enslaved Native and African Americans. Clark and the habitants, however, lacked the kinds of real, tangible power needed to enforce slave codes at the local level. Rapid imperial transfers in the midst of war hastened the breakdown of formal imperial institutions and informal social power, cutting the lines of hierarchy and authority in the Illinois Country.

Shortly after Clark issued his new set of slave codes for Illinois, a series of deaths attributed to poisonings by enslaved men and women created terror among enslavers. The details of the poisonings are clouded by questionable testimony, likely given under duress, by enslaved men and women facing the prospect of horrific torture and execution. Whatever the reality of the situation, enslavers, habitants, and newcomers all agreed that two enslaved men, Moreau and Manuel, had "poisoned several persons."[36] Moreau and Manuel stood accused of concocting a potion and keeping it in "a horn in which there was boiling blood" in the quarters of the enslaved woman Janette. Moreau and Manuel allegedly met with two enslaved persons owned by Monsieur and Madam Nicolle. The unnamed woman enslaved by the Nicolles "complained" that "her mistress" was "very bad" and that she wished "to make her mistress gentle." Moreau and Manuel provided the potion to the unnamed woman with the promise that it would soften her hard-hearted enslavers. The unnamed woman apparently administered the potion; shortly afterward, the Nicolles died. The enslaved woman encountered Moreau and Manuel after the Nicolles' deaths and complained, "We did not ask you to make them die. We wished only that you make them a little gentler." Moreau replied, "You ought to be content now. There are your master and mistress dead." With the Nicolles dead, Moreau bragged that the unnamed enslaved woman could now "take a walk and go where you wish." Authorities also pinned the alleged poisonings of two other enslaved men and several habitants and soldiers on Manuel and Moreau.[37]

Acting Illinois Governor John Todd sentenced Moreau to death. Illustrating the degree to which imperial authorities and local polities cooperated to maintain slavery in the Illinois Country, Todd ordered the head of the habitant militia, Nicolas Janis, "to guard Moreau, a slave condemned to execution," until the sentence was carried out. The manner in which officials executed Manuel remains unclear. One warrant sentenced him to "be hung by the neck until he be dead." Another warrant sentenced him "to be burnt alive, & his ashes scattered."[38] In either case, imperial state power and local polities joined together to bring violence to the bodies of Manuel and Moreau in an effort to remind those who lived of the fates that might await them.[39] Yet the executions of Manuel and Moreau did little to quell the efforts of enslaved men and women in Illinois to claim greater autonomy over their lives. If anything, Manuel's and Moreau's actions exacerbated habitant fears that, in the absence of clear, imperial authority and state power, enslaved Native and African Americans would unravel what remained of their enslaving regime.

Habitant enslavers increasingly looked to themselves, rather than to Virginia authorities, to preserve their regime. In May 1779, the leading habitants of Kaskaskia complained that Virginia officials failed to uphold and enforce the original *Code Noir*, or the more recent proclamations regulating African and Native Americans.[40] Lacking the means to do much of anything in Illinois, Virginia authorities ignored new habitant pleas to subordinate enslaved African and Native Americans. In September 1779, Kaskaskia habitants devised their own set of regulations. The habitant slave codes carried far stiffer penalties for whites who failed to uphold the regime of enslavers, and for enslaved men and women who violated them. The 1779 Kaskaskia regulations prohibited a standard range of interactions between whites and enslaved Native and African Americans. "All persons of whatsoever quality and condition" were forbidden "to sell to, or cause to be sold to, to trade in, to give to, or exchange with, the savages and negro and red slaves, any intoxication liquors or drinks under any pretext whatsoever and in however small quantities." Likewise, "all persons of this district" were prohibited "to buy from, or exchange with, the red or black slaves in any commodities, such as corn, tobacco, pigs, beans, potatoes, or anything else whatsoever." Reiterating the concerns expressed in Clark's earlier proclamation, the habitant regulations made it clear that enslaved men and women were working for themselves, appropriating the fruits of their own labor and using their proceeds to purchase alcohol and other items and to hold gatherings. Whereas Clark's 1778 regulations punished whites with a small monetary fine, the 1779 Kaskaskia regulations fined each white transgressor "twenty-five livres" and sentenced them to eight days of "imprisonment." Any habitant found guilty of a second offense was to be "driven in disgrace from this village as disturbers of the public peace and harmful to their fellow citizens."[41] Habitant enslavers' desperate attempts to preserve their unraveling regime promised stiff penalties, including banishment, for white people who failed to support enslavers.

Such proclamations were of little effect without active imperial state power to back them up. Virginia and then the United States claimed sovereignty over Illinois, but in the 1770s and the 1780s neither was able to establish the kind of effective imperial state power that was necessary for enslavers to enforce their claimed mastery over either enslaved Native and African Americans or non-enslaver whites. Indeed, three years after Kaskaskia enslavers issued their own slave codes, leading habitants once again petitioned Virginia and the United States to issue and enforce a new code. Reiterating a now-standard litany of complaints, the habitant enslavers demanded that Virginia or the United States prevent whites from buying and selling goods with enslaved Native and African Americans, that imperial officials keep enslaved people confined to their enslavers' properties at night, and that authorities prevent the sale of alcohol to enslaved men and women. They also recommended whites be assessed a fine for the first offense and "that they be expelled from the country" for the second offense.[42] However, with no imperial state backing local efforts to regulate them, together, enslaved people and non-enslaving white people created their own social and economic worlds beyond the efforts of enslavers to regulate their laboring and personal lives.

Habitant enslavers and officials continued to issue so many sets of regulations precisely because of their impotence. These regulations—unenforceable without an operative imperial state backing the enslavers—did little to stop enslaved men and women from exercising greater autonomy. In the fall of 1782, an unnamed enslaved man had "let his horse" to a white man "in exchange for meat." After arriving to collect his payment, the enslaved man encountered Madame Louis Gaud and her brother-in-law, who had borrowed the horse. The enslaved man found only "two racoon" pelts at the Gaud farm. The enslaved man demanded the pelts as partial payment. "In spite" of Madame Gaud's objections, the enslaved man took the pelts anyway. Here was an enslaved man, owner of a horse, engaging in transactions with free whites, despite numerous prohibitions against such actions. To collect on his payment, the enslaved man took what he claimed to be his, two raccoon pelts, despite the objections of a white woman. Had he not gone back to collect on the rest of the payment, the enslaved man presumably would have gotten away with these actions. When he returned, the wife's husband was now present. Monsieur Gaud told the enslaved man "several times to leave his house." The enslaved man refused, insisting that he receive satisfactory payment from Monsieur Gaud's brother. The enslaved man persisted until Gaud drew a weapon, beating the enslaved man with "so severe a strike on his head with a club," that the enslaved man "could not work." Ultimately, Gaud and the unnamed enslaved man ended up in court when the enslaver sued Gaud due to his inability to work. While the enslaver received damages, the local judges ordered "that the plaintiff have his negro given twenty-five strokes with the whip to punish his insolence."[43] The court declined to punish the enslaved man publicly, and given his history of defending his autonomy, it is plausible that his enslaver never actually administered the punishment.

Such sentences did little to deter other enslaved men and women from living their lives on their own terms. A remarkable 1785 court case illustrates just how much control over their own lives at least some enslaved men and women managed to gain in the Illinois Country. By the mid-1780s, local and Virginia officials had promulgated numerous regulations outlawing commerce with and between enslaved men and women, as well as prohibiting enslaved men and women from working on their own time. Despite these regulations, the enslavers of two African American men found themselves in Cahokia's ad hoc court to settle a dispute between the two men they enslaved. According to the court records, one enslaved man had taken the coat of the other because the two men "had sold some cloth" in "exchange for some cotton." When the cotton was not delivered as promised, one enslaved man "went and took the coat to hold until he should be paid." With the two enslaved men unable to resolve the dispute between themselves, they turned to their enslavers for adjudication. While one enslaver was willing to resolve the dispute, the other refused because "he never mixed himself up in these affairs" between enslaved people. Ultimately, the two enslavers took the case to the local ad hoc court, which ruled that the coat be returned "and that the masters take a hand to see that the bargain, which the two negroes have made, is carried out."[44]

The details of this case—"these affairs" between enslaved men—underscore just how much of their own laboring lives that enslaved people had reclaimed under the British and then Virginian and U.S. regimes. First, two enslaved African American men clearly participated in their own economic activities, both between themselves and with white community members. As a result of those independent activities, they acquired and traded cloth, cotton, and clothing. Second, their enslavers clearly accepted these independent economic activities. It is unlikely that these were especially permissive enslavers—such a term makes little sense to anyone familiar with the history of slavery. Rather, the unique circumstances found in the Illinois Country in the 1780s—one where no imperial power had proven able to expend any meaningful kind of state power for twenty years—allowed enslaved men and women to claim and sustain a high degree of autonomy and freedom. Indeed, one enslaver refused to help settle the dispute because "he never mixed himself up in these affairs." "These affairs"—independent economic activities undertaken by enslaved men and women—were routine enough that enslavers simply accepted them as part of slavery in Illinois by the 1780s. Absent imperial state power, enslavers in Illinois could only coerce so much uncompensated labor out of the people they enslaved.[45] Finally, the ad hoc court created by Cahokia's leading habitants lacked the power or initiative to condemn the independent economic activities of these two enslaved men, even though a series of previous regulations issued by habitants and Virginia expressly forbade such actions. At minimum, the court's indifference to these activities suggests that they were routine and widespread in Illinois, where imperial authority had been in disarray since French officials and leading habitants relocated for Spanish Upper Louisiana in the 1760s.[46]

By the mid-1780s, enslaved men and women exercised considerable autonomy. Enslavers, including officials such as the captain of the militia of Prairie du Rocher, nonchalantly permitted unsupervised enslaved men to travel between the Illinois settlements. Jean Baptiste Barbeau thus dispatched "one of [his] negroes" to conduct official business for him between Prairie du Rocher and Kaskaskia when Barbeau found himself indisposed.[47] Other enslaved men and women carved out a wide sphere of independent economic activities. In 1787, "Bienvenu Sr.'s negro" took "from the river" a "canoe" that belonged to another habitant for a journey up the St. Mary's River. Neither the enslaver, the aggrieved canoe owner, nor legal officials saw any reason to punish the enslaved man for journeying, on his own, in someone else's canoe. Instead, the two parties and legal officials simply sought to establish who properly owned the canoe and who, if anyone, was owed compensation for the enslaved man's appropriation of the canoe.[48] The previous year, Kaskaskia enslaver Daniel Blouin sought to sell an enslaved woman, Mannon, to Jacques Clamorgan in St. Louis. Mannon and her husband, Raphael, were able to convince the enslavers to sell Raphael as well, and the enslavers "made an exchange of one negro each" so that Mannon and Raphael could remain together. Unable to escape bondage, Mannon and Raphael could nonetheless dictate at least some of its terms.[49] Others simply fled their enslavement. In 1786, George Morgan returned to the Illinois Country. Morgan sought to reclaim the labor of the enslaved man he had left there. The enslaved man had evidently become accustomed to laboring for himself. When Morgan returned and sought to appropriate the enslaved man's labor, he fled, prompting Morgan to hire a voyageur "to go look for his negro."[50]

In the absence of imperial state power, enslavers found themselves constrained in their ability to wreak the violence of slavery on enslaved men and women, to coerce control over enslaved people's laboring and personal lives. As imperial state power diminished, enslaved men and women began the process of unraveling slavery in Illinois. While many remained legally enslaved for life, a status they passed on to their children, by the 1780s they had managed to claim control over a significant portion of their labor and were living increasingly autonomous lives. Few enslavers permitted or recorded formal emancipations of the people they enslaved in Illinois; thus, there is no clear trail of emancipations for historians to follow. What is clear, however, is the increase of independent economic activity among enslaved African Americans. What seems to have developed in Illinois from the 1760s through the early 1800s were informal agreements between enslavers and enslaved men and women that permitted African Americans to labor for themselves most of the time, while their enslavers could call on them for labor when needed or hire them out. Even when hired out, enslaved men and women often worked on the side for themselves.

Great Britain, Virginia, and then the United States claimed sovereignty over Illinois, but none could effectively bolster enslavers and make slavery a central feature of their imperial designs. In response, enslaved men and women slowly and methodically unraveled themselves from at least parts of their enslavement, increasingly dictating the terms of their enslavement to their ostensible enslavers. The unnamed enslaved men who traded horses for meat, or cotton for cloth, remained slaves on paper and in law. Likewise, Mannon and Raphael remained slaves for life, even if they could insist that their enslaver keep them together as husband and wife. But as the frantic regulations issued by habitants and Virginia officials showed, enslaved men and women had consistently negotiated the terms of their enslavement in favor of themselves. They made enslavement an increasingly difficult and tenuous proposition in Illinois. Enslaved men and women had begun to dismantle the small but once-thriving slave societies on the east bank of the Mississippi River.

The 1763 division of the Illinois Country had diminished imperial state power in British Illinois. In contrast, Spanish officials and enslavers strengthened imperial state power in Upper Louisiana. Slavery had been ubiquitous on both banks of the Mississippi River in the 1760s, but it was larger and more important in Illinois. From the 1760s through the 1780s, the weak, ineffective enslaving regimes in Illinois offered only feeble state support for enslavers. Conversely, Spanish imperial authorities worked closely with habitant enslavers to build and preserve the enslaving regime in Upper Louisiana. Spanish imperial officials immediately placed imperial state power into the hands of leading habitants and former French officials. Spanish officials granted titles to habitant grandees, placed both the militia and Spanish soldiers at the disposal of local enslavers, and assisted them both in keeping enslaved people in slavery and in exerting greater control over enslaved people's personal and laboring lives. Slavery thrived in Upper Louisiana. As Illinois enslavers steadily decamped for the west bank, the power of enslavers there grew, and the autonomy of enslaved people remained constrained. Between 1763 and 1790, as enslaved people claimed greater autonomy over their lives in Illinois, habitant enslavers and Spanish officials built a robust and growing enslaving regime in Upper Louisiana.

This regime ensnared an enslaved woman named Lorine in January 1779. On a cold January morning, Lorine and two other enslaved women, Mariane and Fachon, went to a frozen creek. There, they cut holes in the ice and made a fire to clean their enslavers' laundry. After Lorine and Mariane "had a few words" about "the place of the hole" where they were "washing," they exchanged "a few slaps in the face." Lorine then threw Mariane toward the hole in the ice. Another enslaved woman saved Mariane from the freezing water, but Lorine grabbed Mariane and threw her "into the fire." Lorine continued the attack, delivering "several blows" as Mariane struggled in the fire. Mariane was severely injured in the attack, and a surgeon's report found her "abed and gravely ill." Mariane's enslaver was Fernando de Leyba, the lieutenant governor of Upper Louisiana. Leyba had done much to expand the enslaving regime in Spanish Upper Louisiana in the late 1770s, including working with habitants and imperial officials in places such as Madrid and Havana to expand the number of enslaved Africans available for purchase in Upper Louisiana. Already committed to sustaining and expanding the significance of slavery in Upper Louisiana, Leyba promptly ordered an inquest into the assault.[51]

What brought Lorine to the point where she attacked and nearly killed an enslaved woman doing laundry? Her life in St. Louis over the previous decade and a half provides some hints while accentuating the differences between enslaving regimes in Spanish Upper Louisiana and British Illinois. Lorine was sixteen years old in 1766 when she was put up for auction for one year, with the proceeds used to support the minor children of her now-dead enslaver. Two years later, Lorine formally became the property of Marie Anne LaFerne and her new husband. She also gave birth to a son. By 1770 another child had been born, and both were baptized. A few years later, Lorine and her children were seized to cover debts incurred by her enslaver's husband.[52] Over the course of a decade, an enslaving regime had imposed its might on Lorine as she was auctioned, sold, seized, and transferred between enslavers, all while giving birth to two children. St. Louis had existed for barely a decade, but Spanish officials and habitant enslavers had already instituted the rhythms, norms, and legalities of an enslaving regime. By 1777, Lorine had been returned to Marie Anne LaFerne, who was now married to Gaspard Roubieu, a wife-beating, degenerate drunk. Roubieu routinely unleashed "fury and evil designs" on his wife and presumably other female members of his household, a household that included two stepdaughters and Lorine and her children.[53]

Trapped in slavery in Roubieu's household, Lorine had an especially difficult time over the next year. "On several occasions," Roubieu's abuses against Marie Anne "required the interference of her slaves to protect her." In the dead of night in September 1778, Lorine assisted Marie Anne in escaping from her abusive husband. Roubieu, drunk and quarrelsome, had struck Marie Anne in the face with his fist, leaving a bruise. He then attacked LaFerne's daughters, whose "loud screams" "brought at once to their relief her mulatto servant who forced in the door." LaFerne further alleged that "without the protections of her Slaves, who came running at her cries for help," she "would have been grievously beaten." Marie Anne and her daughters escaped Roubieu and found refuge in the "government house." The enslaved women were apparently not so lucky. While Marie Anne and her daughters found shelter, Lorine and her children were left to deal with the drunk and violent Roubieu.[54]

After this latest violent outburst, Marie Anne informed officials of her intention to divorce Roubieu. Authorities then undertook a detailed investigation of Marie Anne's allegations. The official report did not mention the enslaved women who had rescued LaFerne and her daughters from Roubieu. However, Marie Anne's uncle, the lieutenant governor, and other officials downplayed Marie Anne's accusations against her husband, and they apparently talked her out of proceeding with the divorce. On the same day that the depositions were taken, "the suit" was "discontinued, awaiting its withdraw." Marie Anne and Lorine were soon enough living in the same household as the abusive Roubieu. Marie Anne could call on at least some protection from her male relatives, the lieutenant governor, and other officials. Lorine was left to herself to fend off any future attacks.[55]

What drove Lorine to attack another enslaved woman three months after she was forced to return to the home of a drunk, abusive enslaver? The historical record provides no clear motivation, but the stresses of having been auctioned at sixteen, seized by the state to cover debts, returned to her previous enslaver, put in the position of helping her female enslaver escape from an abusive husband, all while likely defending herself, apparently broke Lorine. Marie Anne's testimony is largely silent about any abuses Roubieu might have inflicted on Lorine. Likewise, no official saw fit to record testimony from Lorine herself. But the surviving testimony makes it easy to imagine constant cruel abuse from Roubieu. Enslavement—and the more effective slave regime that Spanish officials were erecting on the west bank of the river—brought a lifetime of pain and suffering to Lorine. The strong enslaving regime erected by Spanish officials and habitant enslavers in Upper Louisiana left Lorine with little recourse or means to escape. If Lorine had been enslaved in Illinois, it is easy to imagine her slipping away from her enslaver, hiring herself out, and finding refuge and comfort with other enslaved people and non-enslaver whites, as others across the river did. But trapped in St. Louis, on a cold January morning, Lorine directed her trauma toward assaulting Mariane. Leyba

cared little about discovering the motivations for Lorine's attack. The arrogance of power gave him little reason to do so. But Leyba, who was in the
midst of fortifying the enslaving regime in Upper Louisiana, brought the full
force of the Spanish imperial state in St. Louis to bear on Lorine. Lorine's
main crime was not that of assaulting another woman; it was attacking the
property of an imperial official and enslaver, thus undermining the authority
of enslavers across Upper Louisiana.

The imperial officials charged with overseeing Lorine's case expressed little
sympathy for her plight. Charged with preserving a regime of enslavers—and
likely seeking to protect his own investment in the body of Mariane—Leyba
and his subordinates launched an extensive inquiry into the attack. Leyba
devoted the resources of the Spanish imperial state to investigating the case.
The investigation was led by "Monsieur Devolsey, cavalier of St. Louis, adjunct
captain of infantry," who was assisted by "Diego Blanco, sergeant of this garrison" at St. Louis, and a leading habitant, Joseph Labuxiere. Together they
interviewed three witnesses and hired the local surgeon to examine Mariane.
Captain Devolsey sentenced Lorine to a horrific public punishment: She was
"to be beaten with a hundred lashes of the whip, which will be given on the
public square." Recognizing that one hundred lashes would likely kill Lorine—
or hoping that two public beatings would be a more forceful deterrent to
enslaved men and women than one—authorities divided her beating between
"fifty lashes today at 4 o'clock in the afternoon and fifty lashes tomorrow."[56] At
roughly the same time that local courts had all but given up on publicly punishing enslaved men and women in Illinois, Spanish officials in Upper Louisiana laid down one hundred lashes on the body of Mariane. The violence
and control that enslavers and enslaving regimes could exert might have been
influenced by cultural practices, legal traditions, and differing forms of capitalism, but in the end, the relative power of enslavers versus enslaved people
came down to the ability of imperial states to empower local officials, for officials to empower enslavers, and for the state to deliver violence and terror on
enslaved bodies. Anglo-American governments in Illinois in the 1760s, 1770s,
and 1780s barely maintained the infrastructure of enslavement in Illinois; the
power of enslavers waned; the autonomy of enslaved people grew. Conversely,
in Upper Louisiana, a Franco-Hispanic government devoted their institutions
and infrastructure to empowering enslavers and controlling enslaved people.

Spanish officials and leading habitants also proved adept at continuing
to enslave African and Native Americans, even after they were legally entitled to emancipation. In 1779, an enslaved Native American woman named

Jeanette somehow or another won her emancipation, though it is possible that her emancipation was a cover for her sale from enslaver De la Joy to Jean Louis DeNoyon. The terms of her emancipation differed little from enslavement. De la Joy and DeNoyon granted Jeanette "*liberté*" "on the condition that the aforementioned girl will stay with [DeNoyon] until the end of her time." They also specified "that she will behave within the good ease and custom" expected of a "*sauvagesse*," the customary term for an enslaved Native American woman. At most, Jeanette might have become free at the end of her unspecified time, as long as she remained submissive and played the part of the good female slave. Even when emancipating Native Americans, Spanish officials and local grandees laid down terms that differed little from slavery.[57]

Ste. Geneviève's most prominent official and enslaver, François Vallé, assisted enslavers by outright denying emancipation to individuals who seemed legally entitled to it. In 1771, at Ste. Geneviève, enslaved woman Marie claimed that she gained her freedom at the death of her former enslaver, Jean Baptiste La Bastille. The grounds on which Marie claimed her freedom remain unclear from surviving documents: It could have been a verbal promise, or it could have been laid out in her enslaver's will. Whatever the case, the heirs of Marie's enslaver contested her emancipation. For individuals like Marie, freedom would be frustrated if someone could make some kind of plausible claim to keep the emancipated individual in slavery, and as long as local and imperial officials empowered claimants. La Bastille's heirs contested the emancipation; local officials sided with them, denying Marie's emancipation. Marie fled to St. Louis. La Bastille's heirs captured Marie there and sought to return her to slavery in Ste. Geneviève. Marie protested her capture, and her case was heard by Leyba. Unfortunately for Marie, her plea for freedom required documentary assistance from François Vallé. Vallé and Leyba decreed that Marie must "stay in her current state" of slavery "without making use of the liberty" until she could better prove that she was indeed legally entitled to her freedom.[58]

Vallé and Leyba, of course, controlled the legal documentation and proceedings by which Marie could prove her right to freedom. It is doubtful that Vallé ever provided Marie with that documentation. Vallé served as something like a social, economic, and political patriarch over the families of Ste. Geneviève. The town's wealthiest man, he owned extensive farming and mining operations and approximately sixty enslaved people. Spanish officials immediately empowered and elevated him as an imperial official and agent. Vallé served as captain of the militia and "special lieutenant and judge." He also headed up the census of enslaved Native Americans in Ste. Geneviève in 1770. As a local patriarch and imperial official, Vallé apparently denied Marie's freedom claim to satisfy the La Bastille family. Local legal indeterminacy—made indeterminate by officials who were themselves enslavers—stalled Marie's emancipation indefinitely.[59] Seven years after claiming that she should be legally emancipated, Marie remained trapped in slavery because Vallé and Leyba possessed the power to assist local enslavers. In Illinois, a weak imperial state allowed enslaved men and women to control their laboring and personal lives. In Upper Louisiana, the imperial state and local notables conspired to deny legal and lawful claims to freedom. The Spanish imperial state and local and habitant potentates empowered *esclavagiste petits* in Upper Louisiana while small enslavers steadily lost their power in Illinois.

Marie was not the only enslaved person denied claims to freedom by local officials who coupled their social and economic power with the Spanish imperial state to keep enslaved people in slavery. Auguste Chouteau was something like Vallé's counterpart in St. Louis. Chouteau had worked with his stepfather in establishing the significance of the village of St. Louis in the 1760s, and his family served as the unquestioned source of the town's social prestige, wealth, and political power. Sometime in the early 1790s, two Native Americans enslaved by Chouteau had the temerity to seek their freedom, though how they did so is not specified in any remaining documents. In any case, with all of the power and arrogance that a prominent subject, imperial agent, and habitant could muster, Chouteau faced off against "his Indian slaves who had been disobedient and claimed their Liberty." After the unnamed Native Americans tried to claim their freedom, Chouteau "had them whipt—being tied to four sticks." They "then had talked no more about their liberty."[60] Who else could they talk to about their liberty? Chouteau was a member of St. Louis's founding family, an important imperial agent for Spain, and patriarch of one of Upper Louisiana's most wealthy and powerful families. Franco-Hispanic enslavement could be every bit as harsh, violent, and encompassing as Anglo-American enslavement. Equally important, Chouteau and Spanish officials had created an imperial state adept at keeping enslaved people in slavery. While an erstwhile enslaving regime faltered in Illinois, Spanish officials, local potentates, and small enslavers built and maintained institutions that empowered enslavers.

In Upper Louisiana, prominent enslavers embodied the imperial Spanish state along with local social, economic, and political power. While the power of enslavers withered in Illinois, in Upper Louisiana enslavers such as

Francisco Cruzat, Chouteau, and Vallé, and hundreds of other *esclavagistes petits*, nurtured the awful growth of a slave society because they were backed by the full force and authority of the Spanish imperial state. Conversely, in Illinois, British and then Virginian officials could not open courts, could not find prominent local enslavers to appoint to office, and watched militia officers and minor bureaucrats such as notaries public flee to Upper Louisiana. The infrastructure of enslavement that once existed in Illinois was reconstituted in Upper Louisiana. No matter how weak the Spanish empire might have been in Upper Louisiana, it was legions stronger than anything Britain, Virginia, or the United States could muster in Illinois. Historians have lauded the legal mechanisms that afforded enslaved men and women avenues for emancipation under Spanish and French regimes, while decrying their absence under British and then U.S. regimes. But imperial legal niceties decreed from Madrid or Paris were far less important than the ability of imperial officials and local slaveholders to exercise power over enslaved peoples. In the Middle Mississippi Valley, local circumstances mattered far more than abstract, imperial legal regimes in shaping the lives of enslavers and the enslaved. With a weak imperial regime in Illinois, enslaved men and women found an ever-growing number of ways to exert control over their laboring and personal lives within their legal enslavement, or to free themselves from slavery altogether. Even if Franco-Hispanic slave codes provided greater theoretical avenues to freedom, enslavers and imperial officials controlled who could access them and how they would be administered. A comparatively strong imperial state in Upper Louisiana forced legally emancipated woman Marie to continue a life of unrequited toil, exiled Marianne to the woods far from Ste. Geneviève, denied her children their freedom, inflicted one hundred lashes on the oft-abused Lorine, and consigned Chouteau's enslaved Native Americans to be tied down and whipped. In the Middle Mississippi Valley, the ability of imperial agents and local polities to prop up the power of enslavers mattered far more than legal regimes, cultural differences, or economic systems.

Much like their counterparts across the river, Spanish officials would issue new sets of slave codes and regulations in 1781 and again in 1787. But reflecting the divergence of the two enslaving regimes, the Spanish codes lacked the sense of urgency found in those issued by Virginian authorities and habitants in Illinois. Nonetheless, the ordinances seeking to govern the behavior of enslaved African and Native Americans on the west bank demonstrate that enslaved men and women in Upper Louisiana found their own ways to claim, exercise, and secure a range of privileges, despite the more stringent oversights of Spanish officials and local potentates. Ordinances issued in St. Louis in 1781 prohibited enslaved men and women from "hold[ing] any assembly at night," from "leave[ing] their cabins at night," or from "reciev[ing] in their cabin other slaves." Enslaved men and women were likewise not "allowed to dance, either by day or night, in the village or elsewhere." Those found in violation of these orders faced "fifty lashes of the whip," to be delivered "in public." If Spanish Missouri was like most slave regimes, regulations governing slave behavior sought to clamp down on actions and activities that were already widespread.[61]

In either case, enslaved African and Native Americans immediately circumvented these new regulations. An ordinance issued three days after authorities banned parties in the woods noted that enslaved Native and African Americans had begun "to dress themselves in a barbarous fashion, adorning themselves with vermillion [red paint] and many feathers which render them unrecognizable, especially in the woods." Enslaved people now took to the woods, where they passed themselves off as free Native Americans who frequently visited St. Louis for extended periods of time. When Spanish officials sought to tighten control over the lives of enslaved Native and African Americans, they retreated to contested spaces outside the village bounds. Spanish authorities now found themselves unable to control the movements of enslaved African and Native Americans who had "metamorphosized" themselves into free people, at least temporarily. Spanish officials thus sought to regulate their dress, "strictly forbidding all savages, whether free or slave, and all negroes of this said post to clothe themselves in any other manner than according to our usage and custom."[62]

Enslaved men and women in Upper Louisiana never managed to gain control over their labor and lives to the extent of their counterparts in Illinois due to far stronger oversight by Spanish officials and habitant enslavers. Nonetheless, within the confines of a stronger enslaving regime that limited the independent economic activities of enslaved people, the mixed commercial agriculture and fur-trade economies required considerable mobility. In 1778 and 1784, Ste. Geneviève and St. Louis issued regulations on fencing in crops and livestock, respectively. The regulations acknowledged the mobility of enslaved people even as it tried to regulate it. Thus, both Ste. Geneviève and St. Louis threatened that "whenever slaves are found to have violated" rules that regulated how individuals moved through fenced-in fields and pastures, "such slaves will be punished by the use of the whip, according to the importance of such violation."[63]

While enslaved men and women were moving freely through fields and pastures, they were also participating in illicit trade, the main venue for independent economic activities among enslaved people. In December 1783, Isabel Bissette Vachard, relative of a prominent St. Louis merchant family, apparently stole a boat laden with goods and headed downriver. Landing at Ste. Geneviève, she traded with enslaved men and women working François Vallé's saline and farms. The enslaved men and women provided Vachard with "salt, corn, meal, and grain"; Vachard provided them with "articles of clothing and dry goods." Authorities contended that her actions caused "manifest injury" to Vallé and his associates, not only in "causing the slaves to steal from their owners" but also in leading some enslaved men and women "to run off to avoid punishment."[64] In the 1780s, the ever-growing presence of Americans, displaced Native Americans and transients, banditti, and other interlopers who traveled through the Middle Mississippi Valley provided increased opportunities for clandestine trade, paid for by the goods that enslaved men and women produced with their own labor. In 1788, Henri Peyroux Coudreniere, commandant at Ste. Geneviève, complained that "savages" and "foreigners" traded "at the Saline" with enslaved men and women. According to Commandant Coudreniere, American interlopers and Native Americans "corrupt the slaves." From the perspective of enslaved men and women, the presence of outsiders not subject to the enslaving Spanish regime provided them an additional opportunity to keep a portion of the salt and grain that they produced so that they could participate in the growing, increasingly diverse economy of the Middle Mississippi Valley. Though autonomy proved far more difficult to come by for enslaved men and women in Spanish Upper Louisiana, they nonetheless seized on whatever opportunities they found or could create, even if such opportunities were harder to come by in Upper Louisiana.[65]

For many enslaved men and women in Upper Louisiana, circumstances and opportunities for freedom rarely presented themselves. In 1785, a group created an opportunity to flee. The response of Spanish imperial authorities and habitant potentates illustrates how the enslaving regimes in the Middle Mississippi Valley were diverging. In November 1785, at least seven Native American men, one Native American woman, and several African Americans escaped their enslavement and fled to the woods. They "set on fire two or three places," either to create a distraction to facilitate their escape or, as imperial authorities alleged, "with a view of destroying the village." Whatever the case, on the way out of St. Louis, they appropriated from "their former masters" "horses, guns, blankets and ammunition." During their "month's absence," they "pillaged an American and his wife on the waters of the Mera-mac" River, attacked "others, subjects of the King," and allegedly "murdered" at least one person. For a month, they eluded Spanish and habitant attempts to capture them. After a month in the woods, "four of them left the others in their place of concealment" and headed toward St. Louis seeking "to per-suade some female slaves to abscond with them." At the village of St. Charles, "one was captured." The lieutenant governor led the interrogation of the cap-tured man, who confessed that they intended to liberate a woman enslaved by the Chouteau family. Authorities ordered Chouteau family member Joseph Papin to hasten to the farm of his mother-in-law, Marie Therese Chouteau.[66]

Matters became confused at the Chouteau farm, when Papin stumbled on an enslaved man named Baptiste, whose enslaver was Marie Therese. The record makes it impossible to know whether Baptiste was assisting the fugi-tives. Whatever the case, when Papin discovered Baptiste in the darkness of a farm where fugitive slaves were expected to liberate an enslaved woman, Baptiste quickly created a story. Baptiste explained to Papin that he was assisting authorities in capturing the fugitives. Authorities dispatched "two detachments" to the Chouteau farm. The soldiers, authorities, and Papin and Silvestre Labaddie then planned an ambush on the fugitives, whom they expected to provide "formidable and violent resistance." One detachment stormed the barn, "discharging their firelocks at the same time." The fugitives "sprang up" when the slavecatchers stormed the barn, but they were "not able to gain" their guns. The fugitives "tried to defend" themselves "by blows," but the more numerous and better-armed slave patrol and Spanish soldiers over-whelmed them. Authorities captured two Native Americans and killed an unspecified number of others, while presumably some escaped to the woods where they remained free. However, during the attack, an errant gunshot killed Baptiste. Authorities spent the next year trying to determine who was liable to compensate Marie Therese for the loss of her property.[67] In Upper Louisiana, enslavers mobilized the powers of the Spanish imperial state and themselves to suppress enslaved peoples' efforts to liberate themselves. When they destroyed valuable enslaved property, they used the imperial state to determine how to compensate Marie Therese Chouteau for her loss.

By the late 1780s, it was clear to enslavers in the Middle Mississippi Valley that the east and west banks of the Mississippi River contained two very differ-ent—and diverging—enslaving regimes. Britain and Virginia failed to imple-ment imperial state power in the Illinois Country. Without an imperial state empowering enslavers at the local level, enslaved men and women claimed, gained, and exercised an ever-growing set of freedoms within slavery. Meanwhile, on the west bank, Spanish authorities, local potentates, and enslavers worked closely to mobilize imperial state power to keep enslaved men and women in slavery and to limit, as much as possible, the freedoms within slavery that enslaved men and women could exercise. By the late 1780s, the enslaving regimes of the Middle Mississippi Valley were clearly branching away from each other, a process that would accelerate over the decade and a half preceding the Louisiana Purchase.

CHAPTER 3

Diverging Regimes

Upper Louisiana and Illinois, 1780–1803

In the contested borderlands of the Middle Mississippi Valley of the late eighteenth century, imperial officials, agents, policy-makers, and enslavers made borders matter in ways that they had not during the previous three decades. In the late 1780s the Confederation Congress and then the new federal government of the United States issued the Northwest Ordinance as a governing compact that would structure U.S. colonization of the region bounded by the Ohio River, the Mississippi River, and the Great Lakes. Article VI decreed that "there shall be neither slavery nor involuntary servitude in the said territory." Historians have harshly criticized the U.S. government for failing to uphold the clear terms of the Northwest Ordinance, allowing slavery to linger on in Illinois well into the 1840s.[1] These criticisms, however, obscure an equally important development. While the United States failed to support or implement emancipation in Illinois, the United States also lacked the resources, institutions, and imperial infrastructures needed to offer anything more than passive state acceptance of the dwindling number of enslavers who remained through British dominion, the U.S. War for Independence, and then the abandonment of the region by Virginian and U.S. officials in the 1780s and 1790s. After the United States developed a more competent administrative-imperial state by the late 1790s, northern antislavery imperialists fought to deny its resources to enslavers in Illinois and the Northwest. Enslavers thrived in the Mississippi Valley when they exercised local self-government in a larger imperial regime that supported them. From the 1770s through the first decade of the 1800s, Virginia and the U.S. government proved incapable and then unwilling to place the resources of the imperial U.S. state at the disposal of enslavers. Even more so than under British rule, the absence of imperial state power in Illinois made enslavement a practice based on personal power. Under such circumstances, the power that enslavers could bring to bear on the people they enslaved became limited. Recognizing as much, migrating enslavers steadfastly avoided Illinois.

Spanish officials responded to the absence of U.S. imperial state power in Illinois by devoting whatever imperial resources they could muster to supporting enslavers on their side of the Mississippi River. Spanish officials used imperial and provincial governments to empower enslavers, who then exercised local power over individuals according to their race, rank, gender, and status. In the contested borderlands of the Middle Mississippi Valley, Spanish officials also made borders matter. They used sovereignty and territoriality to gain an advantage over the United States by protecting the interests of enslavers in Upper Louisiana, while denying them to Illinois enslavers whose business, interests, and slaves carried over to the west bank. In the small, tight-knit world that crossed the two banks of the Middle Mississippi River, enslavers understood that the Spanish regime served them far better than the persons, laws, and imperial institutions that barely existed in Illinois. Enslavers grasped at imperial state power: They followed it to Spanish Upper Louisiana and they fled its absence in U.S. Illinois.

From the 1780s through the early 1800s, enslavers in Illinois—whether habitants or recently arrived Americans—steadily decamped for Upper Louisiana, following Spanish offers of free land, unimpeded access to New Orleans, and active state support for the rights and interests of enslavers. At the same time, enslavers from places like Virginia avoided Illinois because of its prospective ban on slavery and the lack of effective governance. Spanish officials incorporated Americans and habitant enslavers into their imperial enslaving regime by offering them titles and offices, emoluments and rewards, free land, and the resources of an imperial state committed to slavery. Together, Spanish officials, habitants, and enslaver-emigrants from the United States built a stable, effective enslaving regime between the 1780s and the Louisiana Purchase of 1803. The U.S. takeover of Illinois and the Spanish commitment to building a robust enslaving regime accelerated the divergence of Illinois and Upper Louisiana that had begun under British dominion in the 1760s.

The withering of imperial state power in Illinois repelled enslavers. Enslavers, merchants, and imperial officials made slavery the chief concern of empire in the Middle Mississippi Valley from the 1770s through the early 1800s. Like their predecessors, imperial officials, agents, and policy-makers from the

United States and Spain, along with French agents who dreamed of a revived French empire in North America, remained obsessed with counting the number of enslaved people in any given settlement. In doing so, they continued to mark off enslavers and the people they enslaved as valuable assets of empire. In 1786, as the Confederation Congress inquired into the status of the Illinois Country, it took testimony from habitant Gabriel Cerré. Among the questions asked of him was "What is the computed number of inhabitants in the whole Illinois district, and what proportion of them were slaves?" His answer: "There may be in the Towns on the Mississippi about 300 White Inhabitants including American Settlers who may amount to 50. There are moreover about 250 Slaves."[2] What seemed like the near abandonment of the French villages created the circumstances under which U.S. imperial policymakers issued the Northwest Ordinance with the Article VI exclusion on slavery. As a Confederation Congress committee, which was convened to respond to habitant petitions seeking repeal of Article VI, reported, Congress did not realize that "there were at that time Negroes under Servitude to the inhabitants then residing" in Illinois.[3] From the imperial center in 1787, it seemed that enslavers had all but abandoned Illinois.

They had not, but during the two decades of British and Virginian rule, the 1,500 or so habitants and enslaved people who once inhabited the French villages of the Illinois Country had declined by approximately two-thirds. Over the next decade and a half, various imperial agents and interlopers conducted their own inquiries. Their enumerations were all over the place, and the accuracy of any one count is at best doubtful. Nonetheless, a clear pattern emerges in the informal counts and formal censuses. The numbers of enslavers and enslaved people in Illinois continued to decline while the numbers of enslaved people and enslavers in Upper Louisiana increased. Similarly, observers portrayed Illinois settlements as being in a state of terminal decline and Upper Louisiana settlements as vibrant and thriving. Active imperial state power in Upper Louisiana attracted enslavers; its absence in Illinois repelled them.

While colonizers and enslavers were abandoning or bypassing villages in Illinois, they were creating new settlements in Upper Louisiana such as New Madrid, adding to older villages such as Ste. Geneviève, and establishing satellite villages such as St. Charles outside of St. Louis. In 1790, U.S. imperial agent Winthrop Sargent, Secretary of the Northwest Territory, traveled to the Middle Mississippi Valley where he counted two things: the number of men capable of bearing arms in any given settlement, and the number of enslaved men and women. At Cahokia he counted "fifty two families," led by about "100 men" who "possess about 12 Negroes." At an adjacent village he counted "49 men capable of bearing arms & three or four men & women slaves." Enslavers had nearly abandoned Cahokia. Across the river in St. Louis, he enumerated "170 fighting men capable of bearing arms" while "the Blacks at present in the town are said to be 120," an undercount due to the recent establishment of two satellite villages in the St. Louis hinterlands. In either case, Sargent found 15 enslaved people in Cahokia and 120 directly across the river in St. Louis.[4] That same year, a Philadelphia newspaper published an account whose author found "40 American families and about 73 slaves" in the entirety of the Illinois villages. Across the river, he counted "at Genivieve, Lahine, and a small new village (the half of which are black) 850," and at "St. Louis (130 of which are black) 720." Ste. Geneviève, which originated as a satellite village of Kaskaskia, counted more than four hundred enslaved men, women, and children; combined, the Illinois villages contained roughly a quarter of that number.[5] In 1796, Spanish official Charles Dehaute DeLassus entitled his census "Enumeration of the Inhabitants at New Madrid, their Slaves, Cattle, and Crops." In this entirely new settlement, peopled almost exclusively by migrants from Illinois and the United States, Spanish officials counted forty-six enslaved men, women, and children.[6] The following year, Royalist exile Nicolas de Finiels arrived in Upper Louisiana in the employ of the Spanish imperial state. Charged with building fortifications at New Madrid and St. Louis, he penned a general account of Upper Louisiana. He noted that "Black slaves constitute about one-sixth of the population, when an habitant owns two or three to use in agriculture, he thinks he is in a position to undertake anything."[7] In 1803, as the United States prepared to initiate the Louisiana Purchase, U.S. imperial agent Benjamin Stoddert's contacts in the Mississippi Valley provided him a population of 7,876 free whites in Upper Louisiana and 1,497 enslaved people of color.[8] Both Finiels and Stoddert concluded that about one-sixth of the population of Upper Louisiana was enslaved, while Stoddert's number showed that approximately one-quarter of the population of St. Louis and Ste. Geneviève was enslaved. Forty years of successive British, Virginian, and then U.S. dominion had led to the exodus of a substantial portion of Illinois enslavers to Spanish Upper Louisiana, where they were joined by a growing contingent of U.S. enslavers.

British, Virginian, and then U.S. dominion in Illinois from the 1760s to 1803 was characterized by the inability of those imperial governments to extend, build, or maintain even the most rudimentary elements of governance.

Their imperial policy-makers faced a plethora of wide-ranging crises during their tenure in Illinois; they confronted insurmountable difficulties filling basic and high offices. Petitions and requests from habitants and Americans in Illinois routinely took years to receive replies. In the absence of any semblance of an overarching imperial authority, chaos took over the Illinois settlements, especially after Virginian forces abandoned it in the early 1780s. A group of Americans led by John Dodge, hoping to claim the lands around Kaskaskia and Cahokia for speculative purposes, anointed themselves representatives of the government of Virginia. Rather than governing, this group of swindlers and speculators unleashed waves of "general Depredation and Plunder" across the Illinois settlements. Lawlessness reigned, prompting Arthur St. Clair, the first Northwest Territory governor, an enslaver, and a chief U.S. imperial agent in the Mississippi Valley, to write of the deplorable state of the Illinois settlements after his tour there in the winter of 1790. St. Clair found that the Illinois Country had descended into "great Distress ever since it fell under the American Dominion."[9]

To alleviate their "great distress," the habitant and American heads of households in Kaskaskia and Prairie du Rocher appointed recent French emigrant and former U.S. agent Barthelemi Tardiveau to settle outstanding claims and issues with the United States, problems that had lingered since the British evacuation of Illinois in 1778 and that had amplified under formal U.S. dominion since 1783. Initially, Tardiveau, habitants, and the Americans sought confirmation of their land titles and new grants from the U.S. government. The Confederation Congress responded by mandating that land title would pass to settlers only if they remained on the land for a number of years.[10] Whatever the effect of that order, Illinois enslavers became even more dismayed with the United States when the Confederation Congress issued the Northwest Ordinance in 1787.

Illinois enslavers expressed incredulousness at Article VI, which they interpreted to mean "that slavery shall not take place in the Western Territory" of the United States. The U.S regime followed its conditional confirmation of land titles with an ordinance that banned slavery. Habitant and American enslavers expressed outrage. "Many of the inhabitants" of Illinois "have slaves, and some have no property but slaves." Due to the Ordinance, "if they wish to preserve their property" in slaves, "they must transport themselves to the Spanish Side of the Mississippi." But by moving to the Spanish side to preserve their property in slaves, "they Shall lose the lands," which Congress required they inhabit for a set number of years before gaining title. In sum, U.S. policy in the Illinois Country stipulated that habitants and American enslavers must "leave the country, or ye shall forfeit your negroes," or "Stay in the Country," lest "your lands shall be taken from ye."[11] U.S impe-rial agents and officials had created a set of laws and regulations that encour-aged the already-shrinking class of enslavers in Illinois either to migrate to Upper Louisiana or to sell the people they enslaved to other jurisdictions.

Congress and U.S. imperial agents tried to mollify habitant enslavers in Illi-nois by creating a qualified right for habitant enslavers resident in the French villages before 1787. A congressional committee composed of three enslavers ruled that the habitants retained "their right and property in Negro or other Slaves which they were possessed of at the time of passing the said Ordinance." The committee further clarified that the United States would not "manumit or set free" any enslaved person acquired prior to passage of the Northwest Ordi-nance.[12] Likewise, St. Clair promised Illinois habitants that Article VI consti-tuted only "a prohibition to any future introduction" of enslaved people. It was "not to extend to the liberation of those the People were already possessed of, and acquired under the Sanction of the Laws they were subject."[13] Yielding to enslaver demands, Congress and St. Clair interpreted Article VI to pro-hibit only the further importation of enslaved African Americans into Illinois. With that, Article VI attained its character as an exclusionary measure rather than serving as an emancipatory decree. In this regard, it operated much like O'Reilly's 1769 decree banning Native American slavery. Nonetheless, habitant enslavers wanted more than promises that the people they enslaved would not be emancipated. They also wanted the ability to purchase additional enslaved people and to welcome new enslavers. As St. Clair noted, "the circumstance that Slaves cannot be introduced" into Illinois was enough to send additional habitants and Americans to the other side of the river.[14]

In the Middle Mississippi Valley in the late 1780s and early 1790s, U.S. and Spanish imperial agents actively competed, each seeking to lure habitant and American colonizers to their domain. During this period, enslavers and would-be enslavers constituted the main class of colonizers, residents, and emigrants in the trans-Appalachian West. Only the Spanish regime could offer what enslavers sought: clear property rights in enslaved people and the ability to purchase more; regular court sessions; guarantees for property in lands and enslaved men and women; active slave patrols backed by regular soldiers; and the deliberate exclusion of free people who threatened prop-erty in enslaved persons. Conversely, the U.S. imperial regime maintained a ban on the further introduction of enslaved people; left pleas and petitions unanswered; confirmed land grants but placed restrictions that made the terms unacceptable to enslaving habitants and Americans; and failed to hold court sessions or provide any semblance of government. Imperial neglect since the 1760s nearly eviscerated the institutions and infrastructures of imperial state power in Illinois, including slavery.[15]

Enslavers followed state power. Thus, habitants and Americans crossed the Mississippi River for Spanish Upper Louisiana in growing numbers in the late 1780s and early 1790s, rather than negotiating with a far-off government that seemed utterly incapable of upholding titles to land or assisting with efforts to keep enslaved people in slavery while acquiring more. In 1788 and 1789, Spanish officials recorded 33 families and 293 individuals as having migrated from Illinois to Upper Louisiana. Of the 293 individuals, 106 were enslaved; 16 of the 33 families owned enslaved men, women, and children.[16] The Northwest Ordinance, designed to facilitate Indigenous dispossession, colonization, and U.S. empire, instead led to the further abandonment of Illinois. When Sargent visited Illinois in 1790, he described land with "a very beautiful situation" and "an excellent salt spring." He also described Illinois as "abandoned."[17] He derisively wrote that St. Louis "is by no means elegant or handsome, in buildings or situation." He nonetheless lamented that "it very far exceeds everything" on the American side.[18] A functioning imperial state gave Spain a decided advantage over the U.S. regime in attracting colonizers.

Land speculators in the service of Spain used Article VI for their own benefit, further spurring the migration of enslavers from Illinois to Upper Louisiana. Merchant-speculator George Morgan had worked in Illinois in the 1760s as a partner in the firm of Baynton, Wharton, and Morgan, and he had been instrumental in forcibly migrating enslaved African Americans to Illinois via Philadelphia by way of Fort Pitt and the Ohio River. Morgan understood as much as anyone the relationship between empire and enslavement in the Middle Mississippi Valley. After serving in the Continental Army as a colonel and as an agent for Indian affairs operating out of Fort Pitt, he reentered speculation in the Illinois Country in the 1780s. Morgan headed up a group of New Jersey speculators seeking to purchase the entirety of the area settled by European-Americans in Illinois in the late 1780s. When that plan failed, Morgan struck a deal with Spanish Minister Diego de Gardoqui to create *Nouvella Madrid*, "The New Madrid." Situated just below the confluence of the Mississippi and Ohio Rivers, Morgan intended for New Madrid to serve as the main entrepôt of the greater Mississippi Valley.[19] Morgan and Louisiana Governor Esteban Miró made slavery central to their enterprise of colonizing Louisiana with Americans. Miró entitled his vision for New Madrid as the plan "for the admission of planters to people Louisiana." Miró also agreed to "enlarging" the "concession" of any "notable people" capable of forcibly migrating "Negroes" to New Madrid.[20]

To generate interest in his speculative settlement, Morgan used fears of Article VI to entice habitants and Americans in Illinois to colonize New Madrid. Morgan's "chief argument" to Illinois enslavers "was drawn from that Article in the Constitution of the Territory" regarding "slaves." Morgan "assured" Illinois enslavers that, under U.S imperial sovereignty, their slaves "would all be liberated without any Compensation being made to the owners."[21] As the leading francophonic U.S. agent in Illinois explained to U.S. officials, Morgan's warnings created a "rumor that the very moment" new U.S. officials "landed at the Illinois all their slaves would be set free."[22] Morgan was simply one more interloper who issued evanescent promises, but his basic message rang true with enslavers in the Middle Mississippi Valley: The U.S. imperial state was at best indifferent toward enslavers and, at worst, hostile. Conversely, the Spanish imperial state actively supported enslavers who would become Spanish subjects. Morgan's warnings, coming after two decades of neglect and amid swirling rumors about Article VI, nudged additional American and habitant enslavers to cross the river. Major John Hamtramck, the most senior U.S. official in Vincennes, reported that "a number of people had gone and were about going from the Illinois to the Spanish Side, in consequence of a resolve of Congress respecting negroes, who (as it was reported, particularly by Mr. Morgan) were to be free."[23] Eight years later, Hamtramck estimated that "about 250 souls" had departed Illinois for New Madrid.[24] Article VI facilitated the migration of enslavers out of Illinois.

Spanish officials actively sought to lure enslavers to colonize Upper Louisiana by exploiting the weaknesses of U.S. governance in Illinois. From the 1780s through 1803, Spanish officials aided Spanish subjects in their disputes with enslavers from the U.S. side. In 1786, Illinois enslaver Joseph Dupuis and Upper Louisiana merchant Antoine Lachance had a falling-out over the sale of an enslaved person from Illinois. The enslaved person in question had been inherited by children in Kaskaskia. As was standard practice, Dupuis was appointed guardian to manage the children's estate until they reached adulthood. Dupuis had likely rented the enslaved person to Lachance; Dupuis was indebted to Lachance for other matters. Lachance then sold the enslaved person without Dupuis's blessing to cover the debt. Unable to resolve the matter privately, Lachance turned to the governing officials of Upper Louisiana, asking them to return the enslaved person to Dupuis in Illinois. Lieutenant Governor Francisco Cruzat denied Dupuis's petition, informing him that he could seek "redress" against Lachance in Illinois. "When your court of justice is re-established you will be able to make your claim there," wrote Cruzat.[25] But no enslaver in Illinois could expect any court to open and hear his case; no properly construed court had existed in Illinois since the British takeover in the 1760s. And even if a U.S. court ruled in Dupuis's favor, it was unlikely that Upper Louisiana officials would recognize the claim. Eight months later, Dupuis left Kaskaskia "in order to earn his living in some other place," presumably Spanish Louisiana.[26] Spanish laws and imperial officials protected enslavers in Upper Louisiana; they denied the same to enslavers if they remained in Illinois. By Cruzat's action, Upper Louisiana gained one more enslaved person and Illinois lost one. Spanish officials' calculus of empire in the Middle Mississippi Valley dictated transferring enslavers and enslaved people from the east bank to the west bank.

Active Spanish imperial state power and its absence in Illinois facilitated the movement of enslavers and enslaved people across the river in other ways. In the absence of material support or any semblance of law and order from Britain, Virginia, or the United States, the parish at Cahokia declined precipitously since the 1760s. As Cahokia declined under Virginia and then U.S. rule, the parish's priest, Father Forget, sold the majority of the enslaved individuals owned by the parish to continue church operations.[27] The destitution on the U.S. side meant that demand and payment for enslaved individuals was low in Illinois. Father Forget thus sold the unfortunate enslaved families "at St. Louis" or "at New Orleans." In the mid-1780s, the old church's physical structure collapsed. The remaining parishioners sought to erect a new one. To fund the project and to provide labor, the Cahokia parishioners sought to reclaim the enslaved people whom Father Forget had sold. The Cahokia parishioners were especially distressed because the enslaved families that had been sold across the river "have greatly increased by propagation." The parishioners received U.S. warrants to reclaim those sold by Father Forget "on the Spanish side." Spanish officials, however, "refused to do anything" to assist the parishioners in reclaiming the enslaved families. The parishioners received no relief from the United States either. They finally entreated the Archdiocese of Quebec to intervene on their behalf, "to interest yourselves to cause these negroes to re-enter into the power of our mission," by appealing directly to Spanish authorities across the river.[28]

Other Illinois enslavers beseeched U.S. officials to assist them in recovering enslaved people who were stolen from Illinois and then spirited to Upper Louisiana to no avail. Widow Marguerite Beauvais spent six years imploring U.S. authorities to assist her in her claims against John Dodge, who had fled to "the Spanish Part" after he "had kidnapped" several enslaved people claimed by Beauvais. When a U.S. lieutenant ordered Dodge to produce documentation proving his ownership of the people he kidnapped from Beauvais, Dodge "sent off his baggage" to Upper Louisiana, along with another "negresse he had kidnapped."[29] Beauvais sued Dodge, but with no working U.S. courts, the case was heard in Nashville. Andrew Jackson, her attorney, discontinued the case, likely because no one saw any hope in recovering the enslaved persons Dodge had stolen and then spirited away to Upper Louisiana.[30] In 1789, American enslaver, merchant, and land speculator John Edgar received relief from neither U.S. nor Spanish officials after "an attempt" to steal his "property & slaves" at Kaskaskia.[31] Spanish officials looked the other way when enslaved people were spirited across the river from Illinois to Upper Louisiana.

Spanish officials repeatedly rebuffed U.S. officials' efforts to adjudicate disputes between enslavers on the two banks of the Mississippi River. In 1789, an enslaved man owned by Antoine Du Chaufour de Louvieres of Prairie de Rocher ended up in the possession of Jean Baptiste Pratte in Upper Louisiana. Pratte recognized that he had at best a shaky title to the enslaved man, and thus intended to sell him in New Orleans. Louvieres begged U.S. officials to intervene. The best U.S. officials could do was write letters asking Spanish officials to assist enslavers on the American side in recovering enslaved men and women to which Illinois enslavers laid claim. St. Clair framed the matter as one of each side rightfully returning alleged fugitives to the other. St. Clair chided his counterpart in Upper Louisiana that "it is of importance for the inhabitants of each side that their fugitive slaves do not find asylum with the others, and if it happens that some from your side wish to take refuge with us, I shall promise to send them back, and, as I have no doubt that you are willing to do the same."[32] St. Clair appealed to Spanish officials' self-interest as imperial agents of an enslaving regime. If enslavers or enslaved people fled to one side of the river for nefarious reasons, St. Clair promised to return them. But the interests of Spanish officials laid in the opposite direction. Working on building an enslaving regime on the Spanish side by attracting enslavers from the American side, Spanish officials simply ignored the request. Spanish officials had no personal or state interest in assisting their rivals on the other side of the river and had every reason to deny or ignore such requests.

In another example of this lack of cooperation, habitants Jacques Clamorgan and M. Dubreuil of St. Louis agreed to swap cash and settle debts for two enslaved men, two enslaved women, and two enslaved children with Americans George Morgan and Daniel McElduff of Kaskaskia. The deal went bad, but Clamorgan worked with Spanish officials to obtain "a writ of seizure from M. Peyrez, commandant at St. Louis, to obtain possession of said slaves," even though he had failed to pay for them. Clamorgan then headed up a posse who crossed the river and kidnapped a "negress and her child" from the home of McElduff. McElduff begged American officials for relief. But the most that officials on the "American bank" could do was issue a writ for Clamorgan's "arrest on this bank, if he can be discovered here."[33] If McElduff expected the return of the people he enslaved, he could become a Spanish subject who enjoyed the benefits of Spanish state power. Spanish officials turned enslaved African American women and children into pawns of their efforts to undermine the deteriorating enslaving regime in Illinois. In the absence of effective U.S. imperial power in Illinois, such efforts proved simple.

Spanish officials punished Illinois enslavers and rewarded Spanish subjects in other ways. Robert Greer had purchased an unnamed African American man from John Rice Jones in Illinois sometime in the 1790s. Already in debt to Moses Austin, Greer crossed to Spanish Louisiana for business. When Austin discovered Greer's presence in Upper Louisiana with an enslaved man, he received an official order to seize and sell "a negro slave belonging to Mr. Greer." Greer had yet to pay off Jones in Illinois for the enslaved man, as the original bill had not yet come due, but Spanish officials ruled in favor of Austin anyway. Greer objected to Spanish officials' reasoning on the grounds that he "never knew it to be a law in any state, country, or kingdom that property could be sold before the debt is due." But the debt on the enslaved man was due in Illinois; the debt to Austin was due in Upper Louisiana. Spanish authorities acted accordingly, ordering that the enslaved man "be judicially sold" at "public auction" to satisfy the debt to Austin.[34] Spanish officials sent unmistakable messages to enslavers on the U.S. side of the river: Spanish imperial power assisted enslavers in Upper Louisiana; U.S. imperial power remained impotent in the Middle Mississippi Valley. In the 1780s and 1790s, Spanish officials created relationships among enslavement, borders, citizenship, and subjecthood in the Middle Mississippi Valley in ways that they never had before. Equally important, the actions of Spanish officials facilitated the transfer of enslaved people from Illinois to Upper Louisiana.

The rulings of Spanish officials against U.S. enslavers encompassed a larger effort to convert U.S. enslavers into Spanish subjects by providing them with a functioning imperial state. Spanish officials formalized the process of welcoming American and habitant enslavers in 1789. The Spanish imperial state offered "to each family" who migrated to Upper Louisiana "a tract of land from 240 to 800 acres in proportion to their numbers, free from all expense." The greater the number of "slaves" a family migrated with, the larger their land grant. Spanish officials also eliminated duties and customs paid by Americans for access to the Mississippi River and New Orleans. They also promised to provide "a commanding officer" to serve as a commandant and governing official for any settlement that the newcomers might erect.[35] Commanding officers never came alone, and their retinue included soldiers, legal officials, and governing officials who served multiple purposes for enslavers. Officials and agents kept and maintained records for enslavers. Commandants and officials upheld local regulations of enslaved people. They kept records and resolved disputes between enslavers regarding the sale of lands and enslaved persons. They issued emoluments and petty titles to enslavers who served in the militia. They commanded soldiers and militia, who doubled as the slave patrol. They drove out individuals they deemed uncommitted to maintaining slavery. In short, they provided the imperial infrastructure that enabled enslavers to keep enslaved people in slavery.

Numerous prominent habitants embraced Spanish offers, further weakening the enslaving regime in Illinois. Father Pierre Gibault exemplified the troubled state in which many Illinois habitants found themselves in the 1780s and 1790s. Like so many other Illinois habitants, Father Gibault welcomed George Rogers Clark and the Virginian takeover of Illinois from Britain. Gibault raised money and supplies for Clark and his soldiers. He then supported successive Virginia and U.S. regimes. As Gibault explained, he had "at all Times sacrificed his Property," which he gave for the Support of the Troops" who conquered and occupied Illinois. Virginia and U.S. officials, however, paid their debts with "paper Dollars." U.S. and Virginia currency was worthless in Illinois, and Gibault found himself out "seven thousand eight hundred Livres" due to his support for the Virginian and then U.S. garrisons in Cahokia. His destitution "obliged him to sell two good Slaves, who would now be the Support of his old age, and for the want of whom he now finds himself dependent on the Public."[36] Once a prosperous enslaver and prominent potentate, Gibault faulted the U.S. regime for leaving him destitute and slaveless. In the 1780s, he spent progressively more time in Upper Louisiana. In the late 1780s, he permanently relocated to the fledgling settlement at New Madrid, adding Ste. Geneviève to his circuit. He finished his days ministering to the souls of enslavers and the enslaved on the Spanish side of the river.[37]

Father Gibault was exactly the kind of informal imperial agent who was crucial to maintaining slavery in a place like Illinois. Slave societies survived only when preeminent persons demeaned, ostracized, marginalized, and controlled enslaved people, while elevating and praising enslavers. Priests exercised enormous social and political prestige in Illinois and Upper Louisiana. Under the French regime in Illinois, Gibault was an important imperial agent and enslaver whose pronouncements and actions reinforced the social, political, and economic hierarchies that enslaved men and women and kept them in slavery. Under subsequent British, Virginian, and then U.S. regimes, Gibault became a destitute priest in a nearly abandoned parish; his prestige and pronouncements became ineffective at keeping anyone in slavery. Conversely, in Upper Louisiana, he headed a parish supported by the Spanish regime. His leading parishioners included some of the wealthiest, most prestigious enslavers and officers in Upper Louisiana, including the Vallé family. His words and social prestige once more influenced the lives of enslavers and enslaved. In his masses, his visits to the newborn, the sick, the elderly, and the infirm, he elevated enslavers and demeaned enslaved persons. As imperial agents like Father Gibault fled U.S. dominion for Upper Louisiana, their movements weakened the imperial enslaving regime on the U.S. side while strengthening it on the Spanish side. Enslaver power withered when imperial agents like Gibault evacuated U.S. Illinois.

In the 1780s and the 1790s, the persons who embodied and operated the imperial infrastructure of enslavement in Illinois continued to follow Father Gibault to Upper Louisiana. Indeed, Spanish officials built an imperial infrastructure of enslavement in Upper Louisiana in part by enticing officials from the U.S. side to migrate to Upper Louisiana. In the early 1790s, Antoine Gamelin, an Indian agent, interpreter, notary public, probate judge, and clerk at Vincennes, "moved to the Spanish Side with his Family." Officials at New Madrid rewarded Gamelin with two separate land grants, one for 750 arpents and another for 200 arpents.[38] Gamelin was precisely the kind of minor imperial agent and official who helped maintain systems of slavery. His departure from the U.S. side accelerated the dismantling of slavery there; his absence attenuated the state power that Illinois enslavers could impose on the people they enslaved. The migration of other Illinois enslavers also led to the demise of the militia and slave patrol in Illinois and to its subsequent growth in Upper Louisiana. Illinois enslavers often formed the most prominent and literate members of their community, and they staffed the scores of minor offices where imperial state power manifested itself in local communities. One U.S. official lamented the loss of "a number of the Militia" among the 250 who had departed Illinois for New Madrid in the 1790s.[39] By 1797, U.S. officials complained that "the two militia companies" that remained in Illinois were led by "but four officers, not one of whom can either read or write."[40] Spain staffed its militia and slave patrol with a growing number of experienced, bilingual habitant and American enslavers, along with Spanish soldiers; the United States fielded a militia led by four illiterate officers.

Active militias and slave patrols were especially important in the Middle Mississippi Valley in the 1780s and 1790s, not just in their role of keeping enslaved people in slavery, but also in their task of safeguarding enslavers' property in human beings. By the 1780s, roving gangs of banditti had become a persistent problem for enslavers in the Mississippi Valley. Banditti became adept at stealing the most valuable property in the region—enslaved men and women—and then selling them in places such as Pensacola. Spanish officials sought to exclude or deport free people who threatened the interests of enslavers and their ability to keep enslaving people. Spanish officials thus adopted measures to "exclude and send back, those with turbulent and restless spirits who could cause great harm and prejudice" to enslavers who relocated to the Spanish side of the Mississippi. Spanish officials also authorized the use of the militia "to force the vagabonds and all those who have no work relative to the farm to return over the Mississippi" to the American side of the river.[41] With no real militia, U.S. officials and enslavers could do little to protect themselves from the banditti and interlopers who hassled enslavers in the Middle Mississippi Valley.

The extended Janis family exemplified the kinds of prominent enslaver families who fled Illinois, weakening the power that remaining enslavers could exercise over the people they enslaved. Patriarch Nicolas Janis had arrived in Kaskaskia from Canada in the 1750s. Janis became prominent enough that British authorities appointed him a captain in the militia, a position later confirmed by Virginia authorities. The Janis family provided supplies and credit to George Rogers Clark's expedition and garrison during the U.S. War for Independence. In 1779, Illinois Governor John Todd ordered

Nicolas Janis to guard enslaved man Moreau, who was to be executed for his alleged role in murdering several habitants through poisoning. Various Janis men served as officers in the militia and slave patrol. Nicolas's son Jean Baptiste fought with the Virginians in their conquest at Vincennes. Patriarch Nicolas Janis was appointed as a justice of the Virginia courts in Illinois. The Janis family signed numerous petitions directed toward Virginian and U.S. authorities. In 1787, they led the group of habitants who hired Tardiveau to represent their interests and to advocate for their claims before the Confederation Congress. Combined, the family owned at least fourteen lots in and around Kaskaskia, as well as at least fifteen enslaved people.[42] Few habitants tried as hard as the Janis family to maintain their fortunes within the incipient Virginian and U.S. empires in Illinois.

But the breakdown in imperial government drove the Janis family to Spanish Upper Louisiana. The Janis family's land claims in Illinois remained unconfirmed in the early 1790s, even though the Janis family had lived there since the 1750s. Offered better terms from Spain, they unloaded their claims to John Edgar and William Morrison, two American speculators who targeted departing habitants.[43] Janis family Patriarch Nicolas migrated with his extended household, which included ten enslaved adult men and five enslaved adult women, to Upper Louisiana in the late 1780s. In the early 1790s, Jean Baptiste Janis migrated to Ste. Geneviève where he received a land grant in an area prone to flooding. In 1795, Spanish authorities granted him a town lot. Once settled, in 1796, Spanish authorities granted him "eight thousand arpents" of land based on his extended household, which included "a wife and eight children, besides a number of slaves." Four years later, authorities granted the Janis family another 250 arpents, again specifying that the grant was due in part to the Janis family's "number of slaves and animals."[44] Once in Upper Louisiana, at minimum, Jean Baptiste Janis assumed some kind of minor local office.[45]

Like Gibault before them, the Janis family were enslavers, minor agents of an imperial state, and local officeholders who deployed violence, social and political prestige, economic influence, and the powers of an imperial state to keep enslaved men and women in slavery. The Janis family had served as captains and members of the militia, as members of the local slave patrol, and as local magistrates. As *esclavagistes bourgeois*, they were exactly the kind of local imperial officials who maintained slavery by making it so difficult for enslaved men and women to unravel the enslaving regimes and social practices that kept them in bondage. When the Janis clan left for Upper Louisiana, they transferred more than the men and women they enslaved. They also carried with them the accoutrements of imperial state power that kept enslaved people in slavery, everything from their status in the militia and slave patrol, to their arms and the obligation to use violence against enslaved people. When they fled Illinois, so did the practices of enslavement in local polities and knowledge of how those practices operated in larger imperial structures. Article VI worked in the 1790s not as an active emancipatory pronouncement but as a passive imperial decree that facilitated the disintegration of U.S. imperial authority in Illinois.

The absence of imperial state power repelled enslavers just as effectively as imperial decrees that prospectively banned them. U.S imperial policymakers and agents promised Illinois enslavers that Article VI was nonoperative for the people they already enslaved, but enslavers craved an imperial state that actively assisted rather than abandoned them. When combined with the absence of imperial state power, Article VI served to drive enslavers— themselves often the embodiment of imperial state power—out of Illinois. By 1796, the villages on the American side seemed to be all but abandoned. Dr. George Hunter, a speculator, later imperial agent for the United States, and a druggist from Philadelphia, was shocked at the desolation he found on the east bank of the river. In his diary he used the same epitaph to describe Kaskaskia, Cahokia, and St. Phillipe: "A deserted village." After crossing the river and speaking with Spanish officials and recently arrived emigrants, he discovered the reason. "The French inhabitants not being very pleased with the American Laws have chiefly gone over the Mississippi." There, "the Spanish government gives them 400 acres each man & a proportionate quantity for each son & daughter of age & each negro, they bring with them, gratis." Hunter further noted that "many Americans have gone over" to the Spanish side for the same reasons. The contrast between the two banks proved jarring to Hunter. Ste. Geneviève "appears to be in a flourishing state." The town's colonizers were all "very comfortably & Handsomely lodged, their houses are in the same style but much better built than at Kaskaskia." Imperial support for enslaving African Americans brought prosperity for habitants and Americans in Ste. Geneviève. The inability of the U.S regime to do the same in Illinois produced "deserted" villages. The differences between the two regimes became strikingly clear to Hunter when he visited St. Louis. Hunter had met with no American officials in Illinois; none were present. In St. Louis, the commandant "very politely received" his party, invited them to "visit any part of the country," and offered that "he would give us a grant of one thousand acres," and "more if we brought families."[46]

Britain, Virginia, and the United States all proved ill-equipped to protect the interests of enslavers in Illinois. None of those regimes could perform basic imperial and local governing tasks, such as confirming and upholding titles to lands and slaves, assisting enslavers in recovering enslaved people in Spanish domains, holding regular court sessions, or paying off the debts incurred by soldiers and officials during their conquest and occupation of the Illinois Country. The regimes could not gain for their subjects and citizens free access to New Orleans, a gateway to commerce in the broader Atlantic world. Britain in the 1760s and 1770s, and then Virginia and the United States in the 1780s and the 1790s, failed to maintain, let alone expand, the accoutrements of state power on which enslavers depended to keep enslaved men and women in slavery and to grow their enslaving regime. Article VI's passive ban on further slavery alienated enslavers; the absence of imperial state power repelled them.

The presence of imperial state power attracted enslavers. From the 1780s through the Louisiana Purchase, Spanish officials in Upper Louisiana expanded the infrastructure of an enslaving imperial regime, adjusting their laws, practices, and policies to suit the interests of enslavers. Imperial officials and local potentates repeatedly deployed state power on behalf of enslavers, and forged tighter economic connections between Upper and Lower Louisiana. For one, Spanish officials created a robust militia and slave patrol, and they deployed it against enslaved people. Enslaved men and women still struck for freedom whenever circumstances created opportunities to flee. In Upper Louisiana, the heads of local polities worked with imperial officials to deploy local and imperial state power to mitigate efforts of enslaved people who sought to emancipate themselves. In 1792, "a party of maroon slaves" made up of "females and children and seven black men" fled St. Louis. Spanish officials and local potentates swiftly deployed state resources to capture them. François Vallé ordered his subordinates in Ste. Geneviève and surrounding settlements "to do everything you can to find them and arrest them." Vallé added that "we will pay" any person who captured the party of escaped African Americans and brought them to him.[47] It remains unknown if the escaped enslaved people were captured, but Spanish officials used the resources of the imperial state to provide for subjects whose enslaved people rebelled or fled in other ways. In 1795, a group of enslaved African Americans "were sent to New Orleans, for the crime of sedition, to be placed at the disposal of the Governor General." Whatever that "sedition" amounted to remains lost in the historical records; the enslaved people might have been plotting a rebellion, but more likely they planned to flee or were caught doing so. Whatever the case, Spanish officials authorized Vallé to raise funds to compensate the enslavers of the condemned African Americans. Vallé thus ordered that "a tax of six escalins" be levied in the Ste. Geneviève district on "each slave," "of all sexes and ages," to provide compensation to those subjects whose enslaved people were condemned.[48] In Upper Louisiana, imperial and local officials placed the resources of the imperial state at the service of enslavers. When enslaved people fled, they pursued. When enslaved people were killed or condemned, the imperial state compensated the enslavers.

Spanish officials continued to use imperial state power to keep enslaved Indigenous people in slavery well into the 1790s. In 1787 and 1791, Spanish officials undertook an extensive project of re-racializing enslaved Native Americans.[49] That habitants continued to hold, sell, and transfer as slaves individuals of maternal Native American descent in Upper Louisiana remained an open secret throughout the entirety of Spanish dominion. Spanish and habitant officials worked to conceal that secret. In 1801, Auguste Chouteau advised an individual who enslaved a Native American woman seeking her freedom "that little ought to be said about it because it might be a great injury to all those that claimed the service of Indians and to himself." Chouteau—patriarch of St. Louis's most powerful family—advised conscientious neighbors against emancipating those legally entitled to freedom.[50] In Upper Louisiana, imperial, local, and personal power flowed through individuals such as Chouteau, who used his influence to fight off even the mention of individual emancipations to those to whom it was legally due.

Imperial officials and agents ensured that enslaved Native Americans who could not be re-racialized or denied emancipation nonetheless enriched their enslavers. Henri Peyroux, commandant at Ste. Geneviève and a saline operator, claimed ownership of at least one enslaved Native American woman as late as 1795. The enslaved Native American woman's case somehow or another made its way to the governor general of Louisiana. Peyroux "could not present" a "title of the sale" showing that the woman was of maternal African American rather than Native American descent. The governor general of Louisiana, Francisco Luis Héctor de Carondelet, ordered that the woman be emancipated. Spanish officials in Upper Louisiana implemented the order according to their own terms. Ste. Geneviève's most prominent habitant, François Vallé, oversaw the emancipation. Vallé ordered that "this female savage should be freed without any formality," lest her freedom should tip off the numerous other enslaved Native Americans about legal routes to freedom. Vallé also promised to "reimburse" Peyroux for the loss of the enslaved Native American woman, who, of course, received no compensation for her enslavement.[51] Even when the broader imperial state ruled against enslavers, local officials ensured that implementation of those orders fell lightly on enslavers and themselves.

Spanish and habitant officials in Upper Louisiana also worked to close off the routes to emancipation afforded to enslaved people under Spanish law. In 1796, enslaved Native American man Joseph de Lille sought to purchase his *griffe* daughter Victoria out of her "unfortunate yoke of bondage," as was their right under Spanish law. But Victoria and Joseph had to face off against powerful habitants backed by an imperial regime invested in protecting its most prominent subjects. Victoria's enslaver, Gabriel Cerré, was a wealthy and powerful St. Louis merchant, whose daughter had married Auguste Chouteau. When Cerré refused Joseph's entreaties to purchase his enslaved daughter, Joseph petitioned Lieutenant Governor Zenon Trudeau. Trudeau now had to settle the matter. Cerré informed Trudeau that he had "resigned" himself "to the dictates of the law, provided it be executed to the very letter." Trudeau and Cerré would use "the very letter of the law" to make it nearly impossible for Joseph to obtain Victoria's freedom. To purchase Victoria, Cerré proposed a sum of 1,000 piastres, to "be paid . . . in hard money," Spanish gold or silver dollars. Joseph proposed 600 piastres in common currency (skins, furs, or lead), or 500 dollars in specie. Arbitrators appointed by Trudeau adjudicated the differences, settling on a sum of 800 piastres, "in the King's money and in no other kind." Trudeau offered Joseph an opportunity to purchase his daughter's freedom but rigged the process in favor of Cerré. Joseph could purchase Victoria's freedom for 800 piastres in gold or silver coinage, a nearly impossible sum to obtain for someone like de Lille in Upper Louisiana's economy, where specie remained scarce. With her enslaved father very unlikely to come up with 800 piastres in hard cash, Victoria likely remained in slavery. Like so many other Spanish officials, Trudeau both obeyed and complied with the law, but he did so in a way that always benefited enslavers like Cerré. French and Spanish law offered greater legal protections to enslaved men and women while providing them with routes to emancipation. Such laws meant little when powerful enslavers enforced them.[52]

Spanish officials made slavery central to their efforts to expand Upper Louisiana's economy beyond the skin and fur trade, which officials deemed "as dangerous as it is precarious." Commercial agriculture, lead, and salt—all of which required a growing population of enslavers and enslaved people—would become the new cornerstone of Upper Louisiana's economy. Carondelet explained to merchant Jacques Clamorgan that "true riches lie in agriculture, and this requires a competent population and easy outlets." Carondelet also promoted lead production, which offered "great profits" if Upper Louisiana could "furnish the Havannah with this article." The main factor holding back production of both was "want of labor."[53] Spanish officials and Upper Louisiana enslavers worked assiduously to attract a "competent population" of enslavers and to create "easy outlets" for the fruit of the labors of the people they enslaved. Spanish officials and enslaver-grandees used slavery to transform Upper Louisiana from a fur-trading outpost into the chief supplier of foodstuffs, staples, and stores for the growing Mississippi Valley plantation complex.

In the 1780s and 1790s, Spanish officials used the plantation revolutions remaking the Lower Mississippi Valley to expand commercial agriculture in Upper Louisiana. In the Lower Mississippi Valley, Spanish officials were already facilitating the rapid expansion of plantation slavery in the region stretching from New Orleans to Natchez.[54] As Lower Mississippi Valley enslavers devoted increased resources to the production of cash crops such as cotton and sugar, they diverted enslaved men and women away from the production of food for themselves and from the staples and stores that were once the core of the Lower Mississippi Valley's export economy. The growth of plantations in the Lower Mississippi Valley opened new markets for farmers, traders, and enslavers in Upper Louisiana. Upper Louisiana stood as "a country destined to agricultural pursuits and to the breeding of domestic animals" for shipment downriver.[55] The rapidly growing number of plantations in Natchez and Lower Louisiana, and the growth of exports from New Orleans to Atlantic ports, provided Carondelet's "easy outlet" for slave-produced staples, stores, and commodities.

Accordingly, Carondelet and his officers shifted state resources toward supporting the expansion of commercial agriculture, salt production, and lead mining in Upper Louisiana. Barthelemi Tardiveau had been hired by habitant and American enslavers in Illinois in the late 1780s to seek redress for their grievances from the U.S. imperial state. When that venture failed, Tardiveau entered the Spanish service. Working with Carondelet and the commandants of various Spanish posts, Tardiveau launched a new venture to ship the products of Upper Louisiana's increasingly mixed economy to New Orleans and then on to Europe. Spanish officials agreed to pay New Orleans merchants to send "a registered vessel to England, or even Holland, to Hamburg, and to other parts of Europe" to sell "furs, flour, and other articles of the growth of the Country."[56] Less ambitious but equally important, Spanish officials encouraged leading local subjects "to construct flat boats" and "send them down the river as the Americans do." Among the slave-produced bounty of Upper Louisiana bound for Lower Louisiana were "hogs, corn, potatoes, apples, butter, salted meat, etc." The growing export economy out of New Orleans brought in bills of exchange along with the luxuries of the Atlantic world. By the mid-1790s, Upper Louisiana merchants returned from New Orleans with "sugar, coffee, brandy and common material for making clothing &c."[57] Upper Louisiana enslavers now produced foods and stores for New Orleans enslaver-grandees, with any surpluses shipped to Europe. Spanish officials facilitated the more thorough integration of the Middle Mississippi Valley into the Atlantic world of empires and commerce in enslaved people and the commodities they produced.

To sustain and expand their burgeoning economic transformation, Spanish officials self-consciously sought enslavers and enslaved people. However, the ongoing plantation revolutions in the Lower Mississippi Valley diverted the trade in enslaved men and women away from Upper Louisiana and Illinois. Brothers Abijah and John Wesley Hunt moved goods and enslaved people between Kentucky and the Lower Mississippi Valley in the 1790s, which made John Wesley Hunt the first millionaire in the trans-Appalachian West. Going where the greatest profits could be made in the slave trade, the brothers focused their efforts on Natchez, where "Negro men" were "in great demand."[58] Ohio Valley slave traders like the Hunt brothers preferred the longer, more dangerous trip to Natchez, where "negroes of any description" commanded "a high price," over the shorter, less difficult trip to St. Louis and Ste. Geneviève. Thus, when Colonel John Hamtramck, a U.S. imperial agent in the old Northwest, sought to purchase an enslaved "negro girl" in the late 1790s, he could not do so in the Middle Mississippi Valley. Instead, he turned to his personal friend and business associate Abijah Hunt, who had his brother hold back from selling an enslaved teenage girl into the Lower Mississippi Valley trade so that Hamtramck could purchase her in Lexington, Kentucky.[59] In the 1790s, the main currents of free and involuntary migration in the Mississippi Valley were toward New Orleans and Natchez, not Ste. Geneviève, St. Louis, Kaskaskia, or Cahokia.

The lure of plantation profits in the Lower Mississippi Valley also enticed enslavers from the Middle Mississippi Valley to migrate downriver, either to set up their own plantation operations or to sell enslaved people. In 1786, Daniel Blouin agreed to rent an enslaved man to merchant-speculator John Edgar for a "trip to New Orleans." At the conclusion of the trip, Edgar was to sell the enslaved man in a purchase already arranged by Blouin.[60] By 1793, Pierre-Charles Peyroux, brother of the longtime commandant at Ste. Geneviève, had transferred the majority of the people he once enslaved in Upper Louisiana to "his plantation at Natchez" in Spanish West Florida.[61] Two years later, Upper Louisiana surgeon Antoine Reynal violated Spanish and French slave codes, selling enslaved woman Manon away from her son to the commandant at Natchitoches. Commandant Louis de Neuville remained eager to purchase Manon's son, "if he were for sale."[62] Upper Louisiana enslavers found new profits selling human bodies in the burgeoning markets downriver. Meanwhile, Carondelet and Spanish officials in Upper Louisiana desired "a competent population"—colonizers and the people they enslaved—to strengthen the economic ties between Upper and Lower Louisiana. Circumstances in the Ohio and Mississippi Valleys in the 1780s and 1790s, however, made it difficult to increase the population of enslaved African Americans in Upper Louisiana, let alone to retain those already there.

Enslavers in the Middle Mississippi Valley thus went to great lengths to find new sources of enslaved bodies. In 1782, François Vallé traveled to Natchez to recover Leandre, who had been stolen by banditti and then sold in Natchez. Neither Vallé nor Spanish officials could recover Leandre. Vallé thus purchased an enslaved man "named Jacob, aged 25 years old, Creole from the Carolina."[63] In 1790, habitant Jean Boyce traveled to Kentucky to purchase "a Negro, approximately 17 years old, named Ben."[64] Habitants also sought enslaved men, women, and children through the international and circum-Caribbean slave trade via New Orleans. In 1788, Vincent LaFoy of Ste. Geneviève offered to trade a plot of land in Vincennes if a merchant could deliver from New Orleans "a West Indian male Negro" over the course of the following year.[65] With the Atlantic and Ohio-Mississippi Valley slave trades mostly inaccessible to habitants, Spanish officials turned to the growing number of American enslavers in the Ohio Valley to create the "competent population" of enslavers and enslaved people. Spanish officials went to such great lengths to create an active, enslaving regime because they continued to view slavery as the cornerstone on which they would solidify Spanish sovereignty in Upper Louisiana while making the province prosperous. Spanish officials and agents thus actively sought Americans and exiles from the French and Haitian Revolutions who possessed "goods, money, slaves, cattle," and "other effects."[66] One imperial agent articulated Spanish strategy explicitly: Officials sought to attract Americans who were "the well-to-do folks, especially those owning black slaves."[67] Another Spanish agent's 1793 "Plan of Population for the Illinois" recommended offering to enslavers 100 arpents "for each black man or woman, with child," capable of doing "work to the field."[68] The labor of enslaved African Americans would catalyze commercial agriculture in Upper Louisiana while strengthening Spanish sovereignty.

By the late 1790s, enslavers had mostly abandoned Illinois for Upper Louisiana, so Spanish officials turned to enslavers from Kentucky. The plan proved popular enough to prompt one prominent enslaver-speculator from Kentucky to remark on "the rage" of white Kentuckians "for the Spanish settlements and I believe numbers will emigrate to that place in the spring & next summer."[69] In 1797, thirty-eight Kentucky families petitioned Spanish officials in a prearranged exchange. New Madrid Commandant Pierre-Charles DeLassus offered "a man and his wife 240 arpents of land," and to "a man and wife with four or five children, or two or three slaves, 400 arpents, and so on in proportion."[70] Spanish officials valued enslaved people highly, calculating the worth of one enslaved Black person to two free white children. All told, "about thirty American families, taking advantage of the Spanish government's generous land policy of 1796," relocated from Mason County, Kentucky.[71] Spanish policies gradually but steadily increased the population of enslavers and enslaved African Americans in Upper Louisiana in the decade preceding the Louisiana Purchase. The most famous expatriated American in Upper Louisiana, Daniel Boone, entered Upper Louisiana in 1799 with his "*famille et Esclaves*," including his wife, six children, and ten enslaved men, women, and children.[72] In 1799, Jacque Guibourd Dubreuil, a Frenchman and "former inhabitant of Santo Domingo," made his way to Ste. Geneviève, "the place he had chosen for his residence, along with his slaves, and other properties." Spanish authorities granted him 3,000 arpents' of land.[73]

As intended, Spanish policies increased the population of enslaved people in Upper Louisiana. U.S. colonizers often sold land in the United States, used the funds to purchase enslaved men and women in places like Kentucky and Illinois, and then migrated to Spanish Upper Louisiana, thus increasing the size of the land grants awarded to them by Spanish officials. The Smith family of Kentucky purchased "a Negro man Sam & negro woman Rachel" in February 1803 before emigrating to Upper Louisiana. Sam's and Rachel's enslaved bodies entitled the Smiths to "four hundred and seventy-three arpents" of land.[74] Thomas Maddin laid claim to "six thousand arpents" due to his status as an "owner of slaves."[75] Richard Glover received 300 arpents' worth of land in recognition of his having migrated with "five negro slaves" and "a great number of animals."[76] Benjamin Johnston claimed 600 arpents for having forcibly migrated a "great number of slaves" to Upper Louisiana,[77] while Thomas Bevis received 600 arpents for having migrated with his "wife, five children, two negroes, and a large quantity of animals."[78] Colonizers transformed Kentucky land into enslaved bodies, which then inflated land grants in Upper Louisiana.

Enslaver-colonizers from the United States often sold some of those enslaved people to habitants after they obtained their land grants. In 1784, Solomon White sold "a negress and three children" to prominent Ste. Genevesian Antoine Aubuchon,[79] while Samuel Martin sold an enslaved women to Jean Baptiste Lafont.[80] In Ste. Geneviève, in the decade preceding the Louisiana Purchase, Anglophonic settlers sold at least twenty-five enslaved men, women, and children to habitants, though habitants sold only a few enslaved men and women to Anglophonic settlers.[81] Soon enough, Americans in Upper Louisiana began holding public slave sales. In 1799, lead-mine operator Austin Moses purchased an enslaved woman at the "sales" held by Joseph Fenwick, patriarch of an extended clan that claimed immense tracts of land in the Ste. Geneviève district, likely by virtue of having forced numerous enslaved African Americans to migrate to Missouri.[82] By 1800, the prosperity of enslavers in Upper Louisiana had become sufficient enough to attract small-scale, itinerant slave traders from the Ohio Valley. John Coffee, a friend of Andrew Jackson and later a general in the War of 1812, got his start as a merchant selling goods and enslaved people between Nashville, Natchez, and New Orleans. In 1800, he made a diversion, selling to a Ste. Geneviève merchant "a negro girl slave, about fourteen years old" in exchange for "one hundred and seventy five pecks of salt, at fifty livres per peck."[83] In the decade preceding the Louisiana Purchase, Spanish officials created their "competent population" by swapping out expropriated Indigenous land for enslaved African American bodies and the would-be grandees who enslaved them. Spanish land policies created a small-scale slave trade that transferred enslaved bodies from the Ohio Valley to Upper Louisiana.

The Dodge brothers embodied how Spanish officials and American enslaver-colonizers built an enslaving regime in Upper Louisiana. Israel Dodge and John Dodge had made their way from Connecticut to Lake Erie in the early 1770s, where they entered the Indian trade out of Fort Sandusky. In the early 1780s, Virginian authorities appointed John as an Indian agent at Kaskaskia, while Israel shuffled back and forth between Kentucky and Illinois. The Dodge brothers quickly developed a partnership with notorious merchant Thomas Bentley. Bentley had enriched himself in the chaotic Illinois villages in the 1770s. In 1775, he swindled enslaved woman Madeleinne and her two children, Genevieve and Francois, from a habitant merchant.[84] Bentley then increased his estate considerably when he married wealthy habitant Marguerite Beauvais. When Virginian authorities withdrew from Illinois, John Dodge placed himself in charge of the settlements in Illinois. In addition to buying up land warrants issued to Virginia soldiers, the Dodge brothers and Bentley hit on a scheme to purchase unpaid Virginia promissory notes at deeply discounted prices. Sometime in the middle 1780s, Bentley and John Dodge headed off to Virginia, seeking to redeem the notes at face value. Bentley died on the trip, and Dodge returned to Kaskaskia claiming authority over Bentley's estate. Dodge alleged that Bentley had cut Marguerite Beauvais out of his will, due to "her infamous Conduct and Whoredom," and had claimed that she had "dissipated and squander'd away a great part of the Estate." Dodge served as the only imperial agent in Illinois in the mid-1780s, and he used his authority to steal from Beauvais "a Certain Mullattoe Woman named Genevieve with four Children also a Negro Man named Pereault."[85] Beauvais repeatedly sought assistance from U.S. and Spanish officials, to no avail. No U.S. officials were available to hear her pleas. Besides, Spanish officials had apparently already made a deal with the Dodge brothers.

Spanish authorities welcomed the brothers as propertied merchants, farmers, enslavers, and minor officials who would contribute to the region's burgeoning commercial agricultural economy and enslaving regime. Now claiming ownership of at least two enslaved families, the Dodge brothers settled at the state-sponsored settlement of New Bourbon. There, they oversaw the construction of a "flour mill and saw mill," likely built with the labor of the enslaved people they had stolen on the American side. John then sold the mills to François Vallé for 10 arpents' worth of prime land.[86] Shortly after, Spanish officials appointed John as first lieutenant in the New Bourbon militia. John died in 1795, at which point Israel began acquiring land. By 1800, Spanish officials granted Israel more than 7,000 arpents' worth of land, noting that he was not only the "father of a large family" but also the "owner of several slaves."[87] In addition to acquiring and swapping land and contributing to the infrastructure of commercial agriculture, Israel became a regular dealer of enslaved men and women. In 1794, in two separate transactions, Israel sold an enslaved African American man and woman. The following year, he sold two enslaved persons to Antoine Janis.[88] Israel's business dealings and interests extended to the Atlantic states, and in 1795 he worked with a New England merchant to acquire more enslaved men and women. He and Nathaniel Hall struck a deal to establish a shop in New Bourbon. Israel sold Hall land and a home in exchange for cash money, an interest in the business, and, "for six months," the labor of "three of his negroes named Poytour, Tomes and Ralph; and two of his negresses named Sarat and Fanny" while Hall conducted business in New England.[89]

In the early 1780s, the slaveless Dodge brothers were pariahs in Illinois. A decade later, the acquisition of slaves and their removal to Upper Louisiana made them respectable, prosperous, and important subjects of the Spanish empire. Israel engaged in commerce with the most prominent residents of the Ste. Geneviève region, asking François Vallé to secure for him "twenty pounds of sugar and ten pounds of coffee" via Vallé's partners in New Orleans.[90] In 1797, the commandant of New Bourbon noted Israel's service as first lieutenant in the Ste. Geneviève militia; praised him as "a large property owner"; designated him "one of the principal and notable habitants of New Bourbon"; and lauded him for erecting "a flour mill, which is very useful to the public." Lastly, Commandant DeLassus added that Dodge "has a family and several slaves."[91] On the eve of the Louisiana Purchase, Spanish officials joined with habitant and American enslavers to create a stable, thriving economy and society; both rested on enslaved men and women, whose bodies provided forced labor, capital, and the basis of enormous land grants. It also rested on imperial and provincial officials such as DeLassus and the Vallé family, who empowered would-be grandees such as the Janis and Dodge families and then turned those enslavers into local officials who solidified the overlapping social, political, and cultural networks that kept enslaved people in slavery.

Dispossessed land and enslaved bodies underwrote the growth of a diversified economy by the late 1790s. The land grants that Spanish officials offered to habitant and American emigrants began to serve as a form of cash and capital that fed the region's growing agriculture, staple, and consumer economy. Jean-Baptiste Trudeau retired from active participation in the fur trade in the late 1790s and entered into land speculation, lot improvement, and commercial agriculture. Trudeau sold most of his lots to Americans, who supplied the economy with not only enslaved men and women but also cash

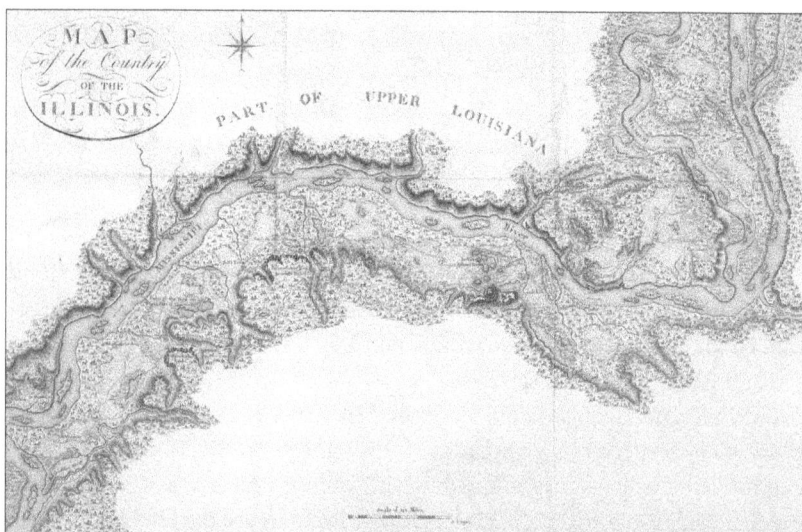

Figure 2. An English print of a 1796 map produced by a French interloper, Georges Henri Victor Collot, 1826, G1375.C6 1826, Geography and Map Division, Library of Congress.

money. Trudeau sold a town lot of "an arpent to an American doctor for 160 dollars." Spanish land grants became cash money. Seeking to sell more lots, Trudeau was willing to accept "spare ribs" along with "corn, tobacco, and vegetables." Some of these goods would be shipped downriver. Others would be sold to newly arriving colonizers from the United States.[92]

Trudeau could retire from the fur trade because enslavers, merchants, and imperial officials had expanded the economy of Upper Louisiana beyond its traditional reliance on the fur trade to a mixed economy based on commercial agriculture, consumer goods, and the increased production of lead and salt. Food and stores, along with skins and furs, went downriver to New Orleans. Lead, a commodity of growing importance, was turned into shot in New Orleans, St. Louis, and Lexington, Kentucky. From there, merchants and governments supplied lead shot to the growing companies of Spanish and U.S. soldiers, local militias, and Native American bands and nations.[93] Manufactured and consumer goods either went downriver via the Ohio, from Philadelphia, Pittsburgh, or Lexington, or upriver from New Orleans. In 1799, recent French emigrant and merchant Louis Tarascon, operating out of Philadelphia, noted that Upper Louisiana's economy produced "piastres [money], lead, salt, corn, flour, and mainly pelts." He expected that it would soon export "cotton, Indigo, [and] hemp."[94] Four years later, another recent emigrant and merchant, Michel Amoureux, noted that Upper Louisiana's abundance included "loads of leather, flour, hemp, cotton, lead, tobacco": All were produced with enslaved labor and destined for markets downriver.[95]

The commodified bodies and labors of enslaved African Americans stood at the center of this new economy. In Upper Louisiana, habitant and American enslavers acquired large land grants from Spanish officials by forcing enslaved men and women to migrate to Upper Louisiana. Enslaved people then produced food, stores, lead, and salt on those land grants. Enslavers and would-be enslavers then swapped land grants, enslaved people, the products of their labor, piastres, and consumer goods, feeding a steadily growing cycle of exchange. Growing demand for these products in distant markets increased the demand for bound labor. The growth in Upper Louisiana's enslaved population expanded the region's production for markets in the Lower Mississippi Valley, in turn creating new demand for enslaved labor. By the 1790s, Spanish policies and habitant enterprise had created a more complex economy, more thoroughly integrated into the growing Mississippi Valley plantation complex, which stretched from Pittsburgh to New Orleans. In the 1780s, enslavers traded enslaved people, typically for furs and skins. Thus, in 1786, Auguste Chouteau used a note to settle a debt for his niece's husband, Joseph Marie Papin, giving him ten years to pay off the loan of 1,204 piastres. Papin secured the loan with "two mulattoes Henry, age approximately thirty years, and Jean his brother, around twenty years old, as well as his two mulatto women, their sisters Agathe, aged nineteen, and Pelagie of sixteen years of age."[96] That same year, merchant Silvestre Sarpy sold "his Negress slave, named Francisca, nineteen to twenty years old, with her son named Luis, age two" for "the price and sum of five hundred pounds of beaver skins."[97] Habitant enslavers had long been nakedly and aggressively acquisitive. They did not need U.S. enslavers or imperialists to teach them the ways of bourgeois capitalism reliant on enslaved labor.

In the years immediately preceding the Louisiana Purchase, economic transactions involving enslaved men and women grew more complex. In 1800, the Duclo, Aubuchon, and Deninelle families sought to settle a series of inheritances and debts. The body and labors of a six-year-old enslaved African American boy, Josephe, served as a form of capital for these middling merchant families. The Duclo and Aubuchon families settled their claims to Josephe for "two hundred dollars" in cash and "distributed" another "one hundred dollars" between themselves. Cecille Aubuchon then used Josephe to settle an outstanding debt incurred by her deceased first husband. Cecille transferred ownership of Josephe to Michel Placette to settle a debt of "one hundred dollars" issued on "lead at the rate of five sols per pound," with "the remaining one hundred dollars to be paid in animals."[98] Whereas the sale of enslaved people had once been mainly for skins and furs, by the late 1790s, transactions often involved cash, lead, salt, and livestock. The following year, Parfait Dufour sold an unnamed enslaved woman, "about eighteen years old, Creole of this dependency," to merchant and speculator Jacques Clamorgan. Clamorgan then paid Parfait's debt for "eight thousand lead weights" and "fifty piastres in shaved deerskins" to Parfait's creditors with a promissory note.[99] In 1800, a Ste. Geneviève enslaver purchased "a negro girl slave, about fourteen years old," for "one hundred and seventy five pecks of salt."[100] Enslaved African Americans became one more commodity to be swapped in a growing commercial economy filled with cash and commodities.

The life of cosmopolitan and peripatetic fur trader Charles Gratiot embodied the changes wrought by empire and enslavement in Spanish Upper Louisiana in the decade preceding the Louisiana Purchase. After spending four years in Cahokia, Gratiot arrived in St. Louis in 1781 and married into the Chouteau family. He became heavily involved in the fur trade, traveling to London and St. Petersburg. After returning to St. Louis in the mid-1790s and removing himself from the fur trade, an associate from London tried to lure him back. Gratiot declined, citing his growing fortunes in Upper Louisiana. "Where is the country that can give me the advantages I possess here?" Gratiot asked. Gratiot owned "a farm in cultivation by some ten slaves." While "this alone would be sufficient for an ambitious man," Gratiot became ecstatic when he considered "what it may be worth in ten years from the population which is rapidly growing here." Gratiot did not foresee the Louisiana Purchase, but he did foresee enslavers flocking to Upper Louisiana and the continuing growth of commercial agriculture. He also tied his future fortunes to "a saline, a considerable mine of stone-coal, and advantageous sites for mills," all of which would be presumably tapped by the labor of enslaved people.[101] Gratiot had commodified the St. Louis hinterlands, including the enslaved people whose labor he expropriated. No longer dependent on the fur trade, Gratiot would grow his fortune by using enslaved men and women for commercial agriculture, salt production, and mining. Over the course of roughly two decades, habitant and American enslavers used the powers of the Spanish imperial state to create a small but thriving slave society in Upper

Louisiana, where the business of empire was enslavement, and where support for enslavers bolstered Spanish sovereignty.

Forty years of Spanish, British, Virginian, and U.S. dominion over the main European settlements in the Middle Mississippi Valley had created dramatic changes in the region. The once-thriving French villages neared abandonment. Conversely, by 1803, enslavers and imperial officials in Upper Louisiana had created an economic system predicated on the continuing emigration of enslavers from the United States and on the growing demand for commodities in the larger Mississippi Valley plantation complex. Habitants, Americans, and Spanish officials used the institutions and infrastructure of the Spanish imperial state to build a system of petty bourgeois capitalism in Upper Louisiana on the bodies of enslaved Black and Indigenous people. Around the time of the Louisiana Purchase, various imperial officials, agents, and observers pegged the American population at anywhere between one-half and two-thirds of the European-descended population of Spanish Upper Louisiana. Overall, enslaved people counted for approximately 16 percent of the population of Upper Louisiana. Around the main settlements of Ste. Geneviève and St. Louis, the population held in slavery ranged between 20 percent and 25 percent.[102] Over the previous three decades, Spanish officials and habitant enslavers had effectively rebuilt and expanded the slave societies of Illinois in Upper Louisiana. Enslavers and imperial officials had created a dynamic and adaptable slave society that formed a key part of the emerging Mississippi Valley plantation complex.

In Upper Louisiana, cultural differences divided habitants and Americans frequently enough. One habitant man penned a poem that expressed his disgust with the Americans who were rapidly settling lands in and around Ste. Geneviève:

Welcome here, dear child of Sodom
Welcome here, man in the midst of Rome
And you hateful damn whore whose cunt disgusts us
Go to the homes of Americans to find those who will fuck you[103]

Male American colonizers shared similarly chauvinistic sentiments toward their habitant neighbors, especially women. After arriving in Ste. Geneviève, William Carr determined that "the French women are undoubtedly the greatest sluts in the world." He wondered if any American would "unite himself for life to one of those ignorant dirty French girls."[104] But habitants and Americans—the white men at least—shared much in common besides ethnic chauvinism, white supremacy, and rank misogyny.

Both groups readily exchanged nominal professions of allegiance to the Spanish empire for protection of their interests, especially their interests in enslaving others. Both groups welcomed Spanish imperial actions that elevated white male enslavers to a privileged position while devoting imperial state resources to marginalizing enslaved African Americans, inflicting violence on them, and keeping them enslaved. By 1803, habitant and American enslavers and would-be enslavers had become Spanish subjects who were loyal enough to a regime that empowered them as bourgeois enslavers. Forty years of Anglo-American rule had decimated the enslaving exclaves in Illinois. Forty years of Spanish rule and support for enslavement had transformed Upper Louisiana from a fur-trading outpost dependent on the enslavement of Native Americans into a nexus for the production of foodstuffs and stores, dependent on enslaved African Americans, and thoroughly integrated into the transnational Mississippi Valley plantation complex. The place of empire and enslavement in the shifting matrix of the imperial Middle Mississippi Valley would soon be determined by a series of unexpected contingencies that few residents of the region saw coming.

CHAPTER 4

The Louisiana Purchase,
the Northwest Ordinance, and the
Middle Mississippi Valley, 1803–1805

Imperial transfers and settlements came rapidly to the Mississippi Valley, while the contours of empire and enslavement proved rife with contingencies between 1803 and 1805. These two years of conflicts centering on the course of empire and enslavement in both Illinois and Upper Louisiana caused concern and consternation for some, hope and opportunities for others. A host of imperial agents, diverse settler-colonizer groups, enslaved African and Native Americans, and sectionalized congressional factions all jostled to protect and advance their particular interests. Proslavery and antislavery imperialists put forth proposals for rescinding Article VI in Illinois or extending it across the river to Upper Louisiana. Enslaved people used imperial transfers to seek new routes to emancipation. From 1803 through 1805, the relationship between empire and enslavement in the Middle Mississippi Valley remained contingent and uncertain. Ultimately, however, the Louisiana Purchase confirmed and crystallized prevailing patterns of empire, enslavement, and colonization far more than it changed them.

Illinois enslavers and speculators saw in the Louisiana Purchase an opportunity for their own transfer. They sought to remove the Illinois counties along the Mississippi River from the Indiana Territory and attach them to a new U.S. territory in Upper Louisiana. Doing so would free them from Article VI and greatly increase the value of the massive land claims that they had accumulated over the previous fifteen years from fleeing habitants, American enslavers, and Virginian land claimants. Enslaved people found their own reasons to welcome U.S. rule, at least initially, and an enslaved family of Native American descent filed a lawsuit seeking emancipation under U.S. law. Between 1803 and 1805, colonizers, enslaved people, and imperial policy-makers sought to leverage the complex and competing laws of slavery and manumission in Illinois and Upper Louisiana to create new avenues for emancipation or to close them off entirely. However, as habitant and American enslavers in Upper Louisiana became ever more concerned about the U.S. imperial state's commitment to enslavers, U.S. imperial agents and leading habitants intervened, pledging that the U.S imperial state would support enslavers and subordinate enslaved people. Upper Louisiana enslavers saw no meaningful distinction between French, Spanish, or U.S. governance; they simply demanded that whatever empire claimed dominion over them place imperial state power at their disposal. From the 1760s through 1803, enslavers followed imperial state power to Upper Louisiana; between 1803 and 1805, they fought to retain their control over it.

While habitants, Americans, and enslaved people in the Middle Mississippi Valley fretted about what U.S. rule meant for slavery in Illinois and Upper Louisiana, sectional factions in Congress fought over what protections and prohibitions they would extend to enslavers. The U.S. Congress had dallied with questions centering on empire and enslavement since the 1790s. The Louisiana Purchase, however, generated a prolonged debate over the borders and extent of enslavement in the sprawling U.S. empire, creating northern and southern factions that Massachusetts Senator John Quincy Adams called "the two parties of slave and anti-slave."[1] The northern faction sought to extend some version of Article VI across the Mississippi River by attaching Upper Louisiana to the Indiana Territory. The southern faction managed to defeat that proposal in the main. The northern faction, however, created a confused territorial government for Upper Louisiana, which suggested that Congress would extend Article VI to Upper Louisiana sometime in the near future.

The status quo prevailed in practice, but constitutional and imperial structures became more muddled. Slavery could continue in Upper Louisiana, but enslavers enjoyed neither the sanction nor the prohibition of an imperial decree on slavery there. Upper Louisiana enslavers found this arrangement acceptable, even though it left open the possibility that Congress could intervene against enslavers in the future. Upper Louisiana enslavers had long demonstrated an ability to preserve their systems of slavery within indifferent and even hostile imperial decrees. Meanwhile, in Illinois, U.S. enslavers and speculators resigned themselves to the reality that northern opponents of an empire for slavery would never consent to rescinding Article VI during the territorial phase of government. They thus began constructing an elaborate system of indentured servitude designed to skirt the clear meaning and intent of Article VI. The conflicts and contingencies surrounding the Louisiana Purchase did little to alter the practices of empire and enslavement in the Middle Mississippi Valley, despite the best efforts of various groups.

In the spring of 1803, word of Spain's retrocession of Louisiana to France reached the Middle Mississippi Valley; habitants, American enslavers, and recently arrived French emigrants both expected and accepted retrocession. Napoleon's ascent to power revived interest in a new French empire centered on the Mississippi Valley. Bonapartists also had designs on a supercolony that replicated its former colonial claims to Louisiana, the western Great Lakes, and the Ohio and Missouri Valleys. Bonapartists' "darling plan of colonizing on the banks of the Mississippi"[2] jettisoned the vestiges of the *ancien régime*, dispensed with the excess of the French Revolution, and promised a new imperial regime on what they pled were more rational and modern Bonapartist terms. In the first years of the nineteenth century, French adventurers penned multiple accounts of the Mississippi Valley that smacked of Bonapartist imperialism: the belief that a new French empire under the direction of Napoleon would be capable of finally realizing the potential of French North America.[3]

When word of the retrocession arrived in the region in early 1803, habitants, Americans, and recent French emigrants took steps to ensure their continuing prosperity and local governance as part of a revived French empire in North America. Slavery stood at the center of their visions of French dominion in Upper Louisiana, and they worked to ensure that local imperial institutions, officers, and governments would continue to serve them. Enslaver and lead-mine operator Moses Austin welcomed "the contemplated change of government from Spanish to French dominion." Heavily dependent on enslaved labor for the operation of his lead mines and smelting operations, Moses expected "that the French government will be ready to take such steps as will be most likely to extend the improvements of this country." Moses sought to bring American enslavers in Upper Louisiana under the good graces of French officials so that he could impress upon them "the many advantages that would accrue from a proper encouragement of commerce and agricultural," both of which were synonymous with the coerced labors of enslaved African Americans. To ensure that French officials would continue Spanish efforts to expand slavery and commerce in the Mississippi Valley,

Moses counseled leading Americans in Upper Louisiana to create "a committee to form a congratulatory address to be presented to our new officers"
from the "French Government." Doing so would "render the Americans in
the country as respectable as possible," ensuring that French officials would
continue to empower prominent local enslavers.[4] The Spanish regime had
been good to enslavers like Austin, and he maneuvered to ensure the same
under French rule.

Recent French emigrants also welcomed French dominion in the Mississippi Valley. In 1793, French merchant Mathurin-Michel Amoureux fled
counterrevolutionaries in Lorient, France; by 1801, he had made his way to
New Madrid. Despite his friendship with Thomas Jefferson, his devotion to
the United States during its War for Independence, and his residence in Philadelphia, Virginia, and Kentucky in the 1790s, Amoureux eagerly welcomed
the restoration of French dominion in Upper Louisiana. Amoureux wrote
to a French prefect, who had not yet arrived in New Orleans, requesting an
appointment to office so that he could become "useful to the public business"
under a new French regime. Amoureux also offered advice on how to turn
Americans into loyal French subjects; how to improve commerce between
Upper and Lower Louisiana; how to capture commerce coming down the
Ohio River; and, finally, where to station French soldiers in Upper Louisiana
in a show of imperial force. Though personally opposed to slavery, Amoureux admitted that "the migrants arriving from United States are usually good
planters. They are not however so good workers." As Amoureux saw matters,
enslaving corrupted the personal morals and work habits of American enslavers. Yet, by coercing labor out of enslaved African Americans, they proved
to be "good planters" who forced enslaved people to "clear our forests and
plow the ground."[5] Amoureux personally opposed slavery but begrudgingly
admitted its necessity for any empire with aspirations in the Middle Mississippi Valley. By mid-1803, habitants, Americans, and recent French emigrants
anticipated French dominion would steadily expand on, but do little to alter,
the enslaving regime that they had built on the west bank of the Mississippi
River over the previous three decades.

Unexpected contingencies shaped the course of empire, if not always
slavery, in the Middle Mississippi Valley. Bonapartist imperialists tied their
interest in a revived North American empire to their desire to reestablish
slavery in Haiti, formerly French Saint-Domingue. France's most valuable
colony and perhaps the most valuable of all European holdings in the Americas in the late 1700s, Saint-Domingue supplied western Europe with the bulk

of its sugar and cotton. Napoleon envisioned using his Mississippi Valley empire to provision Saint-Domingue with foodstuffs and stores. In late 1801, France sent a fleet with a combined twenty thousand men to crush the slave revolt in Haiti, reestablish the island's former cash-crop economy, and create a new, enslaving imperial regime. As Napoleon understood, slavery was the creature of imperial state power and violence. Napoleon also laid plans to send French soldiers to Louisiana and to reinforce the Louisiana troops after French soldiers in Haiti completed their reconquest of the island. In short, Napoleon's plans were Haiti first, then Louisiana and the Mississippi Valley. However, former slaves who had freed themselves became formidable foes to Napoleon's forces. Haitians defeated Napoleon's forces in Haiti, left him fewer troops to secure Louisiana, and dashed his visions for a revived French empire in the Americas.[6]

Haitians begat the Louisiana Purchase. As Alexander Hamilton observed, "those means which were originally destined to the colonization of Louisiana" by France had been "gradually exhausted" in "repeated and fruitless efforts to subjugate St. Domingo." "To the deadly climate of St. Domingo, and to the courage and obstinate resistance made by its black inhabitants are we indebted for the obstacles which delayed the colonization of Louisiana."[7] Without Haiti, Louisiana promised to drain Napoleon's treasury while remaining susceptible to seizure from the United States, Great Britain, or the wannabe princes, interlopers, and adventurers who prowled the Mississippi Valley and Gulf borderlands from the 1780s through 1815.[8] With renewed war in Europe looming, Napoleon offered to sell the entirety of French claims west of the Mississippi to the United States. The United States and France agreed to the Louisiana Purchase Treaty on April 30, 1803. When word of the Louisiana Purchase Treaty reached the Middle Mississippi Valley in August 1803, it provoked new schemes and worries among enslavers about the future of slavery and empire. The Louisiana Purchase threatened to upset the imperial-institutional arrangements forged by enslavers and Spanish officials, while enslaved men and women would seek to use the transfer for their own purposes. At the same time, the imperial rivalries that shaped the transfers of the early 1800s also offered enslavers unique opportunities to extort concessions from the various imperial powers seeking their allegiances and loyalties.

The small cadre of American enslavers and speculators who remained in Illinois took an immediate interest in the Louisiana Purchase. By 1803, the ongoing exodus of habitant enslavers from Illinois to Upper Louisiana was nearly complete. Amos Stoddard, the first American commandant in

Upper Louisiana, reported that "very few French are intermixed with those on the East side of the Mississippi."[9] Seemingly all that remained in Illinois were American speculators with interests that could not be removed across the river. When word of the Louisiana Purchase reached the Middle Mississippi Valley, those Americans tied to Illinois sought to use it to revive slavery while inflating the value of their speculative land purchases. To do so, they proposed creating a trans-Mississippi territory that would join southern and western Illinois to a new U.S. territory in Upper Louisiana.

Land speculators and enslavers Robert Morrison and John Edgar led the scheme, which quickly expanded to include numerous U.S. imperial agents, local speculators, and Kentucky congressmen with interests in Illinois lands. Members of the extended Morrison family left Philadelphia for Kaskaskia around 1790.[10] They immediately began speculating in lands, purchasing and selling enslaved people, and moving goods among Philadelphia, the Middle Mississippi Valley, and New Orleans. William Morrison operated a business out of Cahokia and was active in selling enslaved people into Upper Louisiana, including selling an enslaved family at the slave sales hosted by John Fenwick. The Morrisons also specialized in buying up military land warrants issued by Virginia, along with the claims of enslavers who departed for Upper Louisiana, including the extensive holdings once claimed by the Dodge brothers and the Janis family. By 1805, they had acquired claims to approximately twelve thousand acres of land around Kaskaskia.[11] John Edgar had arrived in Kaskaskia in 1784, and he quickly became the region's leading land speculator. Like Morrison, Edgar purchased land claims staked by habitants and Americans, as well as the land warrants issued to Virginia soldiers. By the early 1800s, Edgar accumulated upward of fifty thousand acres in claims. Edgar and Morrison also launched commercial efforts to supply flour and other foodstuffs to the Lower Mississippi Valley, building a flour mill and hiring crews to move goods downriver.[12] Edgar and Morrison likely would have joined the exodus to Upper Louisiana, but their massive land claims tied them to Illinois. Stuck on the American side, both had been involved in several efforts in the mid-1790s to repeal Article VI in the Illinois settlements, or to lop off a separate Illinois Territory from the Northwest Territory, rescinding Article VI along the east bank of the Mississippi River.[13]

By the early 1800s, Edgar and Morrison had built the commercial infrastructure needed to entice enslavers to Illinois, but they lacked imperial state sanction for slavery and local institutions crafted to empower enslavers. Edgar and Morrison possessed some of the best commercial agricultural land on the North American continent, the "American Bottom." They culti-vated commercial ties with merchants in Upper and Lower Louisiana, cre-ating an easy outlet for foodstuffs, stores, and commodities. Yet settlement in Illinois remained stalled, the villages in a continuing state of decline. In a letter written to eastern newspapers, Morrison complained that, due to Arti-cle VI, "men of respectability and possessing considerable property in slaves, though very much disposed to come and settle" in Illinois, "have been pre-vented merely from the consideration, that they could not bring their slaves with them." American emigrants—primarily enslavers—would continue to bypass Illinois for Upper Louisiana as long as "the other side possess[es] so decided a preference on the score of slavery."[14] In the Middle Mississippi Val-ley, the fortunes of localities hinged on empire and enslavement. Morrison was determined to rejoin enslavement to empire in Illinois.

As soon as they received word of the Louisiana Purchase, Morrison, Edgar, and others hatched a scheme to legalize slavery in Illinois. Under their plan, Congress would remove the southern and western parts of Illinois from the Indiana Territory and the jurisdiction of the Northwest Ordinance. Congress would then make Illinois part of "a New Territorial Government to be formed on both sides of the Mississippi beginning as far South as Lanse Lagrasse [present-day New Madrid] running North as far as inhabited."[15] Under their proposal, "the two western counties" of Illinois, home to the ancient French villages, and the entirety of the American Bottom would be "attached to the upper district" of Louisiana.[16] The Illinois speculators' plan would unite the two banks under a single imperial government and a single set of protections for enslavers, as had been the case under French dominion. Slavery would once again have imperial sanction across the entirety of the Middle Mis-sissippi Valley. Edgar and Morrison brought Kentucky Congressman John Fowler into their scheme, begging Fowler for "a union of these two counties" in Illinois "with the Louisiana."[17] Joining Edgar and Morrison was Matthew Lyon, once a democratic tribune, now an enslaver living in Kentucky. Lyon, who was likely made a partner with the land speculators, remained "anxious to Affix the Counties this Side to the Upper Louisiana." To realize their plan, Lyon pledged to lobby the congressional committee hearing petitions for sep-arating Illinois from Indiana, along with the committee responsible for "the Ceded Country" across the river.[18]

The Illinois speculators' scheme would work only if Congress protected slavery in Upper Louisiana. To that end, the Illinois speculators sought to scare imperial U.S. policy-makers into extending privileges to Upper Louisiana enslavers. U.S. imperial agents and policy-makers in Washington remained wary of their ability to see through the transfer of Louisiana to the United States and then peacefully incorporate the main settlements around New Orleans and in Upper Louisiana into the United States. Habitants and French planters in Lower Mississippi seemed especially wary of the Louisiana Purchase and agitated for retrocession to France; intriguers and interlopers like James Wilkinson sought to form their own polities in the Mississippi Valley; Spain, France, and Britain all retained imperial designs on the Mississippi Valley. In this caldron of imperial intrigue, the Illinois speculators and their allies sought to exploit U.S. imperial fears to win new protections for slavery in Illinois.[19] Whereas habitant and Anglo enslavers had transferred their enslaving polities from Illinois to Upper Louisiana over the previous forty years, Edgar, Morrison, Lyon, and Fowler would extend Upper Louisiana's enslaving regime back to Illinois, this time under the auspices of the U.S. empire.

Edgar and Morrison provided Fowler with a litany of arguments. They advised Fowler to inform Congress that enslavers in Upper Louisiana had come to expect protections and privileges for enslavers from imperial powers in the Middle Mississippi Valley. As Edgar explained, habitants and Americans in Spanish Upper Louisiana "are very much interested in an unlimited slavery," expressing his own desires for Illinois as much as the interests of habitant and American enslavers in Upper Louisiana. "Unlimited slavery"— for Edgar as well as for Upper Louisianan enslavers—referred to the entire retinue of imperial government sanctioning, empowering, supporting, and protecting enslavers in their provincial polities. Edgar added that "many of them hold a considerable part of the estate in that species of property," advising that white Upper Louisianans' personal interests were tied directly to slavery and that Article VI had already alienated many of them from the U.S. regime. According to Edgar, Congress had mistakenly proceeded with Article VI out of ignorance of the circumstances of habitants and Americans in Illinois; he advised Fowler and Congress against making the same mistake in Upper Louisiana.[20] Morrison made a nearly identical plea to the leading Republican newspaper in the mid-Atlantic states, the Philadelphia *Aurora*. "In the province of Louisiana slavery is at present tolerated in its fullest extent, and the interests of the inhabitants are so intimately connected with a continuance of it there, that no doubt it will still be permitted" under whatever territorial government Congress framed.[21] Colonizers' interests demanded imperial sanction and support for slavery in the entirety of the Middle Mississippi Valley.

Edgar, Morrison, and Fowler also brought into their scheme Thomas Davis, a well-connected Virginian who served as a congressional representative from Kentucky before receiving an appointment as a judge and legislator for territorial Illinois. Working as an agent of U.S empire, Davis undertook an extensive campaign to further Edgar's plan to separate the Illinois settlements from Indiana and to ensure that the United States would protect slavery in the proposed trans-Mississippi Territory. Davis first wrote to Kentucky Senator John Breckinridge, whom Jefferson appointed to introduce his bill for the government of Louisiana. Davis advised Breckinridge that he found white Upper Louisianans "very much divided in sentiment on the score of becoming American Citizens—they are wonderfully alarmed lest their slaves should be liberated—the sooner their minds can be quieted on that subject the better." Like his associate John Edgar, Davis asked that "the two western Counties" of Illinois be "added to the Settlements on the Spanish side" to form "one very compact territory."[22] Given Davis's close ties to leading Kentucky and Virginian politicians, he likely expected them to use these letters to cajole northern congressmen into agreeing to southern schemes to sanction slavery in the Middle Mississippi Valley. More likely than not, Breckinridge and Jefferson were in on their scheme and intended to use intelligence from the Mississippi Valley to forestall any efforts to prohibit slavery in Louisiana while aiding efforts to rescind Article VI in Illinois.

The day after writing to Breckinridge, Davis posted a letter about the state of settlement in the Middle Mississippi Valley to the *Virginia Argus*. Noting the "depopulation" of the Illinois settlements since the 1780s, Davis attributed it to "the extension of the American government" there. The "former inhabitants" of Illinois "are all slaveholders, and the adoption of the ordinance" of 1787 "induced them to believe their negroes would be liberated, and they immediately quit [the] place and went on the Spanish side of the Mississippi." Davis then warned that this same "alarm now exists among the inhabitants on the other side of the Mississippi, for they are large slaveholders." Alarmed slaveholders in Upper Louisiana would disrupt the Louisiana transfer: "the sooner some act of the government removes those fears the better."[23] According to Davis, the peaceful transfer of the Upper Louisiana settlements to U.S. dominion required clear and unambiguous protections for enslavers. Davis thus advised Congress against acting out of ignorance of the interests of habitants and Americans in Upper Louisiana; both groups saw imperial support for slavery as central to Upper Louisiana's place in a burgeoning U.S. empire. Speculators from Illinois now served as the chief advocate for enslavers in

Upper Louisiana. A few weeks after posting his letter to Richmond, Davis informed President Thomas Jefferson that he was "presently employed in visiting the Spanish settlements on the other side of the Mississippi." There, he found that "the people are wealthy & the land rich." But he also warned that "most of them are averse to the Cession of Louisiana to the U.S.," as they "are afraid of the liberation of their slaves (of which they have great numbers)."[24] In the course of less than three weeks, Davis posted letters to the senator appointed by Jefferson to introduce a territorial ordinance for Louisiana; to Richmond's leading newspaper; and to President Thomas Jefferson, the chief U.S. imperialist. All three letters contained the same plea and warning: Congress had to sanction slavery in Upper Louisiana and add the Illinois settlements to Louisiana if they wished to see a peaceful and successful transfer.

The Illinois speculators' subterfuge gave rise to rumors that the United States intended to make Upper Louisiana part of the Indiana Territory and to govern Upper Louisiana under the terms of the Northwest Ordinance; it is, of course, likely that the Illinois speculators themselves began circulating the rumor in order to undercut any congressional effort to prohibit slavery in Upper Louisiana. In either case, enslavers, land speculators, and agents of empire spread the rumor and used it to their advantage. Meriwether Lewis spent the winter of 1803–1804 in Illinois, but he frequently crossed the river to attend parties hosted by the leading habitant families of St. Louis.[25] He reported on a swirl of rumors centering on slavery and empire. Given that Lewis had extensive contact with Illinois speculators and Kentucky officials while residing in Illinois, Lewis was likely in on the scheme; given Lewis's close relations with St. Louis's leading family, the Chouteaus, it is likely that they endorsed the plan as well. Whatever the case, Lewis conveyed those rumors directly to Jefferson, likely with the expectation that Jefferson would share them with Congress.

According to Lewis, both habitant and American enslavers "appear to feel very sensibly a report which has been circulated among them on this subject, that *the Americans would emancipate their slaves immediately on taking possession of the country.*" Lewis further shared with Jefferson his "fear that the slaves will form a source of some unwillingness in the French to yield to the wishes of the government." These concerns extended beyond the class of habitant enslavers, encompassing Upper Louisiana's many would-be slaveholders. "There appears to be a general objection not only among the French, but even among the Americans not slaveholders," he continued, "to relinquish the right which they claim relative to slavery in its present unqualified form." Lewis also cautioned against attaching Upper Louisiana to the Indiana Territory. With "slavery being prohibited in the Indiana Territory, (at least the further admission of any Slaves), these proprietors of slaves will be compelled to decide, whether they will reside in an adjacent part of the Indiana Territory" and "sacrifice in some measure their slave property." Lewis once again reiterated that "the slaves appear to me in every view of this subject to be connected with the principal difficulties with which the government will have to contend in" incorporating Upper Louisiana into the U.S. empire. A peaceful and successful transfer of Upper Louisiana required that the United States endorse slavery in Upper Louisiana in its "present unqualified form" and forego extending the Northwest Ordinance across the river.[26] Further imperial intrigue could be quelled by adding the Illinois settlements to Upper Louisiana. Middle Mississippi Valley enslavers and their allies in Washington now possessed the kinds of rumors and intelligence that they needed to defeat imperial bans on slavery in Upper Louisiana and to rescind the ban in Illinois.

By 1803, habitants and American enslavers on both sides of the Mississippi River understood that the politics of empire and enslavement had changed dramatically over the previous decade. From the 1730s through 1787, imperial powers had made support for enslavers central to their imperial designs in the Middle Mississippi Valley, even if they rarely provided all that enslavers demanded. After 1787, the United States did much the same in the southern interior, extending government support to enslavers who sought to dispossess Native Americans of their lands. There was certainly ample commitment to the joint expansion of empire and enslavement in the history of the United States, especially in the decade surrounding the Louisiana Purchase; in that regard, the United States acted in much the same manner as every other imperial power claiming dominion in North America and the Caribbean in the eighteenth and early nineteenth centuries. The business of empire in the eighteenth-century Americas was slavery, and the United States was nothing if not the second British empire in North America. Since the 1500s, imperial officials and colonizers had used imperial state power to create racial hierarchies and to maintain unfree labor systems whenever and wherever they conquered and colonized parts of the Americas.[27] Unsurprisingly, then, from the 1790s through 1815, the United States empowered southern enslavers and their allies in the creation of a massive empire for slavery across the southern interior while European imperial powers hobbled themselves in the Americas during the wars of the French Revolution. In doing so, the United States consolidated and accelerated what Britain, France, and Spain had already been doing in the eighteenth century, laying the foundations of an empire for slavery in the Lower Mississippi Valley and along the Gulf Coast.[28] As an imperial power, the United States conquered Indigenous people, dispossessed them of their lands, and foisted a particularly aggressive and expansive form of racialized slave-labor capitalism across much of the southern interior.[29]

While enslavers and southern imperialists exercised a significant amount of influence over the policies and actions of the U.S. empire from its inception in the 1770s, their control was hardly absolute. Dynamic northern factions consistently managed to fight off southern and local efforts to permit slavery in the Northwest Territory. The constituents of these northern factions remained mired in white supremacy, and they supported efforts at racial exclusion and marginalization for free persons of color.[30] Their commitment to white supremacy and their reticence to interfere with slavery in the southern states did not, however, preclude the development of a meaningful and effective form of antislavery politics, particularly with regards to the place of slavery in the burgeoning U.S. empire. The United States changed the long-standing relationship between empire and enslavement in the greater Mississippi Valley and the broader Americas with passage of the Northwest Ordinance in 1787. The significance of Article VI became manifest in the contentious debates surrounding the relationship between empire and enslavement in the Middle Mississippi Valley set off by the Louisiana Purchase.

Antislavery northern imperialists instinctively applied the new relationship between empire and enslavement begat by the Northwest Ordinance to the Louisiana Purchase. Joel Barlow was a leading Democratic Republican from Connecticut. While serving in the U.S. diplomatic mission in London in 1803, he received word of the Louisiana Purchase in person from James Monroe. Barlow immediately sent a letter to the leader of the Democratic Republican faction in his home state, Alexander Wolcott. Barlow bluntly asked Wolcott, "Is it not possible in the first session of Congress to ordain that in Louisiana there should be no slavery allowed?" Barlow followed this question with a lengthy, detailed argument on the necessity of prohibiting the further expansion of slavery in the Louisianas as the first step toward advancing the cause of gradual abolition in the southern states, ultimately "eradicating it from Spanish America & the Islands" of the Caribbean.[31] For Barlow, the purpose of republican empire and the Louisiana Purchase was to eradicate slavery, not to entrench and expand it. Northern Republicans such as Barlow favored empire as much as any southern enslaver. Yet slavery was antithetical to the empire he envisioned creating on the North American continent. Indeed, for Barlow, republican empire—properly construed and governed—could be the means of eventually eradicating slavery from the Americas. Many other northern whites shared Barlow's commitment to a form of republican empire that contained and eradicated slavery wherever and whenever circumstances permitted. Northern antislavery imperialism was always compromised by a deep anti-Black bias that coupled the elimination of slavery with the removal of emancipated Black people through colonization, joining prohibitions on slavery with the exclusion of Black people. But equating northern white, anti-Black, antislavery imperialism with southern white, proslavery imperialism obscures not only their differences but also their historical significance.

The advocates of slavery in Illinois and Upper Louisiana understood the new politics of empire and enslavement, which is why they fought so hard to undermine the advocates of antislavery imperialism. Illinois enslavers and land speculators had sought the repeal or suspension of Article VI since first receiving word of its passage in 1787. In 1796, John Edgar and Robert Morrison were two of the four signatories on a petition lecturing Congress that Article VI was "contrary to an express fundamental principle in all free countries, 'that no ex post facto laws should ever be made.'"[32] Over the next several years, they devised a host of arguments justifying repeal of Article VI. In 1802, Morrison and Edgar joined with other prominent Americans in Illinois such as Shadrach Bond (who would become Illinois's first governor in 1818) to petition newly appointed Indiana Territory Governor William Henry Harrison to assist them in gaining congressional repeal of Article VI. Harrison immediately took up their plea. In the months preceding Congress's work creating a new government for Upper Louisiana, Harrison and other enslaver-speculators from Illinois lobbied Jefferson and numerous members of Congress to repeal Article VI in Indiana and Illinois.[33] John Rice Jones, another Illinois land speculator and territorial official, delightfully reported to John Davis that "the president is decidedly in favor of the article in our ordinance against Slavery being repealed."[34] Illinois speculator-enslavers won over southern imperialists in the crucial years surrounding the Louisiana Purchase.

A broad group of northern imperialists, however, consistently fought off efforts to repeal Article VI in Illinois and Indiana. This northern faction made it clear that they would assist Indiana and Illinois "in every particular, excepting that of the introduction of slaves."[35] Having won passage of the Northwest Ordinance with Article VI in 1787 and again in 1789, northern antislavery imperialists clung tight to their quarter of the U.S. empire in the west. Northern imperialists would assist Indiana and Illinois in building roads, maintaining commercial access to New Orleans, and dispossessing Native Americans of their lands. Northern imperialists refused, however, to yield on slavery or even a temporary suspension of Article VI. Northern antislavery imperialists scored an important victory in Ohio in 1802, when they joined with local antislavery colonizer-imperialists to exclude slavery from the first state carved out of the Northwest. In 1802, Ohio voters chose a slate of explicitly antislavery candidates for their state constitutional convention, which voted to adopt Article VI into its state constitution. Congress admitted Ohio as the first state from the trans-Appalachian West with a constitution barring slavery just as enslavers from Indiana and Illinois sought repeal of Article VI, and just as the United States was embarking on the Louisiana Purchase.[36] Northern antislavery imperialists understood that the Northwest Ordinance changed the politics of empire and enslavement, promising the exclusion or eradication of slavery in the northern half of the U.S. empire. Proslavery imperialists understood as well. As Thomas Davis noted in his 1803 letter to Virginia seeking repeal of Article VI in Illinois, "in the State of Ohio, the point is settled" against slavery.[37]

The Louisiana Purchase offered Illinois enslavers an opportunity to settle the point in their favor, at least in Illinois. From 1803 through 1805, Illinois enslavers deployed all of their connections in Washington and in Upper Louisiana to encourage imperial policy-makers to protect slavery in Upper Louisiana and to recognize slavery in Illinois. Their increasingly shrill and desperate pleas were intended not to persuade southern imperial policy-makers, such as Thomas Jefferson and John Breckinridge, but for use by them against northern antislavery imperialists. Thus, after warning Jefferson that Upper Louisianans remained "adverse to the Cession of Louisiana to the U.S." because of slavery, Thomas Davis also advised that "by a little attention and moderation they may be easily won over."[38] Davis would leave it to Jefferson and Breckinridge to impress upon northern Republicans that attention to the demands of enslavers would go far in reconciling white Upper Louisianans to U.S. rule. In the process of safeguarding slavery in the Louisiana Purchase, the southern and western counties of Illinois would be joined to the new Upper Louisiana Territory. Illinois speculator-enslavers and their allies also directly lobbied northern policy-makers. Matthew Lyon pressed Congressman Martin Chittenden, an old friend from Vermont, to "report favourably" from his committee when issuing a report on attaching Illinois to

Upper Louisiana.[39] Morrison sent his uncle in Philadelphia copies of the 1803 petition "for the annexation of" Illinois "to Upper Louisiana."[40] He repeatedly implored his uncle to press their "friends in Congress" on "behalf" of the Illinois petitioners seeking separation from Indiana.[41] Morrison also sought a favorable endorsement for their plan from the North's leading Democratic Republican newspaper, the Philadelphia *Aurora*, and its politically influential editor, William Duane.[42] In his lengthy letter to the *Aurora*, Morrison begged that Congress protect slavery in Upper Louisiana and then attach Illinois to Upper Louisiana.

Morrison's letter ran headlong into the new politics of empire and enslavement. Duane strongly rejected Morrison's proposal, denouncing him as "a friend to slavery in its greatest extent in Louisiana and even in the Indiana country." Speaking for northern antislavery imperialists, Duane retorted that the "sentiments" of the Illinois enslavers "are not at all consistent with ours." Duane sought to do more than simply maintain the Article VI exclusion in Illinois. He also expressed his expectation that Congress would "lay the foundation of a gradual abolition of slavery" in Upper Louisiana, just as it had done with the Northwest Ordinance in Illinois. A scheme that began with plans to jettison Article VI in Illinois instead added weight to gathering northern proposals to extend it to Upper Louisiana. Duane expected that "the policy of permitting slavery in Louisiana in its fullest extent" would "no doubt claim the mature attention of Congress." Duane seemingly knew of the plans of some Middle Atlantic Republicans and abolitionists when he added that "the friends of humanity have reason to expect" that the United States "will lay the foundation of a gradual abolition of slavery" "without militating against" the "particular and temporary interests" of enslavers already in Upper Louisiana. Congress would not interfere with enslavers' "particular and temporary interests" by prohibiting slavery immediately. They would, however, move to foster some kind of gradual abolition program in Upper Louisiana by prohibiting the further introduction of enslaved people into Louisiana.[43]

When Congress began debating the Louisiana government bills, the Philadelphia-based American Convention for Promoting the Abolition of Slavery submitted a petition calling on Congress to "prohibit the importation of slaves into the Territory of Louisiana, lately ceded to the United States." They tied their plea directly to Article VI, reminding Congress that "a former Congress judged it expedient to introduce among its regulations, for the government of the Northwestern Territory, a provision resembling that which your memorialists now suggest to you."[44] Philadelphia abolitionists also lobbied northern congressmen; they responded in kind. Pennsylvania Congressman David Bard informed Quaker abolitionist John Parrish that "Our Law for the Govt of Louisiana has some thing favourable on this subject, possibly." Bard also expected that "some more may yet be done," as Congress hashed out the details. In either case, Bard expressed his hope that the Louisiana laws would "be in favr. of preventing the encrease of Slaves, and of the gradual abolition of Slavery" there.[45] Neither Duane, Bard, nor the American Convention called on Congress to emancipate enslaved people already in Upper Louisiana. They would, however, block the further introduction of slavery there, laying the groundwork—to their minds at least—for gradual abolition. In northern antislavery imperialists' understanding of Article VI, it had led to the steady decline of slavery in Illinois. Looking across the Mississippi River to Upper Louisiana, Bard, Duane, and the American Convention expected that the "gradual abolition" of slavery "in [Upper] Louisiana is a measure confidently to be looked for."[46]

Northern antislavery imperialists expected that an Article VI for Upper Louisiana would operate in much the same way that it had in Illinois, Ohio, and Indiana since 1787. Enslavers in Upper Louisiana would complain but generally comply. Meanwhile, slavery would be prohibited from new areas of settlement, and the sale of enslaved men and women into Upper Louisiana would be prohibited. Enslavers in Upper Louisiana would be permitted to keep enslaved people already in their possession. The United States would do little to enforce the prohibition on future slavery, but enslavers would be wary of risking valuable property in territories where territorial ordinances failed to clearly protect the property rights of enslavers, and where slavery existed under the bane of an imperial decree. An imperial decree, the absence of imperial state power in the service of enslavers, and the magical elixir of republicanism would lead to slavery's gradual demise. At some indeterminable date in the future, slavery would somehow, someway, wither away in Upper Louisiana.

Northern imperialists opposed to slavery badly underestimated the difficulties of extending some version of Article VI to Upper Louisiana; the congressional allies of Illinois and Upper Louisiana enslavers had different plans in any case. Massachusetts Senator John Quincy Adams observed that during the debates over the Louisiana governments, the "majority of lawmakers" "divided" into the "two parties, of slave and anti-slave." Northern congressmen introduced "expedient after expedient" to "answer this purpose" of prohibiting slavery in both Louisianas. However, Jefferson's point man in the Senate,

John Breckinridge "concentrated all his wisdom" on defeating these proposals. "This prohibition of the admission of slaves into Louisiana, is like the drawing of a jaw tooth," wrote Adams.[47] Contra recent historiography, which posits that "support for slavery's expansion" served as "one of the best ways to unite southern and northern politicians,"[48] Adams likened resolving the differences between northern and southern factions over slavery in the Louisianas and Illinois to pulling a wisdom tooth.

The most ambitious northern proposal would completely exclude the further introduction of enslaved people into both Louisianas, in effect extending Article VI to Lower and Upper Louisiana. James Sloan, a butcher, Quaker, abolitionist, and recently elected Republican from New Jersey, proposed "inhibiting the admission of slaves into Louisiana, as well as from the United States, as from foreign places." Sloan's ban passed the House 40 to 36.[49] Northern antislavery imperialists expected "that it would require an army to enforce a law excluding slaves" from the Louisianas; they voted for the ban anyway.[50] Breckinridge led southern senators in their efforts to defeat Sloan's ban. To do so, he introduced measures banning the most egregious forms of the international slave trade, while still permitting the domestic slave trade. Northern antislavery imperialists shot down that proposal. Breckinridge and southern enslavers had to settle for a hard-fought, narrowly passed measure permitting "bona fide" U.S. colonizer-enslavers to settle in Louisiana, but prohibiting the sale of enslaved people into the Louisianas. Under the laws that Breckinridge marshalled through Congress for both Louisianas, migrating U.S. enslavers were in; the domestic and international slave trades were out.[51] In the words of Adams, Breckinridge mollified the northern "anti-slave" faction by "providing tolerably well for the introduction of slaves into the territory, under the form of heavy penalties against it. This is now in general the great art of Legislation at this place—To do a thing, by assuming the appearance of preventing it—To prevent a thing by assuming that of doing it."[52] Southern imperialists sanctioned slavery in Louisiana by tucking permission for migrating U.S. enslavers into a host of sanctions against the trade in human flesh.

The northern "anti-slave" faction countered by seeking to create a different government for Upper Louisiana. Their first proposal would "annex" Upper Louisiana "all down to N. Madrid" to the Indiana Territory, while maintaining the Article VI exclusion of slavery on both sides of the Mississippi River.[53] The antislavery implications were clear: "I know that it will estop slavery there, and to that I agree," explained Maryland Senator Samuel Smith.[54] Southern senators countered by trying to create an entirely separate territorial govern-ment for Upper Louisiana where slavery would be recognized, but the north-ern faction fought off that proposal. Framing a territorial government for Upper Louisiana had become analogous to "the drawing of a jaw tooth."[55] To resolve the differences, Congress created the "District of Louisiana" for Upper Louisiana, which was an entity of Louisiana. Under the terms of the territorial ordinance, settler-colonizers could continue to migrate to and settle in Upper Louisiana, but it would be cut off from the slave trade that carried enslaved men and women down the Ohio and Mississippi Valleys. Upper Louisiana would be governed by the officials of a different territory, Indiana, where Arti-cle VI still stood, at least on paper. Imperial agents and enslavers from Indiana had evaded the Article VI prohibition on slavery but had failed to repeal it; they would now govern Upper Louisiana's enslavers.[56]

Much like the new politics of empire and enslavement in the Middle Mississippi Valley, the territorial ordinance for Upper and (Lower) Louisi-ana was muddled and confused, ambiguous and indeterminate, and rife with contradictions and contingencies. It was also expressly temporary, valid for one year to give Congress time to frame less hasty territorial ordinances for the two Louisianas. What Congress would do when it framed a new territo-rial ordinance for Upper Louisiana in the following year was anyone's guess. American and habitant enslavers in Upper Louisiana would do their best to resolve ambiguous and idiosyncratic imperial decrees in their favor. So would enslaved African and Native Americans.

Ambiguous territorial ordinances along with the appearance of a new imperial regime added to the concerns of habitant and American enslav-ers about U.S. rule when the Scypion family used the Louisiana transfer to try to advance their case for emancipation. Their enslavers, members of the extended Chouteau family, sought to use the transfer to solidify their own-ership claims over the Scypion family. Both parties sought to advance their own claims by gaining a sympathetic ruling from U.S. imperial agents. The fate of slavery in U.S. Upper Louisiana seemingly held in the balance.

Since 1799, Marie Jean Scypion and her daughters Celeste, Catiche, and Marguerite had been involved in lawsuits seeking their freedom based on maternal Native American ancestry. Born in the 1740s, Marie Jean was almost certainly the daughter of an enslaved Native American mother and an enslaved African American father. After Marie Jean bore her three daughters, the Tayon family inherited and gifted the mother, sisters, and their children from the 1770s through the 1790s. The Scypion family would grow over the next decade as the Scypion sisters gave birth to their own children. In 1799, after the death of the Tayon family matriarch, the husband made plans to liquidate the estate by selling the enslaved families at auction. Celeste, her sisters, and mother were all of maternal Native American descent, but their enslavers had reclassified them as *pardos* and *mulattos* in the 1770s and again in the early 1790s. Though *mulattos* on paper, everyone in St. Louis knew the family was of maternal Native American lineage. Thus, on the day of the auction, "the mulatto woman Celeste & her Sons Antoine & Paul were not sold, as also, Scipion, Marguerite 18, Catiche 27." For unstated but transparent reasons, Joseph Tayon decided to withhold the Scypion family from auction. By the 1790s, the main route to emancipation for enslaved Native Americans in Upper Louisiana was to be sold, file a freedom suit, and then have their case heard before officials in New Orleans. Anticipating as much, Lieutenant Governor Zenon Trudeau likely advised Tayon that selling the Scypion family all but invited a lawsuit. The Tayon family thus cancelled the sale, retaining possession of the Scypion family.[57]

The Scypion family sued anyway; when mother Marie Jean died in 1802, sisters Celeste, Catiche, and Marguerite continued with their lawsuit. Two female Tayon family members, sisters Helene Chevalier and Marie Louise Chauvin, favored emancipating the family and gave refuge to Celeste and Catiche. Celeste and Catiche were free, as long as they remained in the homes of the Tayon sisters, lest other Tayon family members force them back into slavery. At the same time, Spanish officials could not permit the sale to move forward, which portended trouble with officials in New Orleans. Spanish officials—adept at assisting habitants in keeping Native Americans enslaved—again obeyed and complied with Spanish regulations. The result, as usual, was continued enslavement for Marguerite and her children, while Catiche and Celeste found themselves confined to the homes of two enslavers who agreed to emancipate them.[58] Such was life for enslaved people under the theoretically permissive *Code Noir* and Spanish slave codes prohibiting Native American enslavement; both recognized certain rights for enslaved people and provided routes to emancipation, but their enforcement remained in the hands of local officials with a vested interest in keeping them enslaved. Though long due their freedom, Celeste, Catiche, Marguerite, and their children all remained in indefinite slavery or confinement.

The Chouteau and Tayon families made the case indeterminable, and the sisters' fate would not be resolved until the 1830s when the Missouri

Supreme Court narrowly ruled that the children of enslaved Native Americans were due their freedom under the terms of the 1769 decree. Long before then, when U.S. authorities arrived in St. Louis in March 1804, Joseph Tayon sensed an opportunity to complete the sale and also keep the family legally enslaved. Tayon appealed to Captain Amos Stoddard, the chief American official in Upper Louisiana. Tayon badly misrepresented the facts of the case to Stoddard. Tayon, "being very advanced in age," made a special plea to Stoddard. "Wishing" only "to give during his life full satisfaction to all his children," Tayon hoped "to prevent between them every kind of difficulties after his death." Tayon portrayed himself as an old man on the verge of death, who simply wished to sell the people he enslaved, distribute the proceeds to his heirs, and prevent any acrimony after his death. Tayon thus requested that Stoddard "permit and order the public sale of the slaves in the shortest delay."[59] Tayon hoped to get from U.S. officials what he could not realize under Spanish rule: transferable titles to the lives, bodies, and labors of the Scypion sisters and their children: titles that his ancestors held under French rule; titles that would once again allow him to reduce the family to chattel.

Tayon failed to reveal that two of the enslaved women in dispute had fled to his daughters, who supported the Scypion family's freedom suit. Tayon also omitted the maternal Native American lineage of the enslaved women in question. Stoddard accepted Tayon's facts of the case if only because he had no evidence to counter it. Stoddard thus ordered "that the sale of the said slaves should be made according to the laws" governing slavery in Upper Louisiana. The Chouteaus and Tayons had manipulated laws regarding slavery in the 1770s by having prominent St. Louisans testify that Marie Jean's father was Native American and that her mother was actually African American. They manipulated those laws again in the 1790s when Spanish officials changed their census categories, turning enslaved Native Americans into *pardos* and *mulattos*. Now, Tayon misrepresented the facts of the case. French, Spanish, British, and U.S. imperial law almost always favored enslavers over the enslaved, and initially, at least, Stoddard authorized the sale. As an agent of U.S. empire in Upper Louisiana, Stoddard did what his imperial predecessors, whether French, Spanish, or British, had always done: He used the powers of an imperial state to sustain the authority of a locale's most prominent residents in the hopes that they would support the new imperial regime. Bearing the imprimatur of the U.S. imperial state, Tayon promptly posted a notice for "the public sale of negroes" on the "church door." Imperial states empowered enslavers. With Stoddard's unwitting assistance, Tayon stood on the verge of transforming bonded people of Native American descent into enslaved people of African descent for the third time.[60] Prominent enslavers had long proved adept at manipulating imperial laws in their favor, even when imperial decrees seemed to mitigate against them.

Enslaved people proved equally adept at finding cracks in imperial and local laws. The Scypion sisters responded to Tayon's deception by presenting Stoddard with their own facts of the case, including "three artifacts of their pedigree and freedom." They requested that Stoddard prohibit the sale and emancipate them "according to the laws." Faced with starkly different facts of the case, Stoddard issued an "order to suspend the sale and defer the questions to the future judicial authority." Stoddard thus blocked the sale but refused to emancipate the sisters. He would leave their status undetermined until a properly construed U.S. court could rule on the matter.[61] Stoddard had little inclination to upset the most powerful group in Upper Louisiana, enslavers; Tayon was a lifelong friend of the Chouteau family, and Stoddard also sought to avoid drawing the ire of St. Louis's most powerful family, who would be instrumental in ensuring a peaceful transfer of power from Spain to France to the United States. Furthermore, the treaty of cession had guaranteed to habitants and Americans in Upper Louisiana "free enjoyment of their liberty" and "property." Finally, Stoddard's command in Upper Louisiana operated under strict orders to "take every measure in your power to protect the inhabitants in their rights and privileges as well in relation to religion as property."[62] U.S. imperial interests in conciliating habitants and American enslavers eliminated any chance that Stoddard would emancipate the family. At the same time, the Scypion sisters created ambiguity concerning the uses of imperial state power for emancipation and enslavement. Stoddard added to that ambiguity when he refused to permit the sale to go forward. In doing so, he heightened concerns that U.S. imperial rule in Upper Louisiana might turn out the same way that it did in Illinois. Enslavers in Upper Louisiana had witnessed firsthand how weak or ambiguous imperial state power in Illinois allowed enslaved people to begin untying the gordian knots of imperial and local power that kept them in slavery. Upper Louisiana enslavers also knew that contradictory messages from the U.S. imperial state had hastened the decline of slavery in Illinois. Refusing to rule in favor of either enslavers or enslaved, Stoddard inadvertently fueled the uncertainty feared by enslavers in Upper Louisiana.

In the midst of the Scypion sisters' efforts to emancipate themselves, the terms of the territorial ordinance for "the District of Louisiana" arrived in the region. This ordinance, too, was filled with ambiguities and contradictions. American and habitant enslavers immediately suspected that it was a prelude for extending Article VI across the river. In their own words, enslavers and would-be enslavers were "very much agitated" in "regard to this district's being annexed to the Indiana Territory & the regulations which Congress might adopt relative to slavery."[63] Stoddard expressed concerns to his counterpart in New Orleans that "the late annexation of this country to the Indiana territory has excited much uneasiness in the minds of the people," as they feared that "by coming under the ordinance of Indiana, they will be abridged of some of these important rights secured to them by treaty."[64] American William Carr found nearly all white Upper Louisianans were "apprehensive that slavery would not only be prohibited; but the more ignorant were fearful lest those already in their possession would also be manumitted. I discern from the Law, or that part of it which relates to this district that Congress has been silent on the subject altho' it has been permitted in the territory of Orleans under certain restrictions."[65] Imperial affirmations empowered enslavers. Imperial silence on slavery heralded prohibition and abolition.

Among enslavers in the imperial Middle Mississippi Valley, any insinuation that the United States would extend Article VI across the river bred anxiety. To foster stability, they demanded U.S. policy-makers and agents affirm their commitment to enslavers and place the infrastructure of imperial state power at their disposal. In the first public meeting of the subject-citizens of St. Louis, they rejected efforts "to unite this part of Louisiana to the Indiana Territory" as "contrary to the greatest advantage of this country and its inhabitants."[66] Four days later, the Committee of St. Louis, a self-styled representative body of the white male inhabitants of the town, addressed Governor James Wilkinson, pleading with him to issue a set of regulations "concerning the police which they think necessary to establish on the Slaves."[67] By midsummer, rumors swirled that enslaved Upper Louisianans "will be free before long."[68] As anxiety about the status of slavery grew, so did opposition to U.S. rule in both Lower and Upper Louisiana. Enslavers in both Louisianas grumbled that they would force the United States to retrocede Louisiana to France, mainly because the United States had failed to extend the same privileges to enslavers that Spain had done (and that France presumably would have done).[69]

Stoddard and Auguste Chouteau intervened in this caldron of imperial intrigue, ambiguity, and uncertainty surrounding slavery, at least for Upper Louisiana. To quell white discontent with U.S. rule, in August 1804, Stoddard and Chouteau staged a public exchange clarifying the U.S. imperial state's position on slavery in Upper Louisiana. Born in Connecticut, Stoddard became a harsh critic of slavery; later in life he called for gradual abolition in Upper Louisiana by use of the Article VI precedent from the Northwest Ordinance, devoting an entire chapter to the matter in his 1812 book, *Sketches, Historical and Descriptive, of Louisiana.*[70] However, as the top American official in Upper Louisiana, he knew his primary task was to oversee a peaceful transfer and to reconcile habitants and Americans to U.S. rule. Like every other U.S. imperial official, Stoddard was more committed to fulfilling his official duties and securing the U.S. empire in the trans-Mississippi West than to promoting a plan of gradual abolition that, in the summer of 1804 in Upper Louisiana, threatened rebellion and retrocession. Stoddard had to side with prominent enslavers, local potentates who exercised the influence that would determine the outcome of imperial transitions and the stability of imperial regimes. Stoddard was simply the latest imperial official in Upper Louisiana to find himself beholden to enslavers. Stoddard sublimated his scruples about slavery and joined Chouteau in engaging in the performative politics of empire and enslavement.

Chouteau was the ideal candidate to reconcile habitant and American enslavers to U.S. rule. Chouteaus had married into just about every Spanish, American, and habitant family of importance in Upper Louisiana and Illinois, and they had wives and families among numerous Osage clans. The Chouteaus had fashioned themselves as the undisputed economic, political, and diplomatic power brokers in the region. U.S. officials went out of their way to secure the favor of the patriarch of Upper Louisiana's most wealthy and prominent family. Likewise, Chouteau prepared to further his family's fortunes by carving out favored positions for themselves within the third imperial power to claim the west bank of the Middle Mississippi Valley. As Secretary of the Treasury Albert Gallatin wrote of Chouteau, while he "seems well disposed" toward the United States, "what he wants is power and money." Framing the matter directly, Gallatin explained to Jefferson that Chouteau "may be either useful or dangerous" to the United States. U.S. imperial agents like Stoddard decided to make Chouteau useful rather than dangerous.[71] A useful Chouteau would help mollify habitant and American enslavers in

Upper Louisiana. In a very public exchange of letters and addresses, Chouteau played the role of the loyal provincial supplicant; Stoddard portrayed himself as the agent of benevolent imperial power. Both framed their exchange to alleviate white concerns about the future of slavery, to promise that Article VI would not be extended across the river to Upper Louisiana, and to warn enslaved African and Native Americans that the United States would not pursue gradual emancipation.

Chouteau mobilized local power and then inserted himself into larger imperial structures by organizing the Committee of St. Louis, which operated as a self-appointed government for St. Louis and its surrounding villages during the transition from Spanish to French to U.S. sovereignty. Under the auspices of the committee, Chouteau drew up a petition filled with requests rather than demands. The petitioners expressed commitment to U.S. rule but also voiced concerns about the recent "conduct of their slaves." Enslaved men and women, acting on rumors of the imminent extension of Article VI to Upper Louisiana, had made the white "inhabitants" of Upper Louisiana "uneasy and alarmed." "There exist amongst the Blacks a fermentation," the committee warned, exacerbated "by the report spread by some Whites, that they will be free before long." The petitioners then alluded to the massive rebellion of enslaved people that had just concluded in January of that year with the creation of Haiti. That rebellion began when enslaved people acted on rumors that the revolutionary French republic had issued a general emancipation order that Saint-Domingue enslavers kept secret. Enslaved Upper Louisianans, entertaining the same kinds of rumors, now seemed on the verge of rebellion. The petitioners pleaded that the United States "preserve the New territory" from "the horrors which different American colonies have lately experienced." To do so, the United States had to confirm its commitment to upholding the rights of enslavers and dispense with any talk of extending Article VI across the river.[72]

Upper Louisiana enslavers also sought to write their own laws regarding slavery. The committee reminded Stoddard that "in all countries where slavery exists there is a Code that establishes in a positive manner the Rights of the Masters, and the Duties of the slaves. There is also a Watchful policy, which prevents their nocturnal assemblies, that subject them to their labor." Under "the old French government and Spanish, the Black Code was our guide," they explained. They then asked Stoddard "to have it put in force" under U.S. rule. Only a strong slave code could "keep the slaves in their duty according to their class; in the respect they owe generally to all whites, and more expressly their masters." Demonstrated U.S. commitment to enslavers would place slaves "again under the subordination which they were heretofore." A clear and enforced slave code would also "insure the tranquility of a people who depends entirely on your viligency." Without strict slave codes, enslaved men and women would surely rebel, and Upper Louisiana would be reduced to "nothing but ruins," much like Saint-Domingue.[73] Upper Louisiana enslavers made it remarkably clear that they could maintain their slave society only when imperial states used their power to elevate enslavers and subjugate enslaved people. They also drew on thirty years of experience in dealing with far-off imperial policy-makers and local imperial officials to bring clarity to ambiguous decrees regarding slavery. Finally, they insisted that their inclusion in the U.S. empire was contingent on Article VI being confined to the east bank of the Mississippi River.

Stoddard's reply could have been penned by any of his Spanish predecessors. He readily played the part of benevolent imperial benefactor, offering enslavers what they most wanted: local self-government with imperial officials empowering local enslavers. He acknowledged the concerns of habitant and American enslavers, requesting that they "suggest such rules and regulations as appear necessary to restrain the licentiousness of slaves, and to keep them more steadily to their duty." He assured them "I will add my sanction to whatever may contribute" to "peace and security." Stoddard concluded by admonishing "those Whites who have propagated among the slaves the hope of a speedy emancipation."[74] The United States would empower enslavers in Upper Louisiana; no Article VI for Upper Louisiana would be forthcoming. The following week, the committee presented to Stoddard "the regulations of police concerning the slaves," rules that would "ensure the rights of the masters."[75] As they had done under the Spanish regime, Upper Louisiana enslavers created their own set of slave codes, then elicited a promise from imperial agents to support local enslavers' efforts to enforce them. The committee also again communicated expectations that Congress would abstain from extending Article VI across the river. The committee "restrained itself" in its meeting with Stoddard, presenting only "laws necessary in this moment." Committee members fully expected, however, "the establishment and promulgation" of new laws, "which will be the basis of the rights between the master and the slave, and which will probably make a part of the laws that our political State will want."[76] The contingent factors that might have allowed northern imperialists in Congress to extend Article VI to Upper Louisiana melted away in the summer of 1804. Upper

Louisiana enslavers would incorporate themselves into the U.S. empire on their own terms.

The 1804 territorial ordinance was expressly temporary, necessitating that Congress create a new territorial government for Upper Louisiana in 1805. Having secured Stoddard's support for slavery, habitant and American enslavers now turned toward convincing Congress to recognize the sanctity of slavery in a new territorial ordinance. Habitant and American enslavers had already witnessed how the absence of state power allowed enslaved men and women to begin the process of dismantling the slave societies their ancestors had built in Illinois; they now demanded that the United States—like France and Spain—extend imperial state power to enslavers in Upper Louisiana. Heading into the 1805 congressional session, the enslavers displayed a basic unity of purpose when facing off with U.S. imperial agents and policy-makers. They deployed all of the resources and connections they had forged to force Congress to recognize their rights and interests in Upper Louisiana. They lobbied U.S imperial agents in Upper Louisiana and Illinois; they lobbied lawmakers in Washington; they met with U.S. officials such as Stoddard; they cultivated close ties with officials such as William Henry Harrison; they fired off angry remonstrances and petitions demanding protections for slavery; they participated in the full range of the performative politics of empire to protect their interests as enslavers. In short, they did all they could to block efforts by antislavery imperialists to extend Article VI to Upper Louisiana. They would not replicate the mistakes that were made in Illinois in 1787. Upper Louisiana enslavers understood that it was now, at the moment of imperial transfer, that they could best "obtain a redress of . . . grievances, and ensure success to . . . Remonstrances."[77] Habitant and American enslavers quickly put aside their cultural differences and cooperated on the one thing that mattered most to them: subjugating enslaved people and profiting off of their coerced labor.

"The Representatives Elected by the Freemen of their Respective Districts" in Upper Louisiana drafted a strongly worded "remonstrance and petition" to send to Washington. Protesting "that political system which you have devised," the "remonstrance" alluded that white Upper Louisianas might reject the cession of Louisiana to the United States and seek reunion with France or Spain if their demands were not addressed. The petitioners also warned that the 1804 territorial ordinance seemed "calculated . . . to create the presumption of a disposition in Congress to abolish slavery altogether" in Upper Louisiana. Though "slavery cannot exist in the Indiana Territory" because of Article VI, it already "prevails" in Upper Louisiana. "The laws" of Indiana and Upper Louisiana "must be very dissimilar in a number of respects," they explained. The petitioners demanded that the United States recognize their right "to the free possession of . . . slaves" along with "the right of importing" more. They also reminded Congress that the territorial ordinance, by threatening to withdraw imperial state support from enslavers, stood in violation of the treaty, as "their property of every description has been warranted to them by the treaty between the United States and the French Republic." Under Spanish rule, enslavers had received a large degree of self-government and autonomy within a larger imperial structure that supported their subordination of enslaved African Americans. They demanded nothing less from the United States.[78]

The authors of the "remonstrance" all but admitted to Stoddard that the threats of disunion and retrocession served as unpleasant but necessary parts in the performative politics of empire. Despite their hints at reuniting with France, they did not intend to leave the United States and return to French or Spanish sovereignty. Rather, they hoped to frighten imperial lawmakers from the northern states into foregoing efforts to impose Article VI.[79] Before departing for Washington with their "remonstrance and petition" in hand, the "representatives of the several districts" of Upper Louisiana issued a public letter of gratitude to Stoddard. Referring to the whole remonstrance and petition process as a "painful task," they thanked him for his "judicious, attentive & exemplary dispensation of Justice within this territory during your administration, and the readiness which you have always shown to contribute to the public good." They then asked that "genuine philanthropy—solid parts & unblemished Disinterestedness continue to characterize the governors" of Upper Louisiana.[80] All they wished from the U.S. Congress was the same regards for their interests that Stoddard and his Spanish predecessors had shown them. If Congress would do so, white Upper Louisianans would gladly embrace their place in the expanding American imperial union. Stoddard estimated that "more than four-fifths" of the white inhabitants agreed with the remonstrance's main concerns surrounding "annexation of this country to the Indiana Territory."[81]

The new politics of empire and enslavement produced a unique territorial ordinance for what would become the Louisiana Territory as of July 4, 1805 (Congress designated the present state of Louisiana the "Orleans Territory"). Through the 1840s, territorial ordinances created by Congress addressed slavery in one of two ways. In territories where slavery would be banned,

Congress simply extended the entirety of the Northwest Ordinance, including the Article VI prohibition on slavery to a new territory. Typically, this was done by using language that the new territorial government would be "in all respects similar to that provided by the ordinance of Congress, passed on the thirteenth day of July one thousand seven hundred and eighty-seven, for the government of the territory of the United States north-west of the river Ohio," as was done with Ohio and Indiana in 1800.[82] In territories where Congress protected slavery, it did so indirectly by exempting a territory from Article VI. Thus, when Congress created the Mississippi Territory in 1798, it created "a government in all respects similar to that now exercised in the territory northwest of the river Ohio, excepting and excluding the last Article of the Ordinance."[83] The Upper Louisiana petitioners expressly requested that Congress create for them a territorial "government in all respects similar to that now exercised in the Mississippi Territory," which would have exempted them from Article VI, thus indirectly sanctioning slavery.[84]

However, the 1805 territorial ordinance for Upper Louisiana is unique in that it made no reference to slavery, the Northwest Ordinance, or Article VI, either directly or indirectly. A proposed version of the ordinance would have acknowledged slavery indirectly by creating "a government in all respects similar to that now exercised in the Mississippi Territory." The Senate passed this version of the bill in February 1805. The House and Senate, however, made extensive revisions to the territorial ordinance over the next month. The final version of the territorial ordinance removed all references to the Northwest Ordinance and the Mississippi Territorial Ordinance, omitting all references to slavery in the process. Slavery in Upper Louisiana would now owe its legal existence to the final clause of the territorial ordinance, which held "that the laws and regulations, in force in said district, at the commencement of this act, shall continue in force, until altered, modified, or repealed by the [territorial] legislature."[85] Under the 1805 ordinance, slavery existed legally in Upper Louisiana by force of local law and territorial statute, rather than by territorial ordinance.

The unique and ambiguous 1805 territorial ordinance proved sufficient for habitant and American enslavers, along with their imperial agents and policymakers who favored using state power to protect slavery and enslavers. Under the terms of the first two territorial ordinances, Stoddard and his successor, William Henry Harrison, immediately ratified a series of laws governing enslaved people and empowering enslavers.[86] However, the politics of empire and enslavement in the Middle Mississippi Valley were changing. Northern Republicans created a framework for extending Article VI across the river in the 1804 territorial ordinance for Upper Louisiana. That failed, and in 1805 they forestalled creating a territorial government that endorsed slavery in the territorial ordinance, instead making slavery a local institution, governed by local laws and regulations. Though slavery was not prohibited, the territorial ordinance failed to exempt Upper Louisiana from Article VI. By removing all direct or indirect references to slavery and Article VI in the 1805 territorial ordinance, northern Republicans retained the means by which they could restrict slavery in Upper Louisiana in the future. In 1811 and 1812, Pennsylvania Republicans would seek to prohibit slavery in Upper Louisiana as it moved to the second stage of territorial government and became the Missouri Territory. Congress defeated the proposals, likely because war was imminent.[87] As Missouri moved closer to statehood, commentators interested in empire and enslavement in the 1810s contended that the unique and ambiguous status of slavery in the territorial ordinance was done deliberately by antislavery imperialists so that future Congresses could extend something like Article VI to Upper Louisiana. Northern antislavery imperialists managed to fight off efforts to normalize empire and enslavement in Upper Louisiana, even if they failed to extend some version of Article VI across the river.[88] Meanwhile, northern Republicans continued denying requests from Illinois enslavers to rescind Article VI there. In the aftermath of the Louisiana bills, Matthew Lyon despondently reported to his Illinois associates that "Congress [had] risen without having done much for your quarter of the World."[89]

Ultimately, the Louisiana Purchase did little to alter the larger trajectories of empire and enslavement in the Middle Mississippi Valley that were initiated by the division of the region in 1763 and solidified by the Northwest Ordinance of 1787. Southern white imperialists preserved the status quo in Upper Louisiana; northern white imperialists preserved the Article VI exclusion of slavery in Illinois but created a constitutional mechanism for imposing some kind of future restriction on slavery in Upper Louisiana in the future. Upper Louisiana enslavers might not have won all they sought under U.S. empire, but they received enough to assure them that the United States would continue to prop up enslavers and work with them to close off new routes to emancipation. In March 1805 a woman enslaved by Pierre Chouteau sensed that imperial transfers would not open new routes to freedom and autonomy; she allegedly "lighted with her own hands the fire which devoured" Chouteau's "property and that of the United States."[90] Overall, the status quo prevailed with regards to empire and enslavement in the Middle Mississippi Valley between 1803 and 1805. However, a new group of antislavery imperialists from the United States were beginning to envision a very different future for the Middle Mississippi Valley. Rather than seeing enslavers as assets of empire, these imperialists treated them as detriments. Before then, U.S. enslavers would continue their steady march past Illinois, transforming Upper Louisiana into Missouri.

CHAPTER 5

Expanding Empire, Enterprise, and Enslavement in Missouri, 1805–1818

The Louisiana Purchase did little to alter the practices of empire and enslavement in Upper Louisiana and Missouri.[1] Like their Spanish predecessors, most U.S. imperial agents arrived as enslavers; those who did not quickly joined their ranks. U.S. imperial agents appointed prominent locals—all enslavers—to offices, awarded them government contracts, and recognized, confirmed, and enhanced their prestige. Leading habitants reciprocated, bringing U.S. imperial agents and enslavers into their schemes, commercial ventures, and families. In the process, both groups legitimated U.S. sovereignty and territoriality, and they granted imperial sanction for enslavers and slavery. Land in Missouri remained cheap and accessible due to the circulation of grants and warrants issued first by the Spanish and later by the United States, inviting in a group of small-time enslavers and would-be enslavers from the United States. Enslaved African Americans continued to seek freedom from slavery when possible, as well as greater freedoms within slavery whenever enslavers closed off routes to flight or freedom suits. Against enslaved people stood U.S. imperial agents, prominent habitants, and the growing class of bourgeois enslavers who thickened the web of restraints that kept enslaved people in slavery.

While U.S. sovereignty did little to change the practices of empire and enslavement in Missouri, it significantly altered the scope and size of both. The U.S. imperial state provided something that neither France nor Spain ever could: a continuous wave of colonizers and small but significant numbers of enslaved Black people. The steady stream of migrating enslavers from the United States who crossed the Mississippi River continued to grow slowly in the immediate aftermath of the Louisiana Purchase. The War of 1812 weakened Native American nations in the Missouri Valley and accelerated the

U.S. imperial state's dispossession of Indigenous lands, setting the stage for explosive population growth after 1815. Under U.S. dominion, enslavement and empire pushed hundreds of miles up the Missouri River. When Missouri applied for statehood in 1819, Missouri enslavers held approximately twelve thousand Black people in slavery out of a total Black and white population of sixty thousand.

In the 1810s, a distinct group of bourgeois habitants and Americans dominated empire and enslavement in Missouri: These ambitious, middling Anglophonic enslavers shared much in common with their habitant forbearers and neighbors. Governing them was a small group of prominent French and U.S. officials, including the extended Chouteau family and the extended family of William Clark. Together, southern, northern, and habitant enslavers self-consciously created a middle-class enslaving society. Just like their predecessors, colonizers who made their way to Missouri after 1805 tied slavery to economic incorporation into the U.S. empire and the burgeoning Mississippi Valley plantation complex, the entirety of which now fell under U.S. dominion. Missouri's expansive economy created new opportunities for freedom but also new means for enslavers to squeeze ever more labor from the people they enslaved. Similarly, the growing geography of the Middle Mississippi Valley provided new routes to freedom along with new places for enslavers to exploit and exile the people they enslaved. The terrain, workplaces, and imperial structures and institutions in which enslavers and enslaved people struggled expanded and shifted between the Louisiana Purchase and Missouri statehood. Enslaved people faced new dangers and indignities brought about by enslavers' growing opportunities for easy riches and the rapid influx of newcomers. Like their forebearers, enslaved Missourians struggled against the personal, local, and imperial mechanisms of enslavement: Some found freedom while others struggled for greater autonomy within their continued enslavement.

The political geography of enslavement and empire in the early 1800s attracted certain groups of colonizers, shaping the peculiar characteristics of settler colonialism and enslavement in Missouri. Wealthy enslavers from the Atlantic states preferred settlement in interior South Carolina and Georgia or the Lower Mississippi Valley. There, they used the U.S. imperial state to conquer and carve out a new empire for slavery unlike any other on the North American continent.[2] Colonizers who disliked slavery, Black people, and domineering enslavers preferred settlement in the Northwest territories covered by Article VI, particularly Ohio. By the 1790s, circumstances in Kentucky and Tennessee repelled migrating enslavers while pushing out some already there. Land titles in both states remained tied up in a morass of lawsuits. After 1805, middling and would-be enslavers from the Chesapeake tended to bypass Kentucky and Tennessee, while ambitious Kentuckians and Tennesseans who could not make it there headed off to Missouri.[3] The U.S. empire, simultaneously composite and federal, proved effective at conquering and consolidating the trans-Appalachian West and the Mississippi Valley because it offered different options to different groups of colonizers. Middling enslavers and would-be enslavers from the southern United States dominated the streams of migration to Missouri, but the smaller number of white migrants from the northern states who found themselves in Missouri readily embraced enslaving others.

The population of enslaved African Americans in Missouri grew slowly in the decade after the Louisiana Purchase. As had been the case under previous regimes, between 1805 and 1815, slave trades and the dominant tracks of colonization directed free and enslaved people to places other than Missouri. Small cargoes of "human flesh" regularly floated down the Ohio River as "merchandize." These slave traders rarely stopped in Missouri, instead heading downriver to Natchez and New Orleans.[4] From 1800 through 1820, enslavers and traders forcibly migrated more than 100,000 enslaved African Americans from the Atlantic states to Kentucky, Tennessee, and the Lower Mississippi Valley; only a small fraction made their way to Missouri.[5] With the main currents of the expanding continental slave trade and enslaver-colonizers bypassing the Middle Mississippi Valley, enslavers in Missouri created their own small-scale slave trade based primarily on forced migration and enslaver family ties with relatives in Kentucky and the Atlantic states.

The few wealthy U.S. enslavers who migrated to Missouri sold many of the people they forcibly migrated to Missouri shortly after their arrival. Colonel Samuel Hammond abhorred his transfer to Missouri, but he arrived there under circumstances vastly different from the people he enslaved. Hammond had traveled the route favored by peripatetic, postwar Chesapeake enslavers to the South Carolina and Georgia interior. There, he did battle against Native Americans staving off invasions of Indigenous lands, and he dabbled in Citizen Genet's plan to invade Spanish East Florida. Aggressively imperialistic, interlopers like Hammond did much to expand and consolidate the dominion of enslavement in the U.S. empire.[6] After short stints in the Georgia legislature and the U.S. Congress, Thomas Jefferson appointed Hammond commandant at St. Louis, an appointment that Hammond loathed. Hammond arrived in St. Louis in the early summer of 1805 and immediately laid out his grievances.[7] He moaned to a congressional colleague that he could not "reconcile my being here to anything like prudence or self respect."[8] Hammond intended to make short work of his assignment and then "return to Georgia."[9] A year later, Hammond begged Georgia Senator Abraham Baldwin for a new appointment. "The expense of [his] journey" to Missouri and his lack of adequate "compensation" left him "embarrassed for the common necessities of life."[10]

Hammond, however, had the means to provide "for the common necessities of life" and a whole lot more; the bodies of the people he enslaved served as valuable stores of capital. By 1812, he had sold at least seven of the people he had forced to Missouri to four different enslavers. In 1808, Hammond advertised "for sale" "a likely young negro boy" who "has been accustomed to wait upon a gentleman and is a good house servant."[11] In 1810, he sold enslaved man "Silas" to entrepreneur-enslaver Jacob Horine.[12] Sometime before 1812, he sold mother and wife Catherine, along with her two children, to an habitant. Hammond sold Catherine's husband, Cupid, to a different enslaver.[13] In 1812, Hammond sold father Sam, mother Polly, "and their infant child Juno" to territorial secretary Frederick Bates.[14] Wealthy colonizers and imperial agents from the Atlantic states financed their stay in Missouri by selling the people they enslaved. They also became a key source of enslaved persons for Missouri's would-be enslavers.

The Ellis clan of Georgia joined Hammond as wealthy colonizer-enslavers. Collectively, the Ellises forced at least twenty-nine enslaved men, women, and children to join them on their trek to Cape Girardeau. Within five years, the Ellis family had sold or lost in judgments at least twenty-two of them. Upon arriving in Cape Girardeau in 1804, Elisha Ellis "sold & delivered" to Richard Davies two enslaved men. "One of the negroes died at the mine" where Davies had hired him out.[15] In May 1808, Erasmus Ellis purchased from his family title to twenty-four enslaved men, women, and children, including "Dick, Sam, Nero, Ralph, Jacob, Bob, Abraham, George, Phillis, Clory, Nancy, William, Janey, T__ and her children Little Fancy & Mary, Frederick, Isaac, Cato, Amy, Fanny, and Dice."[16] When Erasmus failed to make good on his notes, the family forced a public sale of twenty of the twenty-four enslaved people. Three enslaved people, Charity, Darcus, and Mint, were "sold at the Mine au Breton," the location of preeminent bourgeois enslaver Moses Austin's mining operation.[17] Seventeen enslaved people were "sold to the highest bidder" at "the courthouse in the town of Cape Girardeau."[18] In a separate action,

Jenny was sold to Richard Davis. Angered at the loss of so many enslaved people, Erasmus kidnapped "Old Ginny" from Davis, adding to the misfortunes of the people he once enslaved.[19] As had happened with Hammond, wealthy enslavers from the Atlantic states became suppliers of enslaved men and women to Missouri's many wannabe and small enslavers. Five years later, when family members in Georgia died, the Ellis family immediately laid claim to the human property left behind. When enslaved man Bob learned that the Ellis family "intended to carry him to that Country in the Spring," he fled. The family's agent in Georgia managed to secure "Bob into [their] possession again," but he "expect[ed] he will get out of the way" if he could flee once more. The Ellis clan expected Bob to "cause considerable trouble to get him" to Missouri. "If ever I do it," counseled Uncle James from Georgia, "I am certain [it] must be done by having him put in irons and carrying of him so all the way."[20] Wealthy enslaving emigrants migrated to Missouri in style; enslaved people like Bob went in chains.

Other wealthy enslavers hired out the people whom they enslaved. William Clark began hiring out people shortly after reaching St. Louis in 1808 to assume his post as Superintendent of Indian Affairs. In 1799, Clark inherited eight enslaved men, women, and children from his father; by 1808, he claimed ownership of at least twenty-three enslaved people. Many of the enslaved people were held in various forms of trust by the Clark family, who extensively trafficked the people they enslaved between Kentucky and Missouri.[21] Within weeks of having arrived in St. Louis, Clark boasted to his brother that he had "hired out most of [his] negroes and shall if possible live in a little snug way."[22] Clark "hired out" at least five enslaved people within months of arriving in Missouri, including "Sillo, Nancy, Aleck, Tenar, & Juba."[23] Less than six months later, Clark sought "to turn negroes into goods."[24] The following month, he advertised his "wish to SELL two likely NEGRO MEN, for Cash."[25] Clark withheld the sale, instead choosing to "hire out" the people he enslaved, including his childhood mate York, whom he repeatedly threatened to sell to Natchez.[26] When the children of Missouri enslavers came of age in the 1810s, they in turn inherited enslaved people from grandparents in places such as Kentucky. Thus, in 1817, John and Benjamin O'Fallon—William Clark's nephews, whom he raised as sons after the death of their father—each inherited an enslaved family from their grandfather. To "Captain John O'Fallon" went "Esther and her children Hannah, Harry, and her infant Son," while "Patsy, Sousen, Frank and Alley" became "the property of Benjamin O'Fallon."[27] The ranks of enslaved Missourians grew through small-scale forced migrations rather than through a deliberate and systematic continental slave trade.

Unlike Hammond, the Ellis family, and the Clark family, most Missouri colonizers arrived rather middling; they quickly used enslaved people to amass if not fortunes, at least respectability. George Sibley's father fled his creditors by hiding out in Spanish Louisiana in the years preceding the Louisiana Purchase. He served as an unofficial U.S. agent in Lower Louisiana, prompting Jefferson to appoint him as an Indian agent at Natchitoches in 1804. Sibley then obtained an appointment for his son as an Indian agent to Fort Bellefontaine at the junctions of the Missouri and Mississippi Rivers. In 1808 Jefferson appointed George Sibley factor at the newly erected Fort Osage near present-day Kansas City.[28] During his travels, Sibley acquired an enslaved man named George, whom Sibley held "as cook and man servant." On a trip to Washington in 1812, Sibley "purchased" Betty, a "black servant girl" from "Gen'l Mason when [he] was last in Georgetown."[29] In 1815, Sibley married Mary Easton, daughter of attorney and frequent officeholder Rufus Easton. To provide household labor at Fort Osage, Sibley "purchased" enslaved woman Clara from Illinois Governor Ninian Edwards, continuing the long-standing practice of Illinois enslavers selling human flesh across the river.[30] Small-scale, forced migrations and sales created a steady increase in the number of enslaved Missourians.

The extension of U.S. empire to the trans-Mississippi West facilitated the intra-imperial traffic in enslaved people three hundred miles up the Missouri River. U.S. empire did not alter the basic practices of empire and enslavement in the Middle Mississippi Valley; ambitious imperial agents had long purchased enslaved people during their appointments in Upper Louisiana. U.S. empire did, however, greatly increase the scope, extent, and territoriality of empire and enslavement, expanding the Middle Mississippi Valley's haphazard slave trade from the Potomac River to the Kansas River. What was the source of enslaved Native Americans in the 1710s had become the destination for enslaved African Americans in the 1810s. George and Betty found themselves approximately one thousand miles from their native Chesapeake region. Like other enslaved people held by Americans in Illinois, Clara was likely purchased in Edwards's native Virginia or Kentucky. Clara, George, and Betty now found themselves enslaved hundreds of miles up the Missouri River around Fort Osage, where Mary and George Sibley ran a farm worked by at least five people whom they enslaved.[31]

No one exemplified the importance of chattel slavery to the ambitious, middling southern white men who dominated colonization of Missouri better than attorney William Carr. Carr traveled a familiar path from Virginia in the 1780s to Kentucky in the 1790s to Missouri in the early 1800s, and he intuitively understood the importance of accumulating and commanding enslaved people to his social prominence and financial well-being. Within a year of arriving in Missouri, he had purchased "a negro boy named Jack, aged about eleven years."[32] Carr augmented his holdings when he married. In 1807, he became engaged to "a little Yankee girl," Ann Maria Elliot, daughter of Dr. Aaron Elliot and niece of Moses Austin. Befitting the Carrs' rising status, William asked his Kentucky-based brother to procure "a negro woman suitable for the kitchen."[33] Carr's brother was unable to obtain the enslaved woman William desired, so he purchased a husband and wife accustomed to field work instead, hoping that William could convert them into house servants. Carr accepted his brother's offer but lamented that "if they do not answer, upon experiment" as house servants, "they must be sold; not withstanding my abhorrence to that kind of traffic." Bourgeois to the last, Carr needed house servants as status symbols. Equally bourgeois, if the husband and wife could not advance Carr's social status, they would improve his economic fortunes, despite his claims of abhorring the very traffic in enslaved human beings that he so readily partook in. In either case, the Carrs' social and economic desires facilitated the small-scale trade in human beings from the Ohio Valley to the Middle Mississippi Valley.[34] Empire and enslavement satisfied the Carrs' bourgeois pretensions; they prospered in an expanded U.S. empire that encompassed and united the Ohio, Missouri, and Mississippi Valleys.

Enslaved men, women, and children were central to Carr's growing fortune and respectability. He speculated in land and enslaved people, swapping both interchangeably. In 1809, he purchased "two negro fellows" in the spring and "another" in the summer for "$333" with "1/3 part on credit for 12 months." Carr "sold again" this enslaved man "for one of those land warrants" valued at $640. He decided to keep the other enslaved men he had purchased because he found them "very likely," expecting their value to increase. In the interim, he hired out the men he enslaved.[35] The following summer, Carr worked as a slave-purchasing agent for John Lucas, an expatriated Frenchman and Jeffersonian appointed to a judgeship in Upper Louisiana. Seeking enslaved people for Lucas while visiting his brother in Kentucky,

Carr "made every inquiry in [his] power on the subject of purchasing negroes in this country." Carr determined that he could not "purchase any tolerably good negro man for less than $500." Carr instead suggested that Lucas purchase an enslaved man "with his wife and two small children," which Carr believed "might be purchased much below their value." Carr counseled that while this particular enslaved family might fail to enhance Lucas's social status, by selling them Lucas could improve his economic fortunes.[36] Two months later, Lucas purchased enslaved man "Kayer, aged twenty five years or there about," from the estate of an enslaver in Mercer County, Kentucky, in a sale likely facilitated by Carr.[37] Carr also supplemented his growing income by defending entrepreneur-enslaver Jacob Horine in a freedom suit lodged by enslaved man William Tarlton in the early 1810s.[38] Small-scale slave traders and speculators like the Carr brothers fed the growth of slavery in Missouri while enhancing their own fortunes and prestige. Meanwhile, an expanded U.S. empire facilitated the growth of slavery in Missouri.

The Carr brothers' side business in trading captive bodies between Kentucky and Missouri received an impetus with the arrival of Captain Theodore Hunt in St. Louis in 1814. Hunt served in the U.S. Navy during the Barbary Wars and had spent time as a captive in Tripoli. After resigning his commission in 1811, Hunt made his way to Lexington, Kentucky, home of the slave-trading enterprise run by his relatives, David and Abijah Hunt.[39] Hunt's time as a captive did not dispel his taste for enslaving others. Shortly after his arrival in St. Louis, he married Anne Marie Lucas, daughter of Judge John Lucas. In the three months preceding his marriage to Anne Marie, Hunt purchased "a negro man named Andrew" from Lexington, Kentucky;[40] "a Mullatto Woman, name Lydia" from Maysville, Kentucky;[41] and a "mulatto boy slave named Wallace," who was owned by Ninian Edwards.[42] It was likely that Hunt's relations in Kentucky arranged the sales; Hunt's soon-to-be father-in-law handled the paperwork. Furthermore, the Carr and Hunt families, with members residing in Lexington and St. Louis, apparently developed an informal slave-trading partnership with one another. Three years after Hunt arrived in St. Louis, William Carr purchased an enslaved family from Fayette County, Kentucky, including husband and wife Frank and Anna, and their children, Ginney, "a small boy Frank," and a nursing infant named Elisa.[43] All told, between 1805 and 1818, Carr purchased at least fifteen enslaved people. At minimum, nine of them were purchased from enslavers in Kentucky or Tennessee; the 1818 sale of the enslaved family seems to have been brokered through the Hunt family.[44]

Carr anticipated and profited from the migration of enslavers and would-be enslavers who beat a similar path from the Chesapeake to Kentucky to Missouri after the settlement of the Louisiana Purchase. In the spring of 1808, Lucas noted that "the emigration in this country was much greater last fall and Winter than usual. The families that have lately come in appear to have much more property with them in slaves &c."[45] Middling enslavers and would-be enslavers from the Chesapeake, Kentucky, and Tennessee found much to like in Missouri between 1805 and 1819. Virginia lawyer Joseph Pollard, Jr., represented the kind of bourgeois enslavers who migrated to Missouri. In 1810, Pollard laid plans to head to Missouri with "5 members" of his "white" family, and his "black one of not more than 12 or 15 slaves." Pollard sought a residence in the town of St. Louis, along with "a little farm in the neighborhood." The farm was to be "sufficiently large to work 6 or 8" enslaved people. The remaining enslaved African Americans would be used at his residence in St. Louis, while his son would practice "that of medicine."[46]

Middling colonizers from the North quickly jettisoned whatever anti-slavery scruples they may have carried with them. Daniel Bissell, from Connecticut, took to enslaving soon after arriving in Missouri. Bissell had served in the Connecticut militia during the War for Independence before obtaining a commission in the U.S. Army in the 1790s. Over the next decade, Bissell continued to move west while he ascended the ranks; in 1808, he was appointed commandant for Missouri. There is no evidence that Bissell owned enslaved people before arriving in Missouri. In 1813, his daughter married preeminent Illinois enslaver and merchant William Morrison, who was a main provisioner of the U.S. Army in Missouri.[47] Within four years Bissell claimed ownership of at least four enslaved African American men: Lewis and Elijah; Joseph, who was purchased from an enslaver in Kentucky; and Frederick Sams, "born in the state of Georgia."[48] Like Spanish and French imperial agents before him, Bissell became an enslaver soon after assuming his appointment in Missouri. Rufus Easton followed the great Yankee exodus from Connecticut to New York in the 1790s and then traveled onward to Vincennes, Indiana. He joined William Henry Harrison's entourage to St. Louis in late 1804 and opted to remain there. Jefferson appointed him to a judgeship; he would go on to serve as the territorial delegate to Congress in the 1810s. As with other northern migrants and officials, there is no evidence that Easton owned enslaved persons before arriving in St. Louis. By 1815, he had purchased at least one enslaved man and one enslaved woman; meanwhile, his daughter Mary married George Sibley, and they claimed ownership of at least five enslaved individuals.[49]

John Lucas was another northern emigrant and U.S. official who immediately took to slavery. Too antimonarchical for France, in 1784, at age twenty-six, Lucas obtained letters of introduction from Benjamin Franklin. Lucas sailed to Philadelphia, eventually making his way to Pittsburgh by 1788. Lucas served as a state representative and judge in western Pennsylvania before winning the congressional seat vacated by friend and fellow francophone Albert Gallatin. In March 1805, Jefferson appointed Lucas to a judgeship. There is no evidence that Lucas owned the bodies or labors of any African Americans during his time in western Pennsylvania.[50] Like so many other northern colonizers in Missouri, Lucas purchased enslaved men and women soon after his arrival. In 1808, Lucas oversaw the sale of enslaved man Sam from a St. Louis widow to Illinois politician Shadrach Bond. With Bond concerned about the legality of Sam's enslavement in Illinois, Lucas purchased Sam from Bond, keeping him in Missouri. Sam then liberated himself after being passed between three enslavers and two sides of the river in a little over a month.[51] With Sam absconded more frequently than he was in Lucas's possession, Lucas purchased enslaved man Kayer from Mercer County, Kentucky, in a sale likely arranged by Carr.[52] Two years later, Lucas hired enslaved man Augustive for at least two months from Madame Veuve Chouteau.[53]

No northern migrants took to slavery as fervently as Vermont native Justus Post and the extended Hempstead clan from Connecticut. After serving in the U.S. Army during the War of 1812, Post moved to Missouri in 1815. By January 1816, he had purchased an enslaved "woman, named Ellen, aged 23 years."[54] John Post intended to join his brother in Missouri, which prompted a warning from Justus that "there is one thing you must reconcile your mind to when you get in this region, that is the owning of slaves." Post had by then purchased "two negro women and three girls." He had "no negro men yet but will have so soon as I can get them. I shall try hard to get two this winter and as many next spring as I can." Having imbibed the close relationship between empire, enslavement, and enterprise in Missouri, Post inveighed his brother to "make up your mind to meet it, for negroes you must have" in Missouri.[55] The following month, Post purchased Peter, "a slave for and during the period of his natural life."[56]

The extended Hempstead clan of Connecticut outdid Post's enthusiasm for enslaving others. They also integrated themselves into and fused the existing worlds of habitant colonialism and the expanding U.S. imperial

state. In 1805, attorney Edward Hempstead arrived in St. Charles, deploy-
ing his services defending habitant land claims. By 1809, three of Edward's
brothers had joined him, one establishing a law practice in Ste. Geneviève,
another entering the Indian trade. Two brothers quickly married into prominent habitant families: Edward married Clarissa DuBriel; Stephen, Jr., married Marie Louise Lefebre.[57] Edward joined St. Louis's town council, where
he worked with habitants Auguste Chouteau and Jean Cabanne, and recent
migrant-enslaver William Christy, in drafting the "Ordinance concerning
Slaves in the town of St. Louis," the St. Louis district's slave codes.[58] In 1810,
Edward rose to the post of attorney general; in one of his first cases, he pros-
ecuted enslaved men George and Joe for an alleged theft from a clothing
shop.[59] Like other American lawyers, Hempstead assisted habitants in settling the estates of deceased relatives, sometimes offering for sale at auction "several Negro slaves, consisting of women and young girls."[60] Edward
implored his parents and sisters to join their sons and brothers. Having
imbibed the ethos of bourgeois enslavers, he promised his parents that
they would "prefer being on a plantation, with hands enough to raise your
subsistence, in a society where you will be greatly respected."[61] The parents
and sisters joined their siblings in Missouri in the fall of 1811. Sister Susan
Hempstead promptly married habitant Henry Gratiot, who, her brothers
noted, owned six enslaved men and women. Widowed sister Mary married
widower, habitant, enslaver, and fur trader Manuel Lisa. By 1817, the male
members of the Hempstead clan had acquired at least seven enslaved people
while the sisters had married prominent enslavers.[62] The accoutrements of
imperial state power in Missouri flowed through local imperial officials
like Edward Hempstead. Whatever the theoretical differences between the
imperial Spanish and U.S. states, in practice, they differed little when it came
to protecting and promoting the interests of enslavers.

Between 1804 and 1818, migrating U.S. families seamlessly integrated
themselves into habitant enslaver-colonialism nurtured by the Spanish imperial state from the 1770s through 1803 while adding to its growth. The ethnic
composition and size of Missouri's population might have changed due to the
Louisiana Purchase, but the basic functions of the imperial state remained
much the same. Middling and prominent bourgeois bureaucrats like Edward
Hempstead embodied the relationship between empire and enslavement.
More broadly, the personas of enslaver-imperial agents and officials like John
Lucas, General Daniel Bissell, Colonel Samuel Hammond, George Sibley and
Mary Easton Sibley, Rufus Easton, Benjamin O'Fallon, and William Clark

reinforced both the tight connections between sovereignty and territoriality and the pretensions and ambitions of middling enslavers that had been
characteristic of stable enslaving regimes in the Middle Mississippi Valley
since the 1720s. Like its predecessors, the U.S. imperial state appointed agents
who arrived as, or quickly became, enslavers. These imperial agent-enslavers
then placed the powers of the U.S. imperial state at the disposal of enslaver
subject-citizens such as the Ellis clan, William Carr, and Justus Post.

Hardly hapless victims of an imperial U.S. state imposed on them, prominent and middling habitants integrated themselves into U.S. imperial structures and institutions. In the process, they used these institutions to protect
enslavers and constructed tighter connections between enslavement and
U.S. empire. Habitants forged close, personal relationships with leading U.S.
officials and their family members, much as they had done with Spanish
officials. Manuel Lisa married Mary Hempstead. Habitants Jean Cabanne
and Auguste Chouteau wrote the 1809 St. Louis slave codes and patrol ordinances with Edward Hempstead and William Christy. Other prominent
habitant enslavers seamlessly integrated themselves into the larger civilian,
military, and commercial structure of the U.S. imperial state as it grasped
its way across the trans-Appalachian West into the trans-Mississippi West.
Louis Lorimier, born of a French father and a Shawnee mother, had beat a
peripatetic trek from Canada in the 1750s, to the Ohio Valley in the 1770s,
along the way marrying into a different branch of the Shawnees. After siding
with the British during the U.S. War for Independence, he sought a path out
of the Ohio Valley. In the late 1780s he negotiated with Spanish officials for
the settlement of 1,200 Shawnee and 600 Delaware around present-day Cape
Girardeau. Spanish officials appointed him commandant at Cape Girardeau,
issuing a customary land grant along the way.[63]

Already an enslaver when he arrived in Upper Louisiana, Lorimier purchased at least two more enslaved women over the next decade.[64] When U.S.
imperial agents arrived in Upper Louisiana, Lorimier immediately solic-
ited their patronage. Lorimier pressed Amos Stoddard to secure his sons
appointments to the U.S. military academy at West Point. Stoddard privately
expressed reservations about an appointment because "he exhibited too much
of the Indian in his color," which "may make his situation among the cadets at
the school rather disagreeable." Stoddard nonetheless lobbied for and won his
appointment, "as his father is one of the most respectable men in this country."[65] In imperial Upper Louisiana, respectability was tied directly to enslaving,

and the Lorimier family fit the bill. Upper Louisiana Governor James Wilkinson recommended Lorimier's appointment as a U.S. Indian agent for numerous reasons, not the least of which was that Lorimier "has secured a fortune in Houses, Lands, & Slaves in the Territory."[66] U.S. officials appointed Lorimier as an Indian agent to the Shawnee and Delaware. After graduating from West Point in 1806, Lorimier, Jr., made his way to the U.S. Indian Factory at Fort Osage, where he served as second-in-command before taking over his father's operations at Cape Girardeau.[67] As had happened under the Spanish regime, the Lorimier family served as imperial agents, which enhanced their power as enslavers; their status as enslavers fitted them for positions as imperial agents; as imperial agents, they acquired more enslaved people. All the while, they strengthened ties among enslavement, empire, and U.S. sovereignty. The Lorimiers moved seamlessly from one empire to the next, from monarchical Spanish imperial governance to the federal, republican U.S. imperial state: All that changed were the titles and the emoluments. Spanish and U.S. imperial agents, enslavers all, intuitively understood one another.

Just as U.S. officials incorporated habitant enslavers into the U.S. imperial state, prominent habitants made leading U.S. officials partners in their business ventures, joining habitant know-how and influence with U.S. imperial state power and capital. The list of partners involved in the Missouri Fur Company, formed by the U.S. government in 1809, reads like a who's who of habitant enslavers and U.S. imperial agents. The partners included Pierre Chouteau; his nephew Auguste Chouteau, Jr.; and their relation, Sylvestre Labbadie, Jr. Manuel Lisa (who married Mary Hempstead) headed up the firm, bringing in his Illinois partners Pierre Menard and William Morrison (two of the largest enslavers in Illinois; Morrison was also married to Mary Bissell, daughter of General Daniel Bissell). Meriwether Lewis's brother Reuben joined the venture, as did William Clark; Clark's brother-in-law, Dennis Fitzhugh; and James Wilkinson's nephew, Benjamin.[68] Mimicking the patterns of empire established under the Spanish regime, U.S. imperial agents incorporated prominent habitant enslavers into imperial governing structures of violence and coercion, whether through the Army or town councils that wrote slave codes. Prominent habitant enslavers then brought U.S. imperial agents into their business ventures and families. Such actions reinforced the reach of empire while empowering local enslavers on the ground. The nexus of empire and enslavement in Illinois had been in doubt since the 1760s; the same nexus was continuously reinforced in Upper Louisiana by successive Spanish and U.S. regimes. The U.S. regime in Upper Louisiana, like its Spanish predecessors, was most accommodating of enslavers; for all intents and purposes, the imperial state under Spanish and U.S. dominion *was* enslavers.

More than any other habitants, Auguste and Pierre Chouteau enmeshed themselves into the U.S. imperial state and channeled its resources to serve the interests of habitant enslavers.[69] Their personal interests intersected with colonial and imperial institutions when the Scypion family continued their freedom suit under U.S. jurisdiction. In 1804, acting U.S. Commandant Amos Stoddard deferred the Scypion freedom suit until the U.S. imperial state established courts in Upper Louisiana. Meanwhile, sisters Catiche and Catherine remained in the homes of Tayon family members who favored their freedom, the sisters Helene Tayon Chevalier and Marie Louise Tayon Chauvin. Joseph Tayon and the Chouteaus, however, continued to hold sister Margueritte in slavery. In the fall of 1805, Catiche and Catherine filed a new freedom suit in U.S. court. Judges Rufus Easton and John Lucas had not yet purchased enslaved men or women, nor had they enmeshed themselves into habitant social circles. Initially, they seem to have approached the case with no clear favor toward enslavers or the Chouteau clan. At the hearing, Jacques Chauvin, husband of Marie Louise Tayon, who supported freedom for the family, attested that the Scypion sisters were free. Judges Easton and Lucas then ruled that "the said" woman "is not detained for any cause whatsoever, she being an Indian woman and free and stays and resides with the said Jacque Chauvin of her own free voluntary consent."[70] A few days later, allies of the Scypion family gained a hearing for Margueritte, whom the Chouteau family held captive. Judge Lucas ruled "that the said Margueritte is a Free woman and therefore order that she be discharged."[71] Within a few months, most if not all of the Scypion sisters' children—Antoine, Paul, Sophie, Carmelite, and four others—had fled their enslavement. The extended Scypion family now lived somewhere in St. Charles, likely at the estates of Helene Chevalier and Marie Louise Chauvin. Initially, U.S. judges seemed inclined to offer fair trials to enslaved people.

Habitant enslavers, however, sought to use U.S. courts for their own purposes, and the Chouteaus infiltrated the institutions of the U.S. imperial state to reclaim the lives, labors, and bodies of the Scypion family. The Chouteau family's determination to keep enslaved Native Americans in slavery matched their prominence and power. Pierre and Auguste Chouteau stood as arguably the most powerful habitants in Upper Louisiana, serving as U.S. Indian agents north of the Arkansas River and as confidants of acting Governor William

Henry Harrison. The Chouteaus were also inarguably the most socially, eco-nomically, and politically prominent European family in Upper Louisiana, claiming close personal and family ties among the Osage. The Chouteau broth-ers likely pressed U.S. authorities to reopen the case. Awarded a new hearing, this time the court ruled that the entire Scypion family were "slaves of the said Joseph Tayon," with the exception of Catherine and Catiche. Neither Judge Lucas nor Judge Easton would attach their name to the case, which reversed their earlier rulings while dismissing legal precedents regarding Indigenous enslavement in Upper Louisiana. The judge issued a warrant for the capture of the family but also required that Tayon post a $4,000 surety bond so that the Chouteaus could not sell the family out of the territory. Pierre Chouteau and Bernard Pratte put up the bond for Tayon.[72]

After ordering the capture and re-enslavement of the bulk of the Scyp-ion family, a judge issued a habeas corpus writ demanding that Pierre Chou-teau bring Margueritte before the court. Chouteau argued that Margueritte was "a negro mulatress and not an Indian nor descended of an Indian mother Grandmother or from any Indian Slave whatsoever." He further asserted "that the said Marguerite is descended from a negro mulatress named Scipion who was acquired by Mr. Joseph Tayon at Fort Chartiers upon a division of the goods and effects of the mother of the wife of said Tayon on or about the year 1760." Finally, Chouteau claimed "that the said Scipion's mother was a Negress and a slave long before that time" and "was always held enjoyed and possessed as a slave."[73] Margueritte retorted that she "ought not be kept in slavery and be deprived of her liberty" because "she is an Indian woman[,] was born free and ever has remained free according to the laws and useages of the Government of Spaniards." Judge Lucas temporarily freed Margueritte from "the caption of Pierre Chouteau" but ruled that she would be returned to slavery, "subject to the Laws of right of property that Joseph Tayon may heretofore establish and prove to have in her person."[74] Lucas then ruled that the entire lot of the free-dom suits would be decided in a jury trial to be held two days later.

The fix was in. Serving as jury foreman was James Morrison of the extended Morrison family, among the largest enslaving families in Cahokia and St. Louis; James Morrison's wife was Emilie Saucier, Pierre Chouteau's sister-in-law.[75] A jury led by one of the largest enslavers in the Middle Missis-sippi Valley, and the son-in-law of an enslaver with a controlling interest in the case, would decide the Scypion family's fate. The Scypion family called thir-teen different witnesses, all of whom testified, in one way or another, "that the mother of Marie Scypion was [an] Indian woman." An eighty-two-year-old habitant testified that Marie's mother was "a Natchez he heard it from his father & by all the ancient people that he knew." Tayon and Chouteau produced two witnesses who testified that "Scipio had short curled hair," implying African ancestry. Three other witnesses claimed that "Marie Scypion was negress and Black." Despite the overwhelming testimony that Marie's mother was an enslaved Natchez woman, the jury denied the Scypion family's Indianness to serve the immediate purposes of the Tayon and Chouteau families.[76] The Scypion family filed numerous appeals, but the court refused to hear them. In July 1806, Joseph Tayon sold the seven Scypion family members he enslaved to Pierre Chouteau, as he had intended to do seven years earlier.[77] Another decade would pass before the Scypion family could get their case before another court, and it was not until 1838 that the Missouri Supreme Court ruled that the remaining Scypions were free based on the 1769 decree.[78] Remarkably little changed in the operations of empire and enslavement in Upper Louisiana in the early 1800s. Prominent subjects and citizens—enslavers all—created, infiltrated, and administered imperial institutions and then used them to serve their own purposes.

Habitant enslavers forged connections to the U.S. imperial regime to protect their interests in other ways. Around the same time that the Chouteaus solidified habitants' hold over enslaved Native Americans in the courts, Charles Gratiot and Gregoire Sarpy "bought two young female Otto savages who had been captured from this nation by their enemies." Gratiot and Sarpy's latest purchase of human flesh hit a snag, however, "when the Otto chiefs came down to St. Louis on invitation of Capt. Lewis." Part of a larger delegation of Native Americans invited to visit Washington, the Otto chiefs expressed outrage to Pierre Chouteau, the acting Indian agent for Upper Missouri. The Otto leaders "demanded of" Chouteau, "with great insistence[,] the liberty of these female savages." Chouteau felt obliged to indulge the Otto leaders because they were ready to depart "for the seat of government" with a contingent that included Indigenous leaders from the Missouri Valley, members of the Lewis and Clark expedition, and prominent habitants. Chouteau likely feared that the specter of an Indigenous leader complaining to President Jefferson and Congress about habitants actively trading enslaved Native Americans would not sit well with the new imperial regime. The enslavement of Ottos also threatened to overturn Chouteau's machinations to have a U.S. court validate habitants' re-racialization of enslaved Indigenous people. Chouteau pressed on Gratiot and Sarpy to free the two enslaved women "by promising them that the government would have considerations for the loss which they would suffer, and the price which they had paid for them would be repaid." Pleading with Governor Wilkinson, Chouteau deemed compensation for the purchasers of human flesh "only justice which is due them."[79] The practices of empire and enslavement changed little; ten years earlier, Chouteau's Ste. Genevièvian counterpart François Vallé had compensated enslaver Henri Peyroux after officials emancipated a Native American woman he enslaved.[80] For the Vallés and the Chouteaus, one of the primary purposes of imperial state power was to protect the interests of enslavers.

The Chouteaus used their connections to protect other habitant enslavers, further reinforcing the ties among sovereignty, enslavement, and empire. In 1813, Robert A. Smith wished to purchase an unnamed enslaved woman and her daughter, Sylvia, from habitant Joseph LeBlond. LeBlond held Sylvia captive with "Chains on her legs," causing "wounds bruises and burns." LeBlond likewise held Sylvia's mother captive with "irons placed on her legs"; "tied her" with a rope around her waist; struck her with "a hot shovel" on the arm; and inflicted "a wound on her head." After consulting with a physician, Smith decided to forego his purchase, as the woman, "if she lived," would "lose her legs." Smith and the physician kept these matters to themselves, and the mother and daughter were left to LeBlond's sadistic whims. Authorities investigated only after LeBlond's neighbors could no longer bear "the piercing cries" echoing from his residence. There, authorities found the corpse of Sylvia, who "came to her death from mortification caused by irons placed on her legs by Joseph LeBlond." As for the mother, "the flesh of her feet and lower part of her legs had mortified and fallen off." Doctors "amputated both of her legs," but she died shortly after. An habitant testified that he "was present when Mr. LeBlond put the irons on" and that they "appeared to" him "at the time to be large enough for both legs." An "inquest" nonetheless found that LeBlond had caused Sylvia's death. Jean Pierre Chouteau and his wife posted a $2,500 surety bond for LeBlond, but there is no surviving evidence that he was tried for the murders. With the protection of prominent habitants like the Chouteaus, lesser habitant enslavers could dodge punishment for slowly torturing and murdering a "young mulatto girl and her infant child."[81] Prominent habitants and U.S. officials—enslavers all—had made the U.S. imperial state in Missouri safe for enslavers—even the most sadistic ones—like Joseph LeBlond.

When the U.S. regime took possession of Louisiana in 1804, a full-blown plantation revolution was already underway in the Lower Mississippi Valley.[82] With the sanctity of slavery under U.S. dominion confirmed, habitant and American enslavers more tightly integrated Missouri into the growing Mississippi Valley plantation complex. Much as the middle and New England colonies of British North America supplied European slave colonies in the Caribbean in the eighteenth century, so, too, would Missouri enslavers self-consciously provision the U.S. slave empire in the Lower Mississippi Valley in the nineteenth century. The great expansion of this slave empire created new "markets for corn flour beef pork butter &c." that were "better" than what "I ever knew there in Virginia," remarked one recent colonizer in Missouri in the summer of 1817.[83] Commercial agriculture brought forth new opportunities for men with capital and enslaved people to work their holdings. "If they purchase in a speculative point of view or to settle them, Capitalists coming to this Country who have sufficiency of lands" would find that "the river at all seasons affords him a quick outlet to any port he pleases." Testifying to the centrality of slavery in Missouri's economy, the speculator concluded by noting that "slaves sell well."[84] Pulling together these developments, Missouri booster Rufus Easton declared that "the upper country" of Missouri had been thoroughly integrated into "the West-India Market" that lay at the core of the Mississippi Valley plantation complex.[85] Missouri enslavers predicated production for the Lower Mississippi Valley on the coerced labor of enslaved men, women, and children.

New and old commodities offered opportunities to coerce labor and profit out of enslaved people. "Salt, iron, coal and salt-petre are found in abundance in many parts of the country, and lead is one of its staples," proclaimed one of the many breathless accounts of the growing economy of the Middle Mississippi Valley.[86] Hemp stood out as a commodity much in demand. In addition to serving as a raw material for cordage, hemp also became canvas bags to store the Lower Mississippi Valley's primary cash crop, cotton. Missouri enslavers partook in hemp cultivation as a supplement to their operations that focused primarily on commercial agriculture. Missouri enslavers also looked to saltpeter, a critical component of gunpowder, as an important commodity to supplement commercial agriculture. Spurred on by the Napoleonic Wars, saltpeter and lead production—and the use of enslaved laborers in the process—increased rapidly in Missouri. Enslavers turned mining and smelting from a seasonal activity to an extended operation.[87] The clay soils that contained lead ore were increasingly used for "making brick." Those bricks lined new furnaces for smelting lead and boiling brine and for building houses in St. Louis, Natchez, and New Orleans.[88] Growing salt, lead, and brick production increased demand for enslaved labor. Local enslavers from Ste. Geneviève had long hired out the people they enslaved to dig and process ores. However, the practice expanded greatly in the first decade of U.S. rule in Upper Louisiana, with enslavers from St. Louis, Kentucky, and Tennessee hiring out enslaved men, women, and children to work in the growing lead operations.[89]

Around 1809, Austin Moses partnered with Colonel Samuel Hammond to establish a new town on the Mississippi River to serve Austin's lead mines. At Herculaneum, Austin and Hammond established new works for processing ore and turning pig lead into shot.[90] In 1815, Austin struck a deal to lease, for ten years, sixty-two enslaved men, women, and children from Kentucky.[91] At the expanded lead operations, Austin and others standardized overseers' "direction and management" to coerce as much labor as possible out of enslaved men and women while minimizing costs.[92] Austin went so far as to draft "memorandums" specifying how much food to allot each enslaved person at the mines, and he ordered "that all the hands" are "at work by sun rise and that they do their duty; and never suffer your orders to be neglected or set aside."[93] Slavery capitalism came in many different forms, all of which produced mass amounts of commodities with enslaved labor. Between January 1817 and June 1818, Herculaneum exported downriver over 2.5 million "lbs. of Pig and bar lead"; "668,350 lbs. of Patent shot"; "5,500 barrels of Flour"; "44,924 gallons of Whiskey"; "500 bushels of Wheat"; "400 barrels of Beef and Pork"; "40,000 wt. of Bacon"; "66,000 feet of Pine boards"; "214,000 ft. of Oak boards and scantling"; and "80,000 lbs. of Gunpowder."[94]

The centrality of slavery to these new and expanded enterprises seemed manifest to colonizers and travelers. Itinerant Yankee scholar Henry Schoolcraft traveled extensively through Missouri, speaking frequently with Americans and habitants. Schoolcraft noted that "slavery was introduced into this Territory at a very early period, and previous to the occupation of the country by the United States. There are a considerable number at present; nearly every good plantation, and many of the mines being wrought by them." Schoolcraft further observed that "many of the plantations and mines are worked by slaves. The introduction of slavery into this section of the western country, appears to have taken place at an early day, and it has led to a state of society which is calculated to require their continued assistance."[95] Under Spanish rule, enslavers had created an economy, society, and polity dependent on enslavement. Slavery had always been central to empire and enterprise in Upper Louisiana. U.S. dominion confirmed these practices while expanding their scope and extent. Coerced labor that produced foodstuffs and lead in the 1780s now produced lumber, gunpowder, bricks, and bacon in the 1810s.

The establishment of the Boon's Lick outposts in the early 1810s expanded the scope of empire and enslavement while deepening the integration of Missouri into the Mississippi Valley plantation complex. In 1804, U.S. colonizers began invading a fifty-mile stretch of the Missouri River in central Missouri, approximately one hundred miles upriver from St. Louis. By 1811 the settlements contained "seventy-five families." Hardly poor squatters, they "are generally persons in good circumstances, most of them have slaves."[96] When the War of 1812 ended, enslavers invaded the region. Superintendent of Indian Affairs William Clark sought to legitimate the settlements and to sell titles to the land. To do so, he declared that an 1808 Osage Treaty included the Sauk and Meskwaki lands that the Boon's Lick colonizers were invading. Pierre Chouteau was in on the scheme, and he rewrote his notes from previous treaties to show that the Boon's Lick settlements on Sauk and Meskwaki lands were indeed part of the 1808 Treaty. Clark's and Chouteau's subterfuges enabled the U.S. imperial state to offer first-rate land at low prices in central Missouri.[97] Boon's Lick attracted hordes of middling enslaver families from the Upper South, enslavers who deliberately bypassed higher-quality land at lower prices in Illinois.

The Boon's Lick settlements immediately became the most desired spots for colonizer-enslavers and would-be enslavers in the Middle Mississippi Valley. Before the war had officially ended, one Kentuckian reported that the "inhabitants" of Kentucky "are all emigrating across the Mississippi."[98] In January 1816, George Sibley expressed astonishment at "the swarms of immigrants that are daily arriving here from Virginia, Tennessee, Kentucky &c."[99] Mary Easton Sibley was especially protective of the Boon's Lick invasion. In 1816, she wrote to her father, Missouri territorial delegate Rufus Easton, demanding that the federal government immediately recognize the claims of the squatter-invaders. Delaying federal recognition would "crush one of the most promising and deserving settlements in the Western country. I mean the Boone's Lick settlement of course."[100] Thanks to lobbying from imperial officials such as Clark and Easton, the federal government recognized the settlements, setting off an even greater "rage for the western Country" among middling and would-be enslavers.[101] The following summer, George Sibley counted "at least five towns laid off on the Missouri, where there was scarcely a White Man's Track seven years ago." Sibley estimated that more than two thousand families had already invaded and settled in the region.[102] By the summer of 1818, speculators scrambled to get in on the rush. Future Missouri Senator Thomas Hart Benton was one of many arriviste speculators who sought investors for his land schemes by promising "that such a body of Land rich in itself, and valuable from its rivers and climate never was before put in market by any government on earth."[103] Meanwhile, Virginia apologist John Randolph lamented "the tide of emigration" from Virginia, which "pours its redundant flood to the wide region that extends from the Gulf of Mexico to the Missouri."[104] The Boon's Lick land rush was on; enslavers and speculators now added Indigenous dispossession to enslavement and empire in Missouri.

The families who invaded and colonized the Boon's Lick settlements either identified as enslavers or expressly wished to become so. "Virginia, Kentucky, Tennessee and the Carolina's had made an agreement to introduce us as soon as possible to the bosom of the American family," enthused the *Missouri Gazette* in 1816. "Every ferry on the river is daily occupied in passing families; carriages, wagons, negroes, carts, &c., &c. respectable people, apparently able to purchase large tracts of land. Come on, we have millions of acres to occupy, provisions are cheap and in abundance." "Respectable" white families, with "negroes" and capital, poured into the Boon's Lick settlements.[105] The Rochester, Carroll, and Fitzhugh families of Maryland exemplified those "respectable" families. The families had scored big in land speculation in the Erie Canal corridor but had rejected settlement in New York because of its climate and New York's passage of an accelerated gradual abolition law in 1817. The families sent Charles Carroll west through the Ohio Valley and into Missouri to scout lands. Carroll rejected Ohio, Indiana, and Illinois and settled on Kentucky or Missouri because, there, "slavery is permitted." Kentucky possessed too many drawbacks, especially its mess of land claims. More than that, however, Carroll extolled that the Boon's Lick settlements attracted the kinds of bourgeois, middle-class enslavers that the families identified with: "The character migrating into the country is of the worthy class from Kentucky, Virg'a, N.C. M'd & Tennessee." Carroll also appreciated that "Slavery being permitted in this Territory in a manner precludes the Yankees, & such is the deep rooted prejudice against them in this section that they would be scarcely tolerated." Carroll secured a post in the Howard County Land Office in 1818, and members of the three families promptly set off for Boon's Lick.[106]

Thousands more followed, and the Boon's Lick land rush ushered the Missouri Territory toward the threshold for statehood. One Virginian estimated that the "population" in Missouri had "doubled" in the "two years" since the end of the war.[107] More accurately, between 1815 and 1818, approximately eighteen thousand enslavers and enslaved people entered the Boon's Lick settlements, accounting for approximately one-third of Missouri's population when the first calls for statehood arose. By late 1818, perhaps twelve thousand of Missouri's sixty thousand non-Indigenous inhabitants were Black and enslaved. In early 1819, Charles Carroll excitedly reported that "the country is populating rapidly with a respectable yeomanry from Kentucky, Vir'a, M'd, Ten'see & N. Carolina."[108] Empire, enslavement, and the integration of Missouri into the Mississippi Valley plantation complex attracted middling American enslavers and accelerated the Boon's Lick land rush, which quickened Missouri's movement toward statehood with a white population committed to statehood with slavery. In Upper Louisiana and Missouri, empire had been tied to enslavement since the 1760s. After 1804, habitant and American enslavers tightened those bonds and then used the U.S. imperial state to force their way up the Missouri Valley. Any suggestions that Congress would somehow constrain the growth of slavery in Missouri would undoubtedly be met with fierce resistance from white Missourians.

Missouri's new economy and the Middle Mississippi Valley's changing geography provided enslaved African Americans with new opportunities for freedom, but it also created new dangers and difficulties in their everyday lives. In 1817, Vermonter Justus Post bragged to his brother that the enslaved people he had recently purchased could be "sure of three things—victuals, clothes, & work in abundance."[109] Missouri enslavers delivered on Post's promise of "work in abundance" as they created new commercial connections in a sprawling U.S. empire that encompassed the entirety of the Mississippi Valley. Enslavers demanded unrelenting physical labor from the people they enslaved. The callousness created by easy riches, combined with the influx of so many new people, fostered excessive cruelty from enslavers, inflicting on enslaved men, women, and children new levels of violence, forced separation from loved ones, indignities, suffering, and general uncertainty.

U.S. empire did not create the cruelty of enslavement in the Middle Mississippi Valley; it did, however, widen its extent. Enslaved woman Betty gave birth to three children in the 1790s. Betty's enslaver sold those children away from her around 1799. Over the next several years, various habitant and American enslavers "swapped" the children between them. Somewhere along the way, two of the children "had the small pox" after a deal had been struck, prompting the purchaser to "rescind his bargain" with the seller. The enslavers sued one another, prompting the judge to call in Betty to testify. Betty's life must have been difficult enough when she lost her three young children around 1799; it must have become unimaginably more so eight years later when she was asked to determine whether two enslaved children who had survived smallpox were her own. Whether due to time or the scars of smallpox, Betty "could not identify" the children as her own.[110] Like enslaved Native American woman Marianne in the 1770s, Betty found herself in a special kind of captive hell. Betty had been separated from her children for eight years, due to their movements within the expanding Mississippi Valley plantation complex at the hands of three different enslavers. The callousness and calculations of these enslavers now bore heaviest on Betty, compelled by a court to witness three enslavers and a judge haggle over "swaps" that left her family separated and her children stricken with scars both physical and mental.

Separation, movement, and uncertainty seemed endemic in the lives of many enslaved Missourians as U.S. empire stretched farther up the Missouri River. George Sibley had purchased Betty, when he "was last in Georgetown" on official business in 1812. Betty's situation was depressingly typical of the young men and women whom Missouri enslavers purchased in Kentucky and the Chesapeake. Sibley compelled Betty to leave all that she knew behind as she moved from Washington to St. Louis. Sibley's party then traveled on to Fort Osage. During the trip, Betty and Sibley's enslaved man, George, developed a relationship and "entered into partnership." Betty's two pregnancies required her return to St. Louis, where she gave birth to sons Edward and George, Jr. Father and husband George, meanwhile, continued on as "cook and man servant" for Sibley at Fort Osage. Sibley praised George for being "much attached to me faithful and industrious and attentive, for which I cheerfully allow him every comfort and indulgence that he ought to have."[111] Eventually, Betty, George, and their young family reunited at Fort Osage, but that domicile would be short-lived. In 1819, Sibley "sold George" to a "gentleman" in the Boon's Lick settlements to satisfy a debt. Meanwhile, Betty and her two sons continued to provide their unrequited labor to George and Mary Sibley at their farm and at Fort Osage, one hundred miles upriver from George.[112] Expanding U.S. empire forced George and Betty hundreds of miles up the Missouri River; the lure of easy profits in the Boon's Lick boom then separated their family.

Expanding empire exposed enslaved people to other dangers. Whenever U.S. empire encroached on Indigenous lands, Native Americans kidnapped and murdered enslaved African Americans, often the most valuable and mobile pieces of property to be found in contested borderlands. Indigenous people frequently targeted property as a form of resistance against expropriation and colonization. In Missouri, Native Americans intuitively understood that white colonizers prized enslaved Black people as a special kind of property that informed the very identity of the colonizers who invaded Indigenous lands. Shortly after European sovereignty over Missouri passed from Spain to the United States, a band of Indigenous warriors "attacked and killed two White peaceable men, and one Negro, on the Missouri." The attacks were part of a larger series of raids targeting the property of European colonizers and were likely motivated by efforts to demarcate what they perceived to be the line of settlement separating Europeans from Indigenous people.[113] Indigenous attacks on enslaved men and women increased as colonizers invaded central Missouri in the aftermath of the War of 1812. In March 1815, Indigenous warriors attacked "settlements" where they "stole a number of horse and killed a negro."[114] The following spring, a group of Iowa and Sauk warriors raided a salt works, another symbol of colonization. One newspaper report noted that "a party of Indians waylaid the Saline and stole our most valuable negroes from the place of wood chopping." After kidnapping the two enslaved men, the warriors "assaulted a Mr. Liggit, robbed him of his hat, threatened to cut his throat if he did not leave that place, made him signs that they would eat the corn he was then working in."[115] A white Missourian confirmed the personal investment that Missouri colonizers made in their human chattel when he wrote that the raids were "an insult" on many levels, but "most of all a loss to the individuals from whom property is thus stolen."[116] The lives of enslaved Black people was incidental compared to the loss of white property. The Sauk and Iowa warriors likely intended to sell or ransom the captives, but when the Boon's Lick militia made "pursuit," the warriors "killed the two negro men with a tomahawk."[117] Enslavers turned African Americans into instruments and symbols of invasion, dispossession, and colonization; enslaved people bore the costs of expanding empire with their lives.

Enslaved African Americans encountered other new dangers in Missouri's expansive economy and the more integrated imperial spaces of the Mississippi Valley. In 1811, Tennessee enslavers hired-out Phill and two others to mine operators in Missouri. The renters hoped to squeeze as much labor as possible out of the enslaved men, keeping them until "a few days before the time was out." Forced to rush back to Tennessee, the enslaved men had to cover considerable distances, even though it was "especially cold & snowing hard." As the three men approached Ste. Geneviève, "an overseer digging another mine, heard of their going" back to Tennessee. He intended to steal another day's labor from them. The overseer "pursued them, overtook them at night after they had walked the whole day thro the snow." Phill "had already given out" due to his arduous trek, "but the overseer made him drink a good deal" to recover. The overseer then "swore" that Phill "should go" to the mine "or die." Under threat of death, Phill began walking to the mine in the cold, snowy night. He never made it: "He failed and was found dead." Phill's owner expressed no concern about the fact of Phill's death, though he seemed relieved that Phill died "just before 6mo. expired." Phill's renter would thus be responsible for Phill's full worth. But the renter only offered one-third of Phill's value. The renter agreed that the overseer's actions were "censurable," but he denied that he could "be charged with wantonly playing with life or designedly taking it away." The renter instead alleged that Phill "had by his inebriation hastened his death," which in any case was caused by the snow and cold. The renter insisted that "the death of Phill can only be considered an act of God." All that remained was to determine the monetary value of chattel and financial responsibility for destroyed property.[118]

The brutality of empire and enslavement sometimes moved beyond calculations of profit to what can only be characterized as wanton cruelty and deliberate indifference to suffering. In 1814, Samuel Means celebrated July 4th by "drinking freely." Meanwhile, Bill, the young man whom Means enslaved, spent the day "pitching quoits with the other boys." Sometime during the night, Means became enraged at some unknown offense and targeted Bill. "A negro woman" tried to get a slumbering partygoer to "prevent Mr. Means from whipping Bill," but Means delivered "30 or 40 pretty severe" blows with a switch. Means also gave "him a kick" to the head, leaving Bill with "dropsy of the brain." Bill died shortly thereafter.[119] A four-person "inquest" concluded that Means had caused Bill's death, but no records of an indictment or trial remain. Much like Joseph LeBlond, Samuel Means apparently dodged a murder charge. Prominent American enslavers proved just as adept as their habitant counterparts at excusing murders committed by enslavers on the children they enslaved. Local potentates mobilized imperial state power in local communities to empower themselves and to protect their neighbors, whether that was the Chouteau family protecting the LeBlonds, or U.S. officials protecting Means.

The violence that enslavers inflicted on those whom they enslaved could provoke retribution. In 1818, enslaved man Elijah and teenager Gabriel conspired to put arsenic into the sausage they "cooked and prepared" for their enslavers, Mary and John Smith. The pair were convicted by a jury who concluded that they were "moved and seduced by the instigation of the devil" to "kill and murder" Mary. The court files suggest that Mary might have been the devil who so moved Elijah and Gabriel. Elijah and Gabriel earned a new trial after their conviction due to Mary's abuses. The court agreed that Mary had inflicted "barbarous treatment" on Elijah and Gabriel, "such as cutting . . . with knives, thrusting . . . flesh with forks, and such like usage." The new jury allowed that Elijah and Gabriel had "acted from the heat of passion." In a retrial, the jury acquitted Gabriel, and prosecutors lessened the charges against Elijah. Gabriel's punishment was twenty-five lashes per day, to be delivered on three straight days.[120] There is no evidence that Mary was in any way punished or condemned for torturing the people she enslaved.

The charlatans who flooded the Mississippi Valley in the early nineteenth century complicated plans for flight. In 1810, an enslaved man, Nat, told a white man, William Dew, that he "would serve any man two or three years that would take him away from his master." Dew agreed to Nat's proposal but harbored other plans. Along with fellow grifter James Monaghan (who went by the alias John Smith), Dew decided that they would "help" Nat escape, lead him to Pensacola in Spanish Florida, and then "sell him" as their property. Over the next few months, Dew gained Nat's trust by "conversing with and feeding" Nat late at night. Dew and Monaghan/Smith helped Nat escape, and Nat remained at large for "5 or 6 months." Meanwhile Dew and Monaghan/Smith tried "to make up money sufficient to bear" their expenses for the trip to Pensacola. Eventually, "the Guard" of enslavers found Nat and deduced Dew's and Monaghan/Smith's plans. The slave patrol, led by enslaver William Neely, summarily "whipped" and beat Monaghan/Smith severely.[121] Neely was elected to represent Cape Girardeau District in the territorial legislature.[122] Nat apparently returned to his life of enslavement. Nat perhaps turned to Dew and Monaghan/Smith because the denser settlements that filled in the Indigenous and once-uninhabited places in Missouri made it more difficult for enslaved men and women who fled to live as maroons. In 1817, enslaved man Waller followed a familiar forced passage from enslavement in Virginia to enslavement in Missouri. Shortly after arriving in Missouri, he decided to flee. To support himself, Waller raided farms at night, procuring enough to sustain himself. One night, Waller scouted out the farm of enslaver William Primm to obtain some sustenance. Primm "took his gun," confronted Waller, and then shot and murdered him "in cold blood." Like just about everyone else who murdered an enslaved person in territorial Missouri, Primm beat the murder charge; he did, however, pay $372.50 in compensation to Waller's enslaver.[123]

The incorporation of Missouri into an expanding U.S. empire caused separation, trauma, and death for some enslaved people, but it also provided new, hard-fought opportunities for greater autonomy. Enslaved man York was determined to live his life on his own terms; enslaver William Clark was just as determined to maintain York's subordination. Clark split up York's family, having York reside in Missouri while his wife and children lived in Louisville with other members of the Clark family. York repeatedly expressed his desire to move to Louisville and "hire himself" out, with his wages going to Clark. Clark refused, partially because York was "serviceable to me at this place" but mostly because Clark was "determined not" to "gratify" York's desire to exercise greater control over his personal and laboring life.[124] To show his domination of York, Clark directed his brother to have York "sent to New Orleans and Sold, or hired out to some severe master" should York become despondent because he missed his wife and children.[125] York finally had himself sent to Louisville, where he extended his one-month stay to five. After returning from Louisville, York became "insolent and sulky," due to his absence from his family. Clark responded with "a severe trouncing."[126] Later that year, York remained low over the separation from his family, so Clark "confined York" to the "Caleboos" and delivered more beatings. The beatings broke York; as Clark reported to his brother, York "has for two or three weeks been the finest negro I ever had." York's breaking proved temporary, as he convinced Clark to yield barely a month later.[127] York would work "as a hand" on "a boat to Wheeling." On his return, he would stay in Louisville, provided York could find someone to purchase or hire him. York's ability to reunite with his family was hard-won, filled with violence, confinement, and suffering.[128] It was also temporary. The following year Clark placed York under the command of his nephew, John O'Fallon. O'Fallon hired out York to a family in St. Louis, who left him "indifferently clothed if at all," and "wretched under the fear" that he would be forced "to leave this quarter for Natchez."[129] Empire and enslavement bred arrogance, and O'Fallon and Clark seemed to delight in York's misfortunes.

The further integration of Missouri into the larger Mississippi Valley plantation complex afforded enslavers like the Clark family with opportunities for profit and new methods of disciplining the people they enslaved. The expanded imperial geography also provided new opportunities for autonomy, though heavily constrained. York spent his life in limbo, despairing of sale downriver to Natchez, pining for trips to Wheeling, hopeful of reuniting with his wife and family in Louisville, all the while subject to the whims of the extended Clark family. Like York, enslaved men, women, and children in Missouri lived under constant fear that they would be sold into the Lower Mississippi Valley. Clark did just that to another man he enslaved, Scipio. In 1819, Scipio "shot himself through the head this morning. Clarke was about sending him to Orleans, on board the steam boat which sailed today, in order to convert his old companion into Cash."[130] It was widely acknowledged in Missouri and Illinois that Scipio's "fears of transportation to New Orleans urged him to the rash act."[131] Rumors were rife in St. Louis that Clark had "lost a female servant sometime ago under circumstances much more atrocious than the above."[132] The expanded geography of empire cut two ways, affording some enslaved people new avenues for autonomy, but also providing enslavers with new means of control that often bled into outright torture or terror.

The changing contours of empire and enslavement could also provide new venues for freedom. Another enslaved man, Dennis, was known to "habitually run away." In 1810, his enslaver in turn sold him to John Hawkins, who was seeking his fortune at "the Mine of Burton." Dennis became fast allies with the other man Hawkins enslaved, and the two "ran away," not to be found.[133] It remains unknown where Dennis and his unnamed accomplice fled to, but if contemporary developments provide any indication, there is a good chance they sought refuge across the river in Illinois. Enslaved man Sam was born in Maryland, forced to St. Louis, and then sold soon after his male enslaver died in early 1808. Judge John Lucas acquired Sam after Illinois territorial delegate Shadrach Bond decided against holding Sam as a slave in Illinois.[134] After moving among three enslavers in the course of a month, Sam fled for the first of many times. In his first escape, Sam found refuge "at one Harris's" farm, somewhere in Illinois. Harris gave Sam refuge in exchange for labor, and Sam apparently lived there as something like a hired hand.[135] Lucas eventually reclaimed Sam, but not for long. Sam had learned French and apparently used it to flee a second time. Sam again managed to stay away for an extended period, spending "several months" in maroonage at "the settlement of Turkey Hill and Richlands," across the river in Illinois.[136] In late 1815, Sam fled yet again. Lucas suspected that Sam had "procured a forged pass as a free Negro" and that he had again fled to Illinois.[137] Lucas somehow or another recovered Sam in early 1816. By April 1816, Sam escaped for the last time, with Lucas once again suspecting that Sam had obtained a pass and fled to Illinois.[138]

Others followed Sam's path to Illinois. In the spring of 1818, an enslaved man calling himself Nathan Ford was caught "stealing fur and bacon" from a farmer in Edwardsville, Illinois, across from the mouth of the Missouri River.

Ford claimed that he had fled from the Boon's Lick settlements, when he happened upon two deserting soldiers and two other enslaved men fleeing bondage. The group had "come down the Missouri," pilfering furs and stealing horses along the way. A group of Illinois farmers found Ford appropriating food and furs from a farm, tied up his wrists, and kept him in a barn overnight. Ford was gone the next morning, having "cut his cords," presumably with assistance from his posse. Ford was not seen again.[139] By the late 1810s, Illinois provided a new route—albeit a difficult one—for enslaved Missourians to flee for freedom. As Illinois and Missouri moved toward statehood in the late 1810s, the differences between the two banks of the Mississippi River were growing ever more pronounced. The relationship between empire and enslavement had been solidified in Missouri while it withered in Illinois. Just as word of the Missouri Crisis reached St. Louis, four people enslaved by Justus Post fled. Peter, Ellen, Sylvia, and Martin made their way to "the state of Illinois," which Missouri enslavers increasingly suspected of harboring runaway enslaved men and women.[140] Whenever possible, enslaved Missourians used an expanding and dividing U.S. empire for their own purposes.

Between the settlement of the Louisiana Purchase in 1805 and white Missourians' application for statehood in late 1818, enslavers and imperial agents consolidated the slave society that Spanish officials and habitants had begun transferring to the west bank of the Mississippi River in the 1760s. In 1819, white Missourians held 12,000 people in slavery; white Illinoisians, fewer than 1,200. Habitant and American enslavers worked with U.S. imperial agents to build a small but thriving slave society that they integrated into the larger Mississippi Valley plantation complex. They could do so because U.S. imperial agents, appointed and elected local officials, and prominent merchants and farmers channeled imperial state power into coercive institutions and relationships designed expressly to keeping people enslaved. At the same time, U.S. empire provided a steady stream of migrating enslavers and further integration into the Mississippi Valley plantation complex.

When the Missouri Crisis erupted in February 1819, a great majority of white Missourians defiantly fought against any imperial restrictions on slavery in Missouri as a condition of statehood. As far as they were concerned, empire and statehood were inseparable from propping up the rights and privileges of enslavers. As they understood matters, the purpose of empire was to facilitate enslavement, not emancipation. As constituent members of the U.S. empire in the trans-Mississippi West, they fully expected statehood to be approved with slavery, without question. They accordingly stood shocked that northern imperialists in Congress wanted to limit the scope of slavery in Missouri. John O'Fallon, on-again and off-again U.S. imperial agent and William Clark's nephew, "expected that the people of this Ty [territory] would revolt and rather separate from the union than submit to the monstrous outrage upon her sacred rights."[141] The purpose of empire *was* enslavement, not emancipation, no matter how far off or how gradual. Like the habitants he so easily meshed with, O'Fallon would rather leave the U.S. empire than suffer under one that denied his sacred rights as an enslaver. Expatriated Virginian John Walker expressed similar sentiments while articulating the new geography of empire and enslavement in the Middle Mississippi Valley. Walker confidently expected that Missouri enslavers would soon enough break "the Shackles of Territorial subjection" and emerge on the righteous side of "the great touchstone" of Missouri statehood, "slavery or no slavery." Walker continued that Missouri's future depended on tight connections among empire, enslavement, and Indigenous dispossession, fed by the continuing "emigration" of southern enslavers. But Walker also noted that Illinois was becoming "a hothouse for runaway negroes and Renegados," Walker's preferred term for whites who opposed slavery.[142] As O'Fallon, Walker, and legions of Missourians, both free and enslaved, recognized, Missouri had become categorically different from Illinois with regards to slavery. Empire and enslavement had once united both sides of the Middle Mississippi Valley. Now, empire and enslavement divided them.

CHAPTER 6

"A Cob Web of Legislation"

Slavery in Illinois, 1805–1818

Between 1805 and the late 1810s, the relationship between empire and enslavement remained stubbornly stagnant in Illinois. Illinois speculator-enslavers continued their schemes to gain imperial sanction for slavery so that they could welcome the steady stream of enslavers moving from the Chesapeake and Kentucky to Missouri. Northern imperialists—who envisioned a new form of North American empire free from slavery and, when coupled with colonization, Black people—continuously shot down their efforts. When it became clear that Congress would not rescind Article VI, Illinois enslavers preserved what remained of their old forms of slavery and devised new legal categories of bondage that differed little from chattel slavery in practice. Though the meaning and intent of Article VI remained clear, Illinois enslavers deliberately made the status of enslaved people ambiguous and indeterminant and then positioned themselves to determine the status of bonded people who sought freedom. In the process, they made Illinois slavery ineradicable for decades.[1]

Between 1805 and 1818, Illinois officials turned the French villages and a few newer settlements into a series of enslaving enclaves in a territory otherwise characterized by the absence of slavery. Within those enclaves, enslavers created a new legal category of enslaved people whom they deemed "French Negroes," contending that they and their descendants remained forever exempt from Article VI. Illinois enslavers also created an ad hoc system of servitude that allowed enslavers to convert chattel slaves into indentured servants, with terms ranging from five years to, in a few cases, ninety-nine years. Illinois enslavers also passed legislation permitting Kentucky enslavers to use enslaved men and women at the United States Saline without losing their claims of ownership. Hardly amounting to some grand scheme that portended the transformation of ostensibly free Illinois into a slave state, enslavers and local imperial officials cobbled together practices and laws to keep already-enslaved people in bondage, in a territory where bondage remained under the bane of an imperial decree. Illinois enslavers themselves conceded that the bundle of laws and practices created nothing more than a "cob web of legislation" that failed to retain or attract enslavers in substantial numbers.[2] No one in Congress, the Middle Mississippi and Ohio Valleys, or regions like the Chesapeake confused Illinois's tangle of laws, practices, and raw assertions of power with an imperial framework for creating a viable slave society. No contemporaries confounded the fragments of eighteenth-century slavery in Illinois with the imperially sanctioned slave society that colonizers were simultaneously creating in Missouri. In 1818, white Missourians held 12,000 people in slavery, approximately 20 percent of the non-Indigenous population; at most, white Illinoisians held perhaps 1,200 people in some form of bondage, perhaps 3 percent of Illinois's non-Indigenous population.

Frequently changing imperial sovereignties, inconsistent imperial decrees, imperial states unwilling or unable to assist enslavers, and assertions of power by local enslavers created a confused and contradictory history of slavery in Illinois from the 1760s through the 1790s, and then again in the 1800s and the 1810s. Between 1805 and statehood in 1818, two developments occurred simultaneously in Illinois: slavery's persistence and even slight growth in a few old settlements and a few new ones, but also its growing irrelevance and decline. After 1805, Illinois slavery proved invidious but also evanescent. Article VI continued to steer enslavers to places such as Missouri, while Illinois enslavers continuously transferred ownership of the people they enslaved in Illinois to Missouri. By the 1810s, Illinois was more similar to states undergoing gradual abolition, such as New Jersey and New York, than places such as Kentucky and Missouri, where slavery was growing. As in states undergoing formal, gradual emancipations, Illinois enslavers crafted measures to steal every last bit of unrequited toil from the people they enslaved, and they cashed in by selling enslaved people into jurisdictions like Missouri where slavery remained fully sanctioned.

As always, imperial policy shaped the contours and geography of enslavement in the Middle Mississippi Valley, but enslaved people, colonizers, and local officials determined practices on the ground. Enslaved Black people infused the region's borders with new meanings when they began suing for their freedom on the basis of Article VI, when they began establishing free Black communities and when Black Missourians fled to Illinois. The reluctance of enslavers to settle in Illinois also allowed for the growth of an increasingly vocal contingent of white colonizers who opposed slavery for a host of different reasons. Meanwhile, a contingent of powerful enslaver-colonizers held local and territorial offices, and they used their political, social, and economic prestige to create and maintain various forms of slavery. Nonetheless, the patterns and practices of emancipation, enslavement, and empire in Illinois and Missouri continued to diverge between the Louisiana Purchase and statehood in the late 1810s. As had happened in Missouri, the Louisiana Purchase did little to alter the practices of enslavement and empire in Illinois; while the scope, extent, and territoriality of enslavement increased in Missouri, it stagnated and shrank in Illinois.

By 1805, Congress had rejected no fewer than a dozen attempts by Illinois enslavers and speculators to gain U.S. imperial sanction for slavery in Illinois. Over the next few years, Illinois enslavers would continue to seek abrogation of Article VI. In early 1805, enslaver and land speculator Robert Morrison worked with his Philadelphia-based uncle to further their scheme "to be annexed to the Government of Upper Louisiana." Morrison again implored his uncle to "interest the feelings" of his "friends in Congress." He also warned that "God only knows" what would become of their extensive landholdings if Congress refused to sanction slavery, thus leaving Illinois in a "deplorable" state.[3] Three months later, Morrison expressed his growing impatience "on the subject of the petition" for the "annexation of the Western Counties in this Territory to Upper Louisiana." Again, Morrison pleaded that "God only knows what will fall our misfortunes" if Congress continued to refuse their pleas. In the meantime, Morrison sought to make up for the refusal of American enslavers to settle in Illinois. He advised his uncle to send "the number of Europeans that are daily Landing in Philadelphia" to Illinois, as Morrison expected he might be able to "sell 8 or 9 thousand acres of Land" to them.[4]

When it became clear that Congress would not add Illinois to Upper Louisiana, Morrison and Illinois enslaver-speculators devised a new strategy: They would seek to separate from Indiana, create a new Illinois Territory, and pursue repeal of Article VI there. Morrison deliberately obfuscated the centrality of slavery to this plan. Rather than asking for imperial sanction for slavery, the late 1805 petition requested that Congress "Rescue from impending ruin a handful of citizens who have been the sport of Fortune since they have been recognized as a part of the American Empire." Morrison extolled "the poor industrious farmer" who "cannot make his way to courts in Vincennes and loses to the man of influence." While asking Congress to protect poor farmers, he was simultaneously pleading with his uncle "to write to your friends on the Subject in Congress." If they managed to split from Indiana and then legalize slavery in Illinois, the Morrisons would all find themselves "in a pleasant situation." Sanctioned slavery in Illinois would "make our property here Valuable, and the Country desirable."[5] Less than a month later, Morrison wrote of yet another petition for separation, warning his uncle that "their all is at Stake." He also pleaded with him to have Robert's latest letter on the subject "published in some Democratic paper in your city."[6] The pleadings of Morrison and his fellow speculators did little to move northern imperialists in Congress.[7]

Antislavery imperialists in Congress might have failed to halt slavery's growth in Upper Louisiana or to eliminate slavery in Illinois, but they remained determined to maintain Article VI. As Kentucky Congressman Matthew Lyon explained, he "laboured faithfully for many years to obtain for that Territory a temporary suspension" of "that part of the Compact" prohibiting slavery. However, "all the States as far as Pennsylvania have long been unanimous on this Subject," and they would never consent to any modification or repeal of Article VI.[8] There was no shared commitment to slavery's expansion among the U.S. empire's policy-makers in the first decade of the 1800s. Northern antislavery imperialists in Congress rejected efforts to rescind Article VI in Indiana and Illinois in 1803, 1804, 1805, 1806, 1807, and 1808. In 1809, Congress created a separate Illinois Territory at the same time that it signaled to Indiana and Illinois enslavers that repeal or modification of Article VI would never happen during the territorial stages of government. Congress split off the two territories only when northern imperialists became confident that a popular antislavery movement in Indiana would fight off any effort to legalize slavery in the territory and then state.[9]

Illinois enslavers—governors, judges, territorial representatives, and other officials—responded to congressional dismissal of their pleas for slavery in Illinois by creating dynamic systems of bondage that ensnared many African Americans in an array of statuses that ranged from chattel slavery, to lifetime indentured servitude, to shorter terms of servitude that sometimes resulted in legal or de facto emancipation. In the aftermath of the Louisiana Purchase, Illinois enslavers and officials responded to Article VI of the Northwest Ordinance in much the same way that Upper Louisiana enslavers and officials confronted Spain's 1769 decree banning Indigenous enslavement. Upper Louisiana enslavers created racial categories that made Indigenous enslavement both indeterminate and ineradicable for decades. They used subterfuge and expedient rulings by local officials to defy the clear intent of the 1769 decree. Spanish officials such as Lieutenant Governor Francisco Cruzat immediately availed themselves of the prevailing forms of Native American bondage in Upper Louisiana by purchasing and selling enslaved Native Americans. Officials such as Cruzat also assisted locally powerful elites like François Vallé and Auguste Chouteau in devising schemes to prolong Native American enslavement. Likewise, in U.S. Illinois, U.S. imperial officials personally defied the ban and assisted enslavers in concocting schemes to evade it. Almost all of these U.S. officials arrived in Illinois as enslavers; nearly all of them hailed from the Chesapeake; all of them used their schemes to evade Article VI for their own personal benefit. Judge John Edgar; Judge Alexander Stuart; territorial representative and congressional delegate Shadrach Bond; territorial representative, delegate, and federal judge Jesse Thomas; territorial secretary and delegate Nathaniel Pope; and Governor Ninian Edwards all held African Americans in various states of slavery in Illinois. They did so under laws, judicial rulings, and customary practices devised by themselves. One of the few northerners appointed to an official position in Illinois, Judge Stanley Griswold of Connecticut, availed himself of Illinois's indentured servitude laws soon after his appointment by "purchasing a Negro or two."[10]

Like their counterparts a generation earlier in Spanish Upper Louisiana, U.S. imperial agents immediately worked with local grandees to protect their shared ideological and material interests under an imperial regime that withdrew sanction for slavery. U.S. imperial officials in Illinois worked extensively with long-resident enslaver potentates such as the Morrison family and Pierre Menard. Robert Morrison served terms variously as a judge and as a colonel in the militia; Menard served as a militia officer, a notary for land claims, a judge, and an appointed member of the territorial legislative council. In the imperial interlude during the winter of 1804, Morrison and Menard served as the Lewis and Clark expedition's main Illinois suppliers and hosts. Both topped the ranks of Illinois's wealthiest merchant speculator-enslavers. Both had either married or had relatives who married into the powerful Chouteau family of St. Louis.[11] Together, they worked with U.S. imperial agents to preserve ownership over enslaved African Americans already in Illinois, and they reclassified chattel slaves from elsewhere as indentured servants. Just like their Spanish counterparts in Upper Louisiana, U.S. imperial officials posted to Illinois helped create and directly participated in systems of enslavement that both defied and concurred with imperial decrees. Just like Spanish officials, too, Illinois imperial officials and enslavers prolonged the enslavement of individuals in Illinois for two generations after imperial decrees portended slavery's demise.

In the aftermath of the Louisiana Purchase, Illinois enslavers worked with U.S. imperial officials to reclassify the people of mixed Native and African lineage whom they enslaved as "French Negroes."[12] They exploited the region's history of confused, overlapping, and oft-changing jurisdictions by cobbling together a series of treaties, reports, and promises issued by imperial officials from the late 1770s through the early 1790s. They then used this confused thicket of sources to create a contrived class of property, allegedly guaranteed to Illinois enslavers in perpetuity. As Ninian Edwards contended, "The right to this species of property was as perfect in Illinois" as it was in "any state of the Union."[13] Illinois enslavers claimed that they had inherited their rights as enslavers from successive French and British jurisdictions and that Virginia and the United States had confirmed those rights. The 1778 Virginia "Act Creating the County of Illinois" granted citizenship to free white men who took "an oath of fidelity" to the Commonwealth of Virginia.[14] Illinois enslavers claimed that upon becoming Virginia citizens in 1778, they gained the same rights as Virginia enslavers. Illinois enslavers next pointed to the 1783 Virginia Treaty of Cession, where Virginia transferred its claims north of the Ohio River to the United States. The Treaty of Cession held "that the French and Canadian Inhabitants and other Settlers" who "have professed themselves Citizens of Virginia shall have their possessions and Titles confirmed to them and be protected in the enjoyment of their rights and liberties."[15] Though this treaty's provisions for the protection of property clearly pertained to land claims, Illinois enslavers retroactively expanded its domain to include enslaved people. As much as anything, this treaty formed the legal basis for Illinois enslavers' prolonging bondage in Illinois for six decades following passage of the Northwest Ordinance.

In 1787, the Confederation Congress issued the Northwest Ordinance; habitant enslavers immediately petitioned the Confederation Congress demanding repeal of Article VI. Illinois enslavers and officials held that the 1783 Virginia Treaty of Cession superseded the Northwest Ordinance, which in their analysis amounted to an *ex post facto* law, rather than a fundamental charter.[16] In response, a Confederation Congress committee staffed by three enslavers issued a report holding that the 1783 Virginia Treaty of Cession protected the rights of enslavers, even though the treaty said nothing directly concerning property in enslaved people. The committee ruled that the Northwest Ordinance of 1787 "shall not be construed to deprive" habitants and Virginians now resident in Illinois "of their Right and property in Negro or other Slaves which they were possessed of" prior to passage of the Northwest Ordinance. In the committee's reading of the Northwest Ordinance, Article VI's purpose was "merely to restrain the Settlers in the future from carrying persons under Servitude into the Western territory."[17] With that, three congressional enslavers transformed a strongly worded ban on slavery in the Northwest Territory into a prohibition on future slavery. In 1789, the First Federal Congress re-passed the Northwest Ordinance and retained the Article VI prohibition on slavery. Speculator George Morgan then used re-passage of Article VI to entice Illinois enslavers and landholders to remove to his new settlement at New Madrid in Upper Louisiana by warning that Article VI portended immediate emancipation. Northwest Territory Governor Arthur St. Clair, himself an enslaver, tried to mollify enslavers to entice them to remain in Illinois. St. Clair assured Illinois enslavers that "the Article respecting Slaves" served only "as a prohibition to any future introduction of them." It did not, he assured them, "extend to the liberation of those the People were already possessed of, and acquired under the Sanction of the Laws they were subject." "At the same time," St. Clair instructed them "that Steps would probably be taken for the gradual Abolition of Slavery, with which they seem perfectly satisfied."[18]

Three years later, St. Clair offered a similar opinion, explaining that Article VI "was no more than the declaration of a principle which was to govern the legislature" after 1787, "but it could have no more retroactive operation whatever." St. Clair further added that "slaves being a species of property countenanced and protected" in Illinois, "by the ancient laws," Congress could not issue a general emancipation. St. Clair concluded that Congress and territorial governments "had a right to determine that property of that kind afterward acquired should not be protected in the future, and that slaves imported into the territory at the declaration might reclaim their freedom."[19] No such declaration would be forthcoming. In the 1790s, Congress, and the federal government more broadly, remained divided between northern whites, willing to take some kinds of action against slavery, and southern whites, who already viewed any action against slavery as an existential threat. Congress, riven by sectional and partisan divisions that made it impossible to pass laws providing for immediate and gradual abolition in a territory it claimed but did not govern, never took up the matter, neither affirming nor denying the rights of Illinois enslavers, or St. Clair's various decrees and opinions.[20] Enslavers and officials on the ground in Illinois would be left to determine the meaning and applicability of Article VI, just as enslavers in Upper Louisiana determined the meaning of the imperial ban on Native American enslavement.

Over the next decade, Illinois enslavers turned a claimed privilege into an expansive right by transforming the series of treaties, ordinances, and rulings into an amorphous mesh of precedents legalizing, protecting, and guaranteeing the rights of enslavers in Illinois. They then used their legal and political authority to determine the meanings and applicability of that which they had made ambiguous, amorphous, and indeterminant. As had happened in Spanish Upper Louisiana with regards to Native American enslavement, long-resident habitant enslavers, arriviste Virginian enslavers, and U.S. imperial officials on the ground employed the precedents and customs they had contrived to their favor. Over time, assertions that the "French Negroes" and their children constituted a protected class of property became practice and custom, gaining the force of law and constitutional right as determined by enslaving local and imperial officials.[21] Both longtime resident enslavers and newer enslavers who purchased "French Negroes" recorded their ownership of the people they enslaved with county clerks and local courts. They reified their ownership in court cases. They recorded the children of "French Negroes" as chattel slaves. They baptized the children they enslaved in churches. They sold the children of "French Negroes" as chattel property.[22] They promised to "severely punish" enslaved people who "misbehaved."[23] In short, they claimed and then asserted over "French Negroes" and their descendants the full range of rights and privileges traditionally accorded to enslavers across North America and the Caribbean. They then used the local governments they controlled to assert and exercise those rights.

By the early 1800s, Illinois enslavers and territorial officials had turned the limited legal concept of "French Negroes" into an elastic, expansive, and permanent status. They repeatedly asserted that "French Negroes" had always been "Negro slaves" and that they and their children could be held as such in perpetuity. An enslaved woman, Mary, was born in 1800 or 1801 to an enslaved mother in Illinois. Mary was then "reared and brought up in a state of slavery" for the next two decades.[24] Like Mary, Aspasia "was born of a negro woman in the Town of Kaskaskia about the year 1806." Aspasia's mother "was held in slavery in said state by one Baptiste Gindreau, who held her till his death." Aspasia was likewise "held and claimed as a slave" into the 1820s.[25] Illinois enslavers also extended the practice to include enslaved people who were in no way "French Negros" but had been forcibly migrated to Illinois after passage of the Northwest Ordinance. In 1809, Maryland enslaver James Rayer settled in Illinois. Rayer forcibly removed the enslaved woman Susan with him "and claimed and exercised authority over" her "as a slave" until 1812, when he moved to Missouri.[26] Illinois enslavers created new categories of enslavement through the raw exercise of power, bottomed on contrived interpretations of their own making.

Illinois enslavers, along with local and territorial officials, mobilized local power to create categories of bondage that skirted the clear meaning and intent of Article VI, just as their predecessors in Spanish Upper Louisiana had manipulated the racial status of the people they enslaved. By the 1810s, Illinois statutes were filled with references to "negro slaves," even though no territorial ordinance or statute ever created a class of enslaved Black people. In 1807, the territorial legislature authorized counties to levy a tax "not exceeding 100 cents" on "every bond servant or slave" in the territory.[27] The territory's 1807 "Act Concerning Servants" specified that no "slave or servant" could travel more than ten miles from their enslaver's residence. All told, the 1807 "Act Concerning Servants" mentioned "slaves" eight times.[28] The following year, lawmakers consolidated their previous efforts to create categories of slaves and servants. The 1808 "Act to Amend an Act, Entitled 'An Act Concerning Servants'" forbade "any slave, or slaves, servant, or servants of colour, to the number of three or more" from holding unsanctioned gatherings, and again used the term "slave" throughout.[29] In 1814, the Illinois legislature passed "An Act Concerning the Kaskaskia Indians," which regulated the sale and transfer of alcohol. This act repeatedly described "any negro or mulatto being the slave or servant of any person whatsoever."[30] Through these repeated legislative assertions, manifested through their enforcement by officials and prominent men in enslaving enclaves, Illinois enslavers and local imperial officials created and reified practices of enslavement.

Illinois enslavers and officials did what enslavers had always done in the Middle Mississippi Valley: They enforced and ignored, manipulated and abused, whatever decrees, treaties, customs, laws, and practices met their needs in the moment. In the late 1780s and early 1790s, Illinois enslavers simply ignored Article VI in the expectation that Congress would rescind it sooner or later. When it became clear in the early 1800s that Congress would never repeal Article VI, Illinois enslavers mobilized their local power to create an elaborate system of chattel slavery. Amos Stoddard, who had witnessed firsthand how Upper Louisiana enslavers perpetuated Native American enslavement, understood exactly what Illinois enslavers had done. Stoddard noted that "the obvious construction" of Article VI "is that the slaves at that period of existence were entitled to their freedom; or at least, that the children of female slaves, born after the adoption of the ordinance, were born free." In effect, Stoddard argued for a built-in gradual abolition mechanism for Article VI, similar to those used in the northern states. Illinois enslavers, however, had created a system that held that "Slave property, while it exists, ought not to be infringed; and if no legal means can be devised to abolish it, let it be perpetual." With this "strained and pernicious construction of the ordinance,"[31] Illinois enslavers managed to keep several hundred men, women, children and their offspring in chattel for several generations.

That was not enough for Illinois enslaver-speculators. Hoping to tap into the growing stream of enslavers who were migrating from the slave states of the Atlantic seaboard to the trans-Appalachian states and territories where slavery was legal and sanctioned, Illinois enslavers also passed a series of laws that permitted the conversion of chattel slaves from places such as Virginia into indentured servants in Indiana and Illinois. Northern imperialists in Congress shot down Illinois enslavers' strongest attempts to modify Article VI in 1803, 1805, and 1807. Indiana and Illinois enslavers responded by creating systems of "voluntary" servitude designed to skirt Article VI's ban on "involuntary servitude." The system was an obvious ruse. Illinois's servitude laws required the consent of enslaved people to convert lifelong, inheritable slavery to terms of servitude that ran to twenty, forty, sixty, and, in a few cases, ninety-nine years. Males and females born to these indentured servants had to serve terms, respectively, of thirty-five and thirty-two years. Furthering the similarities between servitude and slavery, the laws regulating the actions of bonded Black people made no distinction between slaves and servants.[32]

Through law, custom, and practice—created by enslavers who held the contracts of indentured African Americans and upheld by territorial officials—the indentures became real property that could be purchased, sold, and inherited, deepening the similarities between chattel slavery and indentured servitude.[33] By the early 1810s, Missouri and Illinois newspapers regularly ran advertisements listing "FOR SALE," "One indentured Negro Man."[34] As with the informal policy of converting enslaved African Americans into "French Negroes," federal officials sanctioned indentured servitude through their active and abiding use of this system. In 1812, a territorial federal judge, Alexander Stuart, offered for sale "two indented negro women."[35] In 1815,

Connecticut-born judge Stanley Griswold went "about purchasing a Negro or two," adding "they are not slaves in this territory. We hold these only as indentured servants."[36] Enslaving imperial officials like Griswold and Stuart reified and legitimated systems of slavery that contravened imperial decrees. Through the mid-1810s, courts in surrounding slave states also upheld the legality of indentured servitude contracts when African Americans challenged them. St. Louis fur trader and merchant Manuel Lisa "purchased the time" of an enslaved man named Ben "and his wife." Ben and his unnamed wife traveled with Lisa "to New Orleans and thence to St. Louis." Ben and his wife sought their release from the indentures by meeting with officials in both of those places. Those efforts failed, and in 1808 Ben and his wife ran away to Kentucky and sued for their freedom, in part based on their long residence in Indiana and Illinois. Lisa testified to officials in Kentucky "that a removal of slaves from states where slavery is permitted to the Illinois Territory, does not destroy the masters right and title to such slave, but only prevents the masters from compelling involuntary servitude while there." Kentucky officials agreed with Lisa's contrived and convenient argument, and Ben and his wife remained Lisa's captives.[37]

Illinois enslavers created a third category of bondage in territorial Illinois in 1814, again in direct response to northern imperialists' refusal to modify or abridge Article VI. By the 1810s, Illinois and Kentucky enslavers desperately sought congressional approval to permit the use of enslaved men and women to work on federal salt lands, a ten-by-sixteen-mile stretch of land containing brinish streams, marshes, and wells located along the junctions of the Wabash and Saline Rivers with the Ohio River around Shawneetown. Since the early 1800s, Kentucky enslavers hired out or illegally used their own enslaved workers at the salt works. Unwilling to convert enslaved chattel into indentured servants, Kentucky enslavers proved reticent in risking valuable property in Illinois.[38] The salt marshes were largely untapped due to a profound lack of labor, when the federal government appointed Ninian Edwards superintendent of the federal salt reserve. In 1813, Edwards and the Illinois territorial legislature requested that Congress pass a bill permitting "the Partial introduction of Negroes to carry on the salt works."[39] Shadrach Bond, Illinois's territorial delegate in Congress, was familiar with the internal workings of Congress on slavery in the Northwest Territories, and he immediately expressed "doubts about" the bill's success. He also expected that the request "will make a fuss with some," presumably the northern imperialists who had denied every previous request to modify Article VI.[40] Allied enslavers in the

Senate tried to assist their fellow enslavers in Kentucky and Illinois by intro-
ducing a bill permitting "persons held to slavery or service under the laws
of any state" to work the salt marshes, but antislavery imperialists forced the
Senate to table the bill.[41]

After Congress refused Illinois's latest request to modify Article VI, territorial officials passed their own act explicitly permitting the use of enslaved
African Americans at the federal salines. The 1814 law stipulated that the use
of enslaved African Americans in Illinois, for up to one year, "shall not operate in any way whatever to injure the right of property in the master." In other
words, Kentucky enslavers could use enslaved Kentuckians in the Illinois
salt marshes without losing their legal claims to those they enslaved. While
in Illinois, enslaved men and women would "be considered and treated as
indented servants" under the laws of territorial Illinois. Skirting the clear
language of Article VI, the law also stipulated that each enslaved Kentuckian had to "voluntarily hire himself or herself" to salt operators. In effect,
this law locally legalized the use of enslaved African Americans in Illinois for
one-year periods, with no limits on renewal.[42] It is difficult to determine how
many enslaved Kentuckians were forced to work in Illinois salt marshes, but
the Illinois census for 1810 counted 205 enslaved people in Randolph County,
while the 1818 state census counted 321 enslaved people in Gallatin County.[43]
At most, the 1814 law permitted enslavers to use a few hundred enslaved people in the salt marshes for short periods of time. Most enslaved people who
were hired out in Illinois remained for only a few months, primarily during
slack periods of farming work in Kentucky.[44]

Slapdash systems of bondage allowed a small number of enslavers to hold a
small number of persons in slavery, but enslavers proved reluctant to risk their
most valuable property under such shaky premises, especially when the Ohio
and Mississippi Valleys abounded with jurisdictions to exploit enslaved people
legally and more thoroughly. Long-resident enslavers, migrating enslavers, and
enslaved men and women all understood that Illinois's system of indentured
servitude served as a poor substitute for the kinds of imperially sanctioned
slavery that once existed in Illinois, and now existed in Missouri and Kentucky.
Enslavers created enclaves for themselves in Illinois. Here and there, enslavers
held African Americans in bondage where local officials connived at the practice. Thus, in 1806, in the settlements around Shawneetown, a Yankee merchant
encountered "a house of Poverty, where dwelt a Madam of such importance
as to command a one legged Negrow." The next day, he encountered "a civil

family who bear rule over one Negrow." The appearance of enslaved men in southern Illinois proved jarring enough to this Yankee traveler to record their presence in his journal.[45]

More broadly, however, the evasions of Article VI contrived by Illinois enslavers and imperial officials amounted to ad hoc measures that did little to alter the larger trajectories of empire and enslavement that had prevailed in the Middle Mississippi Valley since the 1780s. Kentucky enslavers remained cautious about hiring out the people they enslaved, with good reason. The salt marshes, located in an isolated corner of Illinois with ready access to the Ohio, Wabash, and Saline Rivers, along with roads to Vincennes and Kaskaskia, invited enslaved men and women to flee for freedom. Enslaved woman Dinah, "representing herself as free" and "having papers indicating her freedom," fled the salt marshes and worked as a free woman on a boat traveling the Ohio.[46] Esau, "a preacher for several years in the Methodist society," likewise fled his enslavement at the Illinois salines.[47] Hiring out enslaved people to Illinois salt-marsh operators invited flight.[48]

Kentucky enslavers also sensed that that their transgressions of Article VI created plausible claims for freedom, while work in the salt marshes invited enslaved men and women to loosen the bonds of servitude. Working in isolated salt marshes, far away from the fabric of individuals and institutions that sustained slavery, many enslaved workers claimed and exercised greater freedoms over their laboring and personal lives. Enslaved man Vincent, "after he was some time at the Saline," had "become disobedient and refused to return to the Service of his master."[49] At least four enslaved men and women used by Kentuckians in territorial Illinois in the 1810s sued for their freedom in Missouri in the 1820s. Enslaved man Joe sued for his freedom on the basis "that for some six or seven years in succession" he "was hired out in the State of Illinois at the salt works."[50] Joe died before a decision was rendered. Vincent and Alsey lost initial freedom suits that they later won.[51] Likewise, enslaved man "Ralph had worked at the Saline of Illinois as early as the year 1814 or 1815," and he won his freedom due to residency in Illinois.[52] Few Kentucky enslavers availed themselves of Illinois laws permitting the use of slave labor at the U.S. Saline. Those who did all but invited enslaved people to flee, claim greater autonomy within their legal enslavement, or outright sue for their freedom after they found circumstances and individuals favorable to their lawsuit. Enslavers—crafty, cunning, and well versed in the laws and practices that granted them power over the people they enslaved—found much to dislike, and little to favor, in this particular evasion of Article VI.

Likewise, Illinois's "cob web of legislation" had little effect on its main tar-
get: the thousands of enslaver-colonizers moving into the Ohio and Mississippi Valleys in the first two decades of the nineteenth century. Few people
inside or outside of Illinois thought of it as a place where enslavers could or
should settle as long as Article VI remained in effect. One 1805 piece detailing the migration of enslaver Colonel Samuel Hammond from Georgia to
his post in St. Louis reported that "an act of congress preventing slavery, prevents emigrants, particularly those of opulence," from settling in Illinois.[53] A
Yankee farmer who settled in Illinois urged his friend to run for territorial
delegate in 1812 by championing his "zeal against slavery coming into the Territory."[54] Slavery was present in Illinois, but it was not prevalent and was not
"coming into the Territory" in any appreciable manner. At the end of the War
of 1812, Virginian apologist John Randolph wrote a widely circulated piece
detailing the sacrifices Virginia had made for the Union. Among them, the
cession of "its lands beyond the Ohio," with "conditions" that made it "forbidden ground" to Virginia enslavers.[55] An 1816 article from Virginia that began
"Slavery. An experiment is making in the West," marked "the *Ohio* river" as "a
broad line between the states which hold slaves, and those which have none."
The author continued that "as the States, South of the Ohio not only permit
the existence of slavery, but the introduction of Slaves, most of the emigrants
from the southern Atlantic states will naturally bend their steps to that direction."[56] Article VI steered enslavers away from Illinois despite the best efforts
of Illinois enslaver-speculators to attract them.

Essayists invariably placed Illinois among the states where slavery was
either banned or undergoing a process of emancipation and eradication.
Periodic essays condemning the continuation of slavery in the United States
matter-of-factly placed Illinois among the states where the Northwest Ordinance decreed that "there shall be neither slavery nor involuntary servitude."[57] Eastern newspapers and emigrant guides typically included Illinois
among the nonslaveholding states and territories of the trans-Appalachian
West. "The Illinois Territory, I have no doubt, furnishes greater inducements
to emigration, than any other Territory belonging to the United States, to
such men who are not holders of Slaves," proclaimed one account. After writing off Illinois for enslavers, the author recommended Alabama for colonizers who "have large capital and who hold many slaves."[58] Morris Birkbeck,
who wished to establish a colony for British emigrants in the United States,
declared that because "this curse" of slavery "has taken fast hold of Kentucky,
Tennessee, and all the new states to the south; therefore, my enquiries will be

confined to the western parts of Pennsylvania, and the states of Ohio, Indiana and the territory of Illinois."[59] Widely circulated articles published in eastern newspapers that touted the availability of "lands lying in the Missouri and Illinois territories" added some kind of qualifier that "Slavery is *not* admitted in the Illinois territory" but "Slavery *is* admitted to the Missouri territory."[60] One emigrant guide bluntly claimed that "slavery is not admitted" to the Illinois Territory.[61] In 1817, the Virginia state senate reported that "Ohio, Indiana, and Illinois, are admitted upon terms, which amongst other things, inhibit slavery."[62] More measured accounts of Illinois noted that "slavery was originally prohibited, but the law has been relaxed in favor of the new settlers who have slaves, and there are now 257 slaves in this territory."[63] Another noted that "*indenturing negroes for a term of from* 10 *to* 15 *years*" was now permitted in Illinois.[64] While emigrant guides and booster accounts heralded the riches to be found by enslavers in places such as Missouri, Kentucky, and Lower Louisiana, no one extolled the benefits of Illinois for enslavers.

Some migrating enslavers from the Chesapeake and Kentucky settled in Illinois; most did not. Migrating enslavers bypassed Illinois unless they possessed some kind of vested interest in being there, namely cheaply purchased or inherited land claims. Even enslavers with direct interest in Illinois preferred residing in Missouri. Virginia enslaver Joseph Pollard intended to "go into the practice of law" at Kaskaskia, where he would handle the massive number of land grants in circulation. However, he chose to "reside in the town of Saint Louis" along with "the 12 or 15 slaves" he forced to move with him to Missouri.[65] Like Pollard, the Carroll and Rochester families explicitly ruled out migrating to Illinois, preferring Missouri because "slavery is permitted." Indeed, for the Carroll and Rochester families, "the absence of this necessary evil, to a person of southern habits, is an insuperable objection" to places such as Illinois; as Charles Carroll noted, "I could brook the climate, could I have my negroes to work for me."[66]

By the mid-1810s, a consensus had developed in the Ohio and Middle Mississippi Valleys that enslavers eschewed colonizing Illinois because the U.S. imperial state refused to sanction slavery there. Enslaving colonizers in the Middle Mississippi Valley overwhelmingly looked to Missouri rather than Illinois. Henry Marie Brackenridge, who had periodically traveled to habitant settlements in Illinois and Missouri since the 1790s, concluded that "emigrants from the southern states" preferred Missouri over Illinois because Missouri granted "the permission of holding slaves."[67] Itinerant Yankee preacher Timothy Flint determined that Illinois "laboured under the

inconvenience of excluding the larger slave holders, from its laws interdict-
ing slavery."[68] Another Yankee traveler observed that Illinois "does not suit
the Virginians & Kentuckians as slavery is not tolerated."[69] As Illinois moved
toward statehood, pro- and antislavery factions alike agreed that "were slavery admitted, many emigrants, who now pass through our territory, on their
way to Boon's Lick and other parts of the Missouri territory, followed by a
long concourse of slaves," would likely "settle in Illinois."[70] Article VI deterred
enslavers, despite the extensive efforts of Illinois officials to negate its effects.
Mobile enslaving colonizers avoided jurisdictions that failed to provide clear
imperial sanction for slavery. Passive denial of imperial sanction proved
effective in keeping enslavers mostly out of Illinois.

Migrating enslavers also understood that the indentured servitude laws in
Illinois were at best of dubious legality; the Illinois legislature all but admitted that they were. In 1817, several members of the Illinois territorial assembly sought to repeal the laws that permitted emigrating enslavers to convert
enslaved chattel into long-term servants. Enslaver William Bradsby, the main
supporter of the repeal, charged that Illinois lawmakers knew the law was
a "legal deception which had been practiced upon emigrants" to Illinois.
Bradsby also admitted that "the law is unconstitutional." The conditions under
which indentures were signed amounted to "a species of legal coercion" that
acted "to destroy the voluntary nature of the contract." Bradsby fully expected
that emancipation "must necessarily result from the operation of this cob
web of legislation." Soon enough, either Congress or a future state legislature would nullify the clearly unconstitutional indentures. The speaker of the
Illinois House lamely defended retaining the indenturing laws, but admitted
that Article VI likely rendered them "unconstitutional." He also defended the
indenturing laws on the grounds that repeal would "injure" those "who have
emigrated to the territory under a belief that the law was a good, or constitutional one," even if it clearly was not.[71] The entirety of the Illinois territorial
government understood that Illinois's indenturing laws were temporary, expedient, ad hoc, risky, and largely ineffective evasions of Article VI.

The very authors of the indentured servant laws understood their limits.
Indiana Governor William Henry Harrison helped write the law creating
indentured servitude in Illinois in 1802 and 1803. In 1807, he expressed dismay
to an agent in Kentucky who had purchased an enslaved girl named Molly for
Harrison. Frederick Ridgeley failed to provide Harrison with the details of
Molly's sale and indenturing, leaving her status uncertain. Even if Harrison
could indenture Molly, he feared that her value had declined precipitously,

because "No person in Kenty. will buy an indented servant" who had spent time in Indiana or Illinois.[72] Harrison understood that indenturing an enslaved person substantially lowered their market value, always a foremost consideration of enslavers. Like Harrison, prominent enslaver Robert Morrison understood that indentured servitude laws did not amount to a viable system of slavery. Thus, in 1812 he expressed his preference for "purchasing one that will be considered a slave under the law of the Territory," rather than one bound only by indentured servitude.[73] Illinois enslavers converted the statuses of the people they enslaved into something that roughly conformed with imperial decrees. And while Illinois enslavers certainly wished to gain congressional sanction for slavery in Illinois, they understood that the systems of servitude they created did little more than permit them to hold in slavery the people whom they already enslaved. They also understood that their laws and practices invited future challenges and that the indentures had little force outside of the jurisdictions where they exercised influence and power.

The efficacy of the servitude laws diminished when the legality of these forms of bondage had to be determined by people who had no direct interest in them. In 1803, fur trader Thomas Forsythe purchased an enslaved man named Jeffrey Nash in Detroit. The following year, Nash used his mark to sign an indenture for seven years.[74] By 1808, Forsythe was using Jeffrey's unrequited labors at his farm in Peoria, at the head of the Illinois River. Nash spoke "good French and English, and tolerably good Indian Potawatomie," exactly the kinds of language skills that would facilitate flight, even if he suffered "a halt in his walk." In late 1808, Jeffrey fled, and his enslaver suspected that he "stayed some months at Cahokia."[75] Nash then made his way to New Orleans, where Forsythe's agents tracked him down in 1813. Nash managed to somehow or another get his case heard before a local court and, ultimately, the Louisiana Supreme Court. The Louisiana Supreme Court ruled that Jeffrey's lifetime residence in Indiana, Illinois, and Michigan made him free, because in those territories, "*slavery does not exist*; that it is *forbidden by law*." The court further ruled that Forsythe held Nash under "*de facto*, though not *de jure*" slavery or servitude, and Nash should go free because "tho' purchased as a slave," he was purchased "in a country, which slavery is not tolerated."[76]

Beginning in the late 1810s, scores of enslaved men and women from Illinois who had been removed to Missouri began filing freedom suits based on their residency in Illinois. The majority of the 239 enslaved individuals who sued for their freedom in Missouri courts did so on this basis.[77] In 1819, enslaved woman Milly filed a freedom suit against her enslaver, Mathias Rose.

Rose migrated from Kentucky to Illinois around 1805, indenting child Eliza for seventy years. In 1817, Mathias removed Eliza to Missouri. Two years later, Milly instituted a successful freedom suit on behalf of herself and her children.[78] Numerous other Black people who had their enslavement converted to servitude in Illinois, and were then sold into slavery in Missouri, sued and won their freedom. Husband and wife Labon and Tempe traveled a familiar route from enslavement in the Chesapeake, to enslavement in Kentucky, to servitude in Illinois, to slavery in Missouri. In 1816, Simon Vanorsdale of Cahokia, Illinois, purchased the couple. Vanorsdale indentured Labon for forty years, but "claimed said Labon as his slave and exercised every act of ownership over him." Tempe had been forcibly removed as "a slave, from the state, of Maryland" and indented in Illinois. The following year, Vanorsdale sold Labon and Tempe to St. Louis merchant Risdon Price. Price and Vanorsdale alleged that Tempe and Labon had agreed to serve "the residue of their time" with Rice in St. Louis. Whatever the truth of their agreement, as soon as Labon and Price found themselves in St. Louis, they instituted a freedom suit. A St. Louis jury ruled that the enslavers "had brought" Labon and Tempe "from a slave holding state in to the Northwestern territory of which the state of Illinois was a part," with "an intention to reside" there. As such, the enslaved couple were entitled to their freedom.[79] Lawsuits such as these were easily foreseeable by enslavers, who exercised a keen eye for the many jurisdictional legalities that empowered them to enslave Black people.

The ambiguous status of enslaved people in Illinois meant that few Illinois enslavers purchased enslaved people from Missouri. In 1808, future Illinois Governor Shadrach Bond purchased an enslaved man named Sam from St. Louis widow Elizabeth Harris. St. Louis judge and lawyer John Lucas oversaw the sale; within a month, Bond sold Sam back across the river to Lucas. Bond, a well-connected member of the territorial legislature, decided, with good reason, against using Illinois's servitude laws on enslaved people purchased in Missouri.[80] In the 1810s, the legality of Illinois indentures and enslavement became increasingly suspect in Missouri. In 1815, Missouri enslaver Nicholas Beaugenoux removed enslaved woman Marie from Missouri to Illinois, where "she was detained by and resided with the said Beaugenoux, as his slave in the said Territory of Illinois." The following year, Beaugenoux returned to St. Louis, where he "sold" Marie to Auguste Chouteau. Two years later, as Illinois headed into statehood, Marie filed suit for her freedom and won. St. Louis jurors thought so little of Illinois enslaving laws that they ruled in favor of an enslaved woman against one of St. Louis's most powerful patriarchs.[81] In response to the questionable status of Illinois servitude laws, Missouri enslavers began changing the way they recorded the legal status of the people they enslaved. In 1810, Judge John Lucas purchased enslaved man Kayer, denoting him "as a slave for life."[82] In 1814, Antoine Chenie sold enslaved girl Lucy as "a slave for life, subject to all the incapacities and disabilities of legal slavery," clearly distinguishing her from Illinois servants.[83] When Major William Christy of St. Louis sought to sell enslaved man Davey in New Orleans for continuously "running away," he informed his agent that Davey was a "slave for life," rather than a servant of dubious legal title.[84] Few enslavers on either side of the Mississippi River availed themselves of Illinois's tangle of bondage laws and practices because they understood them to be a series of expedient measures that all but invited freedom suits. Unsurprisingly, when Missouri adopted laws allowing enslaved men and women to petition for their freedom, a significant number of the cases stemmed from enslaved people who claimed their freedom was based on their illegal enslavement in Illinois. Enslaved African Americans in the Middle Mississippi Valley were turning Article VI into a program for personal emancipation whenever circumstances permitted.[85]

No one understood the limits of Illinois's systems of bondage better than the territorial officials who oversaw them. Like so many other federal officials in Illinois and Missouri, Illinois Governor Ninian Edwards was born into the late colonial Chesapeake's gentry, came of age during the political battles between Federalists and Republicans in the 1790s, migrated to Kentucky, became a loyal Jeffersonian, and held a string of increasingly higher offices. In Kentucky, he and other recent enslaver-migrants largely succeeded in replicating the Chesapeake's system of gentry governance bottomed on land speculation and slavery; in 1798 they easily defeated a small movement that tried to limit slavery and land speculation in Kentucky.[86] After rising to Chief Justice of the Kentucky Supreme Court, his cousin, Senator John Pope of Kentucky, secured his appointment as first (and only) governor of the Illinois Territory. He accepted the position reluctantly, preferring an appointment to the Mississippi Territory, where Congress offered full sanction to slavery.[87] Obligated to accept an appointment that family had secured for him, Edwards arrived in Kaskaskia in 1809. Well connected by family and politics to the Democratic-Republican majorities that dominated Congress, Edwards saw no path by which Congress would rescind Article VI and provide imperial sanction for slavery in Illinois, and he never petitioned Congress seeking repeal.

Edwards's doubts about congressional sanction of slavery equaled his qualms about the viability of Illinois's mix of enslaving practices and statutes. Although he was the territory's most powerful official, Edwards quickly determined that bondage in Illinois rested on shaky grounds. Edwards thus sought "most sincerely to be transferred to [Upper] Louisiana as he cannot have benefit in Illinois of his Property in Slaves."[88] The James Madison administration denied Edwards's transfer request, at which point Edwards hit upon a scheme to use and to protect the bulk of his property in enslaved bodies by rotating them between Kentucky and Missouri, with Illinois serving mainly as a transit route for trafficking and temporary work spot. By 1811, Edwards had indented in Illinois at least seven people whom he had enslaved in Kentucky: thirty-five-year-old Anthony; twenty-three-year-old Rose and her eighteen-month-old son, Joseph; fifteen-year-old Marie; forty-year-old Strass; and thirty-six-year-old Charles and thirty-five-year-old Jesse.[89] Edwards indented and transferred these individuals within the thirty-day window required by Illinois's servitude laws. He then immediately hired out the people he indented in Missouri, while retaining title to them in Kentucky as chattel slaves. By hiring enslaved people to Missourians within thirty days of their arrival in Illinois, Edwards exempted them from claims of freedom based on residency in Illinois, thus retaining their status as chattel. In sum, Edwards retained title to enslaved people in Kentucky, held title to the same people as servants in Illinois, and rented them into Missouri as slaves titled in Kentucky. All the while, Edwards availed himself of their labors during their brief residencies in Illinois.

By the summer of 1812, Edwards had hired out "a family of negroes" to Moses Austin. In July 1812, he took out an advertisement in Missouri's newspaper offering to sell five enslaved people he had hired out in Missouri the year before, along with "four very likely young negro men, and several boys."[90] After selling several enslaved people in the summer and fall of 1812, in December he again took out an advertisement offering to sell "several likely young negro men and women."[91] In the first three years of his appointment, Edwards retained at least some individuals as indentured servants in Illinois for his own personal use, but he quickly transferred them to Missouri with an eye toward their future sale. For example, in 1814, Edwards sold a "mulatto slave boy named Wallace" to Theodore Hunt in St. Louis. Wallace, however, was already "in possession of" a Mr. Harry "of Ste. Genevieve," and by all appearances Edwards never held Wallace in Illinois beyond thirty days.[92] Edwards also hired out and then sold a "Mulatto Boy" and "Clara,

a Black woman," to George Sibley in November 1816. Again, by all appearances, Edwards ensured that neither Clara nor the unnamed boy spent more
than thirty days in Illinois.[93] In the 1818 Illinois census, Edwards was listed
as holding four African Americans in either slavery or servitude in Illinois.[94]
But by 1816, Edwards had sold or hired out a large majority of the people he
once enslaved in Kentucky across the river to Missouri, with Illinois serving
mainly as a temporary transit route. Edwards would remain a strong advocate
of legalizing slavery in Illinois, especially during the 1818 and 1824 constitution convention campaigns. Yet, when it came to his own personal finances,
prudence dictated that Edwards sell or hire out the people he enslaved to
Missouri rather than risk losing them in Illinois. By the 1810s, Article VI
served to deter enslavers from seeking to permanently enslave individuals in
Illinois, while facilitating the trafficking of enslaved people to Missouri.

Like Edwards, Judge Alexander Stuart grew wary of the viability of Illinois's systems of bondage. Like so many other federal officials in Illinois,
Stuart hailed from a family of Virginia enslavers. In 1809, President James
Madison appointed him to the newly created Illinois Territory as a judge,
one of three officials who made laws for the territory in consultation with the
governor.[95] Stuart flinched at the prospects for enslavers such as himself in
Illinois, even though he was one of four federal officials in charge of the laws
of the territory and one of three judges who heard court cases. Stuart left several enslaved people in Virginia, but, once settled in Illinois, he indented at
least eight African Americans from Virginia, including enslaved men Adam
and Ben, enslaved women Paige and Lucy, and enslaved children Billy, Scylla,
and William.[96] Facing financial difficulties, in 1812 Stuart advertised for sale in
Missouri "two indented negro women, and one girl slave, about fifteen years
old."[97] No buyers from Missouri expressed interest in purchasing an Illinois
servant, so Stuart sold or transferred ownership over four indented individuals to another territorial official, Shadrach Bond.[98] Around the same time,
he also sent his two children back to Virginia with an unspecified number of
"family slaves." In Virginia, he and his children used a legislative act to reassert
the Stuart family's claims over the enslaved/indentured people they had shut-
tled back and forth between Virginia and Illinois.[99] Stuart found himself in
desperate financial straits the following year, and he directly blamed Illinois's
indentured servitude laws. "In consequence of the misfortunes of a brother,
sister, and my wife's sister," his "annual expense will be so increased" that he
could no longer afford to remain in Illinois. Stuart bluntly stated his reasons
for seeking a transfer: "If I go to Missouri I can take my slaves with me."[100]

Stuart, one of three judges empowered to adopt and enforce laws for the Illinois Territory, had little faith in the efficacy of Illinois's system of bondage. The following year, Stuart secured his transfer to Missouri.

Other enslavers followed Stuart's lead. William Rabb arrived in the settlements outside of Cahokia around 1804. Like other enslavers, Rabb served as a county judge and a territorial official, positions that granted him the kind of local power needed to keep enslaved people in slavery. In 1812, Rabb purchased enslaved man Cupid from enslaver Antoine Chenie, separating Cupid from his pregnant wife, Catherine, and their two children. On at least two occasions, Catherine ran away with her children, with enslavers suspecting she was meeting with her husband. Shortly after, Rabb indentured Cupid for a term of twelve years. Cupid and Catherine fled yet again, disappearing from the historical record. The fates of Cupid, Catherine, and their children are unknown, but Rabb had grown weary of Illinois. In 1818 he moved to the Missouri Territory, became fast friends with enslaver Moses Austin, and served as one of the "Old 300," the cofounders of Austin's enslavers' colony in Tejas. He arrived in Tejas with at least one enslaved person.[101]

While Stuart and Rabb moved to Missouri, and Cupid and Catherine fled their bondage, other Illinois enslavers continued to sell enslaved men and women from Illinois to Missouri. Around 1809, Missouri-based merchant James Callaway sought "to collect" on debts for "pork, whiskey," and "tobacco" he had sold to habitant enslavers Marie Comparie and his wife in Cahokia. To settle the debt, Comparie agreed to transfer ownership of enslaved man Moses, a French Negro, to Callaway. However, the sale became contested after Pierre Chouteau met with the Comparies. After consulting with Chouteau, the Comparies decided to seek the return of the enslaved man. The Comparies cried fraud, accusing Callaway of swindling them with a bill of sale in English rather than French. But Madame Comparie inadvertently revealed the truth in a deposition. The Comparies had willingly transferred Moses to Callaway, but Pierre Chouteau had offered the habitants a better deal: "Pierre Chateau had promised them," Madame Comparie testified, "that in case he recovered the negro in dispute from Callaway," Chouteau "would let the Comparies have the use of the negro during" the remainder of their lives in Cahokia. Chouteau, however, would hold title to enslaved man Moses in Missouri, shielding ownership of him from any changes in Illinois law. Whatever the true facts of the case, one more enslaved man from Illinois made his way to Missouri due to Article VI. "In 1802 or 1803," the Comparies had made a similar deal with William Laramie who "bought a man of them" and then transferred ownership across the river to Missouri while the Comparies continued to use the man's labors.[102] Elderly Illinois habitant enslavers financed their later years by selling enslaved men and women across the river, either directly or through some kind of warped reverse-mortgage scheme. Article VI diminished the number of enslaved people in Illinois by encouraging enslavers to sell the people they enslaved to Missourians. Meanwhile, Article VI served as something like a gradual abolition statute, with enslaved African Americans paying the price for gradually eliminating slavery in Illinois by being transferred to Missouri.

While some Illinois enslavers sold the people they enslaved into Missouri, others dragged out bondage in Illinois for as long as possible. Nathaniel Pope served as a territorial delegate to Congress, a land registrar, and then a federal judge from 1819 until 1850. He held at minimum a man named Felix and his mother in servitude until at least 1827. Pope also routinely "sent" Felix to other prominent men, such as Senator Jesse Thomas, forcing Alex to split his time between Kaskaskia and Edwardsville.[103] When William Morrison died in 1837, he bequeathed to his wife "all the personal property [he] may own," including "slaves and servants, indentured and Register'd."[104] In 1816, enslaver Hezekiah Davis forced "a certain Negro girl named Jane aged sixteen years old" to indenture herself to Davis "for the term of fifty years." The following year, Davis sold Jane to another enslaver for $400; five years later, in 1822, Jane was sold again. In the course of four years, teenager Jane had been passed between three different enslavers and faced, what was for all intents and purposes, a lifetime of slavery.[105] The prolonged terms of indenture could be especially cruel. William Drury or his family had enslaved people in Illinois since at least 1801, when he signed a petition calling on Congress to rescind Article VI. In 1827, Drury drew up a contract transferring his ownership of Mary to Pierre Menard and Jean Baptiste Vallé, the two most wealthy potentates in Kaskaskia and Ste. Geneviève. In the contract, Drury stipulated that Mary "shall be Free and at Liberty to contract or be contracted" as "any free person may do" whenever "she shall pay to me the sum of seventy eight dollars." A month later, Drury "rec'd of Mary a woman of Colour" $78, "by the hands of Menard & Vallé," at which point Mary became free and then entered servitude with Menard and Vallé, who would presumably use her unrequited labors in their business operations in Kaskaskia. The terms of the agreements and transfers suggest that Drury used Mary to settle a debt of $78 to Menard and Vallé, while the papers made it seem that Mary had become free and then chose to indent herself to Menard and Vallé. Bondage in Illinois was as cruel as it was capricious.[106]

Enslavers such as Menard, Vallé, and Pope wrangled whatever labor they could out of the people they held in bondage. At the same time, Illinois enslavement more broadly entered a state of stagnation and decline in the 1800s, not because of active antislavery intervention but because of Congress's passive denial of imperial state sanction to enslavers. By default as much as by design, Article VI created effects like the gradual emancipation laws passed in states such as New Jersey and New York. In both places, enslavers abused the terms of emancipation for their own benefit. Some enslaved people in the Atlantic states managed to secure their freedom rather quickly by fleeing or by navigating their state's legal system and securing assistance from abolition societies. Likewise, some enslaved people in Illinois managed to gain their freedom, especially in the years surrounding statehood.[107] Other enslaved people in Atlantic states, however, faced a different fate. When gradual emancipation laws greatly reduced the value of the people they enslaved, New Jersey and New York enslavers frequently sold them out of state.[108] In other cases, enslavers dragged out the terms of enslavement for people due their freedom under gradual emancipation laws. With the prospect of Article VI enforcement always threatening to upend the "cob web of legislation," some Illinois enslavers cashed in by selling enslaved people into permanent Missouri slavery. Still other enslaved men and women found themselves trapped in various states of servitude that enslavers would draw out into the 1840s. Illinois enslavers squeezed every drop of labor and money they could out of the people they enslaved.

The complex imperial and colonial histories of Illinois enslavement made it both evanescent and invidious. As had happened whenever states passed gradual emancipation laws, enslaved Black people paid the price for gradual abolition in Illinois, as their enslavers either fled or sold them into jurisdictions where slavery remained fully legal and sanctioned by an imperial state. At the same time, Illinois enslavers made Illinois enslavement invidious by creating for themselves a series of enslaving enclaves where they remained among the most prominent citizens, officeholders, merchants, and commercial agriculturalists. Meanwhile, the imperial decree of Article VI kept most migrating enslavers out of Illinois, while encouraging those already there to move elsewhere, thus making Illinois slavery evanescent. Finally, whenever enslaved people could create circumstances favorable to freedom, they did so. The fates of enslaved Illinoisans were as multifaceted as Illinois's history of empire and enslavement.

While Illinois enslavers wrung every last drop of unrequired toil from the people they enslaved, by the 1810s whites on both sides of the Mississippi River—and across the Union—understood that Illinois and Missouri had become categorically different from one another. As the number of enslavers in Illinois remained sufficiently low, a burgeoning antislavery movement appeared in the early 1810s. Mimicking the popular antislavery movements that kept slavery out of Ohio and Indiana when those territories moved toward statehood, these antislavery colonizers railed against enslavers and speculators. In the 1812 campaign for territorial delegate, Andey Kinney, the leader of a group of northern settler-colonizers, requested that John Messinger run for territorial delegate on a platform stressing his opposition to "the great Men about Kaskaskia" and "his zeal against slavery coming into the Territory." Kinney struck on the two themes that would appeal to northern families: opposition to both slavery and land speculators. "If you would Publish that you was pointedly against Slavery and likewise that you would do what you could for the people that is Settled on Congress land," then "it would draw the attention of the people very Much."[109] Messinger declined to run, but Kinney and Messinger continued working against slavery in the territory and state, culminating in the 1824 campaign to kill efforts to hold a state constitutional convention to legalize slavery in Illinois.[110]

The effects of Article VI allowed antislavery colonizers like Messinger and Kinney to expand their movement. By 1812, Illinois's population had climbed to approximately twelve thousand non-Indigenous inhabitants. Illinois's population increased rapidly after the War of 1812, especially after the federal government dispossessed Indigenous Illinoisians and then began surveying and selling bounty and public lands. As Illinois speculators anticipated a great onslaught of colonizers from the East in the aftermath of the War of 1812, they increasingly focused on attracting emigrants who were not enslavers, touting the availability of prime, cheap land in the American Bottom, extolling the commercial value of their landholdings for mills and towns, and steadfastly avoiding mention of slavery and servitude.[111] Illinois public land sales overwhelmingly attracted colonizers opposed to slavery. Newspaper accounts and emigrant guides delineated the differences between Missouri and Illinois, almost always noting that "slavery is not admitted" in Illinois.[112] Illinois in turn drew "Yankees in quest of fortune."[113]

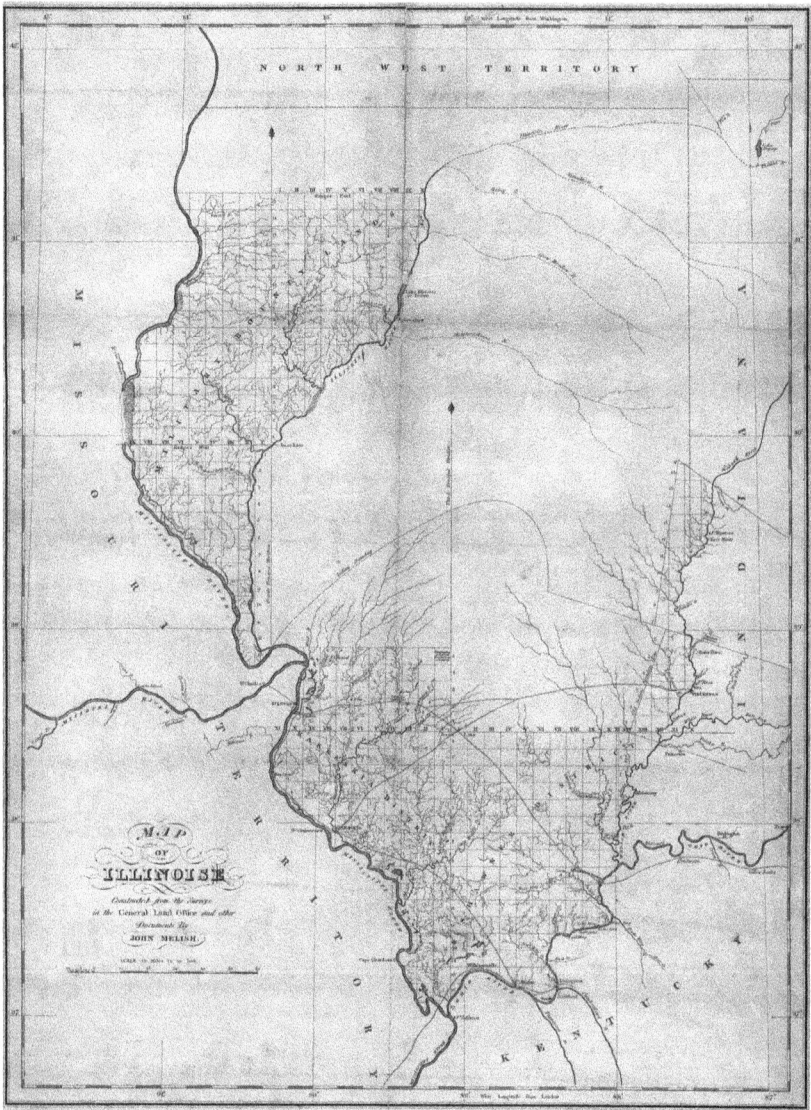

Figure 3. "Map of Illinoise . . . John Melish," 1818, G4100 1818.M4, Geography and Map Division, Library of Congress.

After 1815, the population of nonenslaving colonizers increased rapidly, and a new group of antislavery politicians created and then tapped into antislavery sentiments. Daniel P. Cook, nephew of Nathaniel Pope, took a decidedly antislavery turn as he entered into Illinois politics in 1817. Cook set up Illinois's first newspaper, threw open its pages to antislavery writers, and contributed his own antislavery pieces.[114] In November 1817, the territorial assembly and council voted "to repeal the law authorizing the introduction of negroes and mulattoes into this Territory."[115] The repeal bill admitted that the purpose of indentured servitude in Illinois was "to introduce, and tolerate slavery under pretence of voluntary servitude, in contravention, of the paramount law of the land," the Northwest Ordinance. The bill passed the territorial legislature, indicating growing popular opposition to slavery, but Governor Ninian Edwards blocked it.[116] As Illinois moved toward choosing delegates for its constitutional convention set for July 1818, a coordinated antislavery movement coalesced. Antislavery writers published numerous pieces attacking enslavers. One piece celebrated that "our future population will be principally from the northern states, and avowed enemies of slavery." Meanwhile, "the wealthy southern planter, will not part with the plantation Gods, which he worships, starves, and whips, for the blessings of the western woods" in Illinois. Antislavery writers extolled antislavery colonizers who would soon flock to Illinois while forecasting that enslavers would go elsewhere. As Illinois held elections to choose delegates for the state constitutional convention, the emerging antislavery faction celebrated that it had become "doubtful at this time a majority could be had in favor of the barter of human flesh."[117]

Antislavery articles begat meetings, caucuses, and canvassing. George Churchill had migrated from Vermont to New York to St. Louis after the War of 1812. After finding slavery too entrenched in Missouri, he settled outside of Edwardsville. He promptly and loudly came out "in favor of elections by ballot" and against slavery, publishing articles on both.[118] The elections for the constitutional convention were scheduled for the first week of July 1818, and Churchill and his allies spent much of June canvassing farmers in and between Edwardsville and Alton, a region outside of the personal influence of enslaving potentates like William Morrison. They also held meetings, where they "offered resolutions against slavery"; formed "a committee of correspondence" for local antislavery canvassers; published their antislavery "proceedings"; and pressed candidates to declare their opposition to slavery.[119] On the election days, Churchill visited voters, paying one man "a dime to go to the elections" and arranging transportation for another farmer who "could not go for want of a horse." At the polls, the antislavery men fought off "several bullies" trying to intimidate them for circulating "damned Yankee hand bills" that were "warm" on the slavery question.[120] In the interlude between the elections and the constitutional convention, they called for "the *grand object of universal emancipation*" to be included in the state constitution.[121]

News from Washington bolstered those opposed to slavery. Former Kentucky Congressman Matthew Lyon fired off a hasty letter to his son-in-law John Messinger, who was serving as a member of the Illinois state constitutional convention. Lyon warned that slavery created considerable opposition to Illinois statehood in Washington. The proposed state constitution would either "make you the 21st State in the Union" or push off statehood to "a distance how far off is to the wisest of us uncertain." The issue was stark and unambiguous. Lyon was "alarmed least your Convention[,] under the expectation of bringing Congress to terms on the subject of Slavery[,] will reject the offer of immediately becoming a State. Such a course would be unwise as there is not the least probability that Congress will ever comply." The Middle Atlantic and New England states "have long been unanimous on this subject." The "four Senators from Ohio & Indiana are added to this force." Furthermore, more than a few politicians from "Virginia & Kentucky" supported continuation of Article VI, which provided them with a painless antislavery laurel to deflect mounting criticisms of slavery's entrenchment in their own states and its rapid growth elsewhere. Lyon cautioned that the convention had to accept statehood without slavery. Otherwise, Congress would reject statehood, and "it may be ten years before you get another Offer."[122]

Opposition to Illinois statehood with slavery ran deep in Washington in 1818. On the same day that Congress initiated procedures to advance Illinois to statehood, New Hampshire Representative Arthur Livermore proposed a constitutional amendment that held that "No person shall be held to service or labor as a slave, nor shall slavery be tolerated in any State hereafter admitted into the Union, or made one of the United States of America."[123] Opposition also appeared in the Senate. Territorial delegate Nathaniel Pope wrote an extensive letter to New York Senator Rufus King where Pope erased both slavery and Black people from Illinois. Pope addressed headlong the congressional anti-Illinois faction's plan to deny Illinois statehood on the basis of its small population and its continuing flirtations with legalizing slavery. Pope detailed the populations of previous states upon admission to statehood, noting that at the "last session" Mississippi was admitted "with 25,000 Whites & 20,000 Blacks." Pope nonetheless contended that "the population of Illinois is White." Pope also went on to extol the extensive, progressive plans of post-statehood Illinois, "unlike Colonial Governments admitting slavery."[124] With that, Pope erased both slavery and the 1,200 Black people held in various states of bondage in Illinois. Pope, of course knew, better; he was, after all, himself an enslaver. But Pope also understood that if Illinois was going to gain statehood, the constitutional convention would have to minimize the appearance of slavery and withhold efforts to legalize it in the state constitution.

Illinois enslavers perfectly understood the warnings of Lyon and the expectations of northern white imperialists in Congress. Though challenged by antislavery forces, they retained a narrow majority in the constitutional convention. They drafted a state constitution that preserved the status quo with regards to slavery and bondage, fighting off efforts to eliminate future indentures altogether. The language of the clauses regarding bondage were couched to appease the growing antislavery contingent in Congress, but remained indeterminant enough to permit the continuation of various forms of bondage. An initial draft of the constitution provided that "there shall be neither slavery nor involuntary servitude in this state," which would have incorporated Article VI directly into the constitution while providing those still in slavery a route to emancipation. Enslavers fought to change the language of the clause. By a vote of 17 to 14, they successfully added the caveat that "Neither slavery or involuntary servitude *shall hereafter be introduced into this state.*" Without saying so, Illinois enslavers had inserted a clause that perpetuated the slavery of French Negroes and their descendants while cutting off lawsuits by indentured servants. The constitution also permitted the use of enslaved men and women at the salt marshes for one-year terms until 1825. Antislavery advocates successfully added a clause providing for the freedom of children born to indentured mothers at the age of majority.[125] Overall, the Illinois constitution of 1818 changed little. Illinois slavery would remain both invidious and evanescent.

Pro- and antislavery factions in Illinois could make their own histories; neither, however, could make it on their own terms, thanks to the structural effects of the Northwest Ordinance and the lingering, postcolonial legacies of French, British, and Virginian slavery. The power of enslaver-speculators in Illinois ran deep, and they managed to stave off efforts to abolish existing forms of slavery and servitude in Illinois. But facing pressure from Congress, voters, and convention delegates, they dropped efforts to expand their systems of bondage and focused on preserving what they already had in place.

Proslavery factions retained their claims over the lives and labors of French Negroes and created constitutional protections for the indentures they forced onto enslaved people. Antislavery forces fought off an attempt to repeal Article VI entirely, limited future indentures, and constitutionally mandated emancipation for the children of indentured men and women. The Illinois factions had battled to something like a draw; a Massachusetts newspaper categorized the Illinois constitution by noting that "Slavery though not absolutely rejected, is within limited periods."[126]

The Illinois constitution of 1818 was hardly a victory for either the enslaver-speculators who had spent the previous two decades seeking to overturn Article VI, or the 1,200 Black people who remained in bondage. Enslavers protected the systems of bondage they had already created, and they held open the slim possibility that they might be able to amend the state constitution in the future to sanction slavery fully. Their victory was less than total, however. Even as the constitutional convention was meeting, antislavery politician Daniel P. Cook traveled across Illinois delivering speeches that "excited warm opposition from slavemen, but still warmer support from freemen."[127] Freemen found much to celebrate in the constitution. As Churchill, one of the most committed foes of Illinois slavery, concluded, "Slavery is so far excluded, that hardly any slaveholder will think of settling here, especially while the Missouri Territory offers them so many advantages." "Let us have a few more of the right sort of people," he added, "and we shall be soon able to expel the little remnant of slavery which the Convention have left among us."[128] It was easy to overstate the efficacy of bans on slavery and to understate the difficulties of eradicating such an invidious institution. Nonetheless, committed antislavery voter-politicians in Illinois could herald the constitution for how it portended slavery's ultimate demise, even if they could not foresee how a few enslavers would hold onto slavery in Illinois for another three decades.

Historians' best estimates are that at any given time between 1800 and 1820, enslavers held no more than 1,200 African Americans in some kind of servitude in Illinois.[129] The 1800 federal census of Illinois counted 107 persons held in bondage out of a total white and Black population of approximately 3,100 individuals, or approximately 3 percent of the non-Indigenous population.[130] The 1810 census counted 129 persons held in slavery and another 500 African Americans held in some kind of servitude out of over approximately 12,300 Black and white residents. Combined, enslaved and indentured African

Americans accounted for approximately 5 percent of the population.[131] At statehood in 1818, there were at most 1,200 persons held in some state of bondage among a population around 35,000, or about 3 percent of the population.[132] Whatever the real figures, the population of African Americans held in various states of bondage in U.S. Illinois never approached 10 percent after the 1780s. By 1810, Illinois resembled northern states undergoing processes of gradual abolition such as Pennsylvania and Connecticut, rather than states and territories where enslavers enjoyed full imperial sanction, as in Missouri and Kentucky.[133]

In contrast to Illinois, in 1810 census takers counted 2,875 enslaved persons in Missouri out of an overall non-Indigenous population of approximately 20,000. In 1810, enslaved people accounted for approximately 15 percent of Missouri's population. In the older and more densely colonized parts of Missouri, this amount ranged between 20 percent and 30 percent.[134] When Missouri applied for statehood in 1819, Missouri enslavers held approximately 12,000 individuals in slavery out of a total Black and white population of 60,000. At statehood, approximately 20 percent of Missouri's population was Black and enslaved. From the 1760s through the 1790s, and then again in the 1800s and 1810s, slavery mattered in Missouri in ways that it did not in Illinois. Imperial policies and the deployment of state power mattered. Since the 1760s, successive imperial regimes in Upper Louisiana and Missouri systematically sanctioned slavery and empowered enslavers. In Illinois, successive imperial powers ignored enslavers, even when they sanctioned slavery. Systems of slavery were the creatures of empire. Enslavers followed imperial state power. With imperial support, enslavers flourished; without imperial sanction, slavery languished. Article VI mattered, not as an active, antislavery measure, but through the passive denial of imperial state sanction to enslavers.

Ultimately, African American enslavement in Illinois dissipated in much the same way, and on much the same timeframe, in which Native American slavery faded in Upper Louisiana. Sixty-five years lapsed between the 1769 Spanish decree prohibiting Native American enslavement in Upper Louisiana and a favorable ruling issued to Marguerite and Celeste in an 1834 Missouri Supreme Court ruling that legally ended Native American enslavement in Missouri.[135] In Illinois, sixty-odd years passed between the 1787 issuance of the Northwest Ordinance and a series of court rulings and a new Illinois state constitution in the late 1840s that ended any legal justifications for enslavement in Illinois.[136]

Neither of these rulings produced immediate emancipation; imperial decrees and state supreme court decisions were never self-enforcing, especially when enslavers themselves were in charge of enforcement. Instead, Native American enslavement and Illinois enslavement died out when enslaved people themselves passed on, when they were sold into less scrupulous jurisdictions, or when they legally fought their way out of bondage. The judicial and constitutional abolition of slavery in 1845 and 1848 simply confirmed what had already happened in Illinois over the previous half-century; slavery was eliminated from Illinois by eliminating enslaved people—through death, sale, or removal—far more than it was abolished or by emancipating Black people. Nonetheless, slavery could be eliminated in Illinois because an imperial decree and the passive denial of state power drove the streams of migrating enslavers away from Illinois and toward Missouri and Kentucky from the 1790s through the 1810s, while encouraging Illinois enslavers to sell enslaved people or to migrate elsewhere.

In April 1818, Congress began the process of admitting Illinois to statehood. In January 1819, it would do the same for Missouri. Fifty years earlier, the two banks of the Middle Mississippi River had been united by enslavers but divided between Spain and Britain. Slavery united what empires divided. Over the next three decades, the decline or denial of imperial state power in Illinois resulted in both the dismantling of the systems of slavery once prevalent on the east bank and their reconstruction on the west bank under the protection of the Spanish regime in Upper Louisiana. The Louisiana Purchase reunited the two sides of the river into "this grand valley of our empire."[137] Despite the efforts of enslavers and U.S. imperial agents in Illinois, migrating enslavers preferred to colonize territories where imperial state power directly sanctioned them. As a result, at statehood, Missouri counted ten times as many enslaved people as Illinois. By the end of the 1810s, slavery divided what an empire united. Those divisions would become magnified as imperialists in Congress and across the eastern states debated what each saw as the proper relationship between empire and enslavement in the trans-Mississippi West.

The Middle Mississippi Valley Crisis
and the Future of Empire
and Enslavement, 1818–1820

In November 1818, Congress took up the Illinois statehood bill, where it helped create a maelstrom of debates over what kind of empire the United States would forge on the North American continent. The debates and conflicts that roiled Congress from 1815 through the Missouri Crisis were a long time coming; their indeterminate resolutions would shape the course of empire on the North American continent straight through to the U.S. Civil War. The Seven Years' War led to the U.S. War for Independence, which was an internal civil war over the direction of the British empire in North America as much as it was a colonial independence movement. In claiming the core of Britain's eighteenth-century North American empire in the 1780s, the United States entered into a decades-long conflict with shifting peoples, polities, alliances, and imperial powers, all of whom contended for sovereignty, supremacy, and dominion over the peoples and places of the North American continent. Indigenous nations and confederacies, settler-colonialist polities, sections and regions, Britain, France, Spain, and the United States all sought to shape imperial conflicts in their favor from the 1780s through 1815. In 1815, the United States emerged as the dominant imperial power on the North American continent because its proto-fiscal military state allowed it to deploy imperial state power more effectively than competing European powers, all of whom spent the first quarter of a century of the U.S. federal government's existence consumed by the wars of the French Revolution.[1] From the 1720s through 1815, imperial wars, conflicts, and struggles had shaped the course of empire and enslavement in Illinois and Missouri. After the United

States emerged as the dominant imperial power in 1815, the imperial and local politics of slavery turned inward. Illinois and Missouri statehood would in turn influence conflicts centering on empire, enslavement, and emancipation from the 1820s straight through to 1860.

Much of the business of Congress, the presidency, and the peoples and institutions of the U.S. state after 1815 was consumed by empire: whether scoping out new imperial borders, dispossessing Indigenous people from their lands, or consolidating U.S. sovereignty in once-contested borderlands. Between 1815 and 1818, six western states either obtained statehood or were on the verge of doing so. Southern enslavers laid claim to Florida and insisted that Texas should have been included in the Louisiana Purchase. Meanwhile, Secretary of State John Quincy Adams was concluding negotiations with Britain that would extend U.S. imperial claims to the Pacific. When not consumed by imperial matters, the institutions and infrastructure of the imperial U.S. state frequently found themselves confronting issues related to slavery, including southern enslaver efforts to pass a more aggressive fugitive slave law and northern efforts to regulate the growing domestic slave trade. Often, empire and enslavement became entangled, whether with the illegal international slave trade through Amelia Island, off the Florida-Georgia coast, or Andrew Jackson's invasion of Florida to eradicate "The Negro Fort."[2]

The growing ranks of northern antislavery imperialists had their own agenda. After 1815, northern whites and Blacks took more aggressive stances against slavery and enslavers, especially as the great expansion of slavery into the southern interior laid bare the horrors of slavery and the slave trade to politicians in Washington, D.C., and readers of northern newspapers. At the same time, by the 1810s, gradual abolition laws in the Atlantic states were starting to produce significant effects. After 1815, white and Black abolitionists accelerated these laws, expediting emancipation even as some enslaved men and women remained trapped in slavery. Eastern congressmen like James Tallmadge of New York began considering ways to apply northern gradual abolition laws to the trans-Appalachian and trans-Mississippi West. Joining him were scores of newly elected northern Republicans with no partisan or personal ties to the enslavers who had dominated the Democratic-Republican coalition since 1800. In April 1818, first-term New Hampshire Representative Arthur Livermore proposed a constitutional amendment that held that "No person shall be held to service or labor as a slave, nor shall slavery be tolerated in any State hereafter admitted into the Union, or made one of the United States of America."[3] In New England, at least four newspapers headed Livermore's proposal with the tag *"Abolition of Slavery."*[4] Congress immediately shot down the proposal, but questions regarding empire and enslavement would not go away so easily.

As one of its first orders of business in its second session, the fifteenth Congress took up Illinois statehood. After calling the bill for a first and second reading, the House adjourned on a Friday. All indications suggested that the majority of the House planned to quickly pass Illinois statehood as their first order of business on Monday, seat Illinois's waiting congressmen and senators, and then move on to other issues.[5] Over the weekend, however, Tallmadge actually read the proposed Illinois constitution and apparently investigated the constitutions of Ohio and Indiana, along with the history of the Northwest Ordinance. He immediately challenged Illinois statehood when the House returned to the matter on Monday, catching the House off-guard on what most expected to be a pro forma, third reading of the statehood bill followed by a vote.

Tallmadge seemed genuinely shocked that Illinois's constitution not only recognized slavery and servitude, but also seemed to protect and prolong it. Like most people in the United States outside of Illinois, Missouri, and Kentucky, Tallmadge had never given much thought to the status of slavery in Illinois, as he simply presumed that Article VI had already banned it, an impression that would have been confirmed by the scores of colonizer guides and booster accounts that proliferated after 1815. Tallmadge's reading of the proposed Illinois constitution suggested something nefarious was afoot. Tallmadge noted that "the sixth article of the ordinance" clearly and unequivocally prohibited slavery. For Tallmadge, the mere presence of slavery and servitude "in that instrument" were "sufficient to render the whole inadmissible." Tallmadge also objected "upon the ground that the constitution was not sufficiently conclusive in the rejection of slavery." The Indiana constitution of 1816 prohibited any further indentures of out-of-state enslaved African Americans and included a clause prohibiting any future amendment permitting slavery in the state. Tallmadge thus demanded that Illinois eliminate the use of enslaved labor at the salt marshes, halt any further indentures, and add a clause sanctifying the Article VI exclusion of slavery. For good measure, Tallmadge added that he "hoped that we would no longer leave it in the power of the world to say that while we held the torch of freedom in one hand, we brandished the slave-driver's whip in the other."[6]

Three congressmen, all Virginia natives, deflected Tallmadge's objections. Mississippi Representative George Poindexter answered Tallmadge's

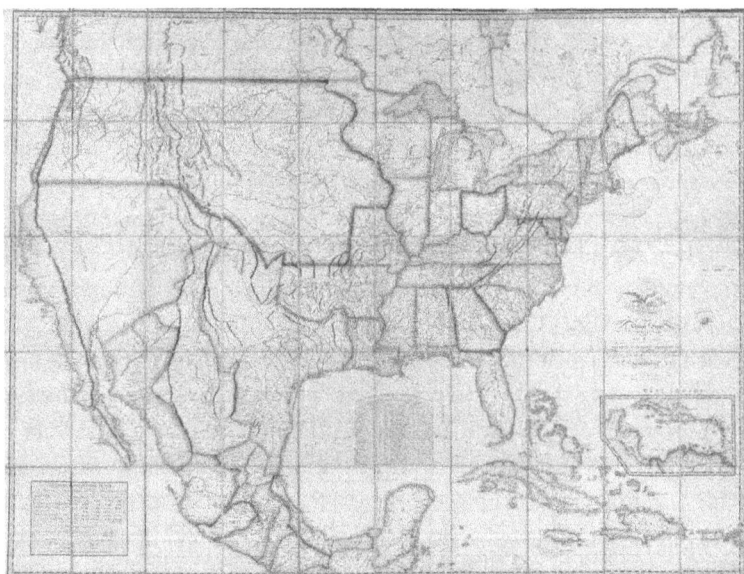

Figures 4 and 5. John Melish's widely reprinted 1816 and 1820 maps of North America portrayed the United States as a transcontinental empire and union. John Quincy Adams used Melish's 1816 map, shown in Figure 4, in negotiations with Spanish and British officials over the western boundaries of the United States and Spanish Mexico. Melish's 1820 map, shown in Figure 5, includes Missouri and extended U.S. borders to the Pacific. John Melish, "Map of the United States of America: With the Contiguous British and Spanish Possessions," 1816, G3700 1816.M4; John Melish, "Map of the United States of America: With the Contiguous British and Spanish Possessions," 1820, G3700 1820.M4e2, Geography and Map Division, Library of Congress.

objections by turning the Illinois constitution into an instrument of eman-cipation. The clauses concerning slavery and servitude "would be attended with the most beneficial consequences," according to Poindexter. By requir-ing the registration of servants and their children, it protected them from kidnapping and sale into states where slavery was fully legal (a crime where Poindexter identified the purchaser of stolen chattel as the victim). The constitution also provided for the emancipation of individuals held by ser-vitude contracts, along with their children. Rather than protecting slavery, Poindexter contended that the constitution provided the means for ridding Illinois of the remnants of slavery that stemmed from its long colonial past while simultaneously protecting the interests of Illinois enslavers. William Henry Harrison, now serving as a representative from Ohio, asserted that the Northwest Ordinance was no longer binding on Illinois as it transitioned to statehood, anticipating arguments that white Missourians and southern enslavers would make in a few months. Richard Clough Anderson of Ken-tucky, a member of the extended Clark family who was heavily involved in land speculation in Illinois and Missouri, went further than Harrison. Anderson pointed out that "slaves were in that territory" at the passage of the Northwest Ordinance. Echoing Illinois enslaver-speculators, Anderson claimed that Article VI amounted to an ex post facto law and violation of the Virginia Treaty of Cession. For good measure, Anderson added that "serious doubts had arisen" concerning "whether Congress had a right to prescribe any condition respecting slavery" in Illinois.[7]

Tallmadge made little headway, and southern enslavers seemed to be on the verge of challenging the constitutionality of Article VI entirely. Many members of the House seemed eager to dispense with the matter, and no one else rose to speak about the issue. Congress promptly admitted Illinois by a vote of 117 to 34.[8] The practices of empire and enslavement in Illinois had changed little over the previous two decades, while the scope of slavery and servitude shrank among Illinois's growing free population. Furthermore, friendly southern congressmen lauded the constitution as providing for grad-ual emancipation of servants and the eventual elimination of servitude in the new state. An Illinois Crisis did not precede the Missouri Crisis because enough northern representatives construed the Illinois constitution to have abided by the spirit of Article VI, if not the letter. That proved sufficient for the majority of northern imperialists who wished to eliminate slavery and Black people from the trans-Appalachian and trans-Mississippian West. Still, over a third of the representatives from the northern states voted against admission. Twenty-six of the thirty-four, including Tallmadge, were in their first or second term in Congress; most would only serve for one or two terms. Like Tallmadge, the new congressmen also found themselves unrestrained by partisan or personal ties to southern enslavers, and were largely unencumbered by the Jeffersonian-Hamiltonian dichotomy that pitted New England against the middle, southern, and western states, which had structured congressional politics since the 1790s. This group of antislavery imperialists from the eastern states would uniformly lead efforts to ban enslavement from empire in the trans-Mississippi West over the next year. They failed to force a direct plan of gradual abolition on Illinois, but they knew they would have a chance to do the same to Missouri, whose pending admission to statehood sat before the House.[9]

The House took up Missouri statehood less than three months after Tallmadge's efforts to eliminate slavery from Illinois failed; this time, he would be better prepared. According to Tallmadge's close confidant, John Taylor of New York, in the week leading up to debate on Missouri statehood, they devised a plan "to arrest slavery in Missouri and Arkansas." Tallmadge and Taylor "discussed" Missouri's "noble rivers, fertile soil, and position by the side of the Northwest Territory, and to which would, doubtless, have been applied the free ordinance of 1787," had "Missouri then belonged to the Union."[10] Archaic imperial boundaries were all that exempted Missouri from Article VI. Taylor and Tallmadge also understood that an effective plan to eliminate slavery from Missouri would require more than a mere prohibition on the future introduction of slavery into Missouri. Both Taylor and Tallmadge had been intimately involved in the long process of gradually abolishing slavery in the Hudson Valley.[11] Having learned from Illinois and New York, they decided to apply Article VI's prohibition on slavery to Missouri and to impose on it a plan of gradual emancipation. Rather than allowing Missouri enslavers to dictate these terms, Congress would do so for them. They also planned on barring slavery from all future territories and states. The Northwest Ordinance might have been "no great moral or political feat" when passed in 1787, but it was politically significant from its passage through Illinois statehood in shaping the Missouri Crisis and for creating a framework for a form of empire without slavery. Indeed, Tallmadge and Taylor used it as the basis for their proposal to decouple enslavement from empire by banning slavery in all states and territories hereafter admitted to the Union.

Tallmadge and Taylor would impose on the imperial trans-Mississippi West the same conditions that had nearly eradicated slavery from the postcolonial Northeast. When the statehood bill came to the floor, Tallmadge proposed that Missouri prohibit the further introduction of enslaved men and women into the state and to provide for the emancipation of all children born to enslaved mothers at the age of twenty-five. Like Article VI before it, Tallmadge's amendment would prohibit "the introduction of slave-holders into that country."[12] Tallmadge and other northern commentators tied restrictions on Missouri slavery to limiting the place of slavery in the expanding and consolidating U.S. empire. Tallmadge "explained his intentions and views, and in the course of his remarks, declared his wish to make the Mississippi the western boundary of slavery, and his hope that the country acquired to the west be settled by freemen."[13] Tallmadge's intent was clear: to eradicate slavery from "the extended empire" between "the two oceans."[14] A New York newspaper celebrated that with Tallmadge's proposal "that foul blot in our national character, can be confined to the boundaries of the Potomac, the Ohio, and the Mississippi."[15]

Under Tallmadge's plan, U.S. empire would proceed without enslavement. The House passed Tallmadge's proposal; the Senate rejected it; then Congress adjourned with the issue unresolved. The sixteenth Congress would return to the issue in January 1820. Before then, Missouri statehood with slavery would ignite questions about empire and enslavement from the Mississippi Valley to the Pacific. Outstanding issues regarding the relationships among empire, enslavement, and emancipation in the Middle Mississippi Valley gave rise to new conflicts about the proper relationships among the three on the broader North American continent. As one observer noted, "Let slavery once pass the Mississippi, & the chains of the negroes will be wielded forever."[16] As another observer noted, if slavery in Missouri was not contained, "from the Atlantic to the Pacific the United States will be cursed with a slave population."[17] A century of empire and enslavement in the Middle Mississippi Valley gave rise to new questions centered on the future of slavery in a U.S. empire with continental aspirations.

Between the fifteenth and sixteenth Congresses, a motley group of northern politicians and voters deemed themselves "restrictionists" and called on Congress to adopt a full, final, and comprehensive prohibition on slavery's expansion, thus decoupling empire from enslavement. Northern calls for containing slavery extended not just to Missouri but also to the remainder of the Louisiana Purchase, to the looming acquisitions of Spanish Florida and Texas, and to any present or future territory "from the Mississippi River to the South Sea."[18] A New York newspaper noted in December 1819 that the upcoming Congress would address not the question of slavery in Missouri but "the Abolition of Slavery in the states or territories which may be hereafter admitted to the Union."[19] This expectation echoed the language and understandings of "the Missouri question" that became widespread across the North as the congressional session neared.[20] In late 1819 and early 1820, local meetings, town and city councils, and state legislatures from across the North adopted resolutions calling on Congress to prohibit the "further extension of slavery in all states and territories hereafter admitted to the Union."[21] Pamphlets and articles that filled northern newspapers repeated this demand. Most confidently expected that "slavery shall not be permitted to spread beyond its present confines."[22] Many commentators linked the Tallmadge restrictions on Missouri slavery to "the glorious work of 'universal emancipation.'"[23] In almost every case, slavery's confinement to the South and eventual abolition was tied to colonization, with free Black people being "instantly transmitted to such a country" where they could live "under a wise and just government" of their "own."[24] Northern imperialists sought to sever the relationship of enslavement to empire and to replace it with emancipation and the expulsion of free Black people. In the long history of European conquest and colonization in North America, empire had facilitated enslavement; U.S. empire would now facilitate emancipation and expulsion.

The northern demands regarding empire and enslavement expressed in the widely circulated resolutions, petitions, articles, and pamphlets shaped congressional debates. The initial committee for addressing the Missouri question was instructed to "inquire into the expediency of prohibiting by law the introduction of slaves into the territories of the United States west of the Mississippi."[25] For Pennsylvania Senator Jonathan Roberts, the "Missouri question" centered on "whether freedom or slavery is to be the lot of the regions beyond the Mississippi."[26] New Jersey Representative Joseph Bloomfield received a letter from a constituent pondering "whether a civil war would be preferable" to the "extension of slavery beyond the Mississippi."[27] Recently retired Pennsylvania Senator Abner LaCock noted that a group of Pennsylvania congressmen similarly sought a general prohibition on "the establishment of slave states over the Mississippi."[28] The Ohio legislature issued a resolution "relative to the admission or extension of slavery in the territories of the United States or any new State which may be hereafter admitted to the Union."[29]

Much like enslavers, northern restrictionists agreed that the purpose of imperial state power was to dispossess Indigenous inhabitants of their lands; to establish territorial borders; to control land and labor; to define the practices of race; to direct voluntary and involuntary migration; and to uphold white autonomy and sovereignty. But they also sought something radical and new. Reversing two centuries using imperial state power to grow and expand systems of slavery on the North American continent, Tallmadge and northern restrictionists proposed that imperial state power be used to halt slavery's growth, to facilitate emancipation, and to draw new borders demarcating the limits of slavery and Black people in an expanding U.S. empire. Northern restrictionists sought to implement a new Northwest Ordinance for the vast regions west of the Mississippi; this one would contain a built-in emancipation mechanism. For northern restrictionists—a self-identified group that included the great majority of northern congressmen and a sizable portion of the electorate—the Missouri question offered Congress an opportunity to halt slavery's expansion fully, finally, and forever. Enslavement would be decoupled from empire; emancipation and expulsion of Black people, along with continuing Indigenous dispossession, would join it.

Southern imperialists understood that northern imperialists sought a general and comprehensive prohibition on slavery's further expansion, a new relationship between empire and enslavement. Southern newspapers reprinted the proceedings of northern restrictionist meetings, dismissing them as "solecisms,"[30] or derivatives of "the Doctrine of the *Hartford convention*" and the machinations of New England secessionists.[31] Their aspirations could not distract from the issue at hand; northern imperialists wanted to limit slavery's place in the U.S. empire. North Carolina Senator Montfort Stokes explained to his governor that "a considerable majority" of northern congressmen "are in favor of restriction as to all the country purchased from France," which for southern politicians like Stokes included Texas.[32] Virginia Senator James Barbour warned members of the Virginia legislature that "in both branches of Congress there was a decided majority for extending the 6th Article of the [Northwest] Ordinance to the territories of the U.S."[33] Virginia representative and future president John Tyler feared that "a joint resolution restricting the territories," "being general in its terms," would soon pass Congress.[34] In a public letter written by President James Monroe or on his behalf, Monroe explained to Virginia enslavers that northern imperialists intended to pass territorial restrictions on slavery and that "the exclusion will be general," covering all future and present territories of the United States.[35] More than simply a debate over the status of slavery in Missouri, the Missouri Crisis centered on the place of enslavement and emancipation in an empire expanding to continental proportions.

When Congress took up the question of Missouri statehood for the second time in January 1820, it faced the immediate issues of Missouri statehood and a prohibition on slavery's future expansion. Southern obfuscation and obstruction, however, caused debate to degenerate into an inchoate mess involving the distinct but related issues of slavery in Missouri; slavery in the remainder of the Louisiana Purchase; slavery in Florida and Texas; the place of slavery in an ill-defined West; the legitimacy of the Northwest Ordinance's Article VI ban on slavery; the constitutionality of restrictions on slavery; and the place of slavery in the past, present, and future of the southern states. As debate dragged on with no resolution in sight, a group of northern and southern congressmen began searching for some type of resolution. By mid-January, even the most ardent northern restrictionists conceded that "Congress have left the favourable time pass. They should have prohibited slavery" in Missouri "when the Territorial government was formed" in 1804. Slavery was already too entrenched in Missouri, and southern enslavers would never accept legislation prohibiting slavery in a territory so near to statehood. Unless northern restrictionists would "compromise to admit Missouri without restriction," it would "be extremely difficult perhaps impracticable to prevent the further introduction of slavery in the Territories." The restrictionists' initial Missouri compromise would trade Missouri statehood without restrictions for a prohibition on "the further introduction of slavery in the Territories."[36] Slavery would be permitted in Missouri, but enslavement would be decoupled from the remainder of the U.S. empire.

By early February, with a compromise agreed to in principle, the main issue facing Congress centered on the extent of territorial restrictions on slavery. LaCock cajoled northern and southern politicians to "let the slave-holding states accept Missouri Arkansaw, & the Floridas, & give an equivalent to the others in the west."[37] Maine Representative Mark Hill expected northerners to admit Missouri without restrictions, "provided slavery shall never exist in what is now the vaccant territory," lands occupied by Indigenous people. Southern enslavers, however, remained concerned about slavery in "the Floridas."[38] By late February, a majority of congressmen agreed to the 36–30 line that would go down in history as the Missouri Compromise. But as Congress went through its final round of votes, a group of northern congressmen sought more extensive prohibitions on slavery's expansion. On multiple occasions, northern restrictions sought "to exclude slavery from the whole country west of the Mississippi, except in Louisiana, Arkansas, and Missouri." This measure would have conceded Florida but prohibited slavery everywhere else, including Texas. These proposals failed, as did a House proposal declaring "that there shall be neither slavery nor involuntary servitude in any of the territories of the United States."[39] With Congress on the verge of settling the issues of slavery in Missouri and the remainder of the Louisiana Purchase, a sufficient number of northerners joined their southern colleagues to defeat these proposals, narrowly at first and more decisively in later votes.[40]

For many northern politicians and voters, the Missouri Compromise stood as a rank failure, a tightening of the ties that bound enslavement to empire, rather than its repudiation. Ohio Congressman John Sloane could barely bring himself to write about "the disgraceful character of the Missouri business."[41] Philadelphia Quaker and abolitionist Daniel B. Smith called for separating from the southern states on the grounds that "a divided empire is more desirable" than an empire that extended and entrenched slavery.[42] Disgust with the Missouri Compromise prompted New York Representative Henry Meigs to put together a proposal for a "grand National effort to eradicate the whole cause of dissension, Slavery." Meigs's plan would finance compensated emancipation and colonization in the entirety of the United States through the sale of "500 millions of acres, west of the Mississippi."[43] For northern imperialists, Indigenous dispossession would fund emancipation and expulsion, not just in Missouri and Illinois but in places such as Virginia as well.

Southern politicians celebrated the Missouri Compromise for the same reasons that northern antislavery imperialists damned it: They had beat back a concerted effort to decouple enslavement from empire. The tight connections between empire and enslavement would remain, at least in the bulk of U.S. claims to the North American continent. "We have carried the question to admit Missouri and all of Louisiana, to the Southward of 36–30 free of restriction from slavery," read a widely circulated letter that was frequently reprinted in southern newspapers. The compromise "will include Arkansaw and the Floridas, and give the Southern interest in a short time an addition of six, and perhaps eight members," hinting at the addition of slave states to be formed out of Texas.[44] While U.S. empire would exclude slavery north of the 36–30 line, it would facilitate enslavement elsewhere. In their private correspondence, southern congressmen also expressed contentment with the Missouri Compromise. Henry Clay deemed "the arrangement which has been made a very good one."[45] Alabama Senator John Walker judged "the compromise on the Missouri question" a "wise and necessary measure."[46] Montfort Stokes celebrated his work in settling the Missouri question. Stokes and his southern colleagues had set out "to rescue from the rapacious grasp of these fanatics a considerable portion of Louisiana"; they had done just that. Stokes accepted the 36–30 line as a "prudent and proper concession." The South had defeated efforts to pass a full prohibition on slavery's expansion, securing Florida, Texas, and the remainder of the Louisiana Purchase "as an asylum for slaves already too numerous to be comfortably supported in some of the southern states."[47] The United States would remain a composite rather than a unitary empire with regards to slavery, and that empire would serve southern enslavers in new ways. For much of the 1700s, slavery had been a tool of enhancing imperial claims. Slavery secured empire. Now, empire would secure slavery, as southern enslavers looked to an expansive empire as the means by which they could manage the dangerously large groups of people they held in slavery.

Voters and politicians in Missouri and Illinois confirmed the divisions made by Congress in the trans-Mississippi West, along with the legacies of empire and enslavement in the Middle Mississippi Valley stretching back to the 1760s. White Missourians drew on a long legacy of local self-government within larger imperial structures, a concerted defiance of imperial regulations that hindered enslavers, and staunch support from southern enslavers. Repeatedly, white Missourians insisted that they would "never become a member of the Union under the restrictions relative to slavery."[48] As far as they were concerned, the question of whether Congress could impose restrictions on Missouri slavery was "very much on the same ground with the old revolutionary question of 75 which produced the separation of the Colonies from the Mother Country." In 1775 and 1776, free white colonists held "that legislation" from Parliament was "inoperable" if it clashed with the interests of free white colonists. Now, white Missourians insisted that Congress was obligated to empower, not enfeeble, enslavers in the U.S. empire.[49] They would become equal members of the U.S. empire on their own terms. Just as habitants had defied Spanish bans on Indigenous slavery, just as Upper Louisiana enslavers had stared down congressional restrictions in 1804, and just as Illinois enslavers had defied Article VI, so, too, would Missouri enslavers ignore congressional efforts to restrict slavery in their portion of the expanding American empire if matters came to that.

In May 1820, Missouri voters held elections to select delegates to write a state constitution; the brief campaign overwhelmingly favored enslavers. In the Boon's Lick settlements, one colonizer "believe[d] that nine tenths of the people of Howard & Cooper are in favor of slavery." He further expected that "no man will be elected from these counties unless he declare himself for slavery & perhaps it will require a property in slaves to qualify him in the eyes of the people."[50] Candidates issued toasts celebrating their defense of enslavers, and they issued handbills declaring "I shall, therefore, if elected, vote for the further admission of slaves, and the future toleration of slavery within the state."[51] In St. Louis County, voters elected a slate of proslavery delegates who received, in total, 7,265 votes. Voters cast 2,026 ballots for restrictionist candidates, who ran on a very limited platform of halting the future introduction of enslaved men and women to Missouri in ten years while eschewing any gradual emancipation mechanisms.[52] Avowed proslavery candidates ran even stronger across the territory, prompting one observer to conclude "that there is not a single *confessed* restrictionist elected throughout the Territory."[53] The delegates wrote a rather standard state constitution protecting slavery, and enslavers continued migrating into the Missouri Valley over the next two decades.[54] Enslaved men and women, particularly in St. Louis, would lead their own personal battles over slavery, filing hundreds of freedom suits from the 1820s through the 1850s. As the state's free population grew, especially around St. Louis due to the immigration of more than fifty thousand German immigrants in the 1840s and 1850s, enslavers became more marginalized, exerting influence primarily in the Missouri Valley. By the 1850s, Missouri itself had become as divided as the Middle Mississippi Valley as the course of empire and enslavement continued southward and westward.[55]

In the 1820s, antislavery Illinois voters continued to gain ground, but the legality and practices of enslavement in Illinois remained stubbornly stagnant. Due to their prominence, proslavery candidates won most of the elections for state and federal office in Illinois in the 1818 elections. However, the Missouri Crisis inflamed existing divisions, emboldening the growing antislavery movement in the state. Daniel Pope Cook ran against and defeated proslavery Congressman John McLean in 1819. Cook, John Messinger, George Churchill, and other early antislavery colonizers led efforts to defeat the proslavery faction's effort in 1824 to hold a new constitutional convention where they intended to legalize slavery fully.[56] African Americans continued to seek emancipation, whether from slavery or indentured servitude. Working with white attorneys, they filed a growing number of cases that challenged the legality of slavery and servitude in the state, culminating in an 1845 Illinois Supreme Court decision that ruled that the descendants of French Negroes born after 1818 were free.

From there, free Black Illinoisians battled against kidnappers, slave traders, and the state's anti-Black laws.[57] Meanwhile, a growing number of northern migrants to Illinois shifted power away from enslavers, setting the path for greater divisions within the state. Given the tangled histories of enslavement and empire in Illinois, it unsurprisingly gave rise to Abraham Lincoln and Stephen Douglas, one an advocate for empire and enslavement, the other an advocate of empire and emancipation.[58] Article VI, largely ineffective in the eighteenth and early nineteenth centuries, had changed the dynamics of empire, enslavement, and emancipation in the Middle Mississippi Valley and on the North American continent in the mid-nineteenth century.

With the Missouri Compromise, the status of empire and enslavement had been presumably established across the vast trans-Mississippi West. Nonetheless, like the Middle Mississippi Valley from which it sprang, the U.S. trans-Mississippi West proved a source of conflict between proslavery and antislavery imperialists. Before the ink even dried on the Missouri Compromise, a Virginia-born senator from Indiana, Waller Taylor, consoled a Virginia enslaver that they could forever block efforts by northern antislavery imperialists to expand empire without slavery in the areas of the Louisiana Purchase where Congress voted to block it. "All the territory in which slavery is excluded, still belongs to the Indians," Taylor explained. With "the Constitution requiring two thirds of the senators present to ratify a treaty, it will always be in the power of the slaveholding States to prevent the acquisition and consequent settlement of any more of this territory."[59] For southern imperialists, enslavement was central to empire. Empire and Article VI had nearly eviscerated slavery from Taylor's Indiana, a situation he found increasingly intolerable. Taylor had fought to preserve slavery in Indiana from his arrival in the territory in 1804. He provided crucial votes in the Senate to defeat northern efforts to ban slavery in all future states and territories during the Missouri Crisis. As much as any senator, he was responsible for southern enslavers' ability to beat back efforts to decouple enslavement from empire.

Reflecting the new dynamics of empire and enslavement, the Indiana legislature voted to censure Taylor due to his votes in favor of slavery in Missouri. At the same time, Taylor lamented the new forms of empire in places such as Indiana, which celebrated the exclusion of slavery. Taylor confessed to a Virginian confidant that "I am unalterably resolved, should I live but a few years, to remove from a state, the manners habits and opinions of the people in which, are so uncongenial with my own. But in what place I shall pitch my tent, I have not yet determined, though as at present advised, most likely in Missouri."[60] Leaving behind an Indiana without slavery, Taylor preferred to live in a Missouri with slavery, though he eventually returned to his native Virginia instead. Hardly unitary when it came to slavery, the United States remained a divided, composite empire, much like the Middle Mississippi Valley.

Taylor understood as well as anyone the new politics of empire and enslavement on the North American continent and within the imperial United States. He also foresaw the direction of the increasingly national politics of empire and enslavement. The next great crisis over empire and enslavement would emerge in the 1840s over Texas. In the 1850s, the United States would undergo another crisis over empire and enslavement regarding the remainder of the Louisiana Purchase. As the United States entered the election of 1860, looming conflicts over empire and enslavement on the North American continent, in Mexico and Central America, and in the Caribbean would result in disunion and a civil war. As much as anything, the U.S. Civil War was the final act of the new politics of empire and enslavement that had been created by the Northwest Ordinance of 1787 and was solidified in the Middle Mississippi Valley Crisis between 1818 and 1820.[61]

ABBREVIATIONS

ALPML   Abraham Lincoln Presidential Museum and Library, Archives, Springfield, Illinois

AP   Austin Papers: Series II, Part I, 1794–1817, Dolph Briscoe Center for American History, University of Texas, Austin

CHM   Abakanowicz Research Center, Chicago History Museum, Chicago, Illinois

CISHL   *Collections of the Illinois State Historical Library*, 38 vols., Illinois State Historical Society, 1903–70, Springfield, Illinois

INDHS   Indiana Historical Society, Archives, Indianapolis, Indiana

JBCLFP   John Baptiste Charles Lucas Family Papers, 1754–1943, Missouri History Museum Archives

KM   Kaskaskia Manuscripts, Foundation for Illinois Colonial and American Studies, Springfield, Illinois (digital microfilm; originals: Randolph County Courthouse, Chester, Illinois)

LOC   Library of Congress, Manuscript Division, Washington, DC

MHMA   Missouri Historical Museum, Archives, St. Louis

MHS   Massachusetts Historical Society, Boston

MSA-JC   Missouri State Archives, Jefferson City, Missouri

MSA-SL   Missouri State Archives, St. Louis, Missouri

PSA   Pennsylvania State Archives, Harrisburg, Pennsylvania

SGA   Sainte Geneviève Archives, State Historical Society of Missouri, Columbia, Missouri

SHSMO   State Historical Society of Missouri, Columbia, Missouri

SLCCHRP   St. Louis Circuit Court Historical Records Project, Circuit Court Case Files, Missouri State Archives, St. Louis, Missouri

SMV   Lawrence Kinnaird, ed., *Spain in the Mississippi Valley, 1765–1794*, 3 vols. (Washington, DC: Government Printing Office, 1946–49)

SRM   Louis Houck, ed., *The Spanish Regime in Missouri*, 2 vols. (Chicago: R. R. Donnelley, 1908)

TPUS   Clarence E. Carter, ed., *The Territorial Papers of the United States*, 28 vols. (Washington, DC: Government Printing Office, 1934–75)

WLCL   William L. Clements Library, University of Michigan, Ann Arbor, Michigan

NOTES

Introduction

1. For a different but complementary conception of this region as "the American Confluence," see Stephen Aron, *American Confluence: The Missouri Frontier from Borderland to Border State* (Bloomington: Indiana University Press, 2006).

2. Following historian Paul A. Kramer, I employ concepts of "the imperial" as "a dimension of power in which asymmetries in the scale of political action, regimes of spatial ordering, and modes of exceptionalizing difference enable and produce relations of hierarchy, discipline, dispossession, extraction, and exploitation." Paul A. Kramer, "Power and Connection: Imperial Histories of the United States in the World," *American Historical Review* 116, no. 5 (December 2011), 1348–1391, quote at 1349. Lisa Ford, *Settler Sovereignty: Jurisdiction and Indigenous People in America and Australia, 1788–1836* (Cambridge, MA: Harvard University Press, 2010), defines sovereignty "as the ordering of Indigenous people in space," quote at page 1. In the Middle Mississippi Valley, and across the greater reaches of imperial North America, European colonizers understood and exercised sovereignty as personal power over racialized and enslaved people, supported by imperial state power and local polities. Sovereignty thus involved ordering, in space, both Indigenous and enslaved African peoples. My understanding of slavery as a series of practices and social interactions has been influenced, most recently, by Joseph C. Miller, *The Problem of Slavery as History: A Global Approach* (New Haven, CT: Yale University Press, 2013); Noel Lenski and Catherine M. Cameron, eds., *What Is a Slave Society? The Practice of Slavery in Global Perspective* (Cambridge, UK: Cambridge University Press, 2018); and Trevor Burnard, *Writing the History of Global Slavery* (Cambridge, UK: Cambridge University Press, 2023).

3. The parts of Missouri and Illinois that are the focus of this book were part of numerous different territories; were marked by dynamic, contested borders; and had many different Native American and European names between the 1600s and Missouri statehood in 1821. In the late 1600s and early 1700s, Osage (Ni-u-kon-ska) and Missouri (Niúachi) inhabited the lower Missouri Valley. Across the Mississippi River, a diverse group of Native Americans that included Kaskaskias, Cahokias, and Peorias lived on the east bank of the Mississippi River and along the Illinois River Valley. Some of these Native Americans were indigenous to the Middle Mississippi Valley, while others were refugees who had fled Haudenosaunee (Iroquois) incursions in the Great Lakes region and the Upper Ohio Valley. Collectively, these Native American nations formed the Illinois, a loose confederacy with no central or formal political structure. For much of the first half of the 1700s, the immediate west bank of the Mississippi River below the Missouri River was largely uninhabited, something of a neutral borderland that kept peace between the Illinois on the east bank and the Osage and Missouri in the Lower Missouri Valley.

In the early 1700s, French traders and missionaries who explored the Mississippi Valley named the region "Louisiana." Around the same time, a different group of traders and missionaries who migrated from French Canada via the Great Lakes established five villages on the east bank of the Mississippi River by the 1720s. They placed their settlements in *le pays des Illinois*, "the country of the Illinois." When habitants began crossing the Mississippi River to establish settlements, such as Ste. Geneviève, around midcentury, they continued to place their settlements in the Illinois Country. At the same time, imperial authorities placed the French settlements on both sides of the Mississippi River under the jurisdiction of the French province of Louisiana, to be governed out of New Orleans. To distinguish the settlements in the Middle Mississippi Valley from French settlements in the Lower Mississippi Valley around New Orleans, French officials and habitants referred to the Middle Mississippi Valley as both Illinois and *La haute Louisiane*, "the high Louisiana," or "Upper Louisiana." Nonetheless, "the Illinois Country" became an oft-used term for both officials and residents for the settlements on both sides of the river.

The 1763 Treaty of Paris divided the Illinois Country along the Mississippi River, with Britain claiming the east bank and Spain claiming the west bank. Spanish officials typically referred to present-day Missouri as Upper Louisiana. However, Spanish officials and colonizers continued to use the terms "Spanish Yllinois." With the Louisiana Purchase of 1803, the United States named what would become the state of Louisiana "Orleans Territory." Everything within the Louisiana Purchase but outside of Orleans became part of "the District of Louisiana," and the region was colloquially referred to as Upper Louisiana. In 1805 Congress transformed the District of Louisiana into the Louisiana Territory, which included all of the land outside of the Orleans Territory, which would become the present-day state of Louisiana. To distinguish the settlements in present-day Missouri from New Orleans and its hinterlands, officials and others referred to present-day Missouri as "Upper Louisiana." When the Orleans Territory became the state of Louisiana in 1811, Congress renamed (Upper) Louisiana the "Missouri Territory," which included much of present-day Arkansas. In 1819, when Missouri applied for statehood, Congress created a separate Arkansas Territory, establishing, more or less, the borders of present-day Missouri. Illinois, on the other hand, became the westernmost counties of Virginia after the British garrison at Kaskaskia surrendered to Virginia forces. In 1784, Virginia ceded its claims to Illinois to the United States, and Illinois became part of the Northwest Territory in 1787. In 1800, Congress created a separate Ohio Territory, and Illinois became part of the Indiana Territory. In 1809, Congress divided the Indiana Territory, creating a separate Illinois Territory. For simplicity and clarity, I use the terms *Illinois* and *Upper Louisiana* for the period through 1805 or so, and then *Missouri* and *Illinois* for the period between 1805 and statehood. For general histories of colonial Missouri and Illinois, see William E. Foley, *The Genesis of Missouri: From Wilderness Outpost to Statehood* (Columbia: University of Missouri Press, 1989); and James E. Davis, *Frontier Illinois* (Bloomington: Indiana University Press, 1998).

4. For works examining enslavement in the Middle Mississippi Valley on its own terms, and from the perspective of Indigenous people and French North America, see Carl J. Ekberg, *French Roots in the Illinois Country: The Mississippi Frontier in Colonial Times* (Urbana: University of Illinois Press, 1998); Carl J. Ekberg, *Stealing Indian Women: Native Slavery in the Illinois Country* (Urbana: University of Illinois Press, 2007); and M. Scott Heerman, *The Alchemy of Slavery: Human Bondage and Emancipation in the Illinois Country, 1730–1865* (Philadelphia: University of Pennsylvania Press, 2018). Heerman's excellent work devotes limited attention to enslavement and empire in Missouri. Ekberg's foundational works on the French colonial Mississippi Valley tend to end with the Louisiana Purchase of 1803.

5. Padraig Riley, *Slavery and the Democratic Conscience: Political Life in Jeffersonian America* (Philadelphia: University of Pennsylvania Press, 2015); George William Van Cleve, *A Slaveholders' Union: Slavery, Politics, and the Constitution in the Early American Republic* (Chicago: University of Chicago Press, 2010); John Craig Hammond, *Slavery, Freedom, and Expansion in the Early American West* (Charlottesville: University of Virginia Press, 2007); Matthew Mason, *Slavery and Politics in the Early American Republic* (Chapel Hill: University of North Carolina Press, 2006).

6. Robert Pierce Forbes, *The Missouri Compromise and Its Aftermath: Slavery and the Meaning of America* (Chapel Hill: University of North Carolina Press, 2007).

7. Nicholas P. Wood, "The Missouri Crisis and the 'Changed Object' of the American Colonization Society," in *New Directions in the Study of African American Recolonization*, ed. Beverly C. Tomek and Matthew J. Hetrick (Gainesville: University Press of Florida, 2017), 146–165; Lacy K. Ford, *"Deliver Us from Evil": The Slavery Question in the Old South* (New York: Oxford University Press, 2009).

8. Jeffrey L. Pasley and John Craig Hammond, eds., *A Fire Bell in the Past: The Missouri Crisis at 200*, vol. 1, *Western Slavery, National Impasse* (Columbia: University of Missouri Press, 2021); Jeffrey L. Pasley and John Craig Hammond, eds., *A Fire Bell in the Past: The Missouri Crisis at 200*, vol. 2, *The Missouri Question and Its Answers* (Columbia: University of Missouri Press, 2021).

9. James Edstrom, *Avenues of Transformation: Illinois's Path from Territory to State* (Carbondale: Southern Illinois University Press, 2022); Suzanne Cooper Guasco, *Confronting Slavery: Edward Coles and the Rise of Antislavery Politics in Nineteenth-Century America* (DeKalb: Northern Illinois University Press, 2013). There remains no single-volume history of slavery in Missouri and Illinois from the 1750s through the Missouri Crisis. For excellent works on the lived experiences of enslaved people in Missouri *after* 1815, see Kelly M. Kennington, *In the Shadow of Dred Scott: St. Louis Freedom Suits and the Legal Culture of Slavery in Antebellum America* (Athens: University of Georgia Press, 2017); Anne Twitty, *Before Dred Scott: Slavery and Legal Culture in the American Confluence, 1787–1857* (New York: Cambridge University Press, 2016); Lea VanderVelde, *Redemption Songs: Suing for Freedom Before Dred Scott* (New York: Oxford University Press, 2014); and Diane Mutti Burke, *On Slavery's Border: Missouri's Small Slaveholding Households, 1815–1865* (Athens: University of Georgia Press, 2010). For African American enslavement and emancipation in Illinois between 1820 and 1860, see Heerman, *The Alchemy of Slavery*.

10. Calvin Schermerhorn, *Unrequited Toil: A History of United States Slavery* (New York: Cambridge University Press, 2018); Calvin Schermerhorn, *The Business of Slavery and the Rise of American Capitalism, 1815–1860* (New Haven, CT: Yale University Press, 2015); Edward Baptist, *The Half Has Never Been Told: Slavery and the Making of American Capitalism* (New York: Basic Books, 2014); Walter Johnson, *River of Dark Dreams: Slavery and Empire in the Cotton Kingdom* (Cambridge, MA: Harvard University Press, 2013).

11. Dale W. Tomich, *Through the Prism of Slavery: Labor, Capital, and World Economy* (Lanham, MD: Rowman and Littlefield, 2004).

12. Walter Johnson, *The Broken Heart of America: St. Louis and the Violent History of the United States* (New York: Basic Books, 2020), 6. Johnson covers the period between the 1763 establishment of a permanent settlement at St. Louis and the 1803 Louisiana Purchase in a single paragraph; he dispenses with the territorial phase of Missouri between 1804 and 1820 in far less than half a chapter.

13. For criticisms of U.S. historians who overlook the significance of Native American enslavement, especially in the Greater Mississippi Valley, see Leila K. Blackbird, "'It Has Always Been Customary to Make Slaves of Savages': The Problem of Indian Slavery in Spanish Louisiana Revisited, 1769–1803," *William and Mary Quarterly*, 3rd ser., 80, no. 3 (July 2023), 525–558; and Nancy E. van Deusen, "In the Tethered Shadow: Native American Slavery, African American Slavery, and the Disappearance of the Past," *William and Mary Quarterly*, 3rd ser., 80, no. 2 (April 2023), 355–388.

14. My understanding of the relationship between capitalism and slavery is influenced by John J. Clegg, "A Theory of Capitalist Slavery," *Journal of Historical Sociology* 33, no. 1 (March 2020), 74–98; and John J. Clegg, "Capitalism and Slavery," *Critical Historical Studies* 2, no. 2 (Fall 2015), 281–304.

15. For similar readings of empire and enslavement in French and Spanish Illinois and Upper Louisiana, which claim that French and Spanish slavery was somehow less predatory and less exploitative than U.S. slavery, see Ekberg, *French Roots in the Illinois Country*; and Ekberg, *Stealing Indian Women*. For criticisms of U.S. historians who overstate the extent of freedoms and paths to manumission under Spanish and French law, see Blackbird, "'It Has Always Been Customary.'" For criticisms of U.S. historians for their propensity to take at face value U.S. imperialists' and colonizers' claims that habitants were indolent and created a noncapitalist economy, see Jay Gitlin, *The Bourgeois Frontier: French Towns, French Traders, and American Expansion* (New Haven, CT: Yale University Press, 2010).

16. For criticism of the tendency of United States historians to write the history of the North American continent outside of the borders of the thirteen colonies of British North America as proto–United States history rather than the history of colonial, imperial, and Indigenous North America, see Peter Kastor, "The Multinational History of Missouri Statehood," in Pasley and Hammond, *A Fire Bell in the Past*, 2:357–383.

17. Baptist, *The Half Has Never Been Told*, 8, 11.

18. For the creation of meaningful antislavery politics in spite of white supremacism, see Kate Masur, *Until Justice Be Done: America's First Civil Rights Movement, from the Revolution to Reconstruction* (New York: Norton, 2021); and Van Gosse, *The First Reconstruction: Black Politics in America from the Revolution to the Civil War* (Chapel Hill: University of North Carolina Press, 2021).

19. For northern white peoples' connections among empire, emancipation, exclusion, and forced removal of Black people through colonization, see Samantha Seeley, *Race, Removal, and the Right to Remain: Migration and the Making of the United States* (Chapel Hill: University of North Carolina Press, 2021); and Brandon Mills, *The World Colonization Made: The Racial Geography of Early American Empire* (Philadelphia: University of Pennsylvania Press, 2020).

20. For the United States as a composite empire, see Steven Hahn, *A Nation Without Borders: The United States and Its World in an Age of Civil Wars, 1830–1910* (New York: Viking, 2016). For the deep divisions and conflicts that were seemingly endemic to the late British empire and then the United States, from the 1760s through the early 1800s, see Alan Taylor, *American Revolutions: A Continental History, 1750–1804* (New York: Norton, 2016); and Alan Taylor, *American Republics: A Continental History of the United States* (New York: Norton, 2021).

21. Max M. Edling, "Peace Pact and Nation: An International Interpretation of the Constitution of the United States," *Past and Present* 240, no. 1 (August 2018), 267–303.

22. For the ways in which competing imperial powers used state support for enslavers to solidify claims of sovereignty in contested regions, see John Craig Hammond, "Slavery,

Sovereignty, and Empires: North American Borderlands and the American Civil War, 1660–1860," *Journal of the Civil War Era* 4, no. 2 (June 2014), 264–298; M. Scott Heerman, "Beyond Plantations: Indian and African Slavery in the Illinois Country, 1720–1780," *Slavery and Abolition* 38, no. 3 (September 2017), 489–509. For the never-ending evasions of Spanish prohibitions against Indigenous enslavement in Lower Louisiana, Texas, and northern Mexico, see Paul Barba, *Country of the Cursed and the Driven: Slavery and the Texas Borderlands* (Lincoln: University of Nebraska Press, 2021); and Andrés Reséndez, *The Other Slavery: The Uncovered Story of Indian Enslavement in America* (Boston: Harcourt, 2016).

23. Changing historiographical perspectives on Article VI began, most notably, with Paul Finkelman, "Slavery and the Northwest Ordinance: A Study in Ambiguity," *Journal of the Early Republic* 6 (Winter 1986), 343–370; and Paul Finkelman, "Evading the Ordinance: The Persistence of Bondage in Indiana and Illinois," *Journal of the Early Republic* 9 (Spring 1989), 21–51; along with Finkelman's many subsequent works. The best analysis of the Northwest Ordinance's origins and significance remains Peter Onuf, *Statehood and Union: A History of the Northwest Ordinance* (Bloomington: Indiana University Press, 1987).

24. Baptist, *The Half Has Never Been Told*, 8.

25. Christopher Phillips, *The Rivers Ran Backward: The Civil War and the Remaking of the American Middle Border* (New York: Oxford University Press, 2016), 15–48; Guasco, *Confronting Slavery*.

26. Kathleen DuVal, *The Native Ground: Indians and Colonists in the Heart of the Continent* (Chapel Hill: University of North Carolina Press, 2006); Aron, *American Confluence*.

27. Jacob F. Lee, *Masters of the Middle Waters: Indian Nations and Colonial Ambitions Along the Mississippi* (Cambridge, MA: Harvard University Press, 2019); John Reda, *From Furs to Farms: The Transformation of the Mississippi Valley, 1762–1825* (DeKalb: Northern Illinois University Press, 2016); Robert Michael Morrissey, *Empire by Collaboration: Indians, Colonists, and Governments in Colonial Illinois Country* (Philadelphia: University of Pennsylvania Press, 2015); Patricia Cleary, *The World, the Flesh, and the Devil: A History of Colonial St. Louis* (Columbia: University of Missouri Press, 2011); Gitlin, *The Bourgeois Frontier*.

28. John Craig Hammond, "Mid-Continent Borderlands: Illinois and the Early American Republic, 1774–1854," *Journal of the Illinois State Historical Society* 111, no. 1–2 (Spring/Summer 2018), 31–54.

29. My understanding of imperial state power in the Americas has been influenced by Gautham Rao, "The New Historiography of the Early Federal Government: Institutions, Contexts, and the Imperial State," *William and Mary Quarterly*, 3rd ser., 77, no. 1 (January 2020), 97–128; Andrew Shankman, "Toward a Social History of Federalism: The State and Capitalism to and from the American Revolution," *Journal of the Early Republic* 37, no. 4 (Winter 2017), 615–653; and Max M. Edling, *A Hercules in the Cradle: War, Money, and the American State, 1783–1867* (Chicago: University of Chicago Press, 2014). For the importance of violence and terror as the primary means by which colonial governments kept enslaved people in slavery, see Jason T. Sharples, *The World That Fear Made: Slave Revolts and Conspiracy Scares in Early America* (Philadelphia: University of Pennsylvania Press, 2020). For the centrality of enslaved people to state formation, in terms of both institutions and infrastructure, in South Carolina, see Ryan A. Quintana, *Making a Slave State: Political Development in Early South Carolina* (Chapel Hill: University of North Carolina Press, 2018).

30. Gregory Ablavsky, *Federal Ground: Governing Property and Violence in the First U.S. Territories* (New York: Oxford University Press, 2021), 2.

Chapter 1

1. For the sake of simplicity, I refer to francophonic individuals of European descent, who lived in French villages in the Middle Mississippi Valley as habitants. Habitants were more or less permanent residents of a village who pursued farming as their main vocation. Informally, especially in the eyes of Spanish and Anglo officials, habitants could include merchants, *voyageurs*, and *coureurs des bois*, licensed and unlicensed traders who engaged in exchanges with Native Americans. The Middle Mississippi Valley also included merchants who engaged in both the Native American trade and commercial agriculture. Many French men took on various roles at various times of the year, and all four groups—farmers, merchants, *voyageurs*, and *coureurs des bois*—actively enslaved Native and African Americans. Though enslaved African and Native Americans often accompanied *voyageurs* and *coureurs des bois* on trips to Native American settlements, the French villages in the Middle Mississippi Valley remained the main sites of enslavement, and French colonizers created and maintained systems of Native and African American enslavement in villages under the jurisdiction of the French imperial state. For the usages of these identities and terms, see Carl J. Ekberg, *French Roots in the Illinois Country: The Mississippi Frontier in Colonial Times* (Urbana: University of Illinois Press, 1998), 138–142.

2. For the Middle Mississippi Valley, the Lower Missouri Valley, and the Great Lakes region in the late 1600s and early 1700s, see Jacob F. Lee, *Masters of the Middle Waters: Indian Nations and Colonial Ambitions Along the Mississippi* (Cambridge, MA: Harvard University Press, 2019); David Nichols, *Peoples of the Inland Seas: Native Americans and Newcomers in the Great Lakes Region, 1600–1870* (Athens: Ohio University Press, 2018); Robert Michael Morrissey, *Empire by Collaboration: Indians, Colonists, and Governments in Colonial Illinois Country* (Philadelphia: University of Pennsylvania Press, 2015); Stephen Aron, *American Confluence: The Missouri Frontier from Borderland to Border State* (Bloomington: Indiana University Press, 2006); and Tanis C. Thorne, *The Many Hands of My Relations: French and Indians on the Lower Missouri* (Columbia: University of Missouri Press, 1996).

3. For the systems of Native American captivity, bondage, and enslavement created by European colonizers, Native American nations, and Indigenous captives and slaves in the 1600s and 1700s, see Leila K. Blackbird, " 'It Has Always Been Customary to Makes Slaves of Savages': The Problem of Indian Slavery in Spanish Louisiana Revisited, 1769–1803," *William and Mary Quarterly*, 3rd ser., 80, no. 3 (July 2023), 525–558; Paul Barba, *Country of the Cursed and the Driven: Slavery and the Texas Borderlands* (Lincoln: University of Nebraska Press, 2021); Andrés Reséndez, *The Other Slavery: The Uncovered Story of Indian Enslavement in America* (Boston: Harcourt, 2016); George Edward Milne, *Natchez Country: Indians, Colonists, and the Landscapes of Race in French Louisiana* (Athens: University of Georgia Press, 2015); Robert Michael Morrissey, "The Power of the Ecotone: Bison, Slavery, and the Rise and Fall of the Grand Village of the Kaskaskia," *Journal of American History* 102, no. 3 (December 2015), 667–692; Brett Rushforth, *Bonds of Alliance: Indigenous and Atlantic Slaveries in New France* (Chapel Hill: University of North Carolina Press, 2013); Christina Snyder, *Slavery in Indian Country: The Changing Face of Captivity in Early America* (Cambridge, MA: Harvard University Press, 2010); Robbie Ethridge and Sheri M. Shuck-Hall, eds., *Mapping the Mississippian Shatter Zone: The Colonial Indian Slave Trade and Regional Instability in the American South* (Lincoln: University of Nebraska Press, 2009); Alan Gallay, ed., *Indian Slavery in Colonial America* (Lincoln: University of Nebraska Press, 2009); Juliana Barr, *Peace Came in the Form of a Woman: Indians and Spaniards in the Texas Borderlands* (Chapel Hill: University of North Carolina Press, 2007); Juliana

Barr, "From Captives to Slaves: Commodifying Indian Women in the Borderlands," *Journal of American History* 92, no. 1 (June 2005), 19–46; Alan Gallay, *The Indian Slave Trade: The Rise of the English Empire in the American South, 1670–1717* (New Haven, CT: Yale University Press, 2002); and James F. Brooks, *Captives and Cousins: Slavery, Kinship, and Community in the Southwest Borderlands* (Chapel Hill: University of North Carolina Press, 2002). For the coexistence and transformation of Native American and African American slavery in Illinois and Missouri, see John Reda, *From Furs to Farms: The Transformation of the Mississippi Valley, 1762–1825* (DeKalb: Northern Illinois University Press, 2016), 14–41; Aron, *American Confluence*, 39–68; Ekberg, *French Roots in the Illinois Country*; Carl J. Ekberg, *Stealing Indian Women: Native Slavery in the Illinois Country* (Urbana: University of Illinois Press, 2007); and M. Scott Heerman, *The Alchemy of Slavery: Human Bondage and Emancipation in the Illinois Country, 1730–1865* (Philadelphia: University of Pennsylvania Press, 2018).

4. Deposition of Pierre Chabot, Concerning a female Chicacha Slave, KM, 40:11:5:1. My understanding of how to read sources written or recorded by colonial enslavers in French Louisiana owes much to Sophie White, *Voices of the Enslaved: Love, Labor, and Longing in French Louisiana* (Chapel Hill: University of North Carolina Press, 2019), especially 1–26.

5. Ruling of Captain Louis Ste. Ange de Belerive, regarding enslaved woman Marie, in Extract from the Registers of the Sessions of the Royal Jurisdiction of the Illinois, 1765, KM, 65:6:8:1.

6. Pierre Gadobert vs. Labastide, Theft of Enslaved Men at Mine LaMotte by Chickasaws, 1771, folder 423, SGA.

7. Barthélemy de Macarty Mactigue to [Pierre de Rigaud, Marquis de] Vaudreuil, Census with a Recapitulation of Villages in the Illinois Country, 1752, Lauden Papers, Americana, Huntington Library, San Marino, California. Macarty's 1752 census counted 446 enslaved Africans and 149 enslaved Native Americans among a total population of 1,380 residents in six French villages.

8. *Ordinance of the Council of State, Appointed by the King of France, to Administer the Company of the Indies, in Favor of the Inhabitants of the Colony of Louisiana, September 2, 1721* (Paris, 1721), Rosemonde E. and Emile Kuntz Collection, French Colonial Period, 1655–1768, Manuscripts Collection 600, Louisiana Research Collection, Tulane University Special Collections Library, New Orleans.

9. For the centrality of slavery to the French enterprise in the Lower Mississippi Valley, and its near collapse due to Natchez resistance, see Christian Pinnen, *Complexion of Empire in Natchez: Race and Slavery in the Mississippi Borderlands* (Athens: University of Georgia Press, 2021); and Milne, *Natchez Country*.

10. Jean-Baptiste Le Moyne, Sieur de Bienville, "Memoir on Louisiana" [1725], in *Mississippi Provincial Archives*, ed. Dunbar Rowland and Albert G. Sanders, 3 vols. (Jackson: Mississippi Department of Archives and History, 1927), 3:523–524.

11. Recorded sales of enslaved Africans in the Illinois Country date to 1720. See Sale of an Enslaved Negro, St. Martin to Bosseron, KM, 20:-:-:1. The arrival, sale, and presence of enslaved Africans in Illinois in the 1720s and 1730s can be tracked in the Kaskaskia Manuscripts. See, for example, Inventory of the Effects of Jacques Bourdon, July 5, 1723, KM, 23:7:1:1; Sale of Enslaved Woman Malade and Her 12-year-old son Pierrot, by Jacques Michel Dufrene, to Antoine Thopart, KM, 41:8:19:1. For foundational work on the origins and operations of African American enslavement in Illinois in the 1710s and 1720s, see Ekberg, *French Roots in the Illinois Country*, 138–170.

12. "Census of Illinois, 1732," *CISHL*, 24:xxii–xxii; Ekberg, *French Roots in the Illinois Country*, 138–170.

13. Agreement between Commandant Dutisne (sic) and Antoine Pelle, July 25, 1725, KM, 25:7:25:1.

14. Pinnen, *Complexion of Empire in Natchez*; Milne, *Natchez Country*.

15. [Jean-Baptiste Le Moyne de] Bienville and Salmon to [Minister Jean Frédéric Phélypeaux, Count of] Maurepas, April 8, 1734, in Rowland and Sanders, *Mississippi Provincial Archives*, 3:667.

16. Maurepas to Vaudreuil, October 9, 1747, *CISHL*, 29:36. For the forced migration of individual enslaved Africans from New Orleans to the Illinois Country in the 1740s, see, for example, Agreement between Jean Baptiste Trudeau Laveau, of Fort de Chartres and Dupas, for purchase of enslaved man Louis Senegal at New Orleans, May 13, 1747, KM, 48:12:5:1.

17. [Jacques-Pierre de Taffanel] La Jonquiere to [Minister Antoine Louis] Rouillé, September 27, 1751, *CISHL*, 29:377–378.

18. La Jonquiere to Rouillé, September 27, 1751, *CISHL*, 29:377–378.

19. Macarty to Vaudreuil, December 8, 1752, *CISHL*, 29:782–783.

20. Macarty to Vaudreuil, March 27, 1752, *CISHL*, 29:563.

21. [Governor Louis Billouart] Kerlérec to Rouillé, June 21, 1754, *CISHL*, 860.

22. George Morgan to [John] Baynton and [Samuel] Wharton, December 2, 1767, April 5, 1768, July 20, 1768; John Baynton to James Rumsey, March 1, 1768, *CISHL*, 16:126, 228–229, 360, 182; Ledger, Sale of Negroes at Kaskaskias, December 1767; List of Negro Bonds, 1767; Cash Account, 1767–1768; Notes and Orders Received of Mr. Rumsey on the Sale of Negroes, 1767–1768; Sale of Negroes, Kaskaskias Dec. 1767; Sale of Merchandise received in Payment for Negroes, November 1768; roll 10, Sequestered Baynton, Wharton, and Morgan Papers, 1725–1827, Manuscript Group 19, PSA.

23. Inventory of the Effects of Jacques Bourdon, July 5, 1723, KM, 23:7:1:1; Sale of an Enslaved Native American Woman, Guion to Etienne Hébert, KM, 23 :—:—: 5.

24. Lee, *Masters of the Middle Waters*, 44–46; Barr, "From Captives to Slaves."

25. For the Southwest, see Brooks, *Captives and Cousins*; Barr, "From Captives to Slaves." For the Southeast, see Gallay, *The Indian Slave Trade*.

26. Deposition Notes, Marie Scipio's Descendants [1806], JBCLFP.

27. For the enslavement of Fox, see, for example, Ruling of Captain Louis Ste. Ange de Belerive, regarding enslaved woman Marie, in Extract from the Registers of the Sessions of the Royal Jurisdiction of the Illinois, 1765, KM, 65:6:8:1. For the enslavement of Chickasaw, see, for example, Deposition of Pierre Chabot, Concerning a female Chicacha Slave, KM, 40:11:5:1. For the enslavement of "a *savagesse* named Jeanette of the Iroquois nation," who was born in Ste. Geneviève in the 1750s or 1760s, see Emancipation Given by Jean Louis de Noyon to an Indian Woman Named Jeanette, October 29, 1779, folder 419, SGA.

28. Macarty to Vaudreuil, January 20, 1752, *CISHL*, 29:452.

29. [Alexandre Xavier] De Guyenne to Vaudreuil, September 10, 1752, *CISHL*, 29:715.

30. Macarty to Vaudreuil, January 20, 1752, *CISHL*, 29:459.

31. Christopher Steinke, "Leading the 'Father': The Pawnee Homeland, Coureurs de Bois, and the Villasur Expedition of 1720," *Great Plains Quarterly* 32, no. 1 (Winter 2012), 43–62; Robert P. Wiegers, "A Proposal for Indian Slave Trading in the Mississippi Valley and Its Impact on the Osage," *Plains Anthropologist* 33, no. 120 (May 1988), 187–202; Thorne, *Many Hands of My Relations*, 20–28, 42–44, 72–75; Barr, "From Captives to Slaves."

32. Case of Joseph Labuniere and Louis Beaudoin, February 20, 1779, box 1, folder 5, Litigation Collection, MHMA; Morrissey, *Empire by Collaboration*, 156–161, 181–182. As late as 1805, "enemies" of the Otoe nation sold "two young female Otto savages" to Charles Gratiot and Grey Sarpy, wealthy habitants involved in the fur trade in the Lower Missouri Valley. The Otoes lived just north of the junction of the Missouri and Kansas Rivers. The two Indigenous women were returned to their nation at the insistence of the "great chief" of the Otoe. See Pierre Chouteau to General Wilkinson, May 12, 1806, box 6, Pierre Chouteau Letterbook, Chouteau Family Papers, MHMA.

33. For habitants declaring a captive Native American woman as an *"esclave sauvage,"* see, for example, Declaration of a female Indian slave belonging to Meliq, KM, 1723:25:16. For the larger motivations and processes by which Spanish, French, and Native American men turned Native American women into captives and slaves, see Barr, "From Captives to Slaves"; and Blackbird, "'It Has Always Been Customary.'"

34. For a lease of enslaved Native Americans, see, for example, Lease Agreement for Five Years between Chasin and Baron, KM, 26:8:3:2. For the gifting of enslaved Native Americans as property, see for example, Deed of Gift from Pierre Laclède Liguest to Madame Marie Therese Bourgeois Chouteau and her Children, May 4, 1768, Instrument #9B, Saint Louis Archives, MHMA; Registration of Marie Thérèse Bourgeois, September 10, 1768, KM, 68:9:10:2. For the transfer of enslaved Native Americans in wills, see, for example, Codicil to Will of Jean Baptiste de Monbrun de St. Laurent, December 21, 1747, KM, 47:12:21:1.

35. For the gendered and imperial dimensions of French enslavement of Indigenous women, along with its long-term consequences, see Leila K. Blackbird, "A Gendered Frontier: Métissage and Indigenous Enslavement in Eighteenth-Century Basse-Louisiane," *Eighteenth-Century Studies* 56, no. 2 (Winter 2023), 205–212; Kathleen DuVal, "Indian Intermarriage and Métissage in Colonial Louisiana," *William and Mary Quarterly*, 3rd ser., 65, no. 2 (April 2008), 267–30; Blackbird, "A Gendered Frontier"; Morrissey, *Empire by Collaboration*, 156–161, 181–182; Ekberg, *Stealing Indian Women*, 9–49; and Heerman, *Alchemy of Slavery*, 17–57.

36. Macarty to Vaudreuil, Census with a Recapitulation of Villages in the Illinois Country, 1752, Lauden Papers, Americana, Huntington Library, San Marino, California.

37. Carl J. Ekberg and Sharon K. Person, *St. Louis Rising: The French Regime of Louis St. Ange de Bellerive* (Urbana: University of Illinois Press, 2015).

38. Henry Marie Brackenridge, *Views of Louisiana: Containing Geographical, Statistical and Historical Notices of That Vast and Important Portion of America* (Baltimore, 1817), 238.

39. Entry for May 24, 1766, Register of the Notary of Ste. Geneviève, 1766 to 1767 [1770], Miscellaneous Bound MS #1, Transcribed and Translated by Vermer J. Genot, WPA, SGA; Lafreniere to Lefebvre and Labuxiere, August 6, 1766, Saint Louis Archives, Instrument #1, MHMA.

40. Notices by The King and our Lords of The Superior Council of Louisiana, November 14 and 16, 1766, in Saint Louis Archives, Instrument #1, MHMA.

41. Inventory of the Effects of Sieur Blouin at the Mines of La Mothe and La Saline, December 17, 1766, St. Louis Archives, Instrument #12, MHMA.

42. Sale from Sieur Joseph Dubord to Joseph Tellier, March 20, 1767, in Saint Louis Archives, Instrument #15, MHMA.

43. Estado General de Todos Los Habitanes de La Colonia de la Luisiana [General State of all the Inhabitants of the Colony of Louisiana], 1766, Santo Domingo, 2595, General Archives of the Indies, National Archives of Spain. Copies of the 1766 Louisiana census are available online at the website of the Missouri Secretary of State: see "1766 Census, Spanish Louisiana Territory,"

Territorial Censuses, Census Records, MSA-JC. For a detailed analysis of the 1766 censuses, see Ekberg, *French Roots in the Illinois Country*, 75, 97. For François Vallé's extensive holdings of enslaved people, see Carl J. Ekberg, *François Vallé and His World: Upper Louisiana Before Lewis and Clark* (Columbia: University of Missouri Press, 2002), 158–202.

44. Agreement between Alexander Langlais and Antoine Hubert [translation], August 14, 1768, folder 1, box 1, Frederick L. Billon Papers, MHMA.

45. Agreement between Gilbert Antoine de St. Maxent and Pierre Laclède Liguest, New Orleans [translation], May 8, 1769, Pierre Laclède Collection, 1769–1969, A0861, MHMA.

46. Louis and James Perrault, Bill of Exchange [translation], September 16, 1772, folder 1, box 1, Frederick L. Billon Papers, MHMA.

47. Estado General de Todos Los Habitanes de La Colonia de la Luisiana, 1766, Santo Domingo, 2595, General Archives of the Indies, National Archives of Spain. For a detailed analysis of the 1766 census, see Ekberg and Person, *St. Louis Rising*, 227–249.

48. Order of Command for M. de Macarty, August 8, 1751, *CISHL*, 29:318.

49. Father Louis Meurin to Bishop Briand, March 23, 1767, *CISHL*, 11:521–525.

50. Papers Documenting the State of the Settlement at St. Vincent on the Ouabache and others in the Illinois Country, CO, 5/87, page 36(71); "British Census of Illinois, 1767," *CISHL*, 11:469.

51. Philip Pittman, *The Present State of the European Settlements on the Mississippi With a Geographical Description of that River* . . . (London, 1770), 43, 47, 50.

52. Thomas Hutchins, *A Topographical Description of Virginia, Pennsylvania, Maryland, and North Carolina, comprehending the rivers Ohio, Kenhawa, Sioto, Cherokee, Wabash, Illinois, Missisippi, &c.* . . . (London, 1778), 17–18.

53. Lieutenant Governor Durnford to the Earl of Hillsborough, February 3, 1770, Colonial Records Office, Class 5, vol. 87, page 97, National Archives, United Kingdom.

54. John Baynton to James Rumsey, March 1, 1768, *CISHL*, 16:126.

55. List of Negro Bonds, 1767; Cash Account, 1767–1768; Notes and Orders Received of Mr. Rumsey on the Sale of Negroes, 1767–1768; Sale of Negroes Kaskaskias Dec. 1767; Sale of Merchandise received in Payment for Negroes, November 1768, roll 10, Sequestered Baynton, Wharton, and Morgan Papers, 1725–1827, Manuscript Group 19, PSA. Morgan to Baynton and Wharton, December 2, 1767, December 6, 1767, April 5, 1768, July 20, 1768; Baynton to Rumsey, March 1, 1768, *CISHL*, 16:126, 128, 228–229, 360, 182.

56. Account of Sundries Distributed to the Negroes, December 6, 1767, roll 10, Sequestered Baynton, Wharton, and Morgan Papers, 1725–1827, Manuscript Group 19, PSA.

57. List of Negro Bonds, 1767; Cash Account, 1767–1768; Notes and Orders Received of Mr. Rumsey on the Sale of Negroes, 1767–1768; Sale of Negroes Kaskaskias December 1767; Sale of Merchandise received in Payment for Negroes, November 1768, roll 10, Sequestered Baynton, Wharton, and Morgan Papers, 1725–1827, Manuscript Group 19, PSA.

58. Ledger Entry, Monsieur Charleville, January 6, 1768, roll 10, Sequestered Baynton, Wharton, and Morgan Papers 1725–1827, Manuscript Group 19, PSA.

59. Agreement with John Campbell, July 20, 1768, roll 10, Sequestered Baynton, Wharton, and Morgan Papers 1725–1827, Manuscript Group 19, PSA.

60. Ensign Hutchins to John Stuart Esq., September 10, 1771, vol. 106, folder 11, Thomas Gage Papers, WLCL; Petition of Fagot La Garciniere, July 22, 1770, KM, 70:7:22:1. It is unclear if the three men were returned to enslavement.

61. Report of Don Pedro Piernas to Gov. O'Reilly, Describing the Spanish Illinois Country, October 31, 1769, *SRM*, 1:70–72.

62. Francisco Cruzat to Bernardo Gálvez, November 23, 1777, *SRM*, 1:159–160.

63. Bernardo Gálvez to Joseph Gálvez, January 27, 1778, *SRM*, 1:158–159.

64. Fernando de Leyba to Bernardo Gálvez, November 16, 1778, *SMV*, 1: 312–313.

65. Special Instructions to Fernando de Leyba from Bernardo Gálvez, March 9, 1778, *SMV*, 1:258–260.

66. Bernardo Gálvez to Fernando de Leyba, January 13, 1779, *SMV*, 1:314.

67. Joseph Gálvez [José de Gálvez] to Francisco Cruzet, April 8, 1778, *SRM*, 1:159–160.

68. Francisco Cruzat to Bernardo Gálvez, November 23, 1777, *SRM*, 1:159–160. For habitants from Kaskaskia purchasing enslaved Africans through the international slave trade, via New Orleans and "the Spanish contract," see Agreement between Pierre Richard and Henry Richard, August 21, 1779, KM, 79:8:21:2. The Richard brothers purchased three enslaved Africans in New Orleans for 2,000 livres.

69. Native American enslavement remained semilegal in Upper Louisiana until 1836 when the Missouri Supreme Court ruled that enslaved persons of maternal Native American descent born after 1769 were due their freedom. See Lea VanderVelde, *Redemption Songs: Suing for Freedom Before Dred Scott* (New York: Oxford University Press, 2014), 39–56, and chapters 4 and 6.

70. Deed of gift from Pierre Laclède Liguest to Madame Marie Therese Bourgeois Chouteau and her Children, May 4, 1768, Instrument #9B, Saint Louis Archives, MHMA; Registration of Marie Thérèse Bourgeois, September 10, 1768, KM, 68:9:10:2.

71. Register of the Notary of Ste. Geneviève, 1766 to 1767 [1770], Miscellaneous Bound MS #1, Transcribed and Translated by Vermer J. Genot, WPA, SGA; List of Documents Contained in the Office of the Register of Ste. Geneviève, kept by Mr. Jean Baptiste Vallé. Given to Thomas Oliver, December 5, 1804, Miscellaneous Bound MS #1, Transcribed and Translated by Vermer J. Genot, WPA, SGA.

72. Deeds # 203–1/2, Relinquishment of Claims in Dower Rights by Mrs. Jautard against Her husband in favor of Pierre Poupet, May 10, 1768 [transcript], SGA.

73. Agreement between Francis Duchouquet and Joseph Pouillot, March 28, 1769 [transcript], folder 1, box 1, Frederick L. Billon Papers, MHMA.

74. For the various and often conflicting forms of bound and slave labor created by Spanish officials and enslavers, see Barba, *Country of the Cursed and Driven*; Reséndez, *The Other Slavery*; and Barr, "From Captives to Slaves."

75. Proclamation by [Gov. Alejandro] O'Reilly, New Orleans, December 7, 1769, *SMV*, 1:125–126. For the circumstances that led O'Reilly to issue his decree, see Blackbird, "'It Has Always Been Customary,'" 533–536.

76. For the origins, meanings, and uses of the phrase "*Obedezco pero no cumplo*" (I obey but I do not comply) among Spanish imperial officials, see John Leddy Phelan, "Authority and Flexibility in the Spanish Imperial Bureaucracy," *Administrative Science Quarterly* 5, no. 1 (June 1960), 47–65. For the flexibility claimed by Spanish officials in implementing imperial decrees in their particular provinces, see Alejandra Irigoin and Regina Grafe, "Bargaining for Absolutism: A Spanish Path to Nation-State and Empire Building," *Hispanic American Historical Review* 88, no. 2 (May 2008), 173–209.

77. Luis de Unzaga to Pedro Piernas, undated letter from late 1770 or early 1771, *SMV*, 1:191.

78. Proclamation by O'Reilly, New Orleans, December 7, 1769, *SMV*, 1:125–126.

79. Pedro Piernas to Luis de Unzaga, July 8, 1770, folder 19, box 5, Louisiana Collection, MSS M-M 508, Bancroft Library, University of California, Berkeley.

80. Confirmation of Gift from Francois Vallé to Marguerite, February 14, 1748, KM, 48:2:14:1.

81. "Indian Slaves at Ste. Genevieve," May 28, 1770, *SMV*, 1:167–170; Census of Indian Slaves at Ste. Geneviève and St. Louis, folder 19, box 5, Louisiana Collection, MSS M-M 508, Bancroft Library, University of California, Berkeley.

82. Agreement between Francis Duchouquet and Joseph Pouillot, March 28, 1769 [transcript], folder 1, box 1, Frederick L. Billon Papers, MHMA.

83. January 17, 1768, Sale of a savage woman by Hunion Huberdeau to Poitvin, List of Documents Contained in the Office of the Register of Ste. Geneviève, kept by Mr. Jean Baptiste Valle, Given to Thomas Oliver, December 5, 1804, Miscellaneous Bound MS #1, Transcribed and Translated by Vermer J. Genot, WPA, SGA.

84. "Indian Slaves at Ste. Genevieve," May 28, 1770, *SMV*, 1:167–170; Census of Indian Slaves at Ste. Geneviève and St. Louis, folder 19, box 5, Louisiana Collection, MSS M-M 508, Bancroft Library, University of California, Berkeley; Estates #4, Probate of the Estate of Antoine Aubuchon, January 12, 1778 [typescript], SGA. The 1766 Census of Ste. Geneviève lists Aubuchon as the owner of two enslaved persons. See Estado General de Todos Los Habitanes de La Colonia de la Luisiana, 1766, Santo Domingo, 2595, General Archives of the Indies, National Archives of Spain. Ekberg, in *Stealing Indian Women*, 183–185, points out that the will of Aubuchon's widow and children provided for the freedom of Marianne's two enslaved sons, but as of the 1787 census, members of the Aubuchon family still had two enslaved *pardos*, the term used by Spanish officials to obscure the Native American ancestry of enslaved people on the east bank of the Mississippi. See A General Census of the Towns of St. Louis and Ste. Geneviève, 1787, and a census of St. Louis and its Districts, 1791, from the Archivo Nacional, Havana, transcribed and translated by Louis Houck, Census Collection, MHMA. For Marianne's flight with the trapper Céledon, see Inquest, Body of an Indian Woman Slave of Widow Aubuchon, Indian Slave escaped in Man's Clothing . . . March 18, 1773, folder 421, SGA. When, in 1773, officials interrogated Marianne concerning the disappearance of another enslaved Native American woman from Kaskaskia, the officials referred to Marianne as a *sauvagesse*, the common term for an enslaved Indigenous woman.

85. Estate Inventory of M. Charles Marois, December 14, 1778, *CISHL*, 2:459; Census of Indian Slaves at Ste. Geneviève and St. Louis, folder 19, box 5, Louisiana Collection, MSS M-M 508, Bancroft Library, University of California, Berkeley.

86. Census of Indian Slaves at Ste. Geneviève and St. Louis, folder 19, box 5, Louisiana Collection, MSS M-M 508, Bancroft Library, University of California, Berkeley; Wills of Don Fernando De Leyba and Louis Ste. Ange De Bellerive [translation], 1774, 1780, folder 6, Frederick L. Billon Papers, MHMA. For St. Ange, see Lee, *Masters of the Middle Waters*, 161–163.

87. Spanish Census of St. Louis and Ste. Geneviève, 1772; Census of Piernas for 1773, *SRM*, 1:53–54, 61.

88. Deposition Notes, Marie Scipio's Descendants [1806], and Deposition Notes, Freedom Suit of Scipio's Children, April 7, 1817, JBCLFP. In the Lucas depositions, every individual who testified, with the exception of Tayon and Chouteau, agreed that it was common knowledge in St. Louis from the 1770s through the 1790s that Marie Scipio's mother "was a Natchez Indian." The freedom suit of Marie Scipio (sometimes Scipion or Sycpion) is covered in subsequent

chapters. For the clearest description and analysis of the case, which was initiated in 1799 and stretched on until the late 1830s, see William E. Foley, "Slave Freedom Suits Before Dred Scott: The Case of Marie Jean Scypion's Descendants," *Missouri Historical Review* 79 (October 1984), 1–23; and VanderVelde, *Redemption Songs*, 39–56.

89. Case of Joseph Labuniere and Louis Beaudoin [translation], February 20, 1779, box 1, folder 5, Litigation Collection, MHMA.

90. Local Ordinances for St. Louis and General Ordinance Published by Lieutenant Governor Don Francisco Cruzat, August 15, 1781, Louis Houck, Papers from Spain, Transcripts, Missouri Historical Society, St. Louis.

91. A Proclamation, September 6, 1779, *CISHL*, 5:118; Proclamation by George R. Clark, December 24, 1779, *CISHL*, 5:65.

92. Agreement between Antoine Renau and Joseph Baugie, August 7, 1783, KM, 83:8:7:1. *Griffe* referred to a person of mixed Native American and African lineage.

93. For the continuation of Native American enslavement in Illinois, see, for example, Sale of an Enslaved Native American Woman by Antoine Rénaux to Joseph Bauge, January 14, 1784, KM, 84:1:14:1; Emancipation of Marianne Sauvagesse by Joseph Marrois, May 15, 1782, KM, 82:5:15:1; Will of Louis Langlois, KM, 73:5:20:1. Langlois's will provided 100 livres for the baptism and religious instruction of the enslaved Native American woman Mannon, but it did not provide for her emancipation.

94. Sale of Slave from Manuel Escalera to Francisco Cruzat, November 25, 1775, St. Louis Archives, 1766–1804, Instrument #170, MHMA.

95. Ekberg, *Stealing Indian Women*, 82–86.

96. Petition of Pélagie Carpentier for Separation from Charles Vallé, 1783 [typescript]; Sale of Various slaves by Pélagie Carpentier to Francois Cruzat, List of Documents Contained in the Office of the Register of Ste. Geneviève, kept by Mr. Jean Baptiste Valle, Given to Thomas Oliver, December 5, 1804, Miscellaneous Bound MS #1, Transcribed and Translated by Vermer J. Genot, WPA, SGA.

97. June 27, 1783, Sale of Various slaves by Pélagie Carpentier to François Cruzat; December 9, 1787, Exchange of Slaves Between Mr. Don Fóis Cruzat and Don Carlos Valle, in List of Documents Contained in the Office of the Register of Ste. Geneviève, kept by Mr. Jean Baptiste Vallé, Given to Thomas Oliver, December 5, 1804, Miscellaneous Bound MS #1, Transcribed and Translated by Vermer J. Genot, WPA, SGA.

98. For the omission of "Indian" or "sauvage" from the list of slave sales after 1780, see List of Documents Contained in the Office of the Register of Ste. Geneviève, kept by Mr. Jean Baptiste Valle, Given to Thomas Oliver, December 5, 1804, Miscellaneous Bound MS #1, Transcribed and Translated by Vermer J. Genot, WPA, SGA.

99. "Accidental Killing of Mrs. Chouteau's negro man, Baptiste, December 27, 1785," in Frederic L. Billon, *Annals of St. Louis, in its Early Days Under the French and Spanish Dominations* (St. Louis, 1886), 233–242, quotes at 233, 236, 238, 239, 234; Census of Indian Slaves at Ste. Geneviève and St. Louis, folder 19, box 5, Louisiana Collection, MSS M-M 508, Bancroft Library, University of California, Berkeley.

100. Local Ordinances for St. Louis and General Ordinance Published by Lieutenant Governor Don Francisco Cruzat, November 24, 1787, Louis Houck, Papers from Spain, Transcripts, Missouri Historical Society, St. Louis.

101. A General Census of the Towns of St. Louis and Ste. Geneviève, 1787, and a census of St. Louis and its Districts, 1791, from the Archivo Nacional, Havana, transcribed and translated

by Louis Houck, Census Collection, MHMA. For the amorphous uses of the term *pardo* in the broader Spanish American empire, see Ann Twinam, *Purchasing Whiteness: Pardos, Mulattos, and the Quest for Social Mobility in the Spanish Indies* (Stanford, CA: Stanford University Press, 2015). *Pardo* had many different meanings in the Spanish American empire, depending on time, place, and the social group who deployed it. Most often, it referred to people who descended from multiple generations of African, European, and Native American ancestry.

102. A General Census of the Towns of St. Louis and Ste. Geneviève, 1787, and a census of St. Louis and its Districts, 1791, from the Archivo Nacional, Havana, transcribed and translated by Louis Houck, Census Collection, MHMA.

103. Emancipation Given by Jean Louis de Noyon to an Indian Woman named Jeanette, October 29, 1779, folder 419, SGA. For the absence of transactions and recordings involving enslaved Native Americans, see List of Documents Contained in the Office of the Register of Ste. Geneviève, kept by Mr. Jean Baptiste Valle, Given to Thomas Oliver, December 5, 1804, Miscellaneous Bound MS #1, Transcribed and Translated by Vermer J. Genot, WPA, SGA.

104. Estate #22, Inventory of the Estate of Widow Bauvais, May 4, 1790 [typescript], SGA.

105. The story of María and her children is recounted in Ekberg, *Stealing Indian Women*, 82–86.

106. For María's, Pierre's, and Baptiste's successful freedom suits, see Proceedings Instituted by Pedro Morsu and Baptista Borguinon to Prove that they are Mestee Indians, In order to Obtain their Emancipation, January 26, 1790, Document # 2369; and Proceedings Instituted by Pedro Morsu (Indian Mestee) In Order to Compel the Heirs of Don Francisco Cruzat to Give Him His Freedom, May 4, 1790, Document # 2491, Louisiana Colonial Documents Digitization Project, Louisiana Historical Center, New Orleans. For analyses of these cases, see Blackbird, " 'It Has Always Been Customary'"; and Stephen Webre, "The Problem of Indian Slavery in Spanish Louisiana, 1769–1803," *Louisiana History* 25, no. 2 (Spring 1984), 117–135.

107. Mrs. Morancy [Marie Rose Devaignay] vs. Simon Hubardeau Concerning an Enslaved Native American Man, 1790, folder 424, SGA.

108. Testimony of Madame [illegible], page 8, Deposition Notes, Marie Scipio's Descendants [1806], JBCLFP.

109. Blackbird, " 'It Has Always Been Customary,'" 546–547; Webre, "Problem of Indian Slavery."

Chapter 2

1. Interrogation of Jean Baxe, Opinion by Terisse de Ternan, and Sentence by the Commandant and Officers, KM, 30:12:22:1, 2, 3.

2. Interrogation and Flogging of several Enslaved Native and African Americans, May 7, 1743, KM, 43:5:7:2.

3. Beauvais to [Pierre de Rigaud, Marquis de] Vaudreuil, November 1752; [Barthélemy de] Macarty [Mactigue] to Vaudreuil, December 7, 1752; Vaudreuil to Beauchamp, January 20, 1753; Kerelérec to [Minister Antoine Louis] Rouillé, August 20, 1753, *CISHL*, 29:741, 755, 756, 757, 776, 808, 809, 810, 823.

4. Beauvais to Vaudreuil, November 1752; Macarty to Vaudreuil, December 7, 1752; Vaudreuil to Beauchamp, January 20, 1753; Kerelérec to Rouillé, August 20, 1753, *CISHL*, 29:741, 755, 756, 757, 776, 808, 809, 810, 823. For the importance of kinship and its role as the antithesis of enslavement, see Christina Snyder, *Slavery in Indian Country: The Changing Face of Captivity in Early America* (Cambridge, MA: Harvard University Press, 2010).

5. The Case of Louis Mahas, 1778, box 1, folder 3, Litigation Collection, MHMA. Transcriptions and translations of the Mahas file can be found in Frederic L. Billon, *Annals of St. Louis, in its Early Days Under the French and Spanish Dominations* (St. Louis, 1886), 156–158.

6. The Case of Louis Mahas, 1778, box 1, folder 3, Litigation Collection, MHMA.

7. The Case of Louis Mahas, 1778, box 1, folder 3, Litigation Collection, MHMA.

8. The Case of Louis Mahas, 1778, box 1, folder 3, Litigation Collection, MHMA.

9. The Case of Louis Mahas, 1778, box 1, folder 3, Litigation Collection, MHMA.

10. For the options available to enslaved men and women who turned themselves into maroons and faced exile in borderlands and hinterlands, see Sylviane A. Diouf, *Slavery's Exiles: The Story of American Maroons* (New York: New York University Press, 2014).

11. Ensign Hutchins to John Stuart Esq., September 10, 1771, vol. 106, folder 11, Thomas Gage Papers, WLCL; Petition of Fagot La Garciniere, July 22, 1770, KM, 70:7:22:1.

12. Inquest, Body of an Indian Woman Slave of Widow Aubuchon, Indian Slave escaped in Man's Clothing . . . March 18, 1773, folder 421, SGA. The details of the party and events that surrounded the flight of Marianne and the unnamed Native American woman are covered in detail in Carl J. Ekberg, *Stealing Indian Women: Native Slavery in the Illinois Country* (Urbana: University of Illinois Press, 2007), 144–146.

13. Inquest, Body of an Indian Woman Slave of Widow Aubuchon, Indian Slave escaped in Man's Clothing . . . March 18, 1773, folder 421, SGA.

14. Inquest, Body of an Indian Woman Slave of Widow Aubuchon, Indian Slave escaped in Man's Clothing . . . March 18, 1773, folder 421, SGA; A General Census of the Towns of St. Louis and Ste. Genevieve, 1787, and a census of St. Louis and its Districts, 1791, from the Archivo Nacional, Havana, transcribed and translated by Louis Houck, Census Collection, MHMA.

15. Inquest, Body of an Indian Woman Slave of Widow Aubuchon, Indian Slave escaped in Man's Clothing . . . March 18, 1773, folder 421, SGA.

16. Robert Michael Morrisey, *Empire by Collaboration: Indians, Colonists, and Governments in Colonial Illinois Country* (Philadelphia: University of Pennsylvania Press, 2015), demonstrates that habitants fled British Illinois for Spanish Upper Louisiana, not because of religion or cultural alienation from the British, but because British officials and agents were unable and unwilling to meet the demands of habitants. Upon the arrival of the British in Illinois in 1765, many habitants envisioned for themselves new commercial opportunities within the British empire, opportunities that British officials failed to deliver. Likewise, habitants eagerly sought British imperial power for their own uses locally. British officials, however, failed to build the infrastructure of imperial state power in Illinois, further alienating habitants.

17. Extract of a Letter from Captain Forbes . . . . Commanding at the Illinois to General Gage, April 15, 1768, in Letters from Major General Thomas Gage August 17–20, 1768, Colonial Records Office, 5/233, 54 (106). This collection of letters to General Thomas Gage, the leading British official in North America, is filled with examples of how badly overextended the British empire in North America had become in the 1760s as it faced crises in the thirteen Atlantic colonies, with Native Americans who had forsaken British counsel stretching from the Haudenosaunee in New York to the Cherokee in Georgia, fears of Spanish conquest of Florida, and the inability of British officials to force colonists anywhere to abide by imperial commercial regulations.

18. Lieutenant Colonel John Wilkins to General Thomas Gage, May 30, 1770, letter 989, Thomas Gage Papers, WLCL.

19. Thomas Stirling to General Thomas Gage, December 15, 1765, Colonial Records Office, 5/84, 108–113.

20. John Evans to ___, May 22, 1770, KM, 70:5:22:1. For Wilkins, see Colton Storm, "The Notorious Colonel Wilkins," *Journal of the Illinois State Historical Society* 40, no. 1 (March 1947), 7–22.

21. The Court of Judicature for the Colony of the Illinois . . . . Kaskaskia, June 6, 1770, Thomas Gage Papers, WLCL.

22. John Evans to ___, May 22, 1770, KM, 70:5:22:1.

23. General Thomas Gage to Colonel Thomas Reid, August 10, 1767, vol. 68, Thomas Gage Papers, WLCL.

24. General Thomas Gage to Colonel Thomas Reid, August 10, 1767, vol. 68, Thomas Gage Papers, WLCL.

25. General Thomas Gage to Colonel Thomas Reid, August 10, 1767, vol. 68, Thomas Gage Papers, WLCL; The Court of Judicature for the Colony of the Illinois . . . . Kaskaskia, June 6, 1770, Thomas Gage Papers, WLCL. Like many other habitants, Derisseaux also faced financial difficulties in the aftermath of the transfer to British authority. By June 1771, he was fighting lawsuits involving more than 1,600 livres' worth of goods stemming from a 1768 transaction involving merchants from the west bank and New Orleans. See Petitions and Affidavits of Paul Derisseaux to Lieutenant Colonel Wilkins, June 9, 1771, Thomas Gage Papers, WLCL.

26. George Morgan to John Baynton and Samuel Wharton, December 6, 1767, *CISHL*, 16:128.

27. Ledger, July 31, 1768, roll 10, Sequestered Baynton, Wharton, and Morgan Papers, 1725–1827, Manuscript Group 19, PSA.

28. Acknowledgement of Josep Dupui, KM, 75:6:16:1.

29. Virginia ceded its claims to Illinois to the Confederation Congress in 1783. The United States issued the Northwest Ordinance in 1787, but U.S. officials did not arrive in Illinois until 1789.

30. Morrissey, *Empire by Collaboration*, 195–223.

31. Proclamation by George R. Clark, December 24, 1778, *CISHL*, 5:64–68.

32. Proclamation by George R. Clark, December 24, 1778, *CISHL*, 5:64–68. For the ways that the disruptions caused by the U.S. War for Independence allowed for enslaved Virginians to claim and exercise greater control over their lives, and in some cases to free themselves from their enslavement entirely, see Woody Holton, *Forced Founders: Indians, Debtors, Slaves, and the Making of the American Revolution in Virginia* (Chapel Hill: University of North Carolina Press, 1999).

33. Proclamation by George R. Clark, December 24, 1778, *CISHL*, 5:64–68.

34. Proclamation by George R. Clark, December 24, 1778, *CISHL*, 5:64–68.

35. Proclamation by George R. Clark, December 24, 1778, *CISHL*, 5:64–68.

36. Transcripts from the Cahokia Record, June 10, 1779, *CISHL*, 2:13–21.

37. Transcripts from the Cahokia Record, June 10, 1779, *CISHL*, 2:13–21.

38. For the conflicting death sentences issued by Todd, see *CISHL*, 2:21n1; Warrant for Execution, John Todd's Record Book, 1778–1779, 18, CHM. For the order to guard Moreau, see John Todd to Nicholas Janis, June 13, 1779, John Todd's Record Book, 19, CHM.

39. For additional sources concerning Manuel and Moreau, see Presentation of J. Girault, State's Attorney, June 11, 1778, KM, 79:6:12:2; Testimony of Several Enslaved Persons, June 10, 1779, KM, 79:6:10:1, 79:6:10:2.

40. Kaskaskia Magistrates to John Todd, May 21, 1779, *CISHL*, 5:91.

41. A Proclamation, September 6, 1779, *CISHL*, 5:117–118.

42. Inhabitants of Kaskaskia to the Magistrates, May 25, 1782, *CISHL*, 5:288.

43. Transcripts from the Cahokia Record, December 14, 1782, *CISHL*, 2:143–145.

44. Court Record, January 8, 1785, *CISHL*, 2:187–189. For the importance of trade in cloth and clothing among subordinated and enslaved people, see Laura F. Edwards, *Only the Clothes on Her Back: Clothing and the Hidden History of Power in the Nineteenth-Century United States* (New York: Oxford University Press, 2022).

45. Court Record, January 8, 1785, *CISHL*, 2:187–189.

46. Court Record, January 8, 1785, *CISHL*, 2:187–189.

47. Jean Baptiste Barbeau to Pierre Langlois, January 1787, *CISHL*, 5:396–397.

48. Deposition of Louis Germain and Antoine Bristout, KM, 87:2:21:1.

49. Exchange of Enslaved Men by Jacques Clamorgan and Daniel Blouin, KM, 86:1:25:1.

50. Power of Attorney of Pierre Degagne to Louis Dore for Payment from Morgan for 8 Piastres, KM, 86:8:21:1.

51. Trial of Enslaved Woman Lorine for an Assault on Enslaved Woman Marianne, . . . January 22, 1779 [translation], folder 2, box 1, Litigation Collection, MHMA.

52. Mr. Condé and Mr. Perrault's Obligation, November 12, 1776, Pierre Laclède Collection, 1769–1969, MHMA.

53. Proceedings Between Gaspard Roubieu and his wife [Marie Anne Laferne] [translation], September 22, 1778, folder 1, box 1, Frederick L. Billon Papers, MHMA. For Lorine's life in St. Louis, see Carl J. Ekberg and Sharon K. Person, *St. Louis Rising: The French Regime of Louis St. Ange de Bellerive* (Urbana: University of Illinois Press, 2015), 150–153; and Patricia Cleary, *The World, the Flesh, and the Devil: A History of Colonial St. Louis* (Columbia: University of Missouri Press, 2011), 212–214.

54. Proceedings Between Gaspard Roubieu and his wife [Marie Anne Laferne] [translation], September 22, 1778, folder 1, box 1, Frederick L. Billon Papers, MHMA.

55. Proceedings Between Gaspard Roubieu and his wife [Marie Anne Laferne] [translation], September 22, 1778, folder 1, box 1, Frederick L. Billon Papers, MHMA.

56. Trial of Enslaved Woman Lorine for an Assault on Enslaved Woman Marianne, . . . January 22, 1779 [translation], folder 2, box 1, Litigation Collection, MHMA.

57. Emancipation Given by Jean Louis de Noyon to an Indian Woman named Jeanette, October 29, 1779, folder 419, SGA. No Jeanette appears in the Ste. Geneviève census of enslaved Native Americans, but two do appear in the St. Louis census.

58. Emancipation of Marie, Order Signed by Fernando De Leyba, Estate of Jean Baptiste La Bastille, 1779, folder 419, SGA. I cannot find evidence that Marie ever secured her emancipation.

59. For Vallé, see Carl J. Ekberg, *François Vallé and His World: Upper Louisiana Before Lewis and Clark* (Columbia: University of Missouri Press, 2002).

60. Testimony of Madame Chauvin, page 12, Deposition Notes, Marie Scipio's Descendants [1806], JBCLFP.

61. Local Ordinances for St. Louis and General Ordinance Published by Lieutenant Governor Don Francisco Cruzat, August 12 and 15, 1781, Louis Houck, Papers from Spain, Transcripts, MHMA.

62. Local Ordinances for St. Louis and General Ordinance Published by Lieutenant Governor Don Francisco Cruzat, August 12 and 15, 1781, Louis Houck, Papers from Spain, Transcripts, MHMA.

63. Documents #27, Rules by the Syndic concerning boundaries and fences, May 9, 1778 [transcript], SGA; Documents #28, Boundary Fences, Copy of Regulations made in St. Louis for the Construction of Fences, April 27, 1784 [transcript], SGA.

64. "Suit Against Isabel Bissette Vachard, 1783–1784," in *Annals of St. Louis, in Its Early Days Under the French and Spanish Dominations*, ed. Frederic L. Billon (St. Louis, 1886), 227–228. Vachard was released after her relatives in St. Louis paid for the damages claimed by Vallé and his partners in Ste. Geneviève.

65. Peyroux Coudreniere to Esteban Miró, March 8, 1788, *SMV*, 2:246.

66. "Killing of Baptiste, December 27, 1785," in Billon, *Annals of St. Louis*, 233–242. For the use of arson as a form of resistance by enslaved people, see Daniel Immerwahr, "Burning Down the House: Slavery and Arson in America," *Journal of American History* 110, no. 3 (December 2023), 449–473.

67. "Killing of Baptiste, December 27, 1785," in Billon, *Annals of St. Louis*, 233–242.

Chapter 3

1. For criticisms of the United States for failing to enforce Article VI, see, most notably, Paul Finkelman, "Slavery and the Northwest Ordinance: A Study in Ambiguity," *Journal of the Early Republic* 6, no. 4 (Winter 1986), 343–370; Paul Finkelman, "Evading the Ordinance: The Persistence of Bondage in Indiana and Illinois," *Journal of the Early Republic* 9, no. 1 (Spring 1989), 21–51, along with Finkelman's many subsequent works on the Northwest Ordinance. For more recent examples, see, for example, Edward Baptist, *The Half Has Never Been Told: Slavery and the Making of American Capitalism* (New York: Basic Books, 2014), especially 8.

2. Gabriel Cerré's Testimony concerning Illinois, Given Before Congress, July 1786, *TPUS*, 2:383.

3. Report of Committee on Memorial of B. Tardiveau, September 1788, *Journals of the Continental Congress*, ed. Worthington C. Ford and others, 34 vols. (Washington, DC: Government Printing Office, 1904–1937), 34:541.

4. Entry for April 13 and April 19, 1790, Winthrop Sargent Diary, reel 1, series II, vol. 1786–1820, Winthrop Sargent Papers, MHS.

5. "The Number of Souls in the Territory of the United States north-west of the river Ohio, in 1790," (Philadelphia) *National Gazette*, November 17, 1791.

6. 1796 Census, New Madrid [translation], box 1, folder 1, Frederick Billon Papers, MHMA.

7. *An Account of Upper Louisiana by Nicolas de Finiels*, ed. and trans. Carl J. Ekberg and William E. Foley (Columbia: University of Missouri Press, 1989), 109.

8. Thomas Jefferson, Queries on Louisiana, 1803; Benjamin Stoddert, Notes on Louisiana, June 3, 1803, Thomas Jefferson Papers, LOC; "Description of Louisiana," *Annals of Congress*, 8th Cong., 2nd sess., Appendix, 1576. There are no census records for the Illinois villages after 1783. In 1790, Northwest Territory Governor Arthur St. Clair sought to conduct a census of the villages, but he relied on counts from 1783. See *TPUS*, 2:257–261. Overall, the reports that St. Clair came into possession of recorded approximately two hundred white families in the Illinois villages.

9. Report of Governor St. Clair to the Secretary of State, February 10, 1791, *TPUS*, 2:324, 332.

10. Contract between the French Inhabitants and Barthelemi Tardiveau, August 27, 1787 and Contract between the Americans and Barthelemi Tardiveau, August 27, 1787, *CISHL*, 5:440–444. For earlier attempts by habitants "to carry their Just complaints against" Virginia

officials "to the governor of Virginia, or before the Congress," see Agreement between the Habitants of Kaskaskia and Richard Macarty and Pierre Prévost, May 5, 1781, KM, 81:5:5:1.

11. Memorial of Barthelemi Tardiveau, July 8, 1788, *CISHL*, 5:488.

12. Report of Committee on Memorial of B. Tardiveau, September 1788, in Ford et al., *Journals of the Continental Congress*, 34:541.

13. Arthur St. Clair to George Washington, May 1, 1790, *TPUS*, 2:247.

14. Report of Governor St. Clair to the Secretary of State, February 10, 1791, *TPUS*, 2:332.

15. For the complete breakdown of the court system, the inability of the United States to pass or send laws, and the inability of the United States to send governing officials to Illinois, see Arthur St. Clair to Winthrop Sargent, May 28, 1792, reel 3, series III, Correspondence and other Papers, 1771–1948, Winthrop Sargent Papers, MHS.

16. "Immigrants from the United States, into Missouri, December 1, 1787 through December 31, 1789," *SMV*, vol. 3, part II, 290.

17. Entry for April 12, 1790, Winthrop Sargent Diary, reel 1, series II, vol. 1786–1820, Winthrop Sargent Papers, MHS.

18. Entry for April 19, 1790, Winthrop Sargent Diary, reel 1, series II, vol. 1786–1820, Winthrop Sargent Papers, MHS.

19. New Madrid Land Office Advertisement, April 22, 1789, George Morgan Papers, Illinois History and Lincoln Collections, University of Illinois, Urbana-Champaign. For Morgan, New Madrid, and the Illinois Country, see Robert Michael Morrisey, "'All Princes and Rulers Are Alike to Us': The Education of George Morgan in the Ohio Valley," *Ohio Valley History* 15, no. 1 (Spring 2015), 41–63.

20. Governor Esteban Miró to George Morgan, May 23, 1789, George Morgan Papers, Illinois History and Lincoln Collections, University of Illinois, Urbana-Champaign.

21. Arthur St. Clair to George Washington, May 1, 1790, *TPUS*, 2:247.

22. Barthelemi Tardiveau to Arthur St. Clair, June 30, 1789, Arthur St. Clair Papers, Ohio History Connection, Columbus.

23. Major John Hamtramck to General Josiah Harmar, August 14, 1789, *CISHL*, 5:508–509.

24. Major John Hamtramck to Winthrop Sargent, April 12, 1797, reel 3, series III, Winthrop Sargent Papers, MHS.

25. Francisco Cruzat to Jean Baptiste Crely and Joseph Dupuis, February 18, 1786, KM, 86:2:18:1.

26. Joseph Dupuis to Mathurin Bouvet, October 17, 1786, *CISHL*, 5:396.

27. In 1757, Father Forget and the parish inherited an unspecified number of "negro slaves" from his fellow priest, Joseph Gagnon. See Execution of will of Joseph Gagnon, March 10, 1757, KM, 57:3:14:1.

28. Inhabitants of Cahokia to the Seminary of Quebec, June 6th, 1787, *CISHL*, 5:564–565.

29. Petition of Marguerite Beauvais to Upper Louisiana Lieutenant Governor Francisco Cruzat, April 23, 1787, KM, 87:4:23:1.

30. Madam Bentley v. John Dodge, Record of Davidson Court, January Term 1790, Davidson County, Tennessee, Court of Pleas and Quarter Sessions, Daily Minutes, 6, vol. A, 342, Copy on file with the Papers of Andrew Jackson Project (PAJ), University of Tennessee, Knoxville, original, Tennessee State Library and Archives. My thanks to PAJ editor Tom Coens for sharing a copy of the minutes book with me.

31. John Edgar to Major John Hamtramck, October 28, 1789, *CISHL*, 5:514.

32. Arthur St. Clair to Henri Peyroux de la Coudrenière, Commandant, Ste. Geneviève, April 1, 1790, *TPUS*, 2:233–234.

33. Transcripts from the Cahokia Record, June 2, 1789, *CISHL*, 2:383–387.

34. Litigation, Moses Austin against Robert Greer (February–March 1799), Washington County Court Collection, box 1, MHMA.

35. Proclamations of the Spanish Governor of Louisiana and West Florida, September 2 and 6, 1789, *TPUS*, 2:214–215.

36. Memorial of Father Pierre Gibault to Arthur St. Clair, May 1, 1790, *TPUS*, 2:243–244.

37. John Rice Jones to Major John Hamtramck, October 29, 1789, *CISHL*, 5:515.

38. Henry Vanderburg to Winthrop Sargent, April 14, 1797, reel 3, series III, Winthrop Sargent Papers, MHS. For Gamelin's presence in Upper Louisiana, see 1796 Census, New Madrid [translation], box 1, folder 1, Frederick Billon Papers, MHMA; Antoine Gamelin, Papers of Original Claimants, 1777–1851, First Board of Land Commissioners, U.S. Recorder of Land Titles, Record Group 951, MSA-JC.

39. Henry Vanderburg to Winthrop Sargent, April 14, 1797, reel 3, series III, Winthrop Sargent Papers, MHS.

40. John Edgar to Winthrop Sargent, August 25, 1797, Winthrop Sargent Papers, reel 4, series III, Correspondence and Other Papers, 1771–1948, Winthrop Sargent Papers, MHS.

41. Baron de Carondelet to François Vallé, June 2, 1797 [translation], François Vallé Papers, 1742–1846, MHMA. For banditti capturing enslaved men and women and then selling them along the Gulf Coast, see, for example, François Vallé to Charles Howard, May 15, 1797 [translation], François Vallé Papers, 1742–1846, MHMA.

42. Receipt, George Rogers Clark to François Trottier Janis, May 20, 1779, box 3, Clark Family Collection, George Rogers Clark Papers, MHMA; Contract between the French Inhabitants and Barthelemi Tardiveau, August 27, 1787, *CISHL*, 5:440–444; John Todd to Nicholas Janis, June 13, 1779, John Todd's Record Book, 1778–1779, page 19, CHM; Petition to the Governor of Virginia from the Inhabitants of Kaskaskia, May 4, 1781, *CISHL*, 5:233; Court of Inquiry, September 11, 1777, *CISHL*, 5:18n4; Lands Claimed by Inhabitants of Kaskaskia, 1790, *TPUS*, 2:254; Memorial of Father Gibault and Others to Governor Arthur St. Clair, June 9, 1790, *TPUS*, 2:281.

43. Improvement of Nicholas, François, Antoine, and Jean Baptiste Janis, No. 2010, *American State Papers: Public Lands* (Washington: U.S. Government Printing Office, 1832), 2:225.

44. Concession #40, February 19, 1795; Concession #41, Petition of Baptiste Janis, September 26, 1796; Concession #42, Petition of Baptiste Janis, November 10, 1800 [typescript], A1461, SGA; "Immigrants from the United States, into Missouri, December 1, 1787 through December 31, 1789," *SMV*, vol. 3, part II, 290; Petition of Jean Baptiste Janis, Sen. of Missouri, April 11, 1836, *Public Documents of the United States Senate*, 24th Cong., 1st sess., vol. 6, Document #299.

45. Jean Baptiste Janis served as a witness at the certification of the will of François Vallé, see Will of François Vallé, February 19, 1804, box 1, Carr-Papin Family Papers, 1776–1877, MHMA.

46. George Hunter, Journal of a tour from Philadelphia to Kentucky & the Illinois Country, 1796, George Hunter Journals, Mss.B.H912, American Philosophical Society Library, Philadelphia. For Hunter's journey to the Middle Mississippi Valley, see John Francis McDermott, ed., "The Western Journals of Dr. George Hunter, 1796–1805," *Transactions of the American Philosophical Society* 53, no. 4 (1963), 1–133.

47. François Vallé to _____, April 29, 1792 [translation], François Vallé Papers, 1742–1846, A1675, MHMA.

48. François Vallé to _____, October 3, 1795 [translation], François Vallé Papers, 1742–1846, A1675, MHMA.

49. A General Census of the Towns of St. Louis and Ste. Genevieve, 1787, and a census of St. Louis and its Districts, 1791, from the Archivo Nacional, Havana, transcribed and translated by Louis Houck, Census Collection, MHMA.

50. Testimony of M'de Chauvin, Deposition Notes, Marie Scipio's Descendants [1806], JBCLFP.

51. François Vallé to _____, November 2, 1795 [translation], François Vallé Papers, 1742–1846, MHMA.

52. Attempted Emancipation of Enslaved Woman Victoria, by her father, Joseph de Lille, June 9, 1796, box 1, Saint Louis History Collection, 1762–1976, MHMA.

53. Baron de Carondelet to Jacques Clamorgan, July 22, 1794, May 11, 1796 [translation], Clamorgan Family Papers, MHMA.

54. Patrick Luck, *Replanting a Slave Society: The Sugar and Cotton Revolutions in the Lower Mississippi Valley* (Charlottesville: University of Virginia Press, 2022).

55. Henri Peyroux de la Coudrenière to Baron de Carondelet, 1796 Census, New Madrid [translation], box 1, folder 1, Frederick Billon Papers, MHMA.

56. Baron de Carondelet to Monsieur [Pierre Dehault] DeLassus, May 25, 1794, Carondelet Series, Alonzo J. Tullock Louisiana History Collection, 1794–2009, MHMA.

57. Baron de Carondelet to Monsieur [Charles Dehault] DeLassus, September 18, 1796, and November 29, 1796, Carondelet Series, Alonzo J. Tullock Louisiana History Collection, 1794–2009, MHMA.

58. Abijah Hunt to John Wesley Hunt, November 9, 1798, September 19, 1799, John Wesley Hunt Papers, Special Collections, Transylvania University, Lexington, Kentucky. For the extended Hunt family's networks of trade, which stretched from Trenton to Natchez, and included cotton, enslaved people, manufactured goods, and provisions for the U.S. Army, see Susan Gaunt Stearns, *Empire of Commerce: The Closing of the Mississippi and the Opening of Atlantic Trade* (Charlottesville: University of Virginia Press, 2024).

59. Abijah Hunt to John Wesley Hunt, November 5, 1798, John Wesley Hunt Papers, Special Collections, Transylvania University, Lexington, Kentucky.

60. Agreement between John Edgar and Daniel Blouin, April 8, 1786, KM, 86:4:8:1.

61. Wills #38, Will of Pierre-Charles Peyroux, December 12, 1793, SGA.

62. Bill of Sale, Antoine Reynal to Louis de Blanc for Enslaved Woman Manon, June 2, 1795, Mss. 366, Louisiana and Lower Mississippi Valley Collections, Louisiana State University Libraries, Baton Rouge.

63. Sale and Exchange of Enslaved Men, Jacob and Leandre, April 16, 1782 [translation], François Vallé Papers, 1742–1846, A1675, MHMA.

64. Depositions Regarding ownership of Enslaved Man Ben, June 28, 1794, box 1, folder 1, Slaves and Slavery Collection, MHMA.

65. Deeds #239, Sale of Land between Vincent LaFoy and Joseph Plait, July 14, 1788 [type-script], SGA, MHMA.

66. François Vallé to Charles Howard, May 15, 1797 [translation], François Vallé Papers, 1742–1846, A1675, MHMA.

67. François Vallé to Baron de Carondelet, November 10, 1796, in Carl Ekberg, ed., *A French Aristocrat in the West: The Shattered Dreams of De Lassus de Luziéres* (Columbia: University of Missouri Press, 2010), 157.

68. Plan de population pour les Illinois, October 4, 1793, folder 283, box 3, Louisiana Papers, 1767–1816, MSS M-M 508, Bancroft Library, University of California, Berkeley.

69. William Lytle to Breckinridge, January 10, 1797, Breckenridge Family Papers, Manuscript Reading Room, LOC.

70. Petition from the Inhabitants of Mason County Kentucky to His Excellency, the Comitant [sic] in & Over the Territories of New Spain, 1797; De Lassus, A Sketch of the Advantages that are Made, and the Quantities of Land that are Granted to Farmers by the Spanish Government, April 8, 1797, folder 354, box 3, Louisiana Papers, 1767–1816, MSS M-M 508, Bancroft Library, University of California, Berkeley.

71. Ekberg and Foley, *Account of Upper Louisiana by Nicolas de Finiels*, 36.

72. Daniel Boone Petition to the Spanish Crown, November 9, 1799, Boone Family Papers, 1777–1930, MHMA.

73. Concession #36, Petition of Jacque Guibourd Dubreuil, November 25, 1799, Filed May 14, 1804 [typescript], SGA.

74. Bill of Sale, Uriah Taylor to George Smith Jr., February 7, 1803, Sale of Enslaved Man Sam and Enslaved Woman Rachel, Slaves and Slavery Collection, MHMA; *American State Papers*, Class VIII, *Public Lands*, 2:474, 563.

75. Concession #50, Petition of Thomas Maddin, New Bourbon, January 7, 1800 [typescript], SGA.

76. Concession #118, Petition of Richard Glover, September 1, 1800 [typescript], SGA.

77. Concession #125, Petition of Benjamin Johnston, July 20, 1801 [typescript], SGA.

78. Concession #115, Petition of Thomas Bevis, March 14, 1801 [typescript], SGA.

79. Sale of a Negress and Three Children by Solomon White, March 19, 1784, Register of the Notary of Ste. Genevieve, 1766 to 1767 [1770], Miscellaneous Bound MS #1, Transcribed and Translated by Vermer J. Genot, WPA, SGA.

80. Sale of a Negress by Samuel White, August 6, 1784, Register of the Notary of Ste. Genevieve, 1766 to 1767 [1770], Miscellaneous Bound MS #1, Transcribed and Translated by Vermer J. Genot, WPA, SGA.

81. Analysis based on Register of the Notary of Ste. Genevieve, 1766 to 1767 [1770], Miscellaneous Bound MS #1, Transcribed and Translated by Vermer J. Genot, WPA, SGA.

82. Receipt of Payment for "a negro wench" between Austin Moses and William Morrison, June 26, 1799 [transcript], AP. For the Fenwick family's extensive land claims, see *American State Papers*, Class VIII, *Public Lands*, 2:120–121, 631. For Fenwick's history of selling enslaved African Americans in Ste. Geneviève, see August 4, 1804, Sale of a Negro by Walter Fenwick to Charles Delassus; and May 27, 1797, Sale of a negro by Walter Fenwick to Guillaume Gerouard. For slave sales at the Fenwick estate, see October 22, 1798, Sale of a negress with her two children by Wm. Morrison to J. Price, all in Register of the Notary of Ste. Genevieve, 1766 to 1767 [1770], Miscellaneous Bound MS #1, Transcribed and Translated by Vermer J. Genot, WPA, SGA.

83. Bill of Sale for Enslaved Girl, Susana, from John Coffee to Jacque Guibourd, February 22, 1800, List of Documents Contained in the Office of the Register of Ste. Genevieve, kept by Mr. Jean Baptiste Valle, Given to Thomas Oliver, December 5, 1804, Miscellaneous Bound MS #1, Transcribed and Translated by Vermer J. Genot, WPA, SGA. For Coffee's career as a speculator and human trafficker, see Gordon T. Chappell, "The Life and Activities of General John Coffee," *Tennessee Historical Quarterly* 1, no. 2 (June 1942), 125–146.

84. Joseph Antoine Maison, transfer of ownership of enslaved people, April 18, 1775, KM, 75:4:18:3.

85. Petition of Marguerite Beauvais to Upper Louisiana Lieutenant Governor Francisco Cruzat, April 23, 1787, KM, 87:4:23:1; Petition of Marguerite Beauvais, Kaskaskia, May 11, 1787, KM, 87:7:11:1; Placard Concerning Marguerite Bentley, April 21, 1787, CISHL, 5:397; Father de la Valineére, Information Concerning Illinois, CISHL, 5:430; Petition of Madame Bentley to Congress, August 31, 1787, CISHL, 5:431–436. For Thomas Bentley, see Robert Englebert, "Merchant Representatives and the French River World, 1763–1803," *Michigan Historical Review* 34, no. 1 (Spring 2008), 63–82.

86. Concession #28, Parcel #9, November 15, 1791, SGA.

87. Concession #27, Copy of concession in favor of Israel Dodge of December 11, 1800 [typescript], SGA; Ekberg, *French Aristocrat in the American West*, 162–163, 166–167.

88. June 16, 1794, Sale of a negress by Israel Dodge to M. Bernard Pratte; July 26, 1794, Sale of a negro Samuel by Israel Dodge and his wife to Delusiere; November 17, 1795, Sale by Israel Dodge of two slaves to Antoine Janis, all in List of Documents Contained in the Office of the Register of Ste. Genevieve, kept by Mr. Jean Baptiste Valle, Given to Thomas Oliver, December 5, 1804, Miscellaneous Bound MS #1, Transcribed and Translated by Vermer J. Genot, WPA, SGA.

89. Deed #131, Sale of land and House between Israel Dodge to Nathaniel Hall [Hull?] May 23, 1795; Concession #27, Petition of Israel Dodge, December 11, 1800, Filed May 14, 1804 [typescript], SGA.

90. Israel Dodge to François Vallé, June 24, 1796, François Vallé Papers, 1742–1846, MHMA.

91. Charles Dehault DeLassus to Baron de Carondelet, October 1, 1797, in Ekberg, *French Aristocrat in the West*, 163.

92. Jean-Baptiste Trudeau [sometimes Truteau] to Manuel Rocque, September 22, 1802, MSS Alpha Trudeau, CHM.

93. For the purchase of lead in the Middle Mississippi Valley and its transportation to Lexington where it was turned into shot, see Robert Buntin to Winthrop Sargent, November 23, 1797, reel 4, series III, Winthrop Sargent Papers, MHS.

94. Entry for October 16, Louis Tarascon, Journal, 1799, Mss. A T177, Filson Historical Society, Louisville, Kentucky.

95. M.[ichel] Amoureux to Pierre Clément Laussat, August 4, 1803, box 6, folder 234, Pierre-Clément de Laussat Papers, MSS 125, Williams Research Center, Historic New Orleans Collection.

96. Financial Agreement between Joseph Marie Papin and Auguste Chouteau, July 30, 1786 [translation], Litigation Collection, AO920, box 2, folder 14, MHMA.

97. Sale of Enslaved Woman Francisca and her son Luis, Between Silvestre Sarpy and Luis Beaudoin [perhaps Bouden], September 14, 1786, folder 1, Slaves and Slavery Collection, MHMA.

98. Bill of Sale for Enslaved Boy Joseph, from Jean Saucier to Antonie Duclo, February 8, 1800; Mortgage Agreement between Antonie Duclo and Cecille Aubuchon [Duclo] with Michel Placette, February 12, 1800 [typescript], SGA.

99. Bill of Sale for Unnamed Enslaved Woman, between Parfait Dufour and Jacques Clamorgan, April 10, 1801 [typescript], SGA.

100. Bill of Sale for Enslaved Girl, Susana, from John Coffee to Jacque Guibourd, February 22, 1800, List of Documents Contained in the Office of the Register of Ste. Genevieve, kept by Mr. Jean Baptiste Valle, Given to Thomas Oliver, December 5, 1804, Miscellaneous Bound MS #1, Transcribed and Translated by Vermer J. Genot, WPA, SGA.

101. Charles Gratiot to John Henry Schneider, September 24, 1794, Letterbook III, Charles Gratiot Papers, MHMA. For Gratiot's selling of Upper Louisiana agricultural lands, salines, and mines to incoming U.S. enslavers, see "Louisiana Lands For Sale," (Lexington, KY) *Reporter*, July 10, 1810.

102. "Extract of a Letter from Thomas T. Davis, Esq., Dated Kaskaskias, Indiana Territory, October 18, 1803," (Richmond) *Virginia Argus*, December 7, 1803; Thomas Jefferson, Queries on Louisiana, 1803; Benjamin Stoddert, Notes on Louisiana, June 3, 1803, Thomas Jefferson Papers, LOC; Amos Stoddard to Sec. of War, Henry Dearborn, June 3, 1804, Amos Stoddard Papers, MHMA; Amos Stoddard to Phoebe Reade Benham, June 16, 1804, Amos Stoddard Papers, MHMA.

103. Undated Poem, Miscellaneous Manuscripts recorded in Ste. Geneviève in the 1790s, Attributed to the Bolduc Family, A1116 Music Collection, 1795–1993, box 3, MHMA. In French, the poem reads as follows: "Soyez 'y' ci les Bien venu cher enfant de sodome // Soyez 'y' ci les Bien venu homme au milieux de rome // Et vous detestable putain don le con nous geoute // Allez chez les ameriquien cherchez gens qui vous foute."

104. William C. Carr to Mrs. Charles Carr, June 21, 1804, William C. Carr Papers, MHMA.

Chapter 4

1. John Quincy Adams to John Adams, January 31, 1804, Adams Family Papers, reel 403, MHS.

2. [Alexander Hamilton], "Purchase of Louisiana," *New York Evening Post*, July 5, 1803.

3. For French adventurers' proposal for a French supercolony encompassing the Mississippi, Ohio, and Missouri Valleys, see, for example, C. C. Robin, *Voyage to Louisiana, 1803–1805*, trans. Stuart O. Landry (1806; reprint ed., New Orleans: Pelican, 1966); and François Marie Perrin du Lac, *Travels through the two Louisianas and among the savage nations of the Missouri; also, in the United States, along the Ohio, and the adjacent provinces, in 1801, 1802, & 1803 . . .* (London, 1807). For Bonapartists' visions for a North American empire, see Lo Faber, *Building the Land of Dreams: New Orleans and the Transformation of Early America* (Princeton, NJ: Princeton University Press, 2015).

4. Moses Austin to James Richardson, August 2, 1803, Louisiana Transfer Collection, MHMA.

5. M.[ichel] Amoureux to [Pierre Clément Laussat, Prefect of Louisiana], August 4, 1803, box 6, folder 234, Pierre-Clément de Laussat Papers, MSS 125, Williams Research Center, Historic New Orleans Collection. For Amoureux's vision of a revived French empire in the Mississippi Valley, see John Craig Hammond and Thomas J. Slancauskas, "'Useful to the Public Business': Mathurin-Michel Amoureux's 1803 Letter from New Madrid," *Missouri Historical Review* 115, no. 4 (July 2021), 296–319.

6. For Bonapartist France and Haiti, see Elizabeth Maddock Dillon and Michael Drexler, eds., *The Haitian Revolution and the Early United States: Histories, Textualities, Geographies* (Philadelphia: University of Pennsylvania Press, 2016); and Laurent DuBois, *Avengers of the New World: The Story of the Haitian Revolution* (Cambridge MA: Harvard University Press, 2004).

7. [Alexander Hamilton], "Purchase of Louisiana," *New York Evening Post*, July 5, 1803.

8. James E. Lewis, Jr., *The Burr Conspiracy: Uncovering the Story of an Early American Crisis* (Princeton, NJ: Princeton University Press, 2017); François Furstenberg, "The Significance of the Trans-Appalachian Frontier in Atlantic History," *American Historical Review* 113, no. 3 (June 2008), 647–677.

9. Amos Stoddard to Phoebe Reade Benham, June 16, 1804, Amos Stoddard Papers, MHMA.

10. Frederic Louis Billon, ed., *Annals of St. Louis in Its Territorial Days, from 1804 to 1821* (St. Louis, 1888), 219–220.

11. Robert Morrison to Joseph Morrison, January 22 and April 7, 1805, Robert Morrison Papers, 1805–1853, ALPML; Robert Morrison to Joseph Morrison, April 1, 1806, Robert Morrison Letters, INDHS; Improvement of Nicholas, François, Antoine, and Jean Baptiste Janis, No. 2010, *American State Papers: Public Lands* (Washington: U.S. Government Printing Office, 1832), 2:225; Bryan and Morrison Records, R0176, SHSMO; Receipt of Payment for "a negro wench" between Austin Moses and William Morrison, June 26, 1799 [transcript], AP; Sale of a negress with her two children by Wm. Morrison to J. Price, List of Documents Contained in the Office of the Register of Ste. Genevieve, kept by Mr. Jean Baptiste Valle, Given to Thomas Oliver, December 5, 1804, Miscellaneous Bound MS #1, Transcribed and Translated by Vermer J. Genot, WPA, SGA.

12. For Edgar's and Morrison's land speculations in Illinois and business operations that extended downriver to New Orleans, see Robert Morrison to Joseph Morrison, April 1, 1806, Robert Morrison Letters, INDHS; James E. Davis, *Frontier Illinois* (Bloomington: Indiana University Press, 1998), 117–122. Edgar and Morrison had purchased warrants issued to Virginia soldiers who participated in the expedition to Illinois. For examples of these warrants, see Illinois Land Commission Indentures, April 8 and August 31, 1789, Darlington Autograph Files Collection, Archives and Special Collections, Hillman Library, University of Pittsburgh.

13. *Congressional Report of the Committee on the Petition of Sundry Inhabitants of the Counties of St. Clair and Randolph . . . May 12, 1796* (Philadelphia, 1796). In 1800, Congress carved the Ohio Territory out of the original Northwest Territory. The remainder they designated the Indiana Territory, which initially included all of the original Northwest Territory, less Ohio. In 1805, Congress lopped off the northern portion of the Indiana Territory into the Michigan Territory, leaving present-day Indiana and Illinois as the Indiana Territory. In 1809, Congress split the Indiana Territory into the Indiana and Illinois Territories. Leading Illinois speculators advocated for a separate Illinois Territory after an antislavery faction won control of the Indiana territorial legislature in 1808. Congress created a separate Illinois Territory in 1809. For efforts to overturn Article VI emanating from Illinois and Indiana, see John Craig Hammond, *Slavery, Freedom, and Expansion in the Early American West* (Charlottesville: University of Virginia Press, 2007), 96–123.

14. "Extract from a letter from a gentleman in the Illinois or Indiana Territory," (Philadelphia) *Aurora and General Advertiser*, November 3, 1803 (quote); "Relating to Louisiana," (Philadelphia) *Aurora and General Advertiser*, October 21, 1803.

15. Matthew Lyon to John Messinger, September 14, 1803, John Messinger Papers, 1797–1878, ALPLM.

16. "Extract from a letter from a gentlemen in the Illinois or Indiana Territory," (Philadelphia) *Aurora and General Advertiser*, November 3, 1803 (quote); "Relating to Louisiana," (Philadelphia) *Aurora and General Advertiser*, October 21, 1803.

17. John Edgar to John Fowler, September 25, 1803, *TPUS*, 13:5–7.

18. Matthew Lyon to John Messinger, November 9, 1803, John Messinger Papers, 1797–1878, ALPML. For Illinois petitions begging to be attached to Upper Louisiana, see Memorial to Congress by Inhabitants of St. Clair and Randolph Counties, *TPUS*, 7:140–145.

19. For enslavers' exploitation of fears for the stability and viability of the U.S. union in the Mississippi Valley to gain protections for slavery in Natchez and Lower Louisiana, see Hammond, *Slavery, Freedom, and Expansion*, 9–54.

20. John Edgar to John Fowler, September 25, 1803, *TPUS*, 13:5–7.

21. "Relating to Louisiana," (Philadelphia) *Aurora and General Advertiser*, October 21, 1803 (quote); "Extract from a letter from a gentlemen in the Illinois or Indiana Territory," (Philadelphia) *Aurora and General Advertiser*, November 3, 1803.

22. Thomas T. Davis to John Breckinridge, October 17, 1803, *TPUS*, 7:124. For a similar letter, see Issac Darnielle to John Breckinridge, October 22, 1803, *TPUS*, 7:129–134.

23. "Extract of a Letter from Thomas T. Davis, Esq., Dated Kaskaskias, Indiana Territory, October 18, 1803," (Richmond) *Virginia Argus*, December 7, 1803.

24. Thomas T. Davis to Thomas Jefferson, November 5, 1803, *TPUS*, 13:7–8.

25. For Lewis and Clark's frequent interactions with leading habitant families as they waited for U.S. officials to take official possession of Upper Louisiana from Spanish and French officials, see Jacob F. Lee, *Masters of the Middle Waters: Indian Nations and Colonial Ambitions Along the Mississippi* (Cambridge, MA: Harvard University Press, 2019), 201–203.

26. Meriwether Lewis to Thomas Jefferson, December 28, 1803, in *Letters of the Lewis and Clark Expedition with Related Documents, 1783–1854*, ed. Donald Jackson (Urbana: University of Illinois Press, 1962), 153.

27. John Craig Hammond, "Slavery, Sovereignty, and Empires: North American Borderlands and the American Civil War, 1660–1860," *Journal of the Civil War Era* 4, no. 2 (June 2014).

28. John Craig Hammond, "Slavery, Settlement, and Empire: The Expansion and Growth of Slavery in the Interior of the North American Continent, 1770–1820," *Journal of the Early Republic* 32, no. 2 (Summer 2012), 175–206.

29. Edward E. Baptist, *The Half Has Never Been Told: Slavery and the Making of American Capitalism* (New York: Basic Books, 2014); Adam Rothman, *Slave Country: American Expansion and the Origins of the Deep South* (Cambridge, MA: Harvard University Press, 2005).

30. For northern white peoples' connections among empire, emancipation, and forced removal of Black people through colonization, along with Black exclusion, see Samantha Seeley, *Race, Removal, and the Right to Remain: Migration and the Making of the United States* (Chapel Hill: University of North Carolina Press, 2021); Brandon Mills, *The World Colonization Made: The Racial Geography of Early American Empire* (Philadelphia: University of Pennsylvania Press, 2020); and Nicholas Guyatt, *Bind Us Apart: How Enlightened Americans Invented Racial Segregation* (New York: Oxford University Press, 2016).

31. Joel Barlow to Alexander Wolcott, July 28, 1803, Joel Barlow Papers, MS Am 1448, #527, Houghton Library, Harvard University, Cambridge, Massachusetts. For the deep connections between northern, white antislavery imperialism, and Black removal and colonization spurred by the Louisiana Purchase, see Padraig Riley, *Slavery and the Democratic Conscience: Political Life in Jeffersonian America* (Philadelphia: University of Pennsylvania Press, 2015), 102–107; and Mills, *The World Colonization Made*, 14–25.

32. *Congressional Report of the Committee on the Petition of Sundry Inhabitants of the Counties of St. Clair and Randolph . . . May 12, 1796* (Philadelphia, 1796).

33. Petition of Shadrach Bond, Sr., et al., November 15, 1802; Memorial and Petition of the Indiana Territorial Convention to Thomas Jefferson, December 28, 1802; Thomas Jefferson to William Henry Harrison, January 12, 1803, reel 2, Papers of William Henry Harrison, 1800–1815, INDHS.

For Harrison lobbying Congress to suspend Article VI in Indiana and Illinois, see, for example, Harrison to [New Jersey Senator] Jonathan Dayton, January 12, 1803; William Henry

Harrison to [Ohio Senator] Thomas Worthington, October 26, 1803, reel 2, William Henry Harrison Papers, INDHS.

34. John Rice Jones to Judge [Thomas] Davis, January 21, 1804, *TPUS*, 7:168–169.

35. William Henry Harrison to Thomas Worthington, October 26, 1803, William Henry Harrison Papers [microfilm], INDHS; *Annals of Congress*, 8th Cong., 1st sess., 779, 1023–1024. For northern Republicans' refusal to suspend Article VI in Ohio, Indiana, and Illinois, see Hammond, *Slavery, Freedom, and Expansion*, 76–123.

36. Hammond, *Slavery, Freedom, and Expansion*, 76–123.

37. "Extract of a Letter from Thomas T. Davis, Esq., Dated Kaskaskias, Indiana Territory, October 18, 1803," (Richmond) *Virginia Argus*, December 7, 1803.

38. Thomas T. Davis to Thomas Jefferson, October 5, 1803, *TPUS*, 13:7.

39. Matthew Lyon to John Messinger, November 9, 1803, John Messinger Papers, 1797–1878, ALPLM,

40. Robert Morrison to Joseph Morrison, April 7, 1805, Robert Morrison Papers, 1805–1953, ALPLM.

41. Robert Morrison to Joseph Morrison, January 22, 1805, Robert Morrison Letters, INDHS.

42. For the importance of the *Aurora* and editor William Duane among Republicans in Pennsylvania, New York, New Jersey, and Delaware, see Riley, *Slavery and the Democratic Conscience.*

43. "Relating to Louisiana," October 21, 1803; "Extract from a letter from a gentlemen in the Illinois or Indiana Territory," (Philadelphia) *Aurora and General Advertiser*, November 3, 1803.

44. "Petition of the American Convention for Promoting the Abolition of Slavery," January 23, 1804, *Annals of Congress*, 8th Cong., Appendix, 1596–1597; *Minutes of the proceedings of the ninth American Convention for Promoting the Abolition of Slavery and Improving the Condition of the African Race: assembled at Philadelphia . . .* (Philadelphia, 1804), 41–43.

45. David Bard to John Parrish, March 26, 1804, box 2, series 2, RG 5/229, Parrish Family Papers, Friends Historical Library, Swarthmore College, Swarthmore, Pennsylvania.

46. "Relating to Louisiana," (Philadelphia) *Aurora and General Advertiser*, October 21, 1803.

47. John Quincy Adams to John Adams, January 31, 1804, Adams Family Papers, reel 403, MHS.

48. Baptist, *Half Has Never Been Told*, 8.

49. *Annals of Congress*, 8th Cong., 1st sess., 1186.

50. Simeon Baldwin to Timothy Pitkin, February 24, 1804, Timothy Pitkin Papers, 1681–1857, Huntington Library, San Marino, California.

51. An Act for the Organization of Orleans Territory and the Louisiana District, March 26, 1804, *TPUS*, 9:209.

52. John Quincy Adams to John Adams, January 31, 1804, Adams Family Papers, reel 403, MHS.

53. Matthew Lyon to Ninian Edwards, February 10, 1804, Ninian Edwards Papers, CHM.

54. Everett S. Brown, ed., "The Senate Debate on the Breckinridge Bill for the Government of Louisiana, 1804," *American Historical Review* 22, no. 2 (1917), 340–364, quote at 360.

55. John Quincy Adams to John Adams, January 31, 1804, Adams Family Papers, reel 403, MHS.

56. An Act for the Organization of Orleans Territory and the Louisiana District, March 26, 1804, *TPUS*, 9:209.

57. Probate Proceedings, Jospeh Tayon, Sr., July 26, 1799, translated by _____ from the original French, St. Louis, April 14, 1825, Zenon Trudeau Papers, Vault MSS 568, L. Tom Perry Special Collections, Harold B. Lee Library, Brigham Young University, Provo, Utah; Deposition Notes, Marie Scipio's Descendants [1806] box 3, JBCLFP; Deposition Notes, Freedom Suit of Scipio's Children, April 7, 1817, box 3, JBCLFP; Marguerite vs Chouteau [various dates], folder 13, box 150, Superior Court Case Files, MSA-JC; Tayon v. Celeste et al., 1806, box RD013, folder 26, MSA-JC. For extensive analyses of the families' multiple freedom suits, see William E. Foley, "Slave Freedom Suits Before Dred Scott: The Case of Marie Jean Scypion's Descendants," *Missouri Historical Review* 79, no. 1 (October 1984), 1–23; and Lea VanderVelde, *Redemption Songs: Suing for Freedom Before Dred Scott* (New York: Oxford University Press, 2014), 39–56.

58. Deposition Notes, Marie Scipio's Descendants [1806], box 3, JBCLFP; Deposition Notes, Freedom Suit of Scipio's Children, April 7, 1817, box 3, JBCLFP; Marguerite vs Chouteau [various dates], folder 13, box 150, Superior Court Case Files, MSA-JC; Tayon v. Celeste et al., 1806, box RD013, folder 26, MSA-JC.

59. Joseph Tayon, Petition to Amos Stoddard, May 11, 1804, box 6, Chouteau Family Papers, 1752–1946, AO274, MHMA (quote); Deposition Notes, Marie Scipio's Descendants [1806], box 3, JBCLFP; Deposition Notes, Freedom Suit of Scipio's Children, April 7, 1817, box 3, JBCLFP; Marguerite vs Chouteau [various dates], folder 13, box 150, Superior Court Case Files, MSA-JC; Tayon v. Celeste et al., 1806, box RD013, folder 26, MSA-JC.

60. Joseph Tayon, Petition to Amos Stoddard, May 11, 1804, box 6, Chouteau Family Papers, 1752–1946, AO274, MHMA (quote); Deposition Notes, Marie Scipio's Descendants [1806], box 3, JBCLFP; Deposition Notes, Freedom Suit of Scipio's Children, April 7, 1817, box 3, JBCLFP; Marguerite vs Chouteau [various dates], folder 13, box 150, Superior Court Case Files, MSA-JC; Tayon v. Celeste et al., 1806, box RD013, folder 26, MSA-JC.

61. Deposition Notes, Marie Scipio's Descendants [1806], box 3, JBCLFP.

62. Secretary of War Henry Dearborn to Amos Stoddard, November 7, 1803, *TPUS*, 13:8.

63. "Remonstrance of the Representatives elected by the Freemen of their Respective Districts in the District of Louisiana," in *American State Papers*, Class X, *Miscellaneous*, 1:401–404.

64. Amos Stoddard to W. C. C. Claiborne, May 19, 1804, Amos Stoddard Papers, MHMA.

65. William Carr to John Breckinridge, July 4, 1804, *TPUS*, 13:29–30.

66. Proceedings of a Meeting of Inhabitants of St. Louis, April 2, 1804, *TPUS*, 35.

67. Address of the Committee of St. Louis, True Translation by J. Rankin, April 6, 1804, page 55, item 62, James Wilkinson Papers, 1779–1823, CHM.

68. Committee of the Town of St. Lewis to Amos Stoddard, True Translation from the original, by authority, J. Rankin, August 4, 1804, Amos Stoddard Papers, MHMA.

69. For the situation in Lower Louisiana, where U.S. officials began to fear that Louisiana planters and merchants would seek to nullify the Louisiana Purchase, see Hammond, *Slavery, Freedom, and Expansion*, 46–54.

70. Amos Stoddard, *Sketches, Historical and Descriptive, of Louisiana* (Philadelphia, 1812), 331–344.

71. Albert Gallatin to Thomas Jefferson, August 20, 1804, Thomas Jefferson Papers, LOC. For the Chouteau family's extensive ties and influence in the region, see Lee, *Masters of the Middle Waters*, 156–230.

72. Committee of the Town of St. Lewis to Amos Stoddard, True Translation from the original, by authority, J. Rankin, August 4, 1804, Amos Stoddard Papers, MHMA. I can find no primary source evidence of "fermentation" among enslaved people for this period, beyond the Scypion family. For an enslaved man and women who fled New Bourbon in the summer of 1804, see "Fifty Dollars Reward," (Vincennes) *Indiana Gazette*, September 18, 1804. In August 1804, Charles Sanguinet asked Jean Baptiste Vallé "to look for a negro woman that I would like to buy, because I have lost mine." Sanguinet gave no indication of how the enslaved woman was "lost," whether she had ran away, passed away, was stolen, or had been seized. See [Charles] Count of Sanguinet to Jean Baptiste Vallé, August 4, 1804 [translation], François Vallé Papers, 1742–1846, A1675, MHMA.

73. Committee of the Town of St. Lewis to Amos Stoddard, True Translation from the original, by authority, J. Rankin, August 4, 1804, Amos Stoddard Papers, MHMA.

74. Amos Stoddard to Auguste Chouteau, August 6, 1804, Amos Stoddard Papers, MHMA.

75. Committee of the Town of St. Lewis to Amos Stoddard, True Translation P. Provenchere, August 11, 1804, Amos Stoddard Papers, MHMA.

76. Committee of the Town of St. Lewis to Amos Stoddard, True Translation P. Provenchere, August 11, 1804, Amos Stoddard Papers, MHMA.

77. Richard J. Waters and Richard Caulk to the citizens of Cape Girardeau, September 6, 1804, Louisiana Transfer Collection, MHMA.

78. "The remonstrance and petition of the representatives elected by the freemen of their respective districts in the District of Louisiana," *American State Papers*, Class X, *Miscellaneous*, 1:400–404.

79. William Henry Harrison, governor of Indiana Territory and acting governor of Upper Louisiana, confided to Chouteau and Jefferson that the angry language of the remonstrance was both necessary and largely insincere. William Henry Harrison to Thomas Jefferson, November 6, 1804, Thomas Jefferson Papers, LOC; William Henry Harrison to Auguste Chouteau, December 21, 1804, March 19, 1805, and April 7, 1805, reel 2, Papers of William Henry Harrison, 1800–1815, INDHS.

80. Committee of the Town of St. Lewis to Amos Stoddard, September 30, 1804, Amos Stoddard Papers, MHMA.

81. Amos Stoddard to William C. C. Claiborne, May 19, 1804, Stoddard Papers, MHMA.

82. Report of the Senate Committee on Bill to Divide the Northwest Territory, *TPUS*, 7:9.

83. An Act for the Government for the Mississippi Territory, April 7, 1798, *TPUS*, 5:20.

84. "The remonstrance and petition of the representatives elected by the freemen of their respective districts in the District of Louisiana," *American State Papers*, Class X, *Miscellaneous*, 1:401–404.

85. An Act for the Government of Louisiana Territory, March 3, 1805, A Bill for the Government of the Territory of Louisiana, February 7, 1805, *TPUS*, 13:92–95, 87–89. The *Annals of Congress* for this period have little to say about the Louisiana Territory bills, as Congress was engaged in the impeachment trial of Justice Samuel Chase at the same time it was drafting and debating territorial ordinances. It seems likely that the territorial ordinance for Upper Louisiana was negotiated in private.

86. Amos Stoddard adopted the first set of Black Codes under U.S. rule in Upper Louisiana in August 1804 when he decreed that the province of Upper Louisiana's *Code Noir* continued in effect under his temporary administration. In October 1804, Indiana Governor William Henry Harrison issued a set of laws for the District of Louisiana, which became the Territory of

Louisiana in 1805. Harrison and the judges from the Indiana Territory adopted, more or less, the Black Codes of Virginia and Kentucky for Upper Louisiana. The most accessible copy of the original territorial Black Codes can be found in *Laws of a Public and General Nature of the District of Louisiana, of the Territory of Louisiana, of the Territory of Missouri, and of the State of Missouri, up to the Year 1824* (Jefferson City, MO: W. Lusk and Son, 1842), 27–33.

87. *Annals of Congress*, 12th Cong., 1st sess., 1248; 16th Cong., 1st sess., 337.

88. [Alexander Mitchell], *An Address to the Inhabitants of the Indiana Territory, on the Subject of Slavery* (Hamilton, OH, 1816); [Robert Walsh], *Free Remarks on the Spirit of the Federal Constitution, the Practice of the Federal Government, and the Obligations of the Union, Respecting the Exclusion of Slavery from the Territories and New States* (Philadelphia, 1819); Stoddard, *Sketches, Historical and Descriptive of Louisiana*.

89. Matthew Lyon to John Messinger, March 29, 1804, John Messinger Papers, 1797–1878, ALPLM.

90. Pierre Chouteau to Henry Dearborn, March 11, 1805 [translation], Pierre Chouteau Letterbook, MHMA. For arson as a form of resistance, see Daniel Immerwahr, "Burning Down the House: Slavery and Arson in America," *Journal of American History* 110, no. 3 (December 2023), 449–473.

Chapter 5

1. In 1805, Congress created the Territory of (Upper) Louisiana to replace the District of Upper Louisiana. In 1812, Congress advanced (Upper) Louisiana to the second stage of territorial government, renaming it the Missouri Territory. For simplicity, I refer to the territory as Missouri throughout the chapter.

2. Patrick Luck, *Replanting a Slave Society: The Sugar and Cotton Revolution in the Lower Mississippi Valley* (Charlottesville: University of Virginia Press, 2022); Edward Baptist, *The Half Has Never Been Told: Slavery and the Making of American Capitalism* (New York: Basic Books, 2014).

3. John Craig Hammond, *Slavery, Freedom, and Expansion in the Early American West* (Charlottesville: University of Virginia Press, 2007).

4. [Unknown], entry for January 4, 1806, Journal of a Trip from Champaign County, Ohio, down the Mississippi River, to New Orleans, November 25, 1805–July 26, 1806, SC 2148, ALPML.

5. Michael Tadman, *Speculators and Slaves: Masters, Traders, and Slaves in the Old South* (Madison: University of Wisconsin Press, 1989), 12.

6. Michael Morris, "Dreams of Glory, Schemes of Empire: The Plan to Liberate Spanish Florida," *Georgia Historical Quarterly* 87, no. 1 (Spring 2003), 1–21.

7. "Extract of a letter from a gentleman in the suit of Colonel Hammond, to his friends in Augusta Georgia, July 15, 1805," (Boston) *Repertory*, October 4, 1805.

8. S[amuel] Hammond to John Archer, December 30, 1805, Rufus Easton Collection, MHMA.

9. S[amuel] Hammond to Abraham Baldwin, December 30, 1805, Rufus Easton Collection, MHMA.

10. S[amuel] Hammond to Abraham Baldwin, December 13, 1806, box 1, folder 18, Abraham Baldwin Papers, Hargrett Rare Book and Manuscript Library, University of Georgia, Athens.

11. "For sale a likely young negro boy," *Missouri Gazette*, October 12, 1808.

12. Bill of Sale, Enslaved Man Silas, S[amuel] Hammond to Jacob Horine, November 3, 1810, Assessment of Estate of Jacob Horine, O'Fallon Family Papers, box 1, Beinecke Rare Book and Manuscript Library, Yale University, New Haven, Connecticut.

13. "For sale or barter," *Missouri Gazette*, May 30, 1812; "Thirty Dollars Reward," *Missouri Gazette*, September 26, 1812; "Ran-away," *Missouri Gazette*, May 7, 1814.

14. Sale of Enslaved Mother, Father, and Child, June 6, 1812, in *The Life and Papers of Frederick Bates*, ed. Thomas Maitland Marshall, 2 vols. (St. Louis: Missouri Historical Society, 1926), 2:225.

15. Court Notes of Judge John B. C. Lucas, Concerning Sale of Two Slaves, Davies vs [Elisha] Ellis, April 7, 1807, JBCLFP.

16. Bill of Sale, Twenty-Four Enslaved Men, Women, and Children, Between Elisha Ellis and Erasmus Ellis, May 10, 1808, folder 6, Legal Papers, Ellis and Ranney Families, Papers, 1787–1948, SHSMO Rolla.

17. "Notice," *Missouri Gazette*, January 15, 1809.

18. "Notice," *Missouri Gazette*, January 18, 1809.

19. Richard Davis v. Erasmus Ellis, Regarding Enslaved Woman Jenny, 1810, Cape Girardeau County, Civil Case, box RD028, folders 9 and 10, Superior Court Case Files, MSA-JC.

20. James E. Welch to Aunt Catherine Beckham, November 17, 1813; Nathaniel Welch to Catherine Beckham, December 31, 1813; James E. Welch to Charles G. Ellis, August 14, 1814, folder 1, Correspondence, Ellis and Ranney Families, Papers, 1787–1948, SHSMO Rolla.

21. Edmund Clark to George Tompkins, July 17–18, 1807, Bodely Family Papers, Filson Historical Society, Louisville, Kentucky; John O'Fallon to William Clark, May 13, 1811, William Clark Papers, MHMA.

22. William Clark to Jonathan Clark, July 2, 1808, in *Dear Brother: Letters of William Clark to Jonathan Clark*, ed. James J. Holmberg (New Haven, CT: Yale University Press, 2002), 139.

23. William Clark to Jonathan Clark, July 21, 1808, in Holmberg, *Dear Brother*, 143–144.

24. William Clark to Jonathan Clark, January 2, 1809, in Holmberg, *Dear Brother*, 190.

25. *Missouri Gazette*, February 22, 1809.

26. John O'Fallon to William Clark, May 13, 1811, William Clark Papers, MHMA.

27. Certificate Dividing John Clark's Slaves According to His Will, June 18, 1817, William Clark Papers, MHMA.

28. David Andrew Nichols, *Engines of Diplomacy: Indian Trading Factories and the Negotiation of American Empire* (Chapel Hill: University of North Carolina Press, 2016), 96–98.

29. George Sibley to Samuel Sibley, September 25, 1813, George Champlain Sibley Papers, 1803–1853, MHMA.

30. Mary Easton Sibley to Rufus Easton, February 11, 1816, George Champlain Sibley Papers, 1803–1853, MHMA; George Sibley, Slaves ___, Entry for January ___, 1820, Commonplace Book No. 1, January 1, 1820 to January 1, 1828, George Champlain Sibley Papers, 1803–1853, MHMA.

31. George Sibley to Samuel Hopkins Sibley, July 10, 1819, George Champlain Sibley Papers, 1803–1853, MHMA; Kristie C. Wolferman, *The Indomitable Mary Easton Sibley: Pioneer of Women's Education in Missouri* (Columbia: University of Missouri Press, 2008).

32. Bill of Sale for Enslaved Child, Jack, Age 11, December 20, 1805, Carr-Papin Family Papers, 1776–1877, box 1, MHMA.

33. William C. Carr to Charles Carr, July 3, 1807, William C. Carr Papers, MHMA.

34. William C. Carr to Charles Carr, September 8, 1807, William C. Carr Papers, MHMA.

35. William C. Carr to Charles Carr, August 25, 1809, William C. Carr Papers, MHMA.

36. William C. Carr to John B. C. Lucas, July 7, 1810, JBCLFP.

37. Bill of Sale, Richard Lowe to John B. C. Lucas, Enslaved Man Kayer, September 26, 1810, JBCLFP.

38. Petition of Billy Tarlton for Freedom, September 22, 1813, folder 1, Slaves and Slavery Collection, MHMA; Petition of William Tarleton, St. Louis, 1813, SLCCHRP.

39. For the Hunt family's networks, which stretched from Trenton to New Orleans, and included cotton, enslaved people, manufactured goods from the East, and provisions for the U.S. Army, see Susan Gaunt Stearns, *Empire of Commerce: The Closing of the Mississippi and the Opening of Atlantic Trade* (Charlottesville: University of Virginia Press, 2024).

40. Bill of Sale between William Cochran and Theodore Hunt for Enslaved Man Andrew, March 6, 1814, JBCLFP.

41. Bill of Sale between Charles Gallagher and Theodore Hunt for Enslaved Woman Lydia, May 7, 1814, JBCLFP.

42. Bill of Sale between Ninian Edwards and Theodore Hunt for Enslaved Child Wallace, May 25, 1814, JBCLFP.

43. Bill of Sale for Frank, Anna, and their Children Ginny, Frank, and Elisa, February 24, 1818, box 1, folder 3, Carr-Papin Family Papers, 1776–1877, MHMA.

44. Bill of Sale for Enslaved Child, Jack, Age 11, December 20, 1805, William C. Carr Papers, MHMA; Bill of Sale for Polly and her son John, February 4, 1811; Bill of Sale for Priscilla, January 30, 1813; Bill of Sale for Polly and her Infant child, June 13, 1815; Bill of Sale for Frank, Anna, and their Children Ginny, Frank, and Elisa, February 24, 1818; Bill of Sale for Steven, March 9, 1818, all in folder 3, box 1, Carr-Papin Family Papers, 1776–1877, MHMA. For Carr's speculation in enslaved people, see William C. Carr to Charles Carr, August 25, 1809, William C. Carr Papers, MHMA; "Fifty Dollars Reward," *St. Louis Enquirer*, November 3, 1819.

45. J. B. C. Lucas to James Mountain, March 3, 1808, JBCLFP.

46. Joseph Pollard, Jr., to William Clark, October 25, 1810, William Clark Papers, 1789–1810, MHMA.

47. Frederic Louis Billon, ed., *Annals of St. Louis in Its Territorial Days, from 1804 to 1821* (St. Louis, 1888), 222.

48. Affidavit of Sherred G. Swain Regarding Dispute with Daniel Bissell and Three Enslaved Men, March 6, 1817, JBCLFP; "100 Dollars Reward," *Missouri Gazette*, March 23, 1816; "$25 Reward," *Missouri Gazette*, February 8, 1817; "Fifty Dollars Reward," *Missouri Gazette*, August 21, 1818.

49. Indictment of Enslaved Black Man George and Enslaved Black Man Joe for theft from Joseph Philibus's Home, March 1810, Fur Trade Collection, MHMA; Irwin V. Wells, in *Reports of Cases Argued And Determined In The Supreme Court Of The State Of Missouri from 1821 to 1827*, ed. Louis Houck (Cape Girardeau, 1870), 22–24.

50. John Francis McDermott, "John B. C. Lucas in Pennsylvania," *Western Pennsylvania Historical Magazine* 21, no. 3 (September 1938), 209–230. The Lucas Papers contain an emancipation from an indenture for Hattie Haynes. It seems that Lucas purchased her indenture in Pennsylvania and then freed her, though it is unclear if she became free in Pennsylvania or St. Louis. See Receipt for Freedom of Hattie Haynes, April 13, 1805, JBCLFP.

51. Bill of Sale for Enslaved man Sam, Elizabeth Harris to Shadrach Bond, February 19, 1808, JBCLFP. For Lucas's ownership of Sam, see I[saac] Darneille to John B. C. Lucas, June 20, 1808, JBCLFP. For Sam's constant efforts to liberate himself, see "20 Dollars Reward," *Missouri Gazette*,

September 5, 1812; Rough Draft Runaway Slave Poster, December 29, 1815, JBCLFP; "50 Dollars Reward," *Missouri Gazette*, May 4, 1816. Sam's successful flight is discussed later in this chapter.

52. Bill of Sale, Richard Lowe to John B. C. Lucas, Enslaved Man Kayer, September 26, 1810, JBCLFP.

53. Madame Veuve Chouteau, Bill for Two Months for Hiring of Enslaved Man Augustive, April 27, 1812, JBCLFP.

54. Bill of Sale, Enslaved Woman Ellen, January 9, 1816, Justus Post Papers, 1807–1821, MHMA.

55. Justus Post to John Post, October 7, 1817, Justus Post Papers, 1807–1821, MHMA.

56. Bill of Sale, Enslaved Man Peter, November 17, 1817, Justus Post Papers, 1807–1821, MHMA.

57. Thomas R. Mahoney, *Provincial Lives: Middle-Class Experience in the Antebellum Middle West* (New York: Cambridge University Press, 1999), 32–38.

58. "Police Regulations," *Missouri Gazette*, December 28, 1809.

59. Indictment of Enslaved Man George and Enslaved Man Joe for theft from Joseph Philibus's Home, March 1810, Fur Trade Collection, MHMA.

60. "Public Sale of Valuable Property, Cavalier & Petit vs. Heirs of Joseph Robideux, dec'd," *Missouri Gazette*, January 4, 1810.

61. Edward Hempstead to My Dear Parents, January 30, 1811, Stephen Hempstead Papers, MHMA.

62. "Notice," *Missouri Gazette*, January 23, 1818; Mahoney, *Provincial Lives*, 32–28.

63. Robert Englebert, "Colonial Encounters and the Changing Contours of Ethnicity: Pierre-Louis de Lorimier and Métissage at the Edges of Empire," *Ohio Valley History* 18, no. 1 (Spring 2018), 45–69.

64. Sale of a negress of Michel Hautius to Lorimer, September 4, 1789; Sale of a negress to L. Lorimier by Scott, January 18, 1798, List of Documents Contained in the Office of the Register of Ste. Genevieve, kept by Mr. Jean Baptiste Valle, Given to Thomas Oliver, December 5, 1804, Miscellaneous Bound MS #1, Transcribed and Translated by Vermer J. Genot, WPA, SGA.

65. Amos Stoddard to Henry Dearborn, May 7, 1804, Amos Stoddard Papers, MHMA.

66. James Wilkinson to Henry Dearborn, August 10, 1805, *TPUS*, 13:183.

67. Lynn Morrow, "Trader William Gilliss and Delaware Migration in Southern Missouri," in *The Ozarks in Missouri History: Discoveries in an American Region*, ed. Lynn Morrow (Columbia: University of Missouri Press, 2013), 19–36.

68. Jacob F. Lee, *Masters of the Middle Waters: Indian Nations and Colonial Ambitions Along the Mississippi* (Cambridge, MA: Harvard University Press, 2019), 195–230.

69. For the thick web of connections forged by the Chouteau family with habitants and Native Americans, and for the ways in which Chouteau incorporated U.S. officials and merchants into his networks, see Lee, *Masters of the Middle Waters*, 195–230.

70. United States vs. Jacques Chauvin, October 30, 1805, and United States vs. Madame Chevalier, October 30, 1805, Missouri Minute Book of the Territorial Supreme Court, MHMA.

71. United States vs. Francois Tayon, November 4, 1805, Missouri Minute Book of the Territorial Supreme Court, MHMA.

72. Motion of Mr. Donaldson on behalf of Joseph Tayon, May 9, 1806, Missouri Minute Book of the Territorial Supreme Court, MHMA. While other cases in the Minute Book have the judge's name assigned, this particular case does not. Given the presence of notes from the case in the John Lucas Papers, it is likely that he was the presiding judge.

73. United States vs. Pierre Chouteau, May 10, 1806, Missouri Minute Book of the Territorial Supreme Court, MHMA.

74. United States vs. Pierre Chouteau, May 10, 1806, Missouri Minute Book of the Territorial Supreme Court, MHMA.

75. Joseph Tayon vs. Celeste & Others, May 16, 1805, Missouri Minute Book of the Territorial Supreme Court, MHMA.

76. Judge Lucas, Deposition Notes, Marie Scipio's Descendants [1806], JBCLFP.

77. Sale of Enslaved Scypion Family Members, Joseph Tayon to Pierre Chouteau, July 3, 1806, Chouteau Family Papers, 1752–1946, MHMA.

78. William E. Foley, "Slave Freedom Suits Before Dred Scott: The Case of Marie Jean Scypion's Descendants," *Missouri Historical Review* 79, no. 1 (October 1984), 1–23; Lea VanderVelde, *Redemption Songs: Suing for Freedom Before Dred Scott* (New York: Oxford University Press, 2014), 39–56.

79. Pierre Chouteau to General Wilkinson, May 12, 1806, box 6, Pierre Chouteau Letterbook [translation], Chouteau Family Papers, MHMA.

80. François Vallé to _____, November 2, 1795 [translation], François Vallé Papers, 1742–1846, MHMA.

81. Superior Court Case Files, United States vs. Joseph LeBlond, 1814, St. Louis County, Criminal Case, Murder of enslaved girl Sylvia, box RD039, folder 37, Superior Court Case Files, MSA-JC; *Missouri Gazette*, November 13, 1813. As of August 1814, LeBlond was free and engaging in business transactions. See "Lost," *Missouri Gazette*, August 13, 1814.

82. Luck, *Replanting a Slave Society*.

83. John Walker to Hugh Stuart, August 8, 1817, box 2, folder 3, Correspondence, Walker Family Papers, Albert and Shirley Small Special Collections Library, University of Virginia, Charlottesville.

84. J. Clemens to J. Pawling, October 4, 1816, Missouri History Collection, MHMA.

85. Rufus Easton, "Missouri and Illinois," *Niles' Weekly Register*, August 24, 1816, 10:260–261. For an additional comparison of the Lower Mississippi Valley to the West Indies, with Missouri supplying food and stores to plantation operations downriver, see [?] to John Holmes, February 26, 1817, John Holmes Papers, New York Public Library, New York City.

86. Rufus Easton, "Missouri and Illinois," *Niles' Weekly Register*, August 24, 1816, 10:260–261.

87. For the importance of hemp, saltpeter, lead, and lead shot as supplemental commodities for commercial farmers, see M.[ichel] Amoureux to Pierre Clément Laussat, August 4, 1803, box 6, folder 234, Pierre-Clément de Laussat Papers, MSS 125, Williams Research Center, Historic New Orleans Collection; J. Clemens to J. Pawling, October 4, 1816, Missouri History Collection, MHMA; "At Herculaneum . . . ," *Missouri Gazette*, March 8, 1809; Rufus Easton, "Missouri and Illinois," *Niles' Weekly Register*, August 24, 1816, 10:260–261; "Salt Petre—Highest Price in Cash," (Lexington, KY) *Reporter*, September 25, 1813.

88. James Cummins to James Bryan, May 22, 1819 [transcript], AP.

89. Henry Marie Brackenridge, *Views of Louisiana, Containing Geographical, Statistical and Historical Notices . . .* , (Baltimore, MD, 1817), 256–269. For St. Louis enslavers hiring out enslaved people to the mines, see, for example, W. Christy to Moses Austin, July 28, 1807 [transcript], AP. For Tennessee enslavers, see N. Wilson to William B. Robertson, July 27, 1811, Slaves and Slavery Collection, MHMA.

90. "At Herculaneum . . . ," (St. Louis) *Missouri Gazette*, March 8, 1809; "The U.S. Mines of Missouri," *Missouri Gazette*, April 17, 1818.

91. Moses Austin to James Bryan, February 1815 [transcript], AP.

92. W. Christy to Moses Austin, July 28, 1807 [transcript], AP.

93. Moses Austin to John Brickey, February 22, 1815 [transcript], AP.

94. Henry R. Schoolcraft, *A View of the Lead Mines of Missouri: ... 1819* (New York: Charles Wiley & Co., 1819), 47–48. For the use of enslaved men to cut wood and produce lumber during slack farming times, see Affidavit of Sherred G. Swain Regarding Dispute with Daniel Bissell and Three Enslaved Men, March 6, 1817, JBCLFP; William Clark to Jonathan Clark, July 21, 1808, in Holmberg, *Dear Brother*, 143–144.

95. Schoolcraft, *View of the Lead Mines of Missouri*, 40, 176.

96. Henry Marie Brackenridge, *Journal of a Voyage up the River Missour ...* (Baltimore, 1817), 34.

97. Robert Lee, "'A Better View of the Country': A Missouri Settlement Map by William Clark," *William and Mary Quarterly*, 3rd ser., 79, no. 1 (January 2022), 89–120.

98. John Corlis to Susan Corlis, January 7, 1815, Corlis-Respress Family Papers, Filson Historical Society, Louisville, Kentucky.

99. George Sibley to Samuel Hopkins Sibley, January 14, 1816, George Champlain Sibley Papers, 1803–1853, MHMA.

100. Mary S. Easton Sibley to Rufus Easton, February 11, 1816, George Champlain Sibley Papers, 1803–1853, MHMA.

101. William Doswell to Thomas W. Claybrooke, June 17, 1817, Claybrooke-Doswell Families, Letters, 1804–1833, Library of Virginia, Richmond.

102. George Sibley to Samuel Hopkins Sibley, July 10, 1817, George Champlain Sibley Papers, 1803–1853, MHMA.

103. Thomas Hart Benton to Abra[ham] Maury, June 18, 1818, Maury Family Papers, 1782–1931, WLCL.

104. John Randolph to Harmanus Bleecker, October 10, 1818, box 5, folder 49, Papers of John Randolph of Roanoke, 1781–1860, Albert and Shirley Small Special Collections Library, University of Virginia, Charlottesville.

105. "St. Louis," *Missouri Gazette*, October 26, 1816.

106. Charles Carroll to Nathaniel Rochester, December 15, 1818; April 15, 1819; May 10, 1820, Rochester Family Papers, 1774–1836, Library of Virginia, Richmond.

107. John Walker to Thomas Walker, December 24, 1818, box 2, Correspondence, Walker Family Papers, Albert and Shirley Small Special Collections Library, University of Virginia, Charlottesville.

108. Charles Carroll to Nathaniel Rochester, February 22, 1819, Rochester Family Papers, 1774–1836, Library of Virginia, Richmond.

109. Justus Post to John Post, October 7, 1817, Justus Post Papers, 1807–1821, MHMA.

110. James McDaniel vs. Juan P. Cabanne, Court Papers Concerning Swapping of Negroes, 1807, JBCLFP.

111. George Sibley to Samuel H. Sibley, September 25, 1813, Sibley Papers, MHMA; Slaves, entry for January ____, 1820, Commonplace Book No. 1, January 1, 1820 to January 1, 1828, Sibley Papers, MHMA.

112. George Sibley to Samuel Hopkins Sibley, July 10, 1819, Sibley Papers, MHMA.

113. Indians #87, Proclamation Against the Muskoe & Creek Indians, April 30, 1804, Issued by Amos Stoddard [transcript], SGA; Amos Stoddard to W. C. C. Claiborne, May 19, 1804, Amos Stoddard Papers, MHMA.

114. "Indian Murders and Warfare," *Missouri Gazette*, March 18, 1815.

115. "St. Louis, June 8," *Savannah Republic*, July 30, 1816; "A Report upon the Claims of Certain Citizens of the United States, who have lost property by Indian Depredations," 22nd Cong., 1st. Sess., House Doc. No. 38, January 4, 1832, 95–104.

116. "A Subscriber," *Missouri Gazette*, June 22, 1816.

117. Deposition of Martin Dorion, October 14, 1817; and Deposition of Maurice Blondeau, October 14, 1817, Indians Collection, MHMA; William Clark to George C. Sibley, August 6, 1816, Sibley Papers, MHMA. For other attacks by Native Americans on enslaved African Americans, see, for example, "Murder!," *Missouri Gazette*, February 17, 1819; Petition of David Norris praying to set free his slave [1817], Series 488, Administration Papers, 1788–1817, Petitions submitted to the General Assembly of the Alabama Territory, Mississippi Department of Archives and History, Jackson, Mississippi.

118. N. Wilson to William B. Robertson, July 27, 1811, Slaves and Slavery Collection, MHMA.

119. United States vs. Samuel Means for Murder of an Enslaved Boy, Bill, 1814, St. Louis County, Criminal Case, box RD039, folder 31, Superior Court Case Files, MSA-JC.

120. United States vs. Elijah, and Gabriel, Superior Court Case Files, August 1818, St. Louis County, Criminal Case, box RD045, folder 33, Superior Court Case Files, MSA-JC.

121. Superior Court Case Files, John Smith v. William Neely, Joseph Sewell, Wright Daniel, John Martin, and John Wilson, 1810, Cape Girardeau County Civil Case, box RD028, folder 03, MSA-JC.

122. "Missouri Legislature," *Missouri Gazette*, December 7, 1816.

123. United States v. William Primm, for Murder, 1820, St. Charles County, Criminal Case, box RD047, folder 18; Francis Nash vs. William Primm, 1821, St. Charles County, Civil Case, box RD092, folder 15, all in Superior Court Case Files, MSA-JC. Judge Nathaniel Beverely Tucker exonerated Primm. For criticism of Tucker's ruling, see "A Dignified Judge," *Edwardsville Spectator*, February 15, 1820.

124. William Clark to Jonathan Clark, November 9, 1808, in Holmberg, *Dear Brother*, 160.

125. William Clark to Jonathan Clark, November 24, 1808, in Holmberg, *Dear Brother*, 172.

126. William Clark to Jonathan Clark, May 28, 1809, in Holmberg, *Dear Brother*, 201.

127. William Clark to Jonathan Clark, July 22, 1809, in Holmberg, *Dear Brother*, 204.

128. William Clark to Jonathan Clark, August 26, 1809, in Holmberg, *Dear Brother*, 210.

129. John O'Fallon to William Clark, May 13, 1811, William Clark Papers, MHMA.

130. Joseph Charless to John B. C. Lucas, April 18, 1819, JBCLFP; Investigation into Death of Scipio, 1819, box RD047, folder 27, Superior Court Case Files, MSA-JC.

131. (Shawneetown) *Illinois Emigrant*, May 8, 1819.

132. Joseph Charless to John B. C. Lucas, April 18, 1819, JBCLFP.

133. John Hawkins v. George Smirl, 1810, Saint Geneviève County, Civil Case, box RD029, folder 1, Superior Court Case Files, MSA-JC.

134. Bill of Sale for Enslaved man Sam, Elizabeth Harris to Shadrach Bond, February 19, 1808, JBCLFP.

135. J. B. C. Lucas, Runaway Slave Notice for Sam, March 31, 1808; I[saac] Darneille to John B. C. Lucas, June 20, 1808; Mse. Staes to J. B. C. Lucas, March 3, 1809, JBCLFP.

136. "Twenty Dollars Reward," *Missouri Gazette*, September 5, 1812; Rough Draft, Runaway Slave Poster, December 29, 1815, JBCLFP.

137. Rough Draft, Runaway Slave Poster for Sam, December 29, 1815, JBCLFP.

138. "50 Dollars Reward," *Missouri Gazette*, May 4, 1816.

139. Entry for May 21 and May 22, 1818, George Churchill Diary, 1818–1841, George Churchill Papers, ALPML.

140. "200 Dollars Reward," *Missouri Gazette*, April 19, 1820.

141. John O'Fallon to Thomas Smith, April 20, 1819, Thomas Adams Smith Papers, folder 16, SHSMO.

142. John Walker to Thomas H. Walker, April 16, 1820, Walker Family Papers, MSS 1532, Special Collections, University of Virginia Library.

Chapter 6

1. For the "radical indeterminacy" of status and conditions for enslaved and bonded people in the Middle Mississippi Valley from the 1780s through the 1850s, see Anne Twitty, *Before Dred Scott: Slavery and Legal Culture in the American Confluence, 1787–1857* (New York: Cambridge University Press, 2016).

2. "Illinois Legislature," (Kaskaskia) *Western Intelligencer*, December 18, 1817.

3. Robert Morrison to Joseph Morrison, January 22, 1805, Robert Morrison Letters, INDHS.

4. Robert Morrison to Joseph Morrison, April 7, 1805, Robert Morrison Papers, 1805–1853, ALPML.

5. Robert Morrison to Joseph Morrison, December 1, 1805; [Undated] Petition, Robert Morrison Letters, INDHS.

6. Robert Morrison to Joseph Morrison, December 31, 1805, Robert Morrison Papers, 1805–1853, ALPML.

7. *Annals of Congress*, 9th Cong., 1st sess., 342.

8. Matthew Lyon to John Messinger, July 31, 1818, folder 3, box 1, John Messinger Papers, 1797–1878, ALPML.

9. John Craig Hammond, *Slavery, Freedom, and Expansion in the Early American West* (Charlottesville: University of Virginia Press, 2007), 103–113.

10. Stanley Griswold to Henry Griswold, March 25, 1815, Griswold Family Papers, 1782–1820, Mss. 821, Family Letters, 1810–1815, Special Collections, Baker Library, Harvard University, Cambridge, Massachusetts.

11. Jacob F. Lee, *Masters of the Middle Waters: Indian Nations and Colonial Ambitions Along the Mississippi* (Cambridge, MA: Harvard University Press, 2019), 209–212.

12. For more on the creation of "French Negroes" by Illinois enslavers in the years following issuance of the Northwest Ordinance, see M. Scott Heerman, *The Alchemy of Slavery: Human Bondage and Emancipation in the Illinois Country, 1730–1865* (Philadelphia: University of Pennsylvania Press, 2018), 58–81.

13. [Proslavery Arguments by Governor Edwards], undated letter draft, before 1818, Ninian Edwards Papers, CHM.

14. "An Act Creating the County of Illinois," *CISHL*, 2:9–11.

15. Treaty of Cession, Executed March 1, 1784, in *The Papers of Thomas Jefferson, 21 May 1781–1 March 1784*, ed. Julian P. Boyd, 45 vols. to date (Princeton, NJ: Princeton University Press, 1952–present), 6:578.

16. Memorial of Barthelemi Tardiveau, July 8, 1788, *CISHL*, 5:488.

17. Report of the Committee: Memorial from Vincennes and the Illinois Country [September 1788], *TPUS*, 2:149.

18. Arthur St. Clair to George Washington, May 1, 1790, *TPUS*, 2:248.

19. Arthur St. Clair to Luke Decker, October 11, 1793, in *The St. Clair Papers: The Life and Public Services of Arthur St. Clair . . .* 2 vols. (Cincinnati: Robert Clarke & Co., 1882), 2:318–319.

20. John Craig Hammond; "Race, Slavery, Sectional Conflict, and National Politics, 1770–1820," in *The Routledge History of Nineteenth Century America*, ed. Daniel Wells (New York: Routledge, 2017), 11–32.

21. For the fullest articulation of this legal theory, see [Proslavery Arguments by Governor Edwards], undated letter draft before 1818, Ninian Edwards Papers, CHM.

22. Heerman, *Alchemy of Slavery*, 70.

23. Robert Morrison to Eliza Morrison, August 29, 1813, Robert Morrison Letters, 1805–1853, ALPML.

24. Mary, A Woman of Color vs. Francois Menard, Andre Landreville, July Term, 1827, SLCCHRP. Mary was born in 1800 or 1801. When Mary's enslaver died in the early 1820s, François Menard purchased her and her three children. When Illinois voted against amending its constitution to permit slavery in 1824, Menard transferred Mary and her children to St. Louis, where Mary initiated her freedom suit, which she ultimately lost.

25. Aspasia, A Free Woman of Color vs. Francois Chouteau, Pierre Menard, March Term, 1828, SLCCHRP.

26. Susan, A Free Woman of Color vs. Henry Hight, February Term, 1818, SLCCHRP.

27. "A Law to Regulate County Levies, September 17, 1807," *CISHL*, 30:332.

28. "An Act Concerning Servants," *CISHL*, 30:651.

29. "An Act to Amend an Act, Entitled 'An Act Concerning Servants,'" *CISHL*, 21:657–658.

30. "An Act Concerning the Kaskaskia Indians," *CISHL*, 28:296. For other references to enslaved African Americans in Illinois, see, for example, "An Act to Prevent the Migration of Free Negroes and Mulattoes into this Territory, December 18, 1813," *CISHL*, 25:92.

31. Amos Stoddard, *Sketches, Historical and Descriptive, of Louisiana* (Philadelphia, 1812), 341.

32. Indiana and Illinois enslavers instituted their first indentured servant laws in 1803 and then modified those laws in 1805 and 1807. "A Law concerning Servants, Adopted from the Virginia code, . . ." *CISHL*, 21:42; "An Act concerning the introduction of Negroes and Mulattoes into this Territory," August 26, 1805, *CISHL*, 21:136–139, and modified in 1807, *CISHL*, 30:467–469.

33. The best guides to the systems of indentured servitude in Illinois are Heerman, *Alchemy of Slavery*, 58–81; and Darrel Dexter, *Bondage in Egypt: Slavery in Southern Illinois* (Cape Girardeau: Center for Regional History, Southeast Missouri State University, 2011). Dexter's work contains a near-exhaustive list of surviving indentures and provides transcripts of numerous indentures. The indentures are also available through the Illinois Servitude and Emancipation Records database maintained by the Illinois State Archives.

34. "For Sale," *Edwardsville* (IL) *Spectator*, July 10, 1819.

35. "At Auction," *Missouri Gazette*, March 21, 1812.

36. Stanley Griswold to Henry Griswold, March 25, 1815, Griswold Family Papers, 1782–1820, Mss. 821, Family Letters, 1810–1815, Special Collections, Baker Library, Harvard University, Cambridge, Massachusetts.

37. Response of Manuel Lisa to Complaint, November 1808, Manuel Lisa Letters, 1807–1812, Vault Manuscript Collection, MSS 529, L. Tom Perry Special Collections, Harold B. Lee Library, Brigham Young University, Provo, Utah.

38. For the use of enslaved labor at salt works, see Thomas Bahde, "'I Would Not Have a White Upon the Premises': The Ohio Valley Salt Industry and Slave Hiring in Illinois, 1780–1825," *Ohio Valley History* 15, no. 2 (2015), 49–69.

39. "Journal of the House of Representatives, 1812," *CISHL*, 3:119.

40. Shadrach Bond to Governor Ninian Edwards, February 7, 1813, Ninian Edwards Papers, CHM.

41. A Resolution of the Legislative Assembly, January 25, 1813, *TPUS*, 16:297; *Annals of Congress*, 12th Cong., 2nd sess., 109, 110, 112.

42. "An Act Concerning Negroes and Mulattos," December 22, 1814, *CISHL*, 25:157–158.

43. Dexter, *Bondage in Egypt*, 475, 479.

44. Bahde, "'I Would Not Have a White Upon the Premises.'"

45. [Unknown], Journal of a Trip from Champaign County, Ohio to New Orleans, November 25, 1805—July 26, 1806, entries for January 7 and 8, 1806, ALPML.

46. "Notice," *Missouri Gazette*, August 9, 1817.

47. "$20 Reward," (Kaskaskia) *Western Intelligencer*, November 6, 1816.

48. For other instances of enslaved people fleeing the salines, see, for example, "$50 Reward," (Vincennes, IN) *Western Sun*, September 18, 1813; "$50 Reward," (Shawneetown) *Illinois Gazette*, August 19, 1820; and "$100 Reward," *Edwardsville* (IL) *Spectator*, March 14, 1820.

49. Vincent, a Man of Color v. James Duncan, November 1829, SLCCHRP.

50. Joe, a Black Man v. Colman Duncan, James Duncan, June Term, 1830, SLCCHRP.

51. Alsey vs. William Randolph, March Term, 1841; Vincent, a Man of Color v. James Duncan, November 1829, SLCCHRP.

52. Ralph, A Man of Colour v. James Coleman and Duncan Coleman, July Term, 1830, SLCCHRP.

53. "Extract of a letter from a gentleman in the suit of Colonel Hammond, to his friends in Augusta Georgia, July 15, 1805," (Boston) *Repertory*, October 4, 1805.

54. Andey Kinney to John Messinger, August 24, 1812, John Messinger Papers, 1797–1878, ALPML.

55. "Randolph's Letter. Letter to a Gentleman in Boston . . . ," *Richmond* (VA) *Enquirer*, December 31, 1814.

56. "Slavery. An Experiment is making in the West," (Washington, DC) *National Intelligencer*, September 16, 1816.

57. "A Reply to 'Thoughts on the subject of educating negroes in the United States, No. V,'" (Wilmington, DE) *American Watchman*, November 2, 1816.

58. "From the Lynchburg Press, The Western Country," (Kaskaskia) *Western Herald*, March 25, 1818.

59. Morris Birkbeck, *Notes on a Journey in America: From the Coast of Virginia to the Territory of Illinois* (London, 1818), 6–7.

60. "Soldier's Bounty Lands," (Washington, DC) *National Intelligencer*, April 1, 1817.

61. Samuel R. Brown, *The Western Gazetteer or Emigrant's Directory Containing a Geographical Description of the Western States and Territories, . . .* (Auburn, NY, 1817), 17.

62. *Journal of Senate of the Commonwealth of Virginia* (Richmond, 1817), 83.

63. John Melish, *Travels through the United States of America, in the years 1806 & 1807, and 1809, 1810, & 1811 . . .* (Philadelphia, 1818), 382.

64. Henry Bradshaw Fearon, *Sketches of America. A Narrative of a Journey of Five Thousand Miles Through the Eastern and Western States of America; . . .* (London, 1818), 262.

65. Joseph Pollard, Jr., to William Clark, October 25, 1810, Clark Family Collection, William Clark Papers, 1789–1810, MHMA.

66. Charles Carroll to Nathaniel Rochester, December 15, 1818; Charles Carroll to Nathaniel Rochester, April 15, 1819, Rochester Family Papers, 1774–1836, Library of Virginia, Richmond.

67. Henry Marie Brackenridge, *Views of Louisiana, Containing Geographical, Statistical and Historical Notices . . .* , (Baltimore, MD, 1817), 213.

68. Timothy Flint, *Recollections of the Last Ten Years: Passed in Occasional Residences and Journeyings in the Valley of the Mississippi . . .* , (Boston, 1826), 211.

69. Abraham Bradley Lindsley to E. Lindsley, January 15, 1819, Small Manuscripts Collection, CHM.

70. "To the People of Illinois, II, Agis," *Illinois Intelligencer*, July 1, 1818.

71. "Illinois Legislature," (Kaskaskia) *Western Intelligencer*, December 18, 1817.

72. William Henry Harrison to Frederick Ridgeley, May 24, 1807, William Henry Harrison Papers, INDHS.

73. Robert Morrison to Eliza Morrison, August 29, 1813, Robert Morrison Letters, 1805–1853, ALPML.

74. John Kinzie and Thomas Forsythe, Indenture of Jeffrey Nash, 1804 [typescript], Illinois History and Lincoln Collections, University of Illinois, Urbana-Champaign.

75. "Forty Dollars Reward," *Missouri Gazette*, April 5, 1809.

76. Forysthe et al. vs. Nash, June 1816, in Francis Xavier Martin, comp., *Louisiana Term Reports, or Cases Argued and Determined in the Supreme Court of the State of Louisiana* 2 vols. (New Orleans, 1819), 2:385–391.

77. The Dred Scott case was the most famous of these cases, but hundreds of suits were filed in the decades preceding the Dred Scott decision. See Kelly M. Kennington, *In the Shadow of Dred Scott: St. Louis Freedom Suits and the Legal Culture of Slavery in Antebellum America* (Athens: University of Georgia Press, 2017); Lea VanderVelde, *Redemption Songs: Suing for Freedom Before Dred Scott* (New York: Oxford University Press, 2014); and Twitty, *Before Dred Scott*.

78. Milly, A Black Woman, for Herself and her Two Infant Children, Eliza and Bob v. Mathias Rose, April 1819, SLCCHRP.

79. Tempe, a Black Woman v. Risden H. Price, filed September 1817; and Labon, a Man of Color v. Risdon H. Price, March Term, 1818, SLCCHRP.

80. Bill of Sale for Enslaved man Sam, Elizabeth Harris to Shadrach Bond, February 19, 1808, JBCLFP. For Lucas's ownership of Sam, see J. B. C. Lucas, Runaway Slave Notice for Sam, March 31, 1808, JBCLFP.

81. Marie, A Mulatto Girl v. Auguste Chouteau, March Term, 1818, SLCCHRP. In 1821, a St. Louis jury upheld Marie's claim of freedom. For similar cases, where Missouri enslavers sold enslaved people to Illinois, and then those Illinois enslavers moved to Missouri, prompting freedom suits, see Pelagie v. Francois Vallois and John P. Cabanne, October 1821, SLCCHRP. See also the four freedom suits filed in 1828 against John Reynolds of Cahokia, who purchased several enslaved people at an estate sale in 1816: Suzette alias Judith Bequette v. John Reynolds, March Term, 1828; Angelique, a free woman of color v. John Reynolds, July Term, 1828; Edmund v. John Reynolds, July Term, 1828; Dolly, a colored woman v. John Young, July Term, 1828; and John, a free boy of color v. John Reynolds, July Term, 1828, SLCCHRP. At least one enslaved man, Moses, ran away almost as soon as Reynolds purchased him: "Fifty Dollars Reward," *Missouri Gazette*, June 8, 1816. For a freedom suit filed by a woman, born in Illinois in

1810, who then sued for her freedom in 1830, see Matilda, A Free Woman of Color v. Charles St. Vrain, March Term, 1831, SLCCHRP.

82. Bill of Sale, Richard Lowe to John B. C. Lucas, Enslaved Man Kayer, September 26, 1810, JBCLFP.

83. Receipt for Sale of Sixteen-Year-Old Enslaved Girl Lucy, from Antoine Chenie to Joseph Brazeaux, January 1814, Slaves and Slavery Collection, MHMA.

84. William Christy to John O'Fallon, February 14, 1821, O'Fallon Family Papers, folder 13, MHMA. For other examples of denoting an enslaved person as "a slave for and during the period of his natural life," see, for example, Bill of Sale, Enslaved Man Peter, November 17, 1817, Justus Post Papers, 1807–1821, MHMA. For Illinois enslavers denoting individuals as "a slave for life," see, for example, Bill of Sale, Between George Bay and James A. James for Enslaved Woman Constance and Child Mary, C298, October 2, 1824, SHSMO.

85. Twitty, *Before Dred Scott.*

86. Stephen Aron, *How the West Was Lost: The Transformation of Kentucky from Daniel Boone to Henry Clay* (Baltimore, MD: Johns Hopkins University Press, 1996), 164.

87. John Pope to James Madison, April 18, 1809, *TPUS*, 16:23.

88. Matthew Lyon to James Madison, January 26, 1810, *TPUS*, 14:365.

89. Anthony to Ninian Edwards; Joseph to Ninian Edwards; Maria to Ninian Edwards; Maria to Ninian Edwards; Rose to Ninian Edwards; Strass to Ninian Edwards; Charles to Ninian Edwards; Jessee to Ninian Edwards, all in Illinois Emancipation and Servitude Records Database, Illinois State Archives.

90. "For Sale," *Missouri Gazette*, July 18, 1812.

91. "Notice," *Missouri Gazette*, December 12, 1812.

92. Bill of Sale Between Ninian Edwards and Theodore Hunt for Enslaved Child Wallace, May 25, 1814, JBCLFP.

93. Thomas Forsythe to Governor Edwards, December 8, 1815, *TPUS*, 17:260; George Sibley, Slaves, Commonplace Book, Entry for January ___, 1820, Sibley Papers, 1803–1853, MHMA.

94. Census of Madison County, 1818, *CISHL*, 26:130.

95. "Virginia Legislature," (Richmond) *Virginia Argus*, December 12, 1809.

96. Adam to Alexander Stuart; Ben to Alexander Stuart; Billy to Alexander Stuart; Lucy to Alexander Stuart; Paige to Alexander Stuart; Scylla to Alexander Stuart; William to Alexander Stuart, all in Emancipation and Servitude Records Database, Illinois State Archives.

97. "At Auction," *Missouri Gazette*, March 21, 1812.

98. Adam, William, Lucy, and Moses, transfer, Alexander Stuart to Shadrach Bond, Jr., Emancipation and Servitude Records Database, Illinois State Archives.

99. "Extracts from the Journal of the House of Delegates, Thursday, December 10," (Richmond, VA) *Enquirer*, December 22, 1812; "An Act concerning Archibald Stuart, jr. & Nancy Stuart," (Richmond, VA) *Enquirer*, February 23, 1813.

100. Alexander Stuart to James Monroe, February 13, 1813, *TPUS*, 16:299.

101. "For Sale or Barter," *Missouri Gazette*, May 30, 1812; "Thirty Dollars Reward," *Missouri Gazette*, September 26, 1812; "Ran-away from the Subscriber," *Missouri Gazette*, May 7, 1814; Cupid to William Rabb, Emancipation and Servitude Records Database, Illinois State Archives; Dexter, *Bondage in Egypt*, 540; Mary Crownover Rabb, *Travels and Adventures in Texas in the 1820's, Being the Reminiscences of Mary Crownover Rabb*, ed. Ramsey Yelvington (Waco, TX: W. M. Morrison, Printers, 1962).

102. Court Notes of Judge John B. C. Lucas, James Callaway vs P. Chouteau & McWhorry [1808], JBCLFP; Wherry and Chouteau v. Callaway, 1810, St. Charles County, Civil Case, box RD028, folder 9, Superior Court Case Files, MSA-JC.

103. Nathaniel Pope to Jesse Burgess Thomas, May 22, 1827, Jesse Burgess Thomas Papers, ALPML.

104. Wills #35, Last Will and Testament William Morrison, dec'd, a copy, attested May 11, 1838 [typescript], SGA.

105. General Indenture Concerning Enslaved Woman Jane, Hezekiah Davis and Samuel Cochran, August 20, 1817, Henry Eddy Papers, ALPML.

106. Indenture and Sale of Enslaved Woman Mary, May 6, 1827, William Drury, Pierre Menard and [Jean Baptiste] Vallé, William Drury Papers, ALPML.

107. For the ways in which enslaved Illinoisians worked to liberate themselves, see Heerman, *Alchemy of Slavery*, 82–134. Heerman counts forty-nine enslaved Illinoisians gaining their freedom between 1815 and 1819, with twelve free African Americans migrating into Illinois. By 1820, free Black Illinoisians had created their own free Black village, Brooklyn, Illinois. The 1820 Illinois census counted 506 free Black people in Illinois, but it is unclear if they were bound by indentures.

108. Sarah L. H. Gronningsater, *The Rising Generation: Gradual Abolition, Black Legal Culture, and the Making of National Freedom* (Philadelphia: University of Pennsylvania Press, 2024); James J. Gigantino II, *The Ragged Road to Abolition: Slavery and Freedom in New Jersey, 1775–1865* (Philadelphia: University of Pennsylvania Press, 2014).

109. Andey Kinney to John Messinger, August 24, 1812, John Messinger Papers, 1797–1878, ALPML.

110. For Messinger's and Kinney's roles in defeating the 1824 effort to hold a new convention, where it was expected enslavers would fully sanction slavery in Illinois, see Suzanne Cooper Guasco, *Confronting Slavery: Edward Coles and the Rise of Antislavery Politics in Nineteenth-Century America* (DeKalb: Northern Illinois University Press, 2013).

111. "Extract of a letter from a gentleman in this place, to his friend in Loudon County Virginia, dated, Kaskaskia, Feb. 3, 1817," (Kaskaskia) *Western Intelligencer*.

112. Brown, *Western Gazetteer*, 17.

113. Abraham Bradley Lindsley to E. Lindsley, January 15, 1819, Small Manuscripts Collection, CHM.

114. In 1817, Daniel Cook published two open letters to James Monroe calling on him to devise a national plan of gradual abolition. See Cook, "For the National Register: To James Monroe, President of the United States," (Washington, DC) *National Register*, September 13 and 20, 1817.

115. "Illinois Legislature," (Kaskaskia) *Western Intelligencer*, December 18, 1817.

116. Illinois General Assembly, Act Regarding Slavery, December 27, 1817 [typescript], Illinois Territory Legislature, Papers, 1807–1818, Illinois History and Lincoln Collections, University of Illinois, Urbana-Champaign.

117. "Caution," (Kaskaskia) *Illinois Intelligencer*, April 15, 1818. For other antislavery pieces, see, for example, "A Republican, For the Western Intelligencer, Slavery," (Kaskaskia) *Western Intelligencer*, April 1, 1818; "Candor," (Kaskaskia) *Western Intelligencer*, April 22 and May 6, 1818.

118. Entries for April 25 and May 3, 1818, George Churchill Diary, 1818–1841, George Churchill Papers, ALPML; "Agis, For the People of Illinois, No. 1," *Illinois Intelligencer*, June 17, 1818; "Agis, No. II," *Illinois Intelligencer*, July 1, 1818.

119. Entries for June 12, 13, 27, 28, 30, and July 6, 1818, George Churchill Diary, 1818–1841, George Churchill Papers, ALPML; "A Citizen," *Illinois Intelligencer*, June 24, 1818.

120. Entries for July 7 and 8, 1818, George Churchill Diary, 1818–1841, George Churchill Papers, ALPML.

121. Response to "A Friend of Enquiry," *Illinois Intelligencer*, July 22, 1818.

122. Matthew Lyon to John Messinger, July 31, 1818, folder 3, box 1, John Messinger Papers, 1797–1878, ALPML.

123. *Annals of Congress*, 15th Cong., 1st sess., 1675–1676; "15th Congress," *City of Washington Gazette*, April 6, 1818.

124. Nathaniel Pope to Rufus King, April 10, 1818, folder 4, box 16, Rufus King Papers, New-York Historical Society, New York.

125. The most readily available copy of the 1818 constitution and convention minutes is in Richard V. Carpenter and J. W. Kitchell, "The Illinois Constitutional Convention of 1818," *Journal of the Illinois State Historical Society* 6, no. 3 (October 1913), 327–424.

126. "Salem, Saturday October 3," (Salem, MA) *Essex Register*, October 3, 1818.

127. Daniel P. Cook to Ninian Edwards, August 3, 1818, Ninian Edwards Papers, CHM.

128. Entry for September 9, 1818, George Churchill Diary, 1818–1841, George Churchill Papers, ALPML; George Churchill to Swift Eldred, September 9, 1818, in "Letter of George Churchill of Madison County, Ill., to Mr. Swift Eldred, Warren Ct.," *Journal of the Illinois State Historical Society* 11, no. 1 (April 1918), 64–67.

129. Heerman, *Alchemy of Slavery*, 58–81; Dexter, *Bondage in Egypt*, 466–533, 538–565.

130. Dexter, *Bondage in Egypt*, 471. Early Illinois census records are scattered. The appendices in Dexter, *Bondage in Egypt*, 472–504, contain the most comprehensive aggregate of the Illinois census returns. For other sources, see Margaret Cross Norton, ed., *Illinois Census Returns, 1810 and 1818* (Springfield: Illinois State Historical Library, 1935); and *CISHL*, vol. 26.

131. Dexter, *Bondage in Egypt*, 471.

132. Dexter, *Bondage in Egypt*, 470.

133. In 1810, Connecticut enslavers held a little more than three hundred African Americans in slavery; in Pennsylvania, enslavers held approximately eight hundred African Americans in slavery. See Ira Berlin, *Generations of Captivity: A History of African-American Slaves* (Cambridge, MA: Harvard University Press, 2003), 276, table 2.

134. Census Schedule, January 10, 1811, *TPUS*, 14:431.

135. VanderVelde, *Redemption Songs*, 39–56.

136. Heerman, *Alchemy of Slavery*, 109–159.

137. "For the Intelligencer, The Republican, No. 2, Pro Patria," (Kaskaskia) *Illinois Intelligencer*, October 6, 1819.

Conclusion

1. John Craig Hammond, "Inveterate Imperialists: Contested Imperialisms, North American History, and the Coming of the U.S. Civil War," in *A Continent in Crisis: The U.S. Civil War in North America*, ed. Brian Schoen, Jewel L. Spangler, and Frank Towers (New York: Fordham University Press, 2022), 36–64; Peter Kastor, "The Multinational History of Missouri Statehood," in *A Fire Bell in the Past: The Missouri Crisis at 200*, vol. 2, *The Missouri Question and Its Answers*, ed. Jeffrey L. Pasley and John Craig Hammond (Columbia: University of Missouri Press, 2021), 357–383; Alan Taylor, *American Republics: A Continental History of the United States, 1783–1850* (New York: Norton, 2021); Alan Taylor, *American Revolutions: A Continental*

History, 1750–1804 (New York: Norton, 2016); Kathleen DuVal, *Independence Lost: Lives on the Edge of the American Revolution* (New York: Random House, 2015); Max M. Edling, *A Hercules in the Cradle: War, Money, and the American State, 1783–1867* (Chicago: University of Chicago Press, 2014); François Furstenberg, "The Significance of the Trans-Appalachian Frontier in Atlantic History," *American Historical Review* 113 (June 2008), 647–677.

2. Jeffrey L. Pasley, "Slavery, War, and Democracy: The Winding Road to the Missouri Crisis," in *A Fire Bell in the Past: The Missouri Crisis at 200*, vol. 1, *Western Slavery, National Impasse*, ed. Jeffrey L. Pasley and John Craig Hammond (Columbia: University of Missouri Press, 2021), 113–157; John Craig Hammond, "President, Planter, Politician: James Monroe, the Missouri Crisis, and the Politics of Slavery," *Journal of American History* 105, no. 4 (March 2019), 843–867.

3. *Annals of Congress*, 15th Cong., 1st sess., 1675–1676; "15th Congress," *City of Washington Gazette*, April 6, 1818.

4. (Amherst, NH) *Farmer's Cabinet*, April 18, 1818; *Portland* (ME) *Gazette*, April 21, 1818; *Bangor* (ME) *Weekley Register*, April 23, 1818; *Concord* (NH) *Gazette*, April 28, 1818.

5. *Annals of Congress*, 15th Cong., 2nd sess., 295–296.

6. "From our Correspondent in Washington," *Alexandria* (VA) *Gazette*, November 25, 1818. The *Alexandria Gazette*'s account of the debate differs somewhat from that found in *Annals of Congress*, 15th Cong., 2nd sess., 308–311. Specifically, either the *Annals* account seems to have significantly toned down Tallmadge's antislavery rhetoric or the *Alexandria Gazette* increased it.

7. "From our Correspondent in Washington," *Alexandria* (VA) *Gazette*, November 25, 1818; *Annals of Congress*, 15th Cong., 2nd sess., 308–311. For Anderson's involvement in land speculation, see David Dodge to Allen Latham, February 17, 1820; F. Cook to Allen Latham, April 23, 1820, Richard Clough Anderson Papers, 1782–1914, Illinois History and Lincoln Collections, University of Illinois, Urbana-Champaign.

8. "From our Correspondent in Washington," *Alexandria* (VA) *Gazette*, November 25, 1818; *Annals of Congress*, 15th Cong., 2nd sess., 308–311.

9. *Annals of Congress*, 15th Cong., 2nd sess., 311. The fifteenth Congress contained 108 new members. For the importance of these new members in bringing an aggressive antislavery agenda to Congress, see Pasley, "Slavery, War, and Democracy."

10. "From the Boston Atlas, Interesting Letter, John Taylor to Charles Hudson, April 15, 1847," *Cleveland* (OH) *Herald*, June 1, 1847.

11. Tallmadge had been an enslaver in New York but had allowed the people he enslaved to emancipate themselves. As a local officeholder, he had overseen the process of gradual abolition in the Hudson Valley by recording emancipations. See Sarah L. H. Gronningsater, "James Tallmadge Jr., and the Personal Politics of Antislavery," in Pasley and Hammond, *A Fire Bell in the Past*, 1:253–284.

12. "From our Correspondent at Washington," *Alexandria* (VA) *Gazette*, February 19, 1819.

13. "From our Correspondent," *Commercial Advertiser* (NY), February 16, 1819.

14. *Annals of Congress*, 15th Cong., 2nd sess., 1166, 1170–1193.

15. "The Proceedings of Congress . . ." *New-York Daily Advertiser*, February 19, 1819.

16. John Thompson Brown to William B. Steptoe, January 28, 1820, Brown, Coalter, Tucker Papers, 1780–1929, MSS 65 B85, Swem Library, William and Mary College, Williamsburg, Virginia.

17. Thomas Hutchinson to John M. O'Connor, February 18, 1820, John M. O'Connor Papers, 1810–1826, WLCL.

18. John Quincy Adams, February 23, 1820, diary entry, in *John Quincy Adams and the Politics of Slavery: Selections from the Diary*, ed. David Waldstreicher and Matthew Mason (New York: Oxford University Press, 2017), 73. For contemporaneous southern calls for the forced annexation of Florida and Texas as a measure designed explicitly to protect and benefit southern enslavers, see, for example, Charles Tait to John Walker, November 19, 1819, Walker Family Papers, Alabama Department of Archives and History, Montgomery, Alabama; John Walker to Charles Tait, January 28, 1821, Tait Family Papers, Alabama Department of Archives and History, Montgomery, Alabama.

19. "Congress of the United States," *Saratoga* (NY) *Sentinel*, December 1, 1819.

20. "Wilmington Meeting," "Resolutions of the Delaware General Assembly," *Niles' Weekly Register*, January 22, 1820.

21. "Legislature of Pennsylvania," *Niles' Weekly Register*, Jan. 1, 1820: 296–297.

22. "Slavery," *Patriot* (Concord, NH), November 30, 1819 [quote]. For a sampling of these resolutions, see, for example, "To the Editors of the American," *American and Commercial Daily Advertiser* (Baltimore), January 3 1820; "From the Rhode Island American," *Niles' Weekly Register*, December 20, 1819; "From a Philadelphia Paper," *Niles' Weekly Register*, December 11, 1819; "Resolutions of the New Jersey Legislature," *Niles' Weekly Register*, January 22, 1820; "Meeting at Camden," *Washington Whig* (Bridgeton, NJ), December 20, 1819; "Resolutions of the New Hampshire Legislature," *Niles' Weekly Register*, July 8, 1820; "Extension of Negro Slavery," *Niles' Weekly Register*, November 27, 1819; "Slavery," (Hartford) *Connecticut Courant*, December 7, 1819; "Town Meeting," *Liberty Hall and Cincinnati Gazette*, December 21, 1819; "Meeting at Keene, New Hampshire," *Concord* (NH) *Observer*, December 20, 1819; "Meeting of the Citizens of Cherry-Valley and Its Vicinity," *Cherry Valley* (NY) *Gazette*, January 4, 1820; (Ohio) *Senate Journal, 1820*, 145–147, 154, 169; (Ohio) *House Journal, 1820*, 166, 176, 198–199; (United States) *Senate Journal*, 16th Cong., 1st sess., 82, 114, 118, 131, 136. For the genesis and operation of these meetings and resolutions, see, for example, Jonathan Mason to William Tudor, November 28, 1819, William Tudor Personal Archive, Personal Correspondence, 1793–1830, Alphabetical Correspondence, 1797–1828, Harvard University Archives, Cambridge, Massachusetts.

23. Nicholas Hansen, July 4th Address, *Edwardsville* (IL) *Spectator*, July 31, 1819.

24. "The Republican, No. 2, Pro Patria," (Kaskaskia) *Illinois Intelligencer*, October 6, 1819.

25. *Annals*, 16th Cong, 1st sess., 732–736.

26. *Annals*, 16th Cong., 1st sess., 336.

27. John Quincy Adams, diary entry, February 20, 1820, in Waldstreicher and Mason, *John Quincy Adams and the Politics of Slavery*, 72–73.

28. Abner LaCock to James Monroe, January 30, 1820, James Monroe Papers, Manuscript Division, LOC.

29. William Trimble to Ethan Allen Brown, January 29, 1820, Ethan Allen Brown Papers, Ohio History Connect, Archives, Columbus.

30. "Missouri Question," *Richmond* (VA) *Enquirer*, December 16, 1819.

31. "Delaware," *Richmond* (VA) *Enquirer*, February 19, 1820.

32. Montfort Stokes to John Branch, February 27, 1820, Slaves and Slavery Collection, MHMA.

33. James Barbour to Spencer Roane, February 13, 1820, Miscellaneous Collection, WLCL.

34. John Tyler to Spencer Roane, February 14, 1820, GLC 03670, Gilder Lehrman Institute, New York City.

35. "Extract of a Letter from a Gentleman in Washington to his friend in Richmond, Washington, February 12, 1820," *Richmond* (VA) *Enquirer*, February 17, 1820. For Monroe's involvement in writing "Extract of a Letter," see George Hay to Monroe, February 16, 1820, James Monroe Papers, Manuscript Division, LOC.

36. William Trimble to Ethan Allen Brown, January 29, 1820, Ethan Allen Brown Papers, Ohio History Connect, Archives, Columbus.

37. Abner LaCock to James Monroe, January 30, 1820, James Monroe Papers, Manuscript Division, LOC.

38. Mark L. Hill to William King, February 4, 1820, William King Papers, Maine Historical Society, Portland.

39. *Annals*, 16th Cong., 1st sess., 424, 426–428, 469, 1171–1172, 1587–1588, 1588–1589.

40. For the course of congressional debates, see Michael J. McManus, " 'We Have Gained All That Was Possible, If Not All That Was Desired': Politics and the Passage of the Missouri Compromise," in Pasley and Hammond, *A Fire Bell in the Past*, 2:37–70.

41. John Sloane to Benjamin Tappan, March 29, 1820, Benjamin Tappan Papers, LOC.

42. D[aniel] B. Smith to Joseph Bringhurst, January 23, 1820, Bringhurst Family Papers, Delaware Historical Society, Wilmington.

43. Henry Meigs to Joseph D. Hay, February 12, 1820, Brock Collection, Huntington Library, San Marino, California.

44. "Copy of a letter from the Honorable Charles Pinckney," *City Gazette and Daily Advertiser* (Charleston), March 10, 1820.

45. Henry Clay to H. M. Brackenridge, March 7, 1820, Henry Marie Brackenridge Papers, Special Collections Library, University of Pittsburgh, Pittsburgh, Pennsylvania.

46. John Walker to Charles Tait, April 17, 1820, Tait Family Papers, Alabama Department of Archives and History, Montgomery.

47. Montfort Stokes to John Branch, February 27, 1820, Slaves and Slavery Collection, MHMA.

48. (Franklin) *Missouri Intelligencer*, June 4, 1819.

49. Isaac A. Coles to Joseph Carrington Cabell, December 20, 1819, Series 1, Wickham Family Papers, 1766–1945, Virginia Historical Society, Richmond.

50. George Tompkins to George C. Sibley, July 30, 1819, George Champlain Sibley Papers, 1803–1853, MHMA.

51. Jonathan S. Findlay, To the Voters of Howard County, April 11, 1820 [Broadside], Abiel Leonard Papers, 1782–1932, SHSMO.

52. "Election for the Convention," *Missouri Gazette*, May 10, 1820.

53. *St. Louis Enquirer*, May 10, 1820.

54. *Journal of the Missouri State Convention* (St. Louis, 1820). For the dominance of enslavers in Missouri politics through the 1840s, and the emergence of free soilism in the 1850s, see Zachary Dowdle, "A Geography of Free Soil: The Legacy of the 1820 Compromise, Political Conflict, and the Decline of Slavery in Missouri," in Pasley and Hammond, *A Fire Bell in the Past*, 2:229–255.

55. Kelly M. Kennington, *In the Shadow of Dred Scott: St. Louis Freedom Suits and the Legal Culture of Slavery in Antebellum America* (Athens: University of Georgia Press, 2017); Anne Twitty, *Before Dred Scott: Slavery and Legal Culture in the American Confluence, 1787–1857* (New York: Cambridge University Press, 2016); Lea VanderVelde, *Redemption Songs: Suing for Freedom Before Dred Scott* (New York: Oxford University Press, 2014).

56. Suzanne Cooper Guasco, *Confronting Slavery: Edward Coles and the Rise of Antislavery Politics in Nineteenth-Century America* (DeKalb: Northern Illinois University Press, 2013).

57. M. Scott Heerman, *The Alchemy of Slavery: Human Bondage and Emancipation in the Illinois Country, 1730–1865* (Philadelphia: University of Pennsylvania Press, 2018).

58. For the ways in which the history of enslavement and empire in the Middle Mississippi Valley from the 1780s into the 1820s structured the positions of Abraham Lincoln and Stephen Douglas in the 1850s, see Anne Twitty, "Placing the Lincoln-Douglas Debates," *American Political Thought* 12, no. 2 (Spring 2023), 267–276.

59. Waller Taylor to Archibald Austin, March 25, 1820, Austin-Twyman Papers, 1765–1939 Subseries 1, Swem Memorial Library, William and Mary College, Williamsburg, Virginia.

60. Waller Taylor to Archibald Austin, March 25, 1820, Austin-Twyman Papers, 1765–1939 Subseries 1, Swem Memorial Library, William and Mary College, Williamsburg, Virginia; "In the Senate of Indiana," *Edwardsville* (IL) *Spectator*, January 1, 1820.

61. For post–Missouri Crisis conflicts over empire and enslavement through the Civil War, see Hammond, "Inveterate Imperialists."

INDEX

Note: Page numbers in italic type indicate illustrations.

ACKNOWLEDGMENTS

It is a great privilege to have worked with so many wonderful people and institutions in putting together this book. Portions of the conclusion appeared previously in John Craig Hammond, "President, Planter, Politician: James Monroe, The Missouri Crisis, and the Politics of Slavery," *Journal of American History* 105 no. 4 (March 2019), 843–67, and is reprinted with the permission of the *Journal of American History*, Oxford University Press, and the Organization of American Historians. Librarians and archivists at the State Historical Society of Missouri, the Chicago History Museum, the W. L. Clemens Library at the University of Michigan, the Huntington Library, the University of California at Berkley, and the University of Illinois at Urbana-Champaign promptly scanned and sent documents I requested. Special thanks are due to Michelle Miler, at the Abraham Lincoln Presidential Museum and Library, and to Dennis Northcutt and the team at the Missouri History Museum Library for sharing their broad knowledge of their archives.

The contributors to *A Firebell in the Past* convinced me that this was a book that needed to be written, none more than my friend and co-editor, Jeff Pasley. My fellow historians gave far too many readings to subpar chapters and then helped improve them. Many thanks to Nick, Peter, Paul, Christa, David, and Matt. Editors make things happen for writers, and Bob Lockhart is one of the best in the business. Bob is a proper professional who made the entire process of writing, revising, and improving this book possible. Along the way, he secured two excellent outside readers. Reader #2, thanks for not being reader #2 and instead providing very useful comments. Anne Twitty went above and beyond in her criticism of my manuscript. It is much stronger as a result.

Penn State New Kensington has been an incredible academic home since 2008. Administrators there have generously funded this project. Allen Larson and Andrea Adolph provided financial support to obtain documents, and they always funded students who assisted me in translating and transcribing those documents. Air Wales was indefatigable once she encountered George Churchill's 1818 diary. T. J. Slancauskas quickly became a first-rate transcriber and an even better historian. Mahima Chowdhury devoted COVID quarantine days to transcribing "runaway slave" advertisements with grace and excellence. Leland Bennett, Shelby Klingensmith, and Ian Callender were sturdy yeoman transcribers, like the agriculturists from which they sprung. Penn State doctoral candidate Emily Peebles was a most excellent translator and is on the path to becoming a first-rate scholar in her own right. Zhaoxu Sui and the team at the Penn State GeoGraphics Lab generously produced the maps for this book. My French football buddies, Alex, Victor, and Julien, assisted in translating nuanced French documents. We had much fun along the way, and we are thankful to Shavit for bringing us all together. Alain Sauret provided a detailed translation of Michel Amoureux's 1803 letter, which led to my interest in this project in the first place. Many thanks, Alain and Marie.

Twenty-plus years on as a historian, it's worth thanking those whose commitment to their craft inspires my own devotion to the historians' craft. The fellows from Minutemen, fIREHOSE, Descendents, and ALL continuously remind me of the importance of dedication to craft. Hopefully this book is a worthy "History Lesson, Part 3." Slavery was about labor, but so much more. Slavery continuously robbed enslaved men and women of their dignity, their families, their friends, their identities. My father and Steamfitters Local Union 420 taught me respect for honest labor and contempt for bourgeois pretentiousness. They also taught me that shared labor produces love, family, friends, and dignity. One of slavery's many great tragedies was that it robbed men, women, and children of the dignity, friends, and family who are created and sustained through daily labors.

My extended group of friends and family on both sides of the Commonwealth of Pennsylvania rarely understand what I do, but they always remain supportive of it. Thanks to the Perkins-Vollmer family and the Nevin Crew for always asking about the next article or book. Bill, Amy, Mike, Kook, Trish, and Balls, thanks for caring about this project and for caring about scholarship. Writing this book constantly reminded me how much my friends and family mean to me.

This book began with my father's ever-present love, support, and pride. It ended shortly after his passing. On behalf of Hallie, Hannah, and Addison, this one's for Pep. Pep, you meant the world to us. We will always love you, miss you, and carry you with us. Thank you for quietly teaching us about love and labor, family and friends. Above all else, thanks for being Pep.